The government of federal capitals

The government of federal capitals

EDITED BY DONALD C. ROWAT

UNIVERSITY OF TORONTO PRESS

© University of Toronto Press 1973
Toronto and Buffalo
Printed in Great Britain
Reprinted in 2018
ISBN 0-8020-1815-7
ISBN 978-1-4875-8228-9 (paper)
Microfiche ISBN 0-8020-0139-4
LC 72-185733

Contents

Contributors ix

Introduction xi

A note on metric measures and currency units xvi

I   Capitals in federal districts

A   Capitals without self-government

1   Brasilia, by Diogo Lordello de Mello 5
    Brazil's federal system 5
    Rio de Janeiro as the federal capital 6
    Why Brasilia? 9
    Brasilia's local government 14
    Brasilia today 20

2   Buenos Aires, by Carlos Mouchet 27
    History and background 27
    Government of the federal district 30
    Local services and finances 33
    Urban planning 34
    The principal problems 35

3   Canberra, by Ruth Atkins 39
    Canberra's characteristics 39
    Constitutional background 44
    The founding of the capital 47
    Canberra's early development and government 50
    Development and government since 1958 53
    Prospects for self-government 59
    Conclusions 61

4   Mexico City, by Gonzalo Martínez Corbalá 63
    Government of the federal district 65
    Politics and political problems 67
    Finances 69
    Planning 71

Problems of government 71
Conclusions 74

5 Washington, by Royce Hanson and Bernard H. Ross 77
The development of the capital 77
The District's constitutional status 78
Federal interest and the national capital area 80
The system of local government 93
The "ungovernment" of the national capital 107

B Capitals with some self-government

6 Caracas, by Allan-Randolph Brewer-Carías 113
Background 113
Historical review 115
Government of the federal district 118
Finances 125
Parties and politics 126
The metropolitan area 127

7 Delhi, by L. M. Singhvi 131
Transfer of the capital from Calcutta 131
The chief commissionership of Delhi 135
The core of the capital 135
Delhi's population 136
Evolution of Delhi's government 139
The Delhi municipal corporation 141
Towards limited self-government 150

II Capitals not in federal districts

A Capitals as states

8 Lagos, by Annmarie Hauck Walsh and Samuel Humes 159
Constitutional history 160
Political background 162
Development problems 165
Government of Lagos as a federal territory 167
Government of Lagos as a state 176

9 Vienna, by Herbert Haller 181
History 181
The legal situation 184
The political situation 190
The functions and problems of Vienna 195
Cultural affairs 200
Conclusion 202

CONTENTS vii

B   Capitals in relatively centralized federations

10 Belgrade, by Miodrag Jovicic   207
    Nature of the federation   208
    The government of Belgrade   211
    Finances   216
    Economic and social planning   218
    A federal district?   219

11 Islamabad, by Muhammad Swaleh   221
    Historical background   221
    The new capital   228
    The second capital   233

12 Kuala Lumpur, by David Harner   235
    The capital and the nation   235
    The Federal Capital Act of 1960   238
    Local government in Malaysia   242
    Kuala Lumpur under federal control   243
    Future problems   245

13 Moscow, by Maurice Hookham   251
    Location and history   251
    Moscow's local government   255
    Finances   263
    Planning   265
    Intergovernmental relations   269

14 Yaoundé, by H. N. A. Enonchong   271
    History and background   271
    The constitutional setting   274
    The municipality of Yaoundé   275
    Control of the municipality   279
    Social characteristics   280
    Future prospects   281

C   Capitals in decentralized federations

15 Bern, by Hermann Boeschenstein   285
    The seat of government in history   285
    The local government   289
    Present federal-city relations   289
    Political problems   291
    Conclusion   293

16 Bonn, by Raimund Beck   295
    The German capital in history   296

The capital in the framework of the constitution 303
The local government 305
Problems of the capital area 306

17 Ottawa, by Donald C. Rowat 315
The problem of divided control 315
The origin of the problem 316
Early attempts to meet the problem 317
The evolution of the national capital region, 1944–58 320
Recent progress and future difficulties 324
The bilingual-bicultural issue 330
A federal district? 336

Conclusion 341
Capitals in federal districts 341
Capitals as city-states 344
Capitals under state law 345
The questions of a federal district and self-government 349

Selected bibliography 353
A   Materials in English 353
B   Materials in other languages 359

Contributors

RUTH ATKINS is Associate Professor of Political Science, University of New South Wales; author of a forthcoming book on Canberra to be published by Longmans.

RAIMUND BECK is Oberregierungsrat in the Federal Administration of Finance; Lecturer in Political Science at the Ruhr University of Bochŭm.

HERMANN BOESCHENSTEIN is a Swiss lawyer and editor in Bern.

ALLAN-RANDOLPH BREWER-CARÍAS is a Professor of Administrative Law, Central University of Venezuela, and author of *El Régimen de Gobierne en el Distrito Federal Venezolano* [The System of Municipal Government in the Federal District of Venezuela] (Caracas, 1968).

GONZALO MARTÍNEZ CORBALÁ is a former member of the Congress for the Federal District, and President of the Executive Council of the Mexican Society of Engineers; former President of the Executive Council, Mexican Planning Society.

H.N.A. ENONCHONG is Solicitor and Advocate of the West Cameroon Supreme Court and the Federal Court of Justice; former Assistant Professor of Law at the Cameroon Federal University, and former Director of Cabinet in the Cameroon Ministry of Justice; author of *Cameroon Constitutional Law* (Yaoundé, 1967).

HERBERT HALLER is Assistant in the Faculty of Law, University of Vienna, and at present working in the Austrian Constitutional Court; fellow of the *Alexander von Humbolt-Stiftung*, University of Munich, 1967-69.

ROYCE HANSON is Professor of Government, American University.

DAVID HARNER was Harvard Development Service Adviser to the Development Administration Unit of the Prime-Minister's Department of Malaysia; formerly City Manager of Jacksonville, Texas, and presently City Manager of Denison, Texas.

MAURICE HOOKHAM is Senior Lecturer in Politics, the University of Leicester.

SAMUEL HUMES is a professor at the Institute of Administration, University of Ife, Ibadan, Nigeria, and is co-author, with Eileen Martin, of *The Structure of Local Government* (The Hague: IULA, 1969).

MIODRAG JOVICIC is at the Institute of Comparative Law, Belgrade.

DIOGO LORDELLO DE MELLO is Executive Director, Brazilian Institute of Municipal Administration, and Professor, Brazilian School of Public Administration, Getulio Vargas Foundation; formerly mayor of Brasilia, 1961.

CARLOS MOUCHET is Special Adviser to the Mayor of Buenos Aires; formerly Director-General of Legal Affairs for the Municipality of Buenos Aires; ex-member of the Governing Council of the Regulatory Plan Organization of the city; ex-Professor of Law and Economics at the University of Buenos Aires; Director of the Study Group on the Metropolitan Area of Buenos Aires for the International Conference on Metropolitan Problems in Toronto, 1967.

BERNARD H. ROSS is Associate Professor of Government and Director, Urban Affairs Program, American University.

DONALD C. ROWAT is Professor of Political Science at Carleton University, Ottawa; author of *The Ombudsman* (Toronto, 1968) and *The Canadian Municipal System* (Toronto, 1969).

L.M. SINGHVI is Senior Advocate, Supreme Court of India; Member of Indian Parliament (1962–67); honorary visiting professor, Delhi University (1967–); founder-chairman, Institute of Constitutional and Parliamentary Studies, Delhi.

MUHAMMAD SWALEH is Senior Parliamentary Draftsman, Government of Tanzania; formerly Deputy Legislative Draftsman, Government of Pakistan.

ANNMARIE H. WALSH is Director, International Urban Studies Project, Institute of Public Administration, New York; author of *The Urban Challenge to Government* (NY: Praeger, 1969) and is co-author, with B.A. Williams, of *Urban Government for Metropolitan Lagos* (NY: Praeger, 1968).

Introduction

Every federal country faces a difficult task in trying to decide how its national capital should be governed. The problem of governing any capital is difficult because there is always a conflict of interests between the national government and the people who live in the capital city. The government wishes to control and develop the capital in the interests of the nation as a whole, while the people of the city naturally wish to govern themselves to the greatest extent possible. In addition, the government of a federal capital presents a special problem which is inherent in the very nature of federalism: if the national capital of a federal union comes under the government of any one state of the union, that state is in a position to dominate the federation's capital, and the central government does not have control over its own seat of government.

John Hamilton Gray, one of the fathers of the Canadian Confederation, foresaw this problem very clearly, and in 1872 gave the following eloquent exposition of it:

At the time of the [Confederation] Convention, one mistake occurred: no provision was made for creating a Federal District for the capital, and withdrawing it from the exclusive control of the local legislature of one of the Provinces. That which was designed to be the capital of the Confederation, might fairly rest its claim for support on the people of the Dominion. Its order, well being, sanitary arrangements, police regulations, adornments and improvements are essential to the comfort and security, not only of the representatives who attend Parliament, but of all those who are compelled to resort to it as the capital of the country in the discharge of the various duties attendant upon the administration of public affairs. Its reputation should be national, not provincial. It belongs no more to Ontario than it does to New Brunswick, Nova Scotia, Quebec or any of the provinces constituting the Confederation ... [yet] the legislation for the capital in all civil matters is entirely under the control of one province, differing in its laws from the others....

Thus we see that the character of a national capital, the security of those who attend it, the elimination of sectional and provincial interests in its government the preservation of the national public property, the protection of the public interests, and the maintenance of the national reputation of its status, are too important to be left to local councils, however good they may be.

Americans have their capital, Canadians have no capital for their country. They borrow a municipality from Ontario, and whether they come from the Provinces of the Atlantic or the Pacific, or whether from Quebec or Manitoba, their representatives in the Dominion Parliament have no power to legislate on any matter touching the property or civil rights of the so-called capital of the Dominion, however great the wrong to be redressed or the evil to be remedied. This should not be.[1]

It was this line of reasoning, then, that was the basis for the federal district idea – the proposition that a federal capital should be governed within a federal district or territory under the exclusive jurisdiction of the central government. The early creation of the District of Columbia in the United States was a recognition of this principle that the federal capital should not be governed for state and local purposes by only one of the states of the union. The South American federations, which were heavily influenced by the United States, also recognized this principle, and some others copied it in their constitutions. It should be noted, however, that many federations did not create a federal district for the capital.

These considerations indicate that two of the most important questions regarding the government of a federal capital are: "Should the capital be in a federal district?" and "How much self-government should the residents of the capital area have?" The second is a question which arises regardless of whether there is a federal district, although it is a more serious question in the federal district kind of arrangement.

If the capital is not in a federal district, the problem becomes one of too much emphasis upon provincial and local views, to the neglect of the national interest. This is the complaint that has been made of Ottawa: that the government of Ontario and the city council of Ottawa do not pay enough attention to the requirements of the national capital as a seat of government and as a symbol of the nation. On the other hand, if the capital is in a federal district, then the reverse problem presents itself. The danger is domination by the central government, lack of self-government in the federal district, and neglect of local interests. In May 1967 the Australian Ministry of Interior, which is responsible for governing the Australian Capital Territory, issued a special report on self-government for Canberra. In that report the problem was expressed this way:

The object of this current and continuing study is to advise on the practicability, desirability and form of government that would assign to the community of the Australian Capital Territory the benefits and responsibilities of accepted democratic processes, while protecting the interests of the Commonwealth. The problem

INTRODUCTION xiii

is thus one of balance. To extend to the community the full range of authority normally exercised through state and municipal governmental organizations would be to place that community in substantial control of the national capital, whereas the national capital was always intended to be the responsibility of the people of the Commonwealth as a whole and to exist for the benefit of the nation as a whole. On the other hand, to consider only the position of Canberra as the seat of government and national capital at the expense of all community participation in government would unjustly deprive the members of the local community of their fundamental democratic rights and responsibilities.[2]

In view of the similar interest in the United States in greater self-government for Washington, it is surprising that no previous comparative study has ever been made of how federal capitals are actually governed.

The present study arose out of the recent revival of the proposal that Canada's capital should be governed as a federal district. Dissatisfaction with the fact that the central government in Canada has no direct control over its own seat of government has existed ever since Confederation, and a federal district has been frequently proposed. But in the discussions of this proposal references are made almost exclusively to Washington and Canberra, and it is usually concluded that a federal district is undesirable because these capital cities have no self-government. I knew that there were several other federations with capital districts and that some of them had more self-government than Washington or Canberra. I also knew that several federal capitals were, like Ottawa, governed by state and local governments. I therefore felt that a survey of how all other federal capitals are governed would be useful.

I also realized that such a comparative survey might be useful to other federations, since neither those whose capitals were governed by one of the states nor those whose capitals were within federal districts seemed entirely satisfied with the system of government for their capital. In fact, several federations were in the process of reorganizing this system. In addition to Canada, such federations included Australia, India, Nigeria, Pakistan, the United States, and West Germany. I therefore set about to gather as much information as I could on the subject.

The number of countries that can be identified as federations, depends, of course, on the definition used. For purposes of this study I tried to include all countries that have a federal constitution. Using this as a basis, I identified seventeen federations: Argentina, Australia, Austria, Brazil, Cameroon, Canada, India, Malaysia, Mexico, Nigeria, Pakistan, Switzerland, the USA, the USSR, Venezuela, West Germany, and Yugoslavia. It should be noted that the study included only existing federations and their present capitals. Though the federation of East and West Pakistan perished in December 1971, after this book had gone to press, West Pakistan had been divided into its four former provinces in April 1970. Hence Pakistan can still be counted as a federation.³ Much can also be learned from a study of how former federal capitals were governed, capitals such as Karachi, Rio de Janeiro, and Berlin under the Weimar Republic.

It would also be useful to study the recent proposals for Brussels, which may become a future federal capital. Because of Belgium's serious bilingual-bicultural problem, some political parties in that country are now proposing that Belgium should be turned into a federation. In February 1970 the government of Belgium proposed that the country should be divided into three semi-autonomous regions, one of which would cover the metropolitan area of Brussels. The northern region would be Dutch-speaking and Flemish, the southern region French-speaking and Walloon, while the region surrounding Brussels would be a bilingual mixture, with about 200,000 Flemings and about a million Walloons. To date, however, this proposal has not been approved by the necessary two-thirds constitutional majority of Parliament. The various proposals made for the government of Brussels within a federation or quasi-federation will be of special interest in Canada, which has a similar bilingual-bicultural problem.

Among the seventeen existing federations, it is interesting that seven have federal capital districts while eight have a capital which comes under the jurisdiction of a state. Some of the latter, however, also come under fairly direct central control. In the two remaining federations, Austria and Nigeria, the capital city is actually one of the states of the union. Vienna has been such a city-state since the beginning of the Austrian federation. Although the city of Lagos had been a federal district until the outbreak of the Nigerian civil war, its metropolitan area has now become one of the twelve states of the new Nigerian federation.

With generous financial help from the Canada Council, I was able to make study-visits to all of these capitals except Lagos and Yaoundé, in Cameroon. Despite this first-hand observation, I realized that, taking into account the number of capitals to be studied and the language problems encountered, it would be impossible to write a satisfactory book on the subject single-handed, and that it would be better to find an expert for each capital who could write an essay on its government.

The two main problems discussed above – the desirability of a federal district and the desirable extent of self-government for the capital – have been used as a general framework for the organization of the book. The capitals have been divided according to whether they are or are not governed within a federal district. Those within a federal district have been further subdivided according to the extent of self-government that they enjoy, while those governed by a state have been subdivided according to whether they are in a relatively centralized or decentralized federation. Because circumstances vary so much from one federal capital to another, I did not ask my authors to adhere to a rigid plan of presentation, but instead submitted to them a series of relevant questions for their consideration. This procedure has permitted the authors to discuss more fully any special characteristics or problems of their capital city, and at the same time has resulted in a reasonably uniform treatment.

This book, like my previous book, *The Ombudsman*, is a product of genuine international collaboration, with essays written by experts in seventeen different countries. Only a person who has participated in such an enterprise can appreciate the difficulties of delay and translation involved. Yet all of my authors have cheerfully contributed their time and expert knowledge to the project, without any guarantee of whether or when the book would be published, and some of them have patiently reviewed, without complaint, "revisions of revisions of translations". All of their essays make original contributions to the published literature on the subject, and in some cases are the only materials available in English. I should therefore like to thank all of them for their contributions to this unique study in comparative government. I should also like to thank my colleague, Mrs Wendy Jones, for translating some of the essays.

February 1972

D.C.R.
Ottawa

1 *Confederation of Canada* (Toronto, 1872), 108–10.
2 *Self-Government for the Australian Capital Territory: A Preliminary Assessment* (Canberra, 1967), para. 8.
3 Cameroon, however, can not. Even more recently, in May 1972, the Cameroonians in a referendum approved a draft constitution to convert Cameroon into a unitary State, and this is expected to occur during 1972. See Dr Enonchong's first footnote to his essay on Yaoundé. Thus two of my federations have disappeared during the course of editing this book!

A NOTE ON METRIC MEASURES AND CURRENCY UNITS

Since many of the capitals dealt with in this volume are in countries that have the metric system, the authors of the essays on these capitals have used metric measurements, such as kilometres (km), square kilometres (km²), and centigrade degrees, for distance, area and temperature. One kilometre equals 0.62137 miles, and one square kilometre equals 0.3861 square miles. Therefore, to convert kilometres to the approximate equivalent in miles multiply by 0.62, and to convert square kilometres to approximate square miles, multiply by 0.39. To convert centigrade into fahrenheit temperatures, multiply by 9/5 and add 32. Where other metric measurements are used, the approximate value of each unit is given the first time that it appears in the text.

In most cases authors have given financial figures in units of the currency used in the country in which the capital is situated. The approximate value of that currency's unit in United States dollars or cents in 1970 is given the first time that it appears in the text.

To assist readers in making comparisons, where the present area of a federal district or capital is given in square kilometres, it is also given in square miles (within brackets).

Part I **Capitals in federal districts**

A Capitals without self-government

1   Diogo Lordello de Mello   **BRASILIA**

BRAZIL'S FEDERAL SYSTEM

Brazil, a large country with a rapidly-growing population of nearly 95 million in 1970, is a federation composed of 22 states, three federal territories, and a federal district. The federation was established in 1889, with the abolition of the monarchy and the proclamation of a republic. The federal idea was the strongest motivation for the reform movement that led to the republican regime, for centralization was the key mark of the monarchy.

The federal system was very much inspired by the United States model. Several of its features were outright copies of that model, including the separation of powers and the presidential system of government. Thus, the parliamentary system that evolved slowly during the monarchy was replaced by a rather strong presidential regime in 1889.

Since then the federation has evolved towards the continuous diminution of the states' rights, mainly to the advantage of the central government. Municipal powers have also increased at the expense of the states.

The federal government is composed of the Congress, the executive and the judiciary. The Congress has a House of Representatives and a Senate. The 310 members of the House are elected by the people of the states and territories and representation is based on population. Senators are elected by the people in each state, only three per state. Elections are by universal suffrage and secret ballot. After the 1964 Revolution a two-party system was established. Elections are partisan at all levels of government, independent candidates not being allowed. The president of the republic used to be elected directly by the people, but under the new regime he is chosen by the Congress.

State organization must follow the same basic principles that apply to the federal government. Thus, separation of powers must be observed, as well as many other principles that apply to the legislative and budgetary process. A much greater degree of uniformity has been imposed by the 1967 Constitution than before, as well as a greater degree of centralization.

Each state elects its own governor and legislative assembly, organizes its own judiciary and adopts its own constitution. The governor is elected by direct vote of the people (except in 1935, and again in 1965 and 1970), as well as the members of the legislative assembly.

The territories are administered by governors appointed by the federal government. They enjoy no autonomy and are little more than departments of the Ministry of the Interior. On the other hand, the municipalities, of which there are 3,902, are autonomous politically and administratively. They elect a mayor and a council and have extensive powers in relation to local matters. Although they are not mentioned as being part of the federal system, they enjoy a unique position when compared to the local governments of most other countries, since their basic powers are guaranteed by the constitution and cannot be curtailed by the states.

The constitution establishes a tri-partite division of powers among the Union, the states and the municipalities. Federal, state and municipal powers are enumerated; residual powers belong to the states. The range of federal competence is far more extensive than that of the states. All civil, criminal and commercial legislation is federal, as well as the laws pertaining to court procedures. In taxation matters the Union also has the lion's share. To it belong the majority of the taxes as well as the most productive ones, such as the excise, income and import taxes. The states are left with the tax on sales, real estate transactions and inheritance. To the municipalities belong the taxes on property and services. Most federal taxes are shared with the states and municipalities, however, according to principles that are evolving towards a system of national rather than federal taxes in many cases. Actually, only the levying and collection of several important taxes are federal, since their product must be constitutionally divided with the other levels of government. The same principle applies to the sales tax, which is levied and collected by the states and shared (20 per cent) with the municipalities.

A system of concurring powers among the three levels of government in relation to the rendering of many public services makes functional boundaries often very fuzzy, especially between the states and local government. Inter-governmental relations, including direct relations between the federal government and the municipalities, are very frequent and a major element of the political process. The participation of the three governmental levels in the execution of common programs is such that Brazilian federalism can easily be included in the category of "co-operative federalism."

RIO DE JANEIRO AS THE FEDERAL CAPITAL

It was in 1763 that the capital of the large Portuguese domains in Brazil was moved from Salvador to Rio de Janeiro. The move was dictated by economic and administrative reasons, since the emergence of gold and diamond mining in Minas Gerais required a stronger presence of the government so that the royal treasury could be better served. Because of this new economic activity Rio de Janeiro had become the principal port in the country by that time.

To indicate the new importance it was attaching to its American domains, the Portuguese crown elevated Brazil to a viceroyalty. In 1808, due to the invasion of Portugal by Napoleon's armies, the Portuguese royal family emigrated to Brazil and settled in Rio de Janeiro, after a short stopover in Salvador, the former capital. Rio de Janeiro gained a new status as the seat of a royal court. In 1815 Brazil was elevated to the category of kingdom, in union with Portugal and Algarves, an old Portuguese province.

With the overthrow of Portuguese domination and the establishment of the Brazilian monarchy in 1822, Rio de Janeiro remained the natural capital, although the thought of the transfer of the capital to the central Brazilian plateau was a recurring one even at that time.

During the political organization that followed the independence movement, the country was divided into provinces, and the city of Rio de Janeiro was politically and administratively detached from the province of the same name and transformed into what was called the Neutral Municipality. This terminology indicated the quality of the city as the national capital. It was governed by a municipal council, an institution that had existed since the creation of the city in the middle of the sixteenth century.

During most of the nineteenth century Rio de Janeiro was the seat of a royal court. This was a unique privilege in the Americas, with the exception of the tragic and short-lived experience of Maximilian in Mexico, and was indeed a matter of some prestige, as the Brazilian kings and emperors were related to some of the most traditional royal houses in Europe. The presence of royalty gave Rio de Janeiro an added pre-eminence among Brazilian cities and has certainly enriched its cultural heritage. Politically, it had also become very important, for the centralized system of government made everything dependent upon "the court," that is, the capital.

With the proclamation of the republic and the introduction of the federal system, the Neutral Municipality was transformed into the Federal District, a change of name that reflected not only the new system but the United States model as well.

As the republican capital, Rio de Janeiro was governed by a popularly elected council and a mayor appointed by the president of the republic with the approval of the Senate. Under the short-lived constitution of 1934 the mayor was also elected, but the prevailing thesis in Brazil has been that national interests in the capital are incompatible with an elected mayor because of the strong powers that are granted chief executives in the political system of the country.

At the time the capital was transferred to Brasilia, Rio de Janeiro's local government system was regulated by two basic laws: an organic law and a law governing judicial organization in the Federal District, besides, of course, the few constitutional provisions referring to the Federal District. Both laws were voted by Congress. The council exercised the legislative powers in the same manner as the state legislative assemblies.

The Rio council was made up of fifty members elected by proportional representation of the parties. It enjoyed complete autonomy for its internal organization but, according to the principle of separation of powers that dominates the political system in Brazil, it exercised no executive or administrative functions, except, of course, in internal matters. It was only a legislative and control organ. In its control functions it was aided by the Tribunal of Accounts, which formed part of the local system of government but which was considered an auxiliary agency of the council. The council had the power to approve or reject the mayor's accounts, which were first examined by the Tribunal of Accounts. Yet, because the mayor was appointed by the president of the republic and not elected, the council could not impeach the mayor, unlike the municipal councils in the country. Removal of the mayor was at the sole discretion of the president, the Senate's approval not being necessary for dismissal.

The mayor (*Prefeito*) was the chief executive and as such the unchallenged head of the local administration (*Prefeitura*). However, in spite of the fact that the terms *Prefeito* and *Prefeitura* applied to all municipal governments in Brazil, technically at least the word "municipal" was not applied to the government of the Federal District, a distinction that reflected its special status. As chief executive, the mayor's powers were very extensive. He appointed and dismissed all local employees (except the council's staff) subject to civil service laws. The preparation and execution of the annual budget was his prerogative, the council's role being that of voting the budget proposal and controlling its execution.

The Federal District's local government was responsible for all city services, including utilities, public education and health, fire protection, most of the police apparatus, including the militia, traffic police and the local court system. Like the municipalities, it enjoyed extensive police powers in relation to planning, building inspection, health and public safety.

Bills voted by the council had to be approved by the mayor, who had the veto power. The revision of this veto, however, did not belong to the council, as in the municipalities, but to the Senate. Thus, the appointment of the mayor by the president with the Senate's approval, and the Senate's power to maintain or reject the mayor's vetoes, were the only legal ways of interference by the national government in the government of the Federal District. De facto interference existed nevertheless, specially in the form of patronage by senators, who often took advantage of the position of the Senate vis-à-vis the Federal District to get appointments and other favours from the city government.

In taxation matters, the district government had at the same time the taxing powers of the states and of the municipalities, so its tax base was a privileged one. But in spite of this advantage and of the fact that the city was very wealthy, it received massive financial assistance from the federal government on the grounds that, as the government of the national capital, it had added responsibilities. Actually, the vast sums spent by the federal government in Rio de Janeiro, directly or through the city government, gave rise to great criticism on the part of many people, who complained of the high cost of the national capital and of its constant embellishment at the expense of the other parts of the country. One such critic pointed out that, in the decade between 1940 and 1950, the federal government spent twice as much in Rio as the yield of local revenues. One of the reasons for popular support for transferring the capital was this concern for the costs of the old one to the nation's taxpayers.

WHY BRASILIA?

Historical background

The idea of moving the capital from Rio de Janeiro to the interior was an old one. The ill-fated revolutionaries of 1789, who wanted independence from Portugal, had already mentioned the moving of the capital as a basic need for the development of the country. Many Portuguese colonial administrators also pointed out the disadvantages that resulted from the installation of the capital on the coast. The busy commercial life of Rio de Janeiro, then already a major port, was not conducive to the study of the many problems of the big country whose boundaries were barely known.

In 1823, the year after Brazil became independent, José Bonifácio de Andrada e Silva, the "patriarch of independence," presented a proposal to the Constituent Assembly "on the needs and means of building a new capital for Brazil" and even suggested Brasilia as its name. The motivation was the occupancy of the vast interior. The proposed location was central Brazil. Publicists and political writers had also defended the idea from the early years of the last century. Hipólito José da Costa, writing in his paper *Correio Brasiliense*, which he founded in London while in exile, said in 1808 that "Rio de Janeiro possessed none of the qualities required for a city destined to be the capital of the Brazilian empire."

Varnhagen, the celebrated Brazilian historian, fought for the idea from 1834 to 1877. He himself made extensive studies of the central plateau where the new capital finally came to be located. In 1852 a bill was introduced in the Senate proposing the transfer, but it was defeated. The new republic, a regime proclaimed in 1889, contemplated the transfer both in the provisional constitution of that year and in the first republican constitution of 1891. The provisional constitution, which transformed the former provinces into states and the former Neutral Municipality into the Federal District, said that Rio "shall continue to be the national capital until Congress decides otherwise." The constitution of 1891 was far more explicit. Its Article 3 said that an area of 14,400 square kilometres in the central plateau belonged to the Union and that it should be demarcated so that the new national capital should be installed there. When this happened, the former Federal District would then become a state.

In compliance with this constitutional provision, the second president of Brazil, Floriano Peixoto, constituted a demarcation commission, whose work lasted for 26 months and ended in December 1894. Nothing happened, however, until 1922. On 7 September of that year, when the first centennial of the independence was being celebrated, the corner stone of the new capital was laid near the town of Planaltina, only a few kilometres from where Brasilia is now located. The gesture was only symbolic, as it turned out. Actual construction never began on that site.

The constitution of 1934, voted after the revolutionary movement of 1930, which brought Vargas to power, prescribed that the capital should be transferred. Disregarding the previous studies, it said that the government should appoint a commission to study possible locations for the new capital, the conclusions to be submitted to the House of Representatives for the selection of the site. It is interesting to note that, contrary to previous manifestations, no commitment was made to the central plateau as the location of the new capital. This is ascribed to the influence of the representation of Minas Gerais, which wanted the capital to be moved to that state.

The commandment of the short-lived constitution of 1934 was never obeyed. Its successor, the dictatorial constitution of 1937, did not mention the transfer explicitly, although the idea was admitted when it said, in Article 7, that "the present Federal District, while capital of Brazil, shall be administered by the Union."

Finally, after dictatorship was overthrown and the 1946 constitution passed, a definite era emerged for the realization of the secular dream. Article 4 of the transitional provisions of the new constitution declared that "the capital shall be transferred to the central plateau." The president was given sixty days to appoint a commission to study the location of the new capital. The findings were to be presented to Congress, which should then set the date for the transfer.

Within the prescribed time the president appointed a commission made up of geographers, agronomists, geologists, hygienists and engineers of high standing, under the chairmanship of General Djalma Poli Coelho. On 4 August 1948, the Commission presented its findings. The location coincided very much with that of the 1892/94 Commission and with previous ideas. On the basis of the Commission's report, President Gaspar Dutra introduced a bill in Congress authorizing the federal government to undertake definitive studies for the location of the new capital in the region of the central plateau, between the parallels 15°30' and 17° south and the meridians W. Gr. 46°30' and 49°30'. The law was approved on 5 January 1953 (No. 1803). The exact site was defined on 30 April 1955, within an area of 5,850 square kilometres (2,260 sq. mi.), between the parallels 15°30' and 16°03'. The state of Goiás, in whose territory the site was located, expropriated the area and donated it to the Union.

On 18 April 1956, President Juscelino Kubitscheck de Oliveira, who had recently been elected and taken office, introduced a bill in Congress creating the Company for the Urbanization of the New Capital – NOVACAP. This bill (No. 2874) was approved on 19 September 1956. The company was incorporated three days later and immediately advertised a national competition for the plan of the new city, which was open only to Brazilians. The jury, composed of eminent city planners from Brazil and abroad, included Sir William Holford from Great Britain, M. André Sive from France, Mr Stamo Papadaki from the United States, and Mr Oscar Niemeyer from Brazil.

The jury convened on 12 March 1957. Twenty-six entries had been made to the competition. In making its choice the jury was guided by two main ideas: first, that the federal capital in a large country like Brazil must convey the force of the national will and must therefore be different from any other city; second, that it must possess its own architectural character. The major feature is its governmental function, around which all other functions are organized and everything should gravitate. The aim was a *civitas* not an *urbs*, in the words of Sir William Holford, who expressed the opinion that the contest reached a very high level. He considered the winning project (Lucio Costa's) one of the most interesting and important contributions made in this century to modern urbanism. The city was planned for a maximum population of 500,000. Growth beyond that point should be checked through the development of satellite towns, of which there are six at present.

Reasons for a new capital

The building of a new capital was, for Brazil, an act of faith and affirmation, more than anything else. It meant a strong desire for effective occupancy, of vast territories that lay empty. It meant moving west, from the saturated coast to the hinterland. It meant the prospect of realizing the great potentialities that lay ahead in a continental country which insists on believing that its manifest destiny is greatness.

Four major arguments have dominated the idea of constructing a new capital: (1) the balanced development of the country through the conquest of the vast interior; (2) strategic considerations, from the view point of national security; (3) the disturbance of the national government by the local problems of the old capital; and (4) the search for a better, more temperate climate.

Paramount was the first argument. It was believed that, by moving the centre of national decisions from the coast to the heart of the country, government power would radiate in a more balanced way, and development could be brought to the enormous and void areas around the new capital. The command of three great river basins – the Amazon, the Prata and the São Francisco – would be greatly facilitated by the location of this centre of decision in the central plateau, where all three basins have their origins. Previous experiences with moving and building state capitals for the same reason enhanced this thesis. Foremost were the examples of Belo Horizonte, inaugurated in 1896, and Goiania in 1940. Both not only became thriving cities very soon but brought progress to their respective regions. Belo Horizonte now has a population of more than a million and Goiania a population of 340,000.

Concern for internal and external security – an argument of importance in the early crusades for the transfer – lost much of its significance as modern warfare introduced new weapons and military concepts.

The third argument – the inadequacy of Rio de Janeiro to serve as the country's capital – became more and more relevant as the city grew into one of the largest metropolises in the world, with the array of problems that accompany rapid urbanization of any major city. With a population of 3,223,000 when the capital was moved in 1960, its government was subject to stresses that automatically overflowed to the national government because of its presence there and also because it was partly responsible for the city, since the mayor was an appointee of the president. It was felt that solving Rio's many local problems took considerable effort and put an extraordinary pressure upon the federal government. Strikes, student demonstrations, street agitations, shortages of basic food commodities, failures or lack of public services, local pressures of all sorts – all these problems tended to find a final outlet at the president's office and to involve the Houses of Congress in acute debate. After all, the large voting audience was present in the most important urban electoral arena in the country. Members of both Houses who were elected by the Federal District could hardly escape considerable involvement in local matters. This situation was believed to be very detrimental to the concentration of the government on national problems. The hectic type of life of a great metropolis extended its agitation to the government, whose work, it was agreed, needed more tranquillity than the city could provide.

The climatic argument was strengthened by the fact that the rigors of a tropical climate are present in Rio during many months of the year, causing discomfort and irritation in many people and reducing productivity. By contrast, the mild annual temperature of the site chosen for the new capital is a comfortable average of 20 degrees centigrade, with a humidity of 76 per cent in summer and 63 per cent in winter.

But beyond these arguments a decisive factor led to the transfer. It was the optimistic enthusiasm of the Kubitscheck government, whose political platform promised fifty years of progress for Brazil in five. The economy in general and the industrial base of the country experienced a great upsurge during those five years, really extraordinary, by Brazilian tradition. Great schemes of national development were not only conceived but carried out in most part. The idea of nation-building moved the government and soon pervaded the nation. In a time of eloquent ideals and considerable achievement like this, a grandiose national project was needed to symbolize the aspirations and the capacity of a people that had been overtaken by the mystique of development. Brasilia was this symbol.

The construction effort

Immediately upon its incorporation in September 1956, the Company for the Urbanization of the New Capital began its task. The country then witnessed an effort unparalleled in its history. A man of proven dynamism and ruthless obstinacy, Israel Pinheiro, was made president of the company and given full authority to carry out his job. He was a personal friend of President Kubitscheck and an experienced politician and administrator, having served for several years as chairman of the powerful budget (ways and means) committee of the House of Deputies. His father presided over the construction of another capital, Belo Horizonte, in the last decade of the nineteenth century.

Huge amounts of material and equipment were transported by air at the beginning of construction, while a highway was opened connecting Belo Horizonte (and thus Rio de Janeiro) to Brasilia. Labourers and all sorts of workers flocked from all over the country, especially from the north-east and the nearby states of Goiás and Minas Gerais, attracted by the ample labour market that had been opened to unskilled and semi-skilled workers. Construction was carried on day and night and on holidays. Time, not cost, was the major concern. To this day, it is not known how much

Brasilia did actually cost to the taxpayers. Its opponents tend to exaggerate, although it is commonly assumed that the construction and installation of the new capital was a major factor in the acceleration of the inflationary process after 1956.

The design of all major public buildings was committed to the Brazilian architect Oscar Niemeyer, who moved onto the site and lived there until after the inauguration, working tirelessly, earning a nominal salary and executing an architectural commission that is unequalled in modern times.

On the date set – 21 April 1960 – Brasilia was inaugurated and the federal government was officially transferred from Rio de Janeiro. Almost a century and a half had passed since serious consideration had been given to the idea of moving the capital, but only three and a half years since the construction had begun.

BRASILIA'S LOCAL GOVERNMENT

Governmental system

The new Federal District is governed by a chief executive appointed by the president of the republic with the approval of the Senate. He can be removed, however, at the will of the president. The new federal constitution of 17 October 1969 changed the name of this chief executive from mayor to governor. There is no local legislative body. Legislation on the administration of the Federal District (taxation, budget, public services and personnel) is passed by a special committee of the Senate, in accordance with Article 17, paragraph 1, of the constitution. This committee thus functions as the city council. Its decisions are not subject to review either by any other committees or by the Senate as a whole, or by the House of Representatives. In fact, however, the other Senate committees do have a say on bills referring to the Federal District, and the Senate as a whole approves or rejects such bills. The Federal District has no representation in either of the two houses of Congress, unlike the federal territories, which have one elected representative each in the House of Representatives.

Therefore there is no self-government in Brasilia. This is a significant departure in relation to the former Federal District, which had a locally elected council and representatives in both houses of Congress, like the states. The organic law of the Federal District (federal law No. 3,751, of 13 April 1960), however, contemplated a locally elected council with legislative functions. This provision was never enforced and was finally revoked by the 1967 and 1969 constitutions. The election of representatives of the Federal District to Congress, although contemplated in the 1946 constitution, was never applied to Brasilia. The new constitution, which went into effect on 17 October 1969, does not include this possibility.

Thus Brasilia has never experienced any measure of self-government. Neither do its satellite towns have representative government. They are administered by officials appointed by the mayor. At present there is no movement of any significance in favour of local autonomy for the Federal District or its satellite towns. The federal government, as the main provider of funds for the maintenance of the capital, does not feel obliged to relinquish its control over the city. Besides, national security reasons would certainly be invoked in favour of the present arrangement. Recent student demonstrations in Brasilia support this view.

Brasilia's citizens could vote in national elections for president and vice-president when these offices were filled by direct vote. They did so in 1960 and in the plebiscite of 1963. In the election of 3 October 1960, they favoured the candidates sponsored by the left (Marshal Lott for president and João Goulart for vice-president, who later in 1963 called the referendum in order to re-establish the full powers of the presidency).

Since the election of the president and the vice-president is now by indirect vote of Congress, the citizens of the Federal District no longer have the possibility of voting. Brasilia is thus the only political subdivision of the country whose citizens do not have the right to vote in any election, at least while the present system of indirect elections for president and vice-president is maintained.

Although the Federal District can be compared to a department of federal government from the point of view of local autonomy, it nevertheless enjoys a great deal of administrative autonomy which puts it in a special status. A comparison with the federal territories serves to illustrate the point. This special position is evidenced by the facts that (1) the Federal District has its own budget and its own taxes, voted by Congress, while the territories are included in the general budget of the federal government and have no tax system of their own; (2) there is a special personnel system for the Federal District, unlike the territories, whose personnel are part of the federal personnel system; and (3) the Federal District has its own Tribunal of Accounts, which examines the governor's accounts. Thus the Federal District is not under the jurisdiction of the Federal Tribunal of Accounts (as are the territories). Reference is here made to the territories to point out an interesting contrast: the territories have representation in Congress but no administrative autonomy, while the Federal District has no representation but ample autonomy in administrative matters. A law reorganizing the territories and granting them more administrative autonomy, especially in budgetary and personnel matters, was passed recently, but it has not been enforced as yet.

It should also be mentioned that the Federal District has its own court system, although the appointment of judges is made by the president of the republic and not by the governor. There is a Court of Justice, with appeal functions and special jurisdiction in certain cases, and ordinary courts for civil, family, criminal and fiscal matters. As in the rest of the country, entrance to the judiciary is based on merit, as ascertained by public competition (with the exception of the highest courts, in which the appointments are freely made by the president). Appointment to Brasilia's Court of Justice follows the general Brazilian pattern adopted in relation to the state supreme courts. Part of the membership is appointed from among the judges of ordinary courts, as a promotion; part from among the public attorneys, who also enter the service by public competition; and part is chosen from among eminent lawyers.

Administration

The governor of the Federal District has full executive power. He appoints all public servants, including the members of the Tribunal of Accounts, without the need of the formal approval of any higher authority. He can also dismiss his cabinet at will. He has the power to issue decrees on many matters, since Congress legislates for the District only in relation to a few important subjects (budget, taxation, personnel, and basic organization).

The administration of the District is constituted by a complex array of organizations under the governor's control. Besides the usual departments, there are eight administrative regions and a host of ad hoc organizations of various kinds. There are twelve departments: Government, Tourism and Recreation, Legal, Administration, Finance, Agriculture and Production, Education and Culture, Health, Social Service, Public Works, Public Services, and Public Safety. The departments are mostly normative, especially the ones responsible for the substantive functions. The actual work of rendering services to the public is usually performed by the ad hoc bodies.

The eight administrative regions have responsibility for rendering certain services, as agents of the District's central departments. The whole Federal District, including the satellite towns and the city of Brasilia itself, is covered by the administrative regions, which perform the role of municipalities in a certain way. They do not have any elective bodies, however. The regional administrator is responsible directly to the Department of Government, which is one of the twelve departments under the governor.

The ad hoc bodies are of the following kinds: semi-autonomous departments, foundations, autarchies, mixed-economy enterprises, and public enterprises. The semi-autonomous departments are seven: Water and Sewage, Sanitation, Public Lottery, National Theatre, Institute for the

Education of the Exceptional, and Public Library. There are also five foundations established, maintained and controlled by the government of the Federal District: the Educational Foundation, in charge of all public education at the primary and secondary levels; the Hospital Foundation, which maintains several public hospitals; the Cultural Foundation, in charge of assorted cultural activities (but not the National Theatre); the Zoobotanical Foundation, which has among its responsibilities the preservation of the fauna and flora of the Federal District; and the Social Service Foundation, with social assistance functions. There is only one autarchy (a body with financial and administrative autonomy), the Highway Department. The mixed-economy enterprises (in which stock can be privately owned) are four: The Telephone Company; the Electricity Company; the Company for the Development of the Central Plateau; and the Regional Bank of Brasilia.

Finally, there are four public enterprises whose capital is totally owned by the government. The most important of these is the Urbanization Company of the New Capital (NOVACAP), which was incorporated by the federal government to build Brasilia. Later, 51 per cent of its capital was transferred to the government of the Federal District. The company operates now as the Public Works Department of Brasilia and as the administrative agency in charge of the sale of land in the Federal District. The other public enterprises are the Transport Company, the Social Housing Company, and the Food Supply Company, which operates a series of public markets.

Taxation and finance

Tax structure

As with the old Federal District, the government of the new District possesses the taxing powers of both a state and a municipality. It can levy and collect the following taxes, fees, and charges:

A sales taxes;
B tax on real estate transactions "inter-vivos" (among living parties);
C inheritance tax on real estate;
D tax on urban buildings and land;
E tax on services (including amusements);
F fees for local services involving the exercise of the police power (vehicle licences, building licences, utilization of public spaces, cemeteries, bureaucratic fees);
G special assessment;
H charges for industrial, social and other services rendered to the public

(water, sewer, telephone, electricity, street cleaning and garbage collection, public transportation, health, secondary education, etc.).

The first three are state taxes, and the taxes on urban buildings and land and services are municipal, but, as has been pointed out, the District government has power to levy both types. The special assessment (betterment tax) can be levied by any of the three levels of government. Therefore, there is no tax especially created for the Federal District.

Revenue composition

The revenue of the Federal District comes from three sources: (1) revenues from taxes, fees and charges that are levied and collected locally; (2) sharing in taxes levied and collected by the federal government; and (3) subsidies from the federal government. Of these, the last source is by far the largest. According to the 1970 budget, the amounts of these three sources of city revenue were as follows (in millions of new cruzeiros and US dollars, at the current rate of one NCr equals 22.7 US cents):

	million NCr	million US $
Locally raised revenues	195.8	44.5
Shared taxes	71.6	16.3
Federal subsidies	157.0	35.7
Total	424.4	96.5

These figures do not include the revenues of the autonomous or semi-autonomous bodies maintained by the District for telephones, water, sewerage, public transportation, electricity, markets, and social services (secondary education and health). These bodies have their own budgets, so that the general budget includes only the subsidies and funds allocated to them by the District government for investments needed to expand their services or for making up any operational deficits.

Of the locally raised revenues, about 90 per cent is represented by the sales tax and only 5 per cent by the tax on urban buildings and land (property tax). This low participation of the property tax is due to the fact that most buildings are tax-exempt since they still belong to the government. A plan is now in operation for the sale of government-owned apartments and houses to public employees, which will make such property taxable.

Expenditures

On the expenditure side, the budget for 1970 equals the total estimated for revenues, and shows the following breakdown of expenditures by programs, as appropriated (in millions of NCrs):

General Administration	104.5
Health and Sanitation	90.4
Education	69.0
Public Safety	58.3
Housing and Urban Development	56.8
Agriculture	17.2
Transportation	11.7
Social Assistance and Social Security	7.4
Energy	6.8
Communications	2.0
Commerce	0.2
Total	424.3

Again it must be noted that these figures do not include the expenditures of the autonomous bodies, but only the subsidies allocated to some of them in the general budget of the Federal District.

Urban planning

Brasilia is a completely planned city and as such the observance of the plan is essential for the keeping of its individuality. Two elements of the plan, among others, contribute to its unmistakable character: the basic concept of Lucio Costa's design and Oscar Niemeyer's architecture of its public buildings.

In order to give continuity to the original concept of the plan and to safeguard it from distortions, a Council of Architecture and Urbanism was created at the same time that the local government was established. The council is chaired by the governor and has as its ex-officio members the author of the city plan (Lucio Costa), the author of the architectural plan (Oscar Niemeyer) and the first president of NOVACAP, the governmental corporation which built Brasilia. Among the specific responsibilities of the council are: (1) to design all major public buildings; (2) to license any private building that by its importance may influence the shape of the city; and (3) to review any alterations of the original plan, as well as the zoning and building regulations.

The council had been able to protect Brasilia's plan and architectural character until recently, when a famous controversy arose about the plan for the construction of the international airport. There were two designs for this building: the air force's and Oscar Niemeyer's. In spite of complete support of Niemeyer's project from public opinion and the press, the air force's plan was adopted, although the council did not review it. It seems that a question of military prestige was involved in the issue. In more normal times Niemeyer would certainly have won.

The day-to-day planning activities are carried out by four divisions of the Department of Public Works. These agencies have responsibility for all routine matters related to building licences, zoning, subdivision control and the design of public works and buildings. Only the major problems are presented to the Council of Architecture and Urbanism. So far, with the unfortunate exception of the airport, it can be said that the city government has been able not only to maintain the original concept of Brasilia's plan but also to develop it accordingly.

BRASILIA TODAY

Brasilia as a city

In 1970 the Federal District had about 480,000 inhabitants. Of these 220,000 lived in Brasilia itself (the planned city). Thus, Brasilia already ranks high among Brazilian cities. The remainder of the District's population live in seven satellite towns and in the rural area. The satellite towns and their respective approximate populations and distances from Brasilia (in kilometres) are: Taguatinga 100,000 (25 km); Gama 60,000 (38 km); Sobradinho 50,000 (22 km); Planaltina 10,000 (42 km); Braslândia 6,000 (42 km); Paranoá 2,000 (32 km); and Jardim 2,000 (63 km).

In the few years since its inauguration Brasilia has acquired all the elements of a planned, governmental city and most of the characteristics of a true city of its size. Its educational system is very good, certainly one of the best in the country at the primary and secondary levels. A notable experiment was made with the creation of the University of Brasilia in 1961. A completely new concept by Brazilian traditions was introduced into the university's organization, based on the American model. The progressive part of the academic community of the country hoped for the success of the experiment, which might become the starting point for the reform of Brazil's archaic university system. Unfortunately, political difficulties since the 1964 Revolution have seriously hampered the development of the university, which has lost most of its excellent faculty and therefore the prestige it briefly enjoyed. Two private universities were created in 1968, with several departments in full operation.

Brasilia has two daily papers, three radio and three television stations, but the Rio de Janeiro and São Paulo major papers are widely read. There are two major libraries, one at the university and the other at the House of Deputies, which is one of the best in Brazil. Other important public libraries are the ones maintained by the British Council, the Alliance Française and the US Information Service.

Opportunities for amusement are found mainly in the many clubs that exist in Brasilia, around the lake and in other parts of the city. Although the children and young people are considered to be fully adjusted to the life of Brasilia and find it easy to amuse themselves and keep busy, it is recognized that for many adults who came from Rio de Janeiro and other larger cities the lack of amusement is a major complaint. On the other hand, many people find that living in Brasilia affords closer family life, which is due in part to the fact that everybody can have lunch at home. There is also an incentive to visit with friends and to live a more leisurely life than in the larger cities.

Despite being planned so fully, Brasilia is in many respects a mirror of the social conditions prevailing in the country in general. Its education system, although of a very high calibre, is still privately operated in a considerable part, especially at the secondary level, which means that the public schools are not sufficient for the population. Housing is a most crucial problem and both outside and within the planned city many *favelas* or slums are found. Under-employment has become chronic for unskilled workers since the pace of construction fell in 1961. Also, the city is unequally developed. There has been a greater concentration of resources in the south wing, where the many beautiful superblocks and other facilities are found, while the north wing still has a rather drab, unfinished look. In spite of all this, social inequalities are certainly less in Brasilia than in any other large Brazilian city. Being inhabited mainly by functionaries, it has practically no wealthy people. At the same time, the general standard of living is one of the highest in the country.

The federal government in Brasilia

Upon the inauguration of the new capital on 21 April 1960, the highest organs of the three powers of government moved to Brasilia. Both houses of Congress occupied their bowl-shaped building, the Supreme Court moved into its new palace, and the president of the republic occupied his official residence at the Palace of the Dawn and moved the presidential offices to the Plateau Palace at the Three Powers Square. The ministries established offices in their respective buildings and several other federal agencies started to move. Suit was followed by the Federal Court of Appeals, the Superior Electoral Court and the Federal Court of Accounts.

Today, five governments and ten years later, the moving still continues at an uninterrupted if often hesitant pace, and the transfer of the capital has become an irreversible fact. During this period the president many times conducted his business in the former capital, and his ministers are generally found more often in Rio de Janeiro than in Brasilia. But the judiciary, the Congress and the Federal Court of Accounts have not budged from their new home since they moved. The conduct of executive business at Brasilia, at least at the higher governmental levels, is dictated mainly by the attitude of the president. If the president chooses to stay in Brasilia, then the ministers and other high-ranking officials are bound to spend more time there; this was so during the short-lived Quadros government. If, on the contrary, the president prefers to be frequently in Rio de Janeiro, as with Goulart, Castello Branco, Costa e Silva and even Kubitscheck himself in 1960, then the hubbub of governmental activity is heard in Rio. The new president, Garrastazu Medici, who took office in November 1969 for a term lasting until 1975, speeded up the move to a pace never seen since the inauguration of the capital. He ordered most of the ministries, including the critical ones, such as planning and finance, to be in Brasilia by the end of the first quarter of 1970.

Two other major factors, however, determine the pace of transfer to Brasilia. One is the lack of housing for the functionaries, in spite of the fact that there is sufficient office space for most services to move into. The other is the resistance of many top government officials to living in Brasilia. Cheap rents and double salary were incentives that were used in the beginning to lure federal employees to move. The double salary was later discontinued as a costly device. As for housing, the government decided to sell the units to the employees on very favourable conditions, instead of renting, as a new stimulus to call people to Brasilia.

The present government has plans to move the policy-making and control agencies of all ministries to Brasilia within the next two years, in accordance with the principles set forth by the administrative reform now under way. The reform calls for a great deal of decentralization of the decision-making process, which will have an effect on geographic decentralization as well. Thus the idea of keeping away from Brasilia all offices of a markedly executive or regional nature will have a favourable effect in speeding up the transfer, which may well be completed within twelve years after the inauguration.

Finally, the recent inauguration of the beautiful Itamaraty Palace, where the Ministry of Foreign Affairs is located, is an important thrust to the effective moving of the capital. By the end of March 1970 the Ministry had moved completely to Brasilia. A rule is being considered according to which two years after that date all diplomatic actions have to be taken in Brasilia, in order to be valid. This means that either all diplomatic missions will have moved also or that a trip to Brasilia will be necessary for the performance of any diplomatic act. As a further step to force the move of foreign missions, the government decided to withdraw diplomatic recognitions from those missions which are not in Brasilia by the end of September 1972.

The government has granted all sorts of facilities for the installation of the diplomatic missions in the new capital. A plot of land was donated to each mission in the embassy sector, where both the mission and the official residence of the mission chief can be built. This land and its buildings are tax-free, according to the existing laws.

Japan, the United States and Yugoslavia have already built their embassies, while the Scandinavian countries, France and several others are building theirs. The Ministry of Foreign Affairs has reached an agreement with all missions that their buildings in Brasilia must express the modern architecture of their countries. The Ministry provides customs exemptions and other facilities to the teams of architects and designers who come to Brasilia to study the sites. Great names of each country's architecture have been commissioned for these projects. Moreover, many countries already have a small staff in Brasilia, and several have built residences for their diplomatic personnel. As a result, Brasilia has already gained as one of its features that habit of the cocktail circuit which is a distinctive mark of diplomatic and international activity.

Brasilia as the national capital

The wisdom of building Brasilia is still questioned by many people, but it seems that there is a growing consensus about the fulfilment of the objectives which motivated the decision to move the capital to the central plateau.

One of the objectives which is being fully achieved is the development of the hinterland. Three major roads have been built to link the vast interior with Rio de Janeiro, São Paulo, and Belem. The Belem-Brasilia highway, 2,086 kilometres long, cuts through the vast Amazonic wilderness and opens an immense area to civilization. The Brasilia-Acre road, still longer, links the westernmost part of the country to the capital. It connects the remote city of Cuiabá in the western state of Mato Grosso, to Brasilia and thus to the big metropolitan centres to the east and south. The opening up of these roads has had a significant effect on the region. Sleepy old towns have come to life and dozens of new communities have emerged along the highways, teeming with life and vitality. Traffic is intense, even on the Belem–Brasilia link, which is still a dirt road with many problems. The western part of Minas Gerais and a large area of Goiás, around Brasilia, have shown great signs of development. Goiânia, the capital of Goiás – 220 km from Brasilia – has experienced what is considered a really spectacular boom.

It is contended that this awakening of the hinterland could well be achieved by just building the roads and investing in other reproductive projects, without incurring the great expenses of building Brasilia. This argument, however, has a serious flaw in that a motivation like Brasilia was needed to make everything happen. Statesmen and politicians are not guided by purely rational ideas alone, but by rapture and inspiration as well. They might easily have asked the rhetorical question: "If there is to be no Brasilia, why build the roads?"

Another aspect to be considered is the efficiency of Brasilia as a capital. A definitive judgement on this is still impossible, since the executive branch of the government is still in the process of moving. This causes an inevitable ambiguity, the effects of which are often enervating to those who must deal with certain governmental offices and therefore commute between Rio and Brasilia in search of the officials and the papers.

Congress has had to change its pace and method of work, so as to allow many of its members who still have houses in Rio to spend the weekends there. Work is therefore concentrated on Tuesdays, Wednesdays, and Thursdays, although sessions are regularly held on Mondays and Fridays to attend to minor business. This difficulty will of course be overcome as the representation is renewed and fewer and fewer congressmen have a house in Rio de Janeiro.

The transfer to Brasilia has also meant a certain isolation for the Congress. In Rio de Janeiro it functioned before a large political audience and in a centre that radiated information to the whole country. Individual members had access to a large television network and appeared before the great vehicles of mass communication. The possibilities for this in Brasilia are much smaller. As a compensation, Congress was granted half an hour on the national radio network, Monday through Friday from 7.30 to 8.00 pm, to parallel what is done for the executive, which occupies the radio waves on those days from 7.00 to 7.30 pm. During this half hour the most relevant news about the day's activities of both houses of Congress is broadcast over all radio stations of the country.

On the other hand, the productivity of the higher courts has greatly increased. These bodies have moved completely, and since their members do not need the contact with Rio de Janeiro as a major political centre as the congressmen do, they can devote themselves to their work in much calmer surroundings than previously.

Conclusions

Misgivings about the feasibility of Brasilia as the capital have almost disappeared. The prevailing feeling now is that it is there to stay. Some people find the pace of moving the capital a slow one, perhaps because the early rhythm of construction was so hectic. It must be remembered, however, that compared with other new capitals, such as Washington, New Delhi, and Canberra, Brasilia fares exceedingly well. Carl Sandburg says, in his biography of Lincoln, that the grounds in front of the White House were a pasture when Lincoln was president. New Delhi, whose construction began in 1913, had its government palace completely built only in 1930. Canberra, inaugurated in 1927, is still being completed.

The quality of life in Brasilia improves constantly. The pace of construction has increased in the last three years. Industry is beginning to move in, although cautiously. Tourists from all parts of Brazil and from all over the world visit it in ever larger numbers. The place becomes more urbanized every day, with many improvements made of its infra-structure.

By most counts, Brasilia is a dream coming true.

HISTORY AND BACKGROUND

Buenos Aires as the federal capital

The federalization of Buenos Aires was the culmination of a long and grave political problem, called the "Capital Question," that even resulted in a civil war.

Since Argentina's independence, all antecedents and factors of a physical, historical, economic, social, and cultural nature have pointed to the city of Buenos Aires as the capital of the republic. Formerly, under the Spanish regime, it had been the capital of the Viceroyship of the River Plate. After independence it was the capital of the province of Buenos Aires and the seat of the national authorities, but was not declared the capital of the republic. It was the most important city, however, thus assuring the province of Buenos Aires a decisive, even an excessive, influence in the control of the republic. In 1880 the city had a population of 256,000 out of a total of 2.5 million for the whole country. Even then it was considered that this constituted an excessive concentration making for disequilibrium.

In 1826, under an ephemeral unitary regime, the city of Buenos Aires, plus an extensive adjacent rural territory, was declared the national capital, but it only functioned as such for a short time until the unitary government was overthrown. Later, when the country was organized under the federal Constitution of 1853 and the province of Buenos Aires was temporarily separated from confederation, the city of Parana in the province of Entre Rios was temporarily federalized (national decree of 24 March 1854, and law of 4 October 1858).

From 1860 until 1880 the national authorities resided in and governed from Buenos Aires as the provisional capital of the country, except for a very brief installation of the federal authorities in the municipality of Belgrano, which had not then been incorporated into the city of Buenos Aires. This short installation originated from an armed conflict between the national authorities and those of the province of Buenos Aires. Before 1880 there had been some initiatives to federalize other cities or to build a new city as the capital of the nation. However, these initiatives were unsuccessful, and Buenos Aires was formally declared the federal capital of the Argentine Republic by law No. 1029 of 21 September 1880.

In Article 1 of this law the capital of the republic was declared to be "the municipality of the city of Buenos Aires, within actual limits to be prescribed after compliance with the constitutional requirements of Article 8." Article 8 refers to the necessary cession of the territory by the legislature of the province, in conformity with Article 3 of the national constitution. Article 3 establishes that "The federal authorities shall reside in the city that has been declared the capital of the republic by a special law of Congress, which shall provide for the transfer by one or more provincial legislatures of territory to be federalized." Until this time the city of Buenos Aires had belonged to the province of Buenos Aires and was functioning as the provincial capital. However, without prejudice to this fact and under agreed conditions, the national authorities were installed in the same city. The provincial law which authorized the transfer of territory was passed by the legislature of the province of Buenos Aires on 26 November 1880.

Later the territory of the federal capital was increased by new transfers from the province of Buenos Aires. By provincial law No. 1899, the territories of the departments or neighbouring municipalities of San José de Flores and Belgrano were ceded to the nation. This transfer was accepted by national law No. 2089 of 29 September 1887.

The federalization of the city signified a serious sacrifice for the province, which for its part had to create and construct "from the bottom up" a new capital as the seat of provincial government, namely the city of La Plata, some 50 km from Buenos Aires. Meanwhile the provincial government continued to occupy the buildings necessary for its operations and to function without jurisdiction in the city of Buenos Aires until it was moved to its new seat (Article 6 of national law No. 1029). On the other hand, the separation of the city from the territory of the province did not prevent an accelerated growth of population in the federal capital's environs: physically, socially, and economically the city overflowed its political and administrative limits to become what is known as the "metropolitan area."

Constitutional background

The majority of the Argentine provinces predate the national organization set up by the constitution of 1853. Other provinces were created afterwards out of "national territories."

By Article 104 of the national constitution, "the provinces retain all power not given to the federal government by the constitution, or those which were specifically reserved by special pacts at the time of its incorporation." The autonomous sphere of the provinces within the federation is also laid down in Articles 105 to 110 inclusive. Article 5 established that "each province shall draw up for itself a constitution in the manner of the republican representative system, and in accord with the principles, declarations and guarantees of the national constitution; and which shall assure the administration of justice, a municipal regime and primary education. Under these conditions, the federal government guarantees to each province the enjoyment and exercise of its own constitution."

Argentina is made up of 22 provinces, a federal territory, i.e. "the National Territory of Tierra del Fuego, Antarctica and the Islands of the South Atlantic" governed directly by the national government, and the federal capital territory. In conformity with Article 67 para. 27, of the constitution, the national Congress is empowered to "exercise exclusive legislation in all the territory of the capital of the nation and all other places acquired by purchase or transfer in whatever province for the establishment of forts, arsenals, stores or other establishments for national use."

On 28 June 1966 there was a revolution which had serious and far-reaching effects on the national political scene and which posed important questions for the leaders. The revolutionary junta dictated the so-called Statute of the Argentine Revolution on that day, and named the president of the nation. By virtue of this statute the national, provincial, and municipal legislative organizations were suppressed and political parties dissolved. According to Article 9 of the statute, "the national government is responsible for matters which concern the provincial governments and nominates the respective governors, who will exercise the powers conceded by the respective provincial constitutions to the executive and legislative authorities."

The system of government for the federal capital shows the influence of the US system. The difference is that Buenos Aires was a city which predated federalization, whereas Washington was newly established.

National significance of Buenos Aires

According to the 1960 census the total population of the country was 21 million, and in 1970 it was over 24 million. According to the same census Buenos Aires as a municipality has an area of 200 square kilometres (77.2 sq. mi.) and had a population of 2.8 million, while in 1970 its population was more than 3.5 million.

But Buenos Aires as a "city" – as a physical, economic, and social phenomenon – now constitutes a metropolitan area which greatly exceeds the political and administrative limits of the municipality and includes a number of neighbouring municipalities in the province of Buenos Aires. The municipality is linked with these by uninterrupted urban population and the whole area has become an inter-related complex. Using the criteria accepted by the Regulatory Plan Organization of the city, one finds that the metropolitan area covers more than 4,000 km² and has a population of over seven million, nearly one-third of the population of the whole country.

According to the 1960 census, next in importance to the metropolitan conglomerate of Buenos Aires are only two cities with populations between 500,000 and 600,000 (Córdoba and Rosario) and three with populations between 200,000 and 300,000 (Tucumán, Santa Fe, and Mar del Plata).

In external trade, the port of Buenos Aires holds a monopolistic position: 80 per cent of the import tonnage and 35 to 40 per cent of the export tonnage pass through it. The Regulatory Plan Organization's figures show the following economic concentration in the region of Buenos Aires as compared with the rest of the country: 40 per cent of all industrial establishments, 50 per cent of power, 60 per cent of the working population, and 60 per cent of industrial production.

The growing disparity between metropolitan Buenos Aires and the rest of the country is due to a whole complex of causes. Its position as the national capital is not the only factor. Others are: (a) it is located on the banks of the great river Plate, which is formed by the convergence of two great rivers of South America, the Paraná and the Uruguay; (b) it is the most important port in the country; (c) it is the centre of a national and international economic structure, based mainly on the export of agricultural products and cattle; (d) it is the terminus of the national railway systems; (e) it is the chief industrial centre of the country (particularly in the vicinity of the capital); and (f) it is the principal financial and cultural centre of the country.

GOVERNMENT OF THE FEDERAL DISTRICT

Distinction between the political and municipal government

It is necessary to differentiate between the political government of the capital which is reserved by the national government, and the administrative government of the city, which is delegated to the municipal authorities.

Under the constitution of 1853 the national government laid down the local legislation for the federal capital, and the president of the republic is the local head of the federal capital. Within the local legislation which the national government laid down there is the municipal regime of the city. The following are the constitutional references: Article 67, para. 27, gives the national Congress the right "to exercise exclusive legislative power in all the territory of the national capital"; and Article 86, para. 3, states that the president "is the immediate local head of the federal capital." All of the courts which function in the federal capital are national, and the judges are appointed by the national government.

As a result of the revolution of 28 June 1966, the national Congress was dissolved, as were also the provincial legislatures and the political parties. According to the Statute of the Argentine Revolution, "the national president shall exercise all legislative authority that the national constitution grants to Congress ..." (Article 5).

Municipal government and the question of self-government

The organic legislation for the government and municipal administration of the city of Buenos Aires was passed by Congress in exercise of its authority under Article 67, para. 27, of the constitution. It springs from Organic Law No. 1260 of 1882, augmented by later laws on various matters: impositions, expropriations, restrictions of jurisdiction, elections, organizations of courts, etc.

The constitution refers in Article 5 to municipal systems in the provinces, but there is no specific reference to the municipal system in the city of Buenos Aires; this fact started a long controversy as to whether Buenos Aires has the right, constitutionally speaking, to an autonomous municipal government or whether the national government has the power to establish any form of local administration, even to abolish the characteristics of a municipal government. The supporters of the first point of view were inspired by the municipal thinking which dominated the constitution-makers in 1853, and harked back to the tradition of municipal government which the city of Buenos Aires formerly enjoyed. The supporters of the latter view were inspired by the example of Washington.

Ignoring these doctrinal discussions, it is certain that until now the national government has assumed to itself, by virtue of the two articles of the constitution already mentioned, the power to regulate the system of local government and administration for the city of Buenos Aires. The exercise of this authority by the national government has done away with genuine municipal authority, since it is not guaranteed by the constitution, as it is for example in the constitution of Brazil.

Under the Organic Law of 1882 the government of the municipality of Buenos Aires is divided into two branches: an executive, whose titular head is the municipal intendant, designated by the president with the agreement of the Senate (Article 53); and a municipal council, elected by the people of the capital. The electoral process is regulated mainly by law

No. 10240. The consultative council, however, was dissolved by the revolutionary junta of 28 June 1966. Within the limits of the municipality there are no other governments or local authorities nor any territorial decentralization.

Federal control of the municipal administration

Federal control is exercised by means of both legislative authority over the capital territory and the appointment of the municipal intendant by the national president (law No. 1260, Article 53).

With the dissolution of the municipal council, the greater part of its powers were transferred by law No. 16897 of July 1966 to the president. The president has reserved to himself control of the following matters through the Ministry of the Interior:

A Ratification or modification of fiscal or tariff ordinances;
B Authorization of the general expense budget, or its modification in regard to any increase in expenditures;
C Ratification of all the orders to pay issued by the municipal intendant and carried out by the accountant-general of the municipality;
D Approval or alteration of the basic systems of contracting, including those for public works contracts;
E Examination, approval or non-acceptance of the projects in municipal budgets;
F Arrangement of loans;
G Approval or alteration of basic systems regarding municipal personnel, including establishment, rights, obligations, salaries and social security;
H Granting of concessions for municipal services, except those which must be awarded by public tender.

However, there is a recourse of a judicial character against the decisions of the municipal intendant on matters of administrative dispute. Article 4 of law No. 16897 establishes that such matters "shall be brought for settlement directly to the National Court of Civil Appeals, to which recourse is given by Article 8, para. 3 of the law of 1893." The law of 1893 refers to the organization of the courts in the federal capital.

Political aspects of the municipal government

There are no divisions or conflicts of a religious or ethnic nature in the country, which could have any serious consequences of a political nature. There are only, as everywhere, diverse tendencies of a political and social character. The Catholic religion is virtually predominant.

In the city of Buenos Aires there is a cosmopolitan spirit, and a tolerance in matters religious and racial. With regard to political and social differences which have led to revolutionary movements, only occasionally has true violence occurred. Generally speaking, in major electoral decisions (e.g. on the president of the nation), the capital has reflected the political tendency prevailing throughout the country.

Nevertheless, there have been occasions when the voters of the federal capital have been manifestly against the party in power in the national government. In the elections of 1928 the Independent Socialists, a party with limited support, won in the capital, thus overthrowing the Radical party of President Irigoyen. Also, just prior to the Argentine Revolution of 28 June 1966, some of the non-governmental parties represented in the municipal council frequently paralysed the action of the executive branch by using obstructionist tactics in a manner similar to that adopted in the national Parliament. In some elections political groups formed to operate only in the local municipal sphere, or with support only in that sphere, have put up candidates. Incidentally, in municipal elections foreigners who fulfilled specified requirements were allowed to vote. As mentioned, all political parties were dissolved in 1966, and no elections are now being held.

LOCAL SERVICES AND FINANCES

Urban public services in Buenos Aires are provided by national enterprises and by municipal organizations. For technical and financial reasons several public services which were formerly provided by the municipality or one of its agencies have passed by degrees into the national sphere when their extension has gone beyond the municipal boundaries or they have become part of large technical-financial systems. Such has been the case with electricity and gas services, passenger bus transport, etc. Sewers and water have been provided since their establishment by a national enterprise, National Sanitation Works, which extends throughout the country. Telephone service is provided by a nationalized agency.

Apart from exercising police authority in matters of security, hygiene, and morality, the principal services provided by the municipality are: public lighting, street cleaning, garbage collection, cemeteries, and the provision of cultural services (theatres, museums and libraries). In transportation, only taxis remain under its jurisdiction. The municipality also has the task of providing a register of the civil status of its residents.

Financing of local services

The services provided by the municipality are financed partly from municipal revenues and partly by a share of the taxes which are imposed by the national government. Among its "own" resources the most important are of a tax nature. The most lucrative of the levies are, in order of importance, a tax on business activities, taxes for lighting and street cleaning, and taxes on automobiles. Also there are other assessments which are raised on real property, and income arising from the occupation of public places, the renting of property to private concerns by the municipality, and payments received for special services.

Its share of national tax revenue until 1967 provided 16 per cent of the total income of the municipality. In 1968 this share was reduced 50 per cent by virtue of the imposition of law No. 17578. This loss of income will seriously affect municipal plans, since in the previous two years a more satisfactory financial situation had been enjoyed as compared with former years in which serious problems had developed because of an excess of expenses over income.

For some time now the municipality has not used credit to any significant extent (partly due to a national policy of limiting its use by municipalities). Recently external financing has been used for the construction of housing, by means of a credit from the Interamerican Development Bank.

The fiscal ordinance exempts from payment of all taxes diplomatic representatives of foreign countries (Article 34, para. 2), with the sole exception of payment for special services provided by the municipality at their request. This general tax exemption includes the provision of car licences, not only special plates for cars of the diplomatic missions but also licences for private cars belonging to members of these missions (Articles 34 and 99 of the fiscal ordinance, text of 1967). As regards the consular corps, the fiscal ordinance states that "special plates will be given free of charge to foreign consuls and vice-consuls (non-honorary) provided that the respective countries act reciprocally." No serious financial or other problems appear to have arisen in relations between the municipality and foreign diplomats.

URBAN PLANNING

After some unsuccessful attempts, in 1959 the municipality established the "Regulatory Plan Organization for the city of Buenos Aires" as an agency for regional planning. The organization was assigned the basic task of preparing a Master Plan for the city and also the specifications and estimates for putting the plan into effect, at the same time taking into account various regional projects which the urban development of the city would require. Its studies encompass both the national functions of the city and the fact that the municipality forms part of the metropolitan area. In 1962 the Master Plan (Preliminary) was approved together with the documents and complementary studies, destined to orient municipal activity within the development of the city. The enactment of a law of urban planning is anticipated, which in time will authorize a municipal code of urban planning, replacing the present one.

Despite the limited time which has passed since its creation, the work done by this local planning organization is considered to be effective. Throughout the municipal administration there is a consciousness of the necessity of adjusting urban action to provisions and plans made in line with up-to-date technical concepts. The municipal authorities have striven to provide the organization with the human, technical, and financial resources necessary to act in co-ordination with the national government and the province of Buenos Aires not only around the perimeter of the municipality but also throughout the whole metropolitan area.

The urban planning of the city will in future be integrated into the regional planning of the metropolitan area by virtue of the requirements of the National System of Planning and Development Action (Law No. 16964 of 30 September 1966 and decree 1907 of 1967). The National Development Council will provide the general guide lines for the development of the area.

THE PRINCIPAL PROBLEMS

In general the political, financial, and technical problems which confront the city of Buenos Aires are common to all big cities of the world. The most critical problems are those of housing, traffic, and transportation. Also, the telephone services are inadequate. Until recently there was a shortage of electricity but this has been overcome. There are important sections of the city – such as the so-called "southern quarter," very close to the central zone – which, due to obsolescence, call for programs of urban renewal. As much in the municipality as in the rest of the metropolitan area, "poverty-stricken towns" have developed – wretched districts with a total population of some 700,000 persons. In addition, there is a constant crisis in municipal finances, due to the rising cost of services in the face of a limited financial basis.

In the past, certain demagogic forces in the elective branch, desirous of acting at times as a "miniature parliament" and not as an administrative body, have impaired the image of the municipal council in the eyes of the public. The present national government, however much it has endorsed the basic importance of the existence of municipal organization, has not expressed any official policy on the Argentine municipal system and on the reform of the municipal system of Buenos Aires. But it is evident to all that the present basic municipal law, which dates from 1882, should be revised and enforced.

This calls for a reform of the structure of the city's government. Universal experience indicates the convenience of participation by neighbourhoods in a common government, but experience also indicates the necessity of having a more technical and less political city government and administration. Although a new structure of municipal government needs to be imposed, at the same time the city's operations must be developed in a manner consistent with the methods and standards called for by the modern techniques of administrative rationalization. The growing demand for services does not necessarily signify an increase in personnel and costs if these services are provided in a better and more efficient way. With this in mind, consideration of the problems of the city and its environs should be raised to a metropolitan level. It would be absurd to try to find separate solutions for each one of the municipalities which make up the area. Soon the need for establishing an authority of a technical character for the metropolitan area will have to be faced.

In the past, proposals have been advanced for the reform of the city's municipal system, originating for the most part with the traditional political parties. These proposals would retain the general lines of the present structure of the municipal organization. For a long time the problem that preoccupied the political parties and some authors was the reinforcement of so-called "municipal autonomy" by such means as direct popular election of the municipal intendant, but no party once it formed a government would decide to carry out the idea. Election of the intendant is attractive to partisans of municipal autonomy but is repugnant to those who see a danger for national government in a city which has a very strong and independent municipal authority; they foresee collisions and conflicts of power. In any case, the idea has never received any legislative endorsement.

Proposals have also been made for an increase in the taxation powers of the municipality, in order to meet the constant rises in the costs of administration, and there has been no lack of authoritative voices who have raised the problem, so often debated in other countries, of the reconciliation of democracy with efficiency in municipal government. In addition, a reform of the constitution has been proposed in order to define the city's municipal system, which has been up to now so much a subject of controversy, and to guarantee the municipality a secure place within the governmental structure of the country.

The question of a new capital

Confronted with the increasing growth of Buenos Aires and its metropolitan area and with its disproportion to the rest of the country, some people have suggested that its growth might be contained by depriving it of the federal capital and by establishing the capital in the interior of the country, either in an existing city or in a newly constructed city on the model of Brasilia. This second project is seen not only as a form of decentralization but also as a means of developing the country. Some studies of this matter exist, and there have been some parliamentary initiatives to undertake an examination of the possibilities of carrying out such a scheme.

In my view, this would be neither an effective nor practical solution to the problem. The disproportionate growth of Buenos Aires does not stem mainly from its being the seat of the national government but is due basically to an exceptional geographical location, aided by a wide-ranging policy of centralization which has created factors that are difficult if not impossible to remove directly. At the same time, recent statistical data show that, while the population of the surrounding district is increasing, the population of Buenos Aires is remaining stable. The creation of a new federal capital, with the consequent transfer of the national administration and of the executive offices of private firms and organizations concerned with government, would represent an incalculable financial cost that the country could not undertake.

Solutions must be found elsewhere, and must be related to a national policy that would stimulate the development of other regions of the country by means of new industrial centres and ports and by granting them preferential status. One could realize by this method what is called by the French "a metropolis in equilibrium." Additional measures which could be taken without raising contentious local issues, would be to facilitate only the installation of new industries called for by the immediate needs of Buenos Aires, to control building density and to encourage foreign immigration to settle in the interior of the country.

Whatever methods are adopted, the city of Buenos Aires is not likely to lose its position as the first city of the republic. Although its greatness is a cause for national pride, it may also be one of the causes of the breakdown of the equilibrium required for a good federal system of government.

3 Ruth Atkins* CANBERRA

CANBERRA'S CHARACTERISTICS

Introduction

Canberra is a planned new city developed as Australia's capital in a specially created federal district. It is most fortunately situated, and the delights of varied landscape, of tree-lined streets and green hills, of distant views to mountains, of the central sweep of lakes, lively with sail boats by day and bright reflections by night, are notable parts of its charm. It has been fortunate also in many other ways. The federal territory acquired for the capital comprises an inland strip of 910 square miles, with another small coastal area at Jervis Bay, about 80 miles away. This land was virtually unoccupied when it became the property of the federal government. The original plan for the capital city was an imaginative concept, and, in spite of difficulties, it has remained influential in later development. In recent years a single national authority has been responsible for planning, development and construction, and has strong financial and administrative support from the Commonwealth government whose headquarters the city has become.

There are no difficulties here arising from competing jurisdictions among different levels of government or from the expansion of the capital beyond the federal area. Expropriation has never been a major problem. Crown lands in the territory were transferred to the Commonwealth without cost. A leasehold system of occupancy was established in the capital city area from the outset, and has been extended to other sections of the territory as

* The author requests it to be noted that the essay was completed early in 1969 and hence makes no mention of two important events that occurred late in 1970. The first was the issuing of a statement of municipal accounts for Canberra in which the Department of the Interior estimated the revenues and expenditures for the capital that in other Australian cities would be local government revenues or expenditures. Those estimates revealed a considerable subsidizing of "local" functions by the national treasury. The second event was the government's announcement of its decision to abolish land rent in Canberra (except for a token annual payment designed to retain the leasehold system for the control of land use) and to adjust local charges so that the return from them will approximate the amounts that would have been received from land rent, rates, and water and sewerage charges.

required. Planning in the capital territory has never faced the difficult hurdles of entrenched private ownership or established urban settlement. It will not be difficult or expensive for the Commonwealth government to extend some planned new settlements into rural areas where lands have remained under freehold occupancy. Moreover, Canberra at a very early stage was efficiently and generously supplied with the basic equipment for water supply, sewerage, drainage and power.

These are enormous advantages, that might well be envied by those concerned with other national capitals, and with other cities in Australia, or elsewhere. What has been achieved in Canberra might seem disappointing unless we recognize that two of these advantages were lacking until very recent years, the crucial factors of unified development control and strong government support for the capital project.

For almost fifty years after the site was chosen, development was slow and half-hearted, with governments usually vacillating or neglectful, finance inadequate and the attitudes of Australian citizens varying from amused tolerance to scorn or opposition. As with the creation of Australia's federal system from the six British Australian colonies, there was agreement in principle, but there was little sense of urgency. It is probably a sign of Australia's peaceful good fortune that neither its federation, nor the establishment of its federal capital was pushed along by any urgent necessity. It took eight years for the capital's site to be determined; another five before the foundation ceremonies were held. Fourteen years later in 1927 the present parliament house was opened and the federal parliament began meeting in Canberra instead of in Melbourne. But there was no accompanying transfer of more than a few sections of the federal government departments.

Between 1930 and 1950 the population grew only from 7300 to 22,000, and it remained a collection of scattered settlements around an almost empty capital centre. It did not become an effective working headquarters of national government until the 1960s, and it was noticeably lacking in commercial and business life until these recent years. In spite of its official age Canberra is a city whose principal growth as a major government centre and as a city in its own right has occurred only since about 1958. Population figures indicate this concentrated growth; by 1968 there were more than 100,000 people in Canberra, and a doubling of this figure is confidently expected in less than 20 years.

Canberra today

Canberra is now a more complete government headquarters and a more flourishing city than even the most confident predictions of ten years ago would have suggested. Though it still lacks many of the planned buildings of the capital centre, the lakes have tied the place together, provided an attractive and varied centre-piece, and a splendid setting for buildings that are being planned. The new national library is an impressive addition, and a national gallery and new parliament house are currently being planned, though neither is likely to appear for years. There is, however, a recognizable character now in the capital city, not the impression of a small town.

In the main commercial centre only in the last few years there have appeared tall office blocks, department stores, and varied shopping and other commercial enterprises. A new theatre centre opened in 1955 has helped to put Canberra on the national circuit for visiting musical and theatrical performances, and there is more varied entertainment than in any Australian city of comparable size. Those who criticize the lack of night life and sophistication in Canberra are often using Sydney or Melbourne as their yardsticks; each of these is 25 times the size of Canberra.

For many people there are unique charms in the combination of arcadian surroundings, unspoiled by careless "development," and the bright clean garden-city character of Canberra. For others the variety and challenge of an unplanned metropolis are lacking, the expanding suburbs too orderly and dull, even the tree-planting too formal. But there is no doubt that more and more people are finding Canberra an attractive place to live in and to visit, however justified some of the detailed criticisms may be.

The capital is no longer just a government town. The Commonwealth public service still provides and is likely to go on providing the main source of growth. But the proportion of the work-force in government office employment has declined in ten years from over 40 per cent to just over 30 per cent. Private enterprise is playing a much greater part than ever before. Investment is profitable in providing hotels, shops, restaurants, and other services for a growing local population and a visiting population of more than half a million each year. The tourist trade is flourishing, partly because of the attractions of the capital and its surroundings, partly because Canberra is on the way from Sydney to Melbourne, from Sydney and the north to the Snowy Mountains area, and to attractive parts of the south coast of New South Wales. More and more headquarters offices are being established in Canberra, which is becoming increasingly a conference centre and meeting place. The Australian National University was one of the first really important "non-government" organizations in the capital, but from the beginning the national observatory at Mount Stromlo, the Commonwealth Scientific and Industrial Research Organization, and the Institute of Anatomy helped to make Canberra a centre for scientific research. Within a few miles of Canberra city there are now tracking stations participating in United States-Australian space research.

Manufacturing industry has only a small part in the capital's economy. It is however becoming a centre for regional marketing and for commercial and professional services. Within 20 years Canberra's market influence may extend over a region with a population of 650,000 of which 250,000 will be in the capital itself. Naturally, providing for this rapid growth in the capital requires a large building and construction force. But the building of the capital and its extensions is no longer mainly a government enterprise. A considerable part of the new developments, whether national buildings or shopping centres, is provided through private firms of architects, town planners, builders, and so on, under the general direction of the National Capital Development Commission.

If Canberra should reach – or even double – its predicted size of 250,000 in the next twenty years, it would still not be a large city on national or international standards. But it is rapidly moving into a position of importance among Australian cities. It is already the largest inland city in the country, and only eight other cities are ahead of it in size. Australia has a unique pattern of urban concentration. Of its 12.3 million population in 1969, more than 2.5 million lived in Sydney, and almost as many in Melbourne. Together these two state capitals account for over 40 per cent of the whole Australian population. In each of the states there is only one major urban-metropolitan region, centred in the state capital. In New South Wales, three-quarters of the state's population lives in the central coast region of Newcastle-Sydney-Wollongong. Between that New South Wales region and Melbourne, more than 500 miles south, there is no urban centre comparable with Canberra in population, growth rate, or attraction for visitors and residents. The 1966 census gives the following figures for Australia's state capitals, apart from Sydney and Melbourne:

Brisbane	777,935
Adelaide	770,628
Perth	558,297
Hobart	141,238

These are far distant from the national capital. Canberra is in an extremely favourable position for becoming an influential and important regional centre for reasons that are apart from, but of course supported by, its character as a planned national capital.

The lack of self-government

There is no elected government for the city of Canberra or for the capital territory. A partly elected Advisory Council was established in 1930, but its functions have always been limited to advising, and in 1969 the elected members resigned in protest against alleged failures on the government's part to consider their advice or to keep them informed. Since 1949 a member for the Australian Capital Territory has been elected to the federal House of Representatives, and since 1960 he has had full voting rights. There is a lively press, whose editors and contributors have often voiced local grievances and demands. Especially in recent years most government departments and authorities have been careful to provide for consultation with individuals and groups affected by their programmes. Local representation has been arranged on some special boards and committees. Even without any formal self-government it is probable that citizens in the capital have easier access to those who decide matters affecting them than would the citizens in Australia's larger cities. Canberra is relatively small. Only one level of government exists. Recent governments have been concerned to win public acceptance, or at least not to let grievances build up. But this does not amount to self-government, and its absence may need explanation.

Some factors made self-government unlikely. In this national capital, created by a national government to be its headquarters, the decisions for a long time were necessarily those of this government. They chose the site; they decided on the plan; they determined the laws to operate in the territory; they allocated funds; they decided what would be established, and when. In the initial stages of any new town it is not appropriate to establish local self-government. This was especially inappropriate for a national capital where almost all the work force was government-employed, occupying government houses, and often temporarily and even reluctantly resident in the capital.

In Canberra these initial stages were protracted over 50 years. In this long period of slow development the system of administration by federal authorities became entrenched, but it was almost the only workable arrangement. Elected self-government could not have remedied the defects that were noticeable – the inadequacies of housing and office accommodation, the difficulties of travel to the capital from other population centres, the lack of community facilities, the neglect of the capital centre. Only national government decisions to promote and manage the capital enterprise could do this. Local residents might have wanted the national government to act more vigorously and consistently, but their demands were not for self-government.

Moreover there is no great strength in the tradition of local government in Australia. Municipal local government developed here as an imposed duty rather than an asserted right, as a device used by higher governments (first colonial then state) to encourage and then to require local citizens to accept some responsibility for financing and administering, for their area, such things as roads, streets, lighting, refuse disposal, sewerage, and health controls. Acceptance of this imposed duty was encouraged if this was the only way of getting such local services. But in Canberra from the beginning these things were provided, and comparatively well provided, by the Commonwealth government, and for many decades without direct payments from local residents. The residents of the capital were not faced with a situation where local self-government seemed the likeliest way to have their needs met. National governments until the 1950s might have been slow and ineffective in their policies and practices connected with the capital's development, but no national government moved to transfer responsibility to the local residents.

Australians are not used to powerful or independent city governments. There is no system of home-rule charters or of optional forms of local government. There has been little experimentation in city government. Local councils are part of a state-controlled system, in which the local authorities have very limited discretion. Those residents of Canberra who had lived in other Australian cities would not necessarily feel deprived of an important democratic opportunity because there was no local elected authority. And since most of the residents until very recent years were employed in the federal bureaucracy they may well have found a different form of political activity in support of their local interests both more congenial and more effective. It is not surprising that self-government was not demanded while Canberra remained a half-completed government centre. It may be more surprising that self-government still did not seem very likely in 1969 when the population had increased rapidly in numbers and diversity and when the capital had become a thriving city.

CONSTITUTIONAL BACKGROUND

Canberra is the capital of the Australian Federal Commonwealth which was established in 1901 when the six Australian colonies were formally linked under a federal constitution enacted by the British parliament. The decision to have a specially created federal capital was part of these constitutional arrangements, but in 1901 the site, design and building of the capital were left for future decision. Until this capital was established the new federation had its governmental headquarters in Melbourne, the state capital of Victoria.

Each of these six colonies – New South Wales, Victoria, Queensland, Tasmania, Western Australia and South Australia – had acquired parliamentary self-government in the years after 1855. Each became a state in the new federation in 1901, but their internal constitutional arrangements were not much changed, except by the ceding of some powers to the newly created federal Commonwealth parliament. Together these six constituent parts of the federation covered the whole area of Australia. In 1907 the Northern Territory was transferred from South Australia to the Commonwealth, but otherwise the state boundaries remained unchanged. No new states have been added, mainly because the formation of any new state, except from this Northern Territory, would require some division of an existing state, and such division has proved constitutionally and politically difficult. It is probable that at some time in the future the Northern Territory will acquire statehood, but the prospect is not immediate.

Canberra and the Australian capital territory have been governed from the outset under Acts and Ordinances of the Commonwealth government. Except for a brief period of government by a specially appointed commission, the capital has been administered by federal government departments, with varying arrangements for coordination, parliamentary supervision and local representation, but no territorial or city self-government. The only other federal territory in Australia, the Northern Territory, is so different from the capital territory that the governmental arrangements for one are not likely to be appropriate for another. The Northern Territory is a large, relatively undeveloped area, whose principal town, Darwin, depends on the development of the natural resources (mining, cattle, etc.) of the hinterland. By contrast the development of the capital territory depends on the growth of Canberra. The legislative council arrangement in the Northern Territory is the traditional half-way house between direct central administration and responsible self-government as a state, and there is some probability that this Northern Territory will eventually become a seventh state of the Commonwealth. But such interim arrangements are not appropriate for the Australian capital territory and are not currently being suggested by government or citizens.

The six Australian colonies had a common form of parliamentary government, with a few local variations, before they federated and became states. The new federal constitution was not intended to make revolutionary changes, but principally to add – with Britain's blessing and encouragement – a new national parliament to carry out some national functions. The form of government retained a strong British imprint, and relations with Britain remained firm. Only very gradually did Australian governments move beyond the management of internal affairs to take full responsibility for international relations and defence without dependence on British policy and leadership.

Australia's federal constitution has proved resistant to formal amendment. The requirement (in the constitution) that a majority of total voters, and of voters in a majority of states must approve proposed amendments has proved difficult to fulfil. Only four significant amendments have been made in nearly 70 years. But the balance of power has been changed noticeably, and the federal system in practice is now very different from that of the first decade of its existence. Two world wars and the depression of the 1930s encouraged the exercise of increased national power. The defence powers in the constitution have given federal governments ample authority for wartime controls. The financial arrangements, including the power of the Commonwealth to make grants to the states "on such terms and conditions as they (the Commonwealth) see fit" have from a very early stage offered the possibility of centralized power.

The most noticeable feature of Australia's federalism now is that the states are dependent for much of their finance on what the Commonwealth allocates, and that their loan policies are also nationally controlled. The Commonwealth government controls all the most lucrative tax sources, including income tax, company tax, sales tax, customs, and excise. The Commonwealth Reserve Bank has important financial powers. In the federal-state Loan Council the Commonwealth has the decisive voice. Each year state premiers and their advisers seek to modify in their favour the allocations, general and specific, which the Commonwealth determines. All states are likely to agree in criticizing the general distribution as between the Commonwealth's activities and those of the states, but not all are equally dissatisfied with the cutting-up of the cake among the separate states. Dissatisfaction is probably strongest in the two most populous and industrialized states, New South Wales and Victoria.

The expansion and improvement of Canberra since 1958 as a capital and a "home-town" has been possible only by increasing and assured financial support from the federal government. This has not been paralleled by federal subsidizing of urban growth elsewhere in Australia. A recent change in Commonwealth road allocations has made some concessions to urban needs, but federal governments have for many years responded more generously to demands for rural subsidies and assistance for research in and marketing of primary products, than to claims based on urban needs. State governments and local authorities have been left with the major responsibilities for dealing with urban expansion. These responsibilities are most difficult and complex in the two urban giants, Sydney and Melbourne, which together have about 5 million of the total 12 million Australian population. There does not seem to be much likelihood that the Canberra example will encourage a different national government approach to urban problems.

THE FOUNDING OF THE CAPITAL

Choosing the site

At the Constitutional Conventions of the 1890s which eventually resulted in Australia's federation in 1901, agreement had been reached that a federal territory of at least 100 square miles should be created within New South Wales, and that the federal capital city (not yet named) should be at least 100 miles from Sydney. Until the capital was ready the new parliament was to meet in Victoria's capital, Melbourne.

The principle of a specially created capital was established, but every move to translate that idea into reality met with difficulties and delays. A continuing difficulty was the reluctance of some politicians and administrators to hasten the day when they might have to transfer from Melbourne, where parliament continued to meet till 1927 and where a high proportion of federal government officials remained until the 1950s. Every question connected with the choice of site, the transfer of territory and the planning and building of the capital took a long time to answer, and was the occasion for dispute.

The first big question about the capital territory was "Where?" Associated questions were these: How big was the territory to be? Who would have the deciding voice, the donor-state or the Commonwealth government? On what terms should the transfer be made? Should the territory have access to the coast? Where in the territory should the capital city be placed?

While the final negotiations for the new federation were going on, New South Wales commissioned a report on three possible sites, Bombala, Orange, and Yass. A choice among these was offered to the new prime minister and his government when they assumed office in 1901. There was no apparent reluctance behind these offers, the potential advantage of the capital as a development centre being seen as sufficient recompense. Nor was there any serious objection from New South Wales to this report's recommendation that much more than 100 square miles should be transferred. It seemed that a simple choice was all that was required. But soon the expectation of benefits to any chosen area caused other sites to be proposed, and members of parliament to advocate their claims. The new federal government was said to be "like a bridal couple returning from their honeymoon to be besieged by enterprising real estate agents with offers of eligible sites for their new home."

In the next few years there were parliamentary inspection tours of possible sites, and another commission of enquiry. By 1904 the federal government had chosen Dalgety and passed a federal act authorising the establishment of the capital there. But New South Wales had not offered this site, and, resenting the Commonwealth's high-handedness, resubmitted an offer of three sites (not including Dalgety), and reduced the area from the tacitly agreed 1,000 square miles to a mere 200. It seemed like a deadlock, but by 1906 more tactful and patient negotiations resulted in agreement on the present site, more than 900 square miles in the Yass-Molonglo area. At a later stage the addition of 28 square miles at Jervis Bay, for a naval base, was agreed upon, and access rights granted to the Commonwealth over the land between the main territory and this small coastal area.

To recommend a location for the capital city within the territory the New South Wales government loaned a district surveyor, Scrivener. His imaginative appraisal and his wisdom in choosing the present site has been commended many times, not least by the winner of the design competition for the capital's plan, who was delighted and inspired by the possibilities of the area.

The arrangements for the territory included agreement that all land was to become Commonwealth territory, and all crown lands were transferred without cost. Land-owners expropriated were to receive the market value as of 1907. With these arrangements and a sparsely settled area, the expense of acquisition was not great. Only £740,000[1] was spent in compensation in the early years. Another agreement gave the Commonwealth rights over waters into the Snowy Mountains, for water supply and hydro-electric schemes. The necessary enabling Acts to establish the Australian capital territory were passed by the Commonwealth and New South Wales governments in 1908-9.

Designs for the capital

The site was chosen, agreements concluded. Next came the question of design. After a few basic surveys had been made, and some essential works (for water, sewerage, etc.) commenced, a world-wide competition was announced for the capital's design. In spite of some unfortunate details connected with the competition – for example, the minister for Home Affairs being the principal judge, and insisting on the possibility of selecting items from any of the three prize winning designs – the result in 1913 was the award of first prize to Walter Burley Griffin of Chicago (with Saarinen of Finland second and Agache of Paris third).

From this time on Griffin's plan had a principal role in Canberra's story. From 1913 until 1920 it was the centre of a battle between Griffin and his supporters on one side and departmental officials on the other, with the minister supporting first one side and then the other. Though Griffin left Canberra in 1920 disappointed and disillusioned, at least some of his basic ideas have had a continuing influence on the shape and style of Canberra.

The garden-city character, the lakes, the vast triangular central arrangement, the use of separate and distinct areas for separate functions, the emphasis on topography and on retaining the hilltops as focal points, ... all these characteristics of Canberra's design are a Griffin legacy. We cannot blame him if we think Canberra's architecture unimaginative, or its buildings in the capital centre inadequate. None of Griffin's proposed buildings have been erected. But if anyone else had designed Canberra, the capital might have been compact, formal, European in style. Because Griffin won the prize, and influenced later decision-makers, Canberra became a garden city, on a large expansive plan, with a lake as a centrepiece.

Griffin had studied the site-model on view in Chicago, and had immediately grasped the possibilities of the site. His central idea was a bold triangular scheme using hilltops as "terminating climaxes" for wide avenues. Recognizing that the Molonglo flood plain would not be suitable for buildings, he proposed a linked series of rather formally-shaped lakes. At the apex of his triangle was the Parliamentary precinct; at the base points were the civic and commercial centres. The residential areas, on garden-city lines, had a rather complex pattern of wide tree-lined avenues and circuits that for many years made difficulties for visitors trying to find their way, especially by car, around this wide-spread unfinished town. Recently it has been comparatively easy to convert Griffin's road plan to something more suitable for the fast motor traffic he could not be expected to envisage in 1913, and with this reorganization and a few more clear landmarks, the road map of Canberra is becoming easier to comprehend.

It was a vast scheme. The sides of Griffin's triangle were each two miles long. Griffin's vision was large, and his sights were set on the future. He was reluctant to make concessions to immediate needs, fearing (with some reason) that any compromise would encourage makeshift development, and destroy the possibility of achieving the kind of city he had planned for.

Departmental officials, however, thought his plan visionary and impractical, and wanted to concentrate on achieving a workable township as quickly as possible. They saw the design competition as providing them and the minister with ideas they might use or discard or combine as they thought fit, not as something providing a unified design they should implement. The resulting conflict was unfortunate, because rigidity on one side encouraged rigidity on the other. The battle of the plans could be represented by a zig-zag graph pattern. At first the minister chose Griffin's plan, but the same minister then accepted a departmental proposal for a hybrid "concocted" scheme. When the official foundation stones were laid ceremonially in February, 1913, and the capital's name declared, the authorized plan was not Griffin's but this departmental hybrid. A change of government pushed the Griffin scheme to another peak of influence, and Griffin, late in 1913, was appointed Federal Capital Director of Design and Construction on a three-year contract, renewable. His title seemed authoritative, but in the next three years he met strong resistance. A Royal Commission reporting in 1917 strongly criticized some government officials for undermining Griffin's authority and obstructing his work. Australia had entered World War I in 1914, and, partly because of this, attention was diverted from the capital project. The budget available for Griffin was never more than £3,000 per year. Though his contract was renewed, Griffin was in difficulties for most of his term. He did manage to establish the general shape of his roads and streets, the sites for some buildings and for the lakes. But from 1913 to 1924 there was no certainty that his plan would endure.

However, in 1925, when support for the Griffin scheme was temporarily strong, his basic street plan was "gazetted" so that modifications required Parliamentary approval, a requirement that has been effective ever since. Slow growth helped also to retain the influence of the basic plan once it was established. In the period of tentative development from 1920 to the late 1950s, there was little pressure for the use of land areas in ways contrary to those suggested by Griffin's plan. The area that subsequently became the lakes remained virtually empty, even though few people believed that the lakes would ever be created. Also, since Griffin's scheme was imaginative and original, it appealed to those who much later were called on to advise on Canberra's development, when really serious attention was given to the future planning of Canberra.

When the Senate Committee reported on Canberra's development in 1955, when Sir William Holford (now Lord Holford) advised the federal government in 1957, 1960, and later, when the National Capital Development Commission began its task in 1958, one principal point always referred to was the need for adherence to Griffin's basic design. No one would assert that his winning design has been implemented fully. But his general scheme has been influential. Even the expanding pattern of new urban centres beyond the original capital city is thought of by some planners as following on a grander scale the basic principles which Griffin supported.

CANBERRA'S EARLY DEVELOPMENT AND GOVERNMENT

The years from 1911 to 1921 in Canberra had seen the "battle of the plans" and some very slow beginnings in basic services, roads and accommodation. In 1921 a Federal Capital Advisory Committee was appointed and its first report recommended a three-stage development plan which, if acted upon, would have had Canberra equipped as a government headquarters by 1924. But the proposals were not acted upon. Funds allotted were inadequate; construction labour was not readily available; and the committee had to advise or persuade at least four separate ministries among which the functions affecting the capital were spread.

The Federal Capital Commission

A new government in 1923 decided that the federal Parliament should meet in Canberra within three or four years, and therefore replaced the scattered departmental administrative scheme with a strong Federal Capital Commission with a clear mandate to get the (temporary) Parliament House built, and enough houses, offices and other buildings for Canberra to be a working capital in 1927.

The Commission provided the most unified administration in Canberra's history, even more unified than the present arrangements. From 1925 on they were responsible for education, police, transport and accommodation, as well as general construction. They began the process (still not quite complete in 1968) of devising legislation and ordinances specifically for the capital territory to replace those laws of New South Wales that had been made temporarily applicable in 1911. The Commission tried to provide offices and housing for the staff of four principal departments – prime minister's, attorney-general's, treasury and home affairs – and for a headquarters staff in several other Commonwealth departments. But the stop-and-go tactics of earlier years had left Canberra without labour to complete such projects and the wave of this government's enthusiasm did not spread far beyond the completion of the Parliament House.

The ceremonial opening of the Parliament House on 9 May 1927 was a grand occasion. The Duke of York (later George VI) performed the ceremonies. The Parliaments of most of the British dominions were represented. But many journalists and visitors were amused at the contrast between the pomp and ceremony on the one hand and the frontier-village setting on the other. Some noted that New Delhi had recently begun full operation though its planning was only being considered when Canberra's foundation stones had been laid in 1913. In Canberra the Parliament House was now open, but the supporting departmental organizations were not there, nor the accommodation that would make their presence possible.

Soon after this parliamentary opening the last ripples of strong government support died away. By 1929–30 national problems related to the depression pushed aside any schemes for building the capital. In 1930 the Commission was dismissed, with accusations of autocracy and extravagance. The generality of the Commission's powers, the strong personality of its chairman, and the pace at which they tried to move had inevitably caused some dissatisfactions. It is significant that the return to departmental administration was accompanied by the establishment of a partly-elected Advisory Council, to give local citizens some representative spokesmen.

At this distance the Commission's regime, though probably autocratic, does not seem one of extravagance. It was the only period between 1911 and 1958 when vigorous and determined efforts were made to build the capital. Canberra was still a scattered, not-very-comfortable place, but this burst of development coincided with and perhaps helped to create a lively sense of community life. For the first time there developed a number of local societies interested in art, literature, music, and science, as well as in the progress of the city. There was a small-town atmosphere, but some of the leaders in this small town's activities were remarkable men and women.

Departmental administration

From 1930 until 1958 administration of the capital was again shared among a number of federal departments. As economic conditions improved in the mid-thirties there was some increased building, but the pace of growth remained slow. World War II found Canberra still most inadequately supplied with office space, houses and other facilities even for those already stationed in the capital. There was no way of accommodating the rapid increase of federal employment caused by the war, and certainly none for providing for significant moves from Sydney or Melbourne. The Commonwealth government exercised wide and general powers in the war, especially after Pearl Harbor in December 1941 brought a real threat close to Australia. A rapid expansion of Commonwealth employment and of the functions of the national government was inevitable. The result was that office space had to be acquired temporarily in Sydney and Melbourne. In Canberra additional offices could only be provided by building, and that was too slow.

For the duration of the war, then, a three-capital arrangement developed in Australia, with cabinet ministers and their advisers following an exhausting, time-wasting, and costly program of journeys between Canberra, Sydney, and Melbourne. As soon as post-war needs came up for discussion, the chairman of the Public Service Board urged that for efficiency as well as economy it was necessary to end this division and to concentrate national government in Canberra. Immediate plans were recommended for wholesale transfers to Canberra, especially from Melbourne. But in 1952 the board reported that progress was negligible; housing quite inadequate. Two years later the situation had not changed much.

A Select Committee of the Commonwealth Senate was set up in 1954 under the gifted leadership of Senator J. A. McCallum to report on the development of Canberra. Their report in 1955 was forthright and critical; their recommendations clear. They criticized especially the divided control, the poor standards in building design, and the lack of any clear plan of development. Officers responsible for parts of Canberra's development and administration had, they said, so many other duties as officers of national departments that their tasks for Canberra were seen as by no means the most important of their obligations. Offices being constructed were blatantly temporary in appearance but destined to last longer than desirable. Waiting lists for houses got longer, not shorter, each year. There seemed to be "no positive determination to complete the national capital." Instead of carefully worked out plans of needs and priorities there seemed to be "merely a vague aspiration that somehow it would be possible" to house the public servants being transferred.

The committee found that Canberra's development had not been worthy of its national capital status, that considerations of expediency had been allowed to defer permanent construction and to cause a mushroom growth of temporary buildings. Aesthetic values had been neglected. Architectural and planning controls were inadequate. The city lacked not only the major buildings appropriate to a capital city but also many of the facilities needed to make it an attractive and comfortable place for residents and tourists.

Urging prompt and decisive action the committee asserted that the time had come "to take the responsibility of planning the national capital from the unborn backs of future generations and place it fairly and squarely on the shoulders of people alive today." Their primary concern was to encourage vigorous development, and high standards of building and of civic design. Though they favoured arrangements for some greater local participation in decisions affecting the city's development, and for more public information, their discussion of self-government is almost perfunctory compared with their thorough study and firm recommendations about planning, construction, and administration.

This was understandable for reasons already suggested. The things this committee wanted would require strong national government decisions on finance, employment policy, and administration. The Legislative Council, they suggested, without much discussion could help encourage local interest and responsibility, but this was not their first priority.

DEVELOPMENT AND GOVERNMENT SINCE 1958

The Senate Committee expressed ideas that had already been approved by the Public Service Board, some other departmental officers, and a number of politicians, notably the Prime Minister, Menzies. The government did not create a single all-purpose authority to replace departmental control, but in the next few years it moved to give effect to many of the principles enunciated. Firm decisions on a transfer policy were made, and on finance Sir William Holford was invited to report on the planning of Canberra. His 1957 report placed before the government the choice between allowing a slow and makeshift policy to continue and taking bold and necessarily costly steps to develop a unified Canberra, joined by the lakes and bridges and built to a standard that would be worthy of a national capital. A strong plea was made for the bold step forward.

The National Capital Development Commission

In the same year the government legislated to create the National Capital Development Commission, a statutory body to be responsible for planning, development, and construction. Other administrative responsibilities remained, as they still did in 1969, with various Commonwealth departments. But in spite of this sharing, the capital's management has been much more co-ordinated than it was previously. Griffin's plan for Canberra had survived the difficulties of the early years and received formal gazettal in 1925. The slow growth of Canberra had aided the retention of the general scheme, even though some variations had occurred. The Senate Committee and Holford both recommended that it should be used as a guide in future planning, and in setting up the NCDC the government formally continued the conditions introduced when the plan was gazetted. When the Commissioner, John Overall, and his two assistant commissioners took office in 1958, they appointed, as chief town planner, Peter Harrison, whose knowledge of and enthusiasm for Griffin's basic concepts had impressed Sir William Holford in earlier years. The Commission thus began their task with an acknowledged intention to use the original plan as a guide-line, and this intention has been adhered to.

The functions of the Commission were described in the 1957 Act as "to undertake and carry out the planning, development and construction of the city of Canberra as the National Capital of the Commonwealth." They were empowered to carry out building development, roads, bridges and service works, and "all things necessary or convenient ... or incidental to" their functions. Their principal tasks at first were to build houses, schools, offices, and other facilities urgently needed, and at the same time to make long-range plans for the city's expansion and for the development of the capital sector, the parliamentary triangle.

Though their statutory powers seem comprehensive they share some of them. The Department of Works is the main road maintenance authority, and Interior has important functions related to housing. A good deal of the Commission's construction work is done as the agent for other government bodies.

From the start the Commission has worked on five-year programs with annual plans based on these. It has kept its staff organization small and highly qualified, relying a great deal on consultants, commissioned studies, and in recent years on using private firms, in close consultation with the Commission, for design and construction even of some new neighbourhoods. The Commission has been conscious of the uniqueness of its tasks and the long-term effect of its choices, and has followed the practice of having its programs and policies assessed and reported upon by outside experts. The lakes scheme and its landscaping, economic aspects of the Commission's work, questions related to the general administration of Canberra, are only a sample of matters on which the Commission has sought general or specific comment.

Since the Commission's task was long-term planning it had population estimates placed before it as quickly as possible, and revises these continuously. The first detailed growth study made in 1958 surprised most people by estimating a population of 100,000 by 1973-74. In 1960 this end-date was changed to 1970. The 100,000 was in fact reached by 1967.

Given the unprecedented rate of growth, which shows few signs of diminishing, the Commission has been faced with immediate demands for housing and office construction, and ancillary works, and with the need to plan and develop new areas of settlement for a projected population of more than 250,000 by the end of the century. At the same time it had to plan for the filling-in of the central city area with some of the proposed capital buildings, the creation of the lakes, the commercial and recreational development of the main city, and the continued landscaping of the area.

The Commissioners have been helped in their tasks, of course, by the fact that the Commonwealth government is the sole land-owner. But this has placed a big responsibility on the Commission in servicing and making available land-blocks for lease. The price which leases bring at auction cannot help being related to the supply which the Commission's activities make available, and this, as well as the conditions attached to leases, has not always resulted in public approval. Once a lease is bought, the Commissioners have no direct control over subsequent changes of use, though they can oppose or support owners' applications to the appropriate tribunal of review.

Commonwealth ownership of much of the extensive national capital territory gave the Commissioners a choice of possible lines of growth for Canberra's expansion. In this as in other matters they sought expert advice and commissioned studies, especially of transportation schemes. Eventually they developed (1965) a plan for Canberra which has a series of linked urban centres to the north and south of the central city, separated by landscaped open space to preserve the general garden-city character. They hope for some decentralization of government employment and the plan includes reservation of road space that may accommodate a rapid-transit system later on.

In their first years of operation the Commissioners had to emphasize the building of houses, offices, and other buildings needed to equip the city as a working headquarters. Increasingly they have sought the co-operation of private enterprise in these tasks, so that they could pay more attention to the central capital area, the building of the lakes scheme, and the general long-term planning of the new metropolis.

It is unlikely that any authority dealing with Canberra has built up such acceptance and support as the Commission has done. It has developed an effective system of consultation and liaison with community groups and with other federal authorities. It has also won approval from the professionally knowledgeable for its long-term planning, and for the care with which it investigates future possibilities.

The Commission is, of course, criticized and attacked from time to time. Detailed questions of land use, or of variations in leasehold conditions, as well as questions of the siting of the permanent Parliament House, can arouse strong feelings and strong opposition to the planners' recommendations. More generally, not everyone approves of the Commission's plans for the capital's expansion. Not everyone welcomes the lavish use of land that will spread, in separate clusters, up to 500,000 people over an area that in other Australian cities may house 3 or 5 million. Some people wish for more concentrated development; for a different order of priorities, a different landscape treatment or a different style of office building. But in spite of these inevitable disagreements, the National Capital Development Commission has built up acceptance and support and even gratitude for its work in and for the capital.

Federal administration and finance

The National Capital Development Commission has so much influence on the shape and working of the capital that some people think of the Commission as the territory's governing authority. But many federal departments and agencies share responsibilities for the capital's administration and services. The Department of Health administers hospitals and enforces health regulations. The attorney-general's department deals with courts, law enforcement, and the drafting of legislation affecting the capital, and in the late 1960s was undertaking some revision and consolidation of these laws and ordinances. The Treasury, Department of Primary Industry, the

Auditor-General, the Public Service Board, and ten other government instrumentalities each occasionally has some concern with capital territory matters. Co-ordination is not a serious problem, however, for several reasons. The broadest and most continuing responsibilities for the capital come under the Department of the Interior to which the National Capital Development Commission is responsible, and with which it works closely. Of course there are disagreements to be ironed out, but they have been much less noticeable in recent years because the different agencies were not having to battle for part of a very small allocation: the general government policy has been to spend much more money on the capital than was ever spent before. Without this the present stage of growth could never have been reached.

Just how much is spent annually is difficult to estimate. We can discover that in 1966–67 the NCDC spent something like (Aus.) $42 million on construction and a little over $1 million on administration, whereas in the previous year the construction expenditure was $37 million. We can contrast this with amounts of less than half of this in some earlier years. But the general costs of Canberra have not yet been separated from those of other functions in the many federal departments that have some capital responsibilities. Nor will this be easy to do.

The Department of the Interior issued a pamphlet in 1967 on *Self-Government for the Australian Capital Territory*. This indicates that from the general financial records of the Commonwealth, including those of Interior, "it is not feasible to extract ... details of the Australian Capital Territory components in a manner which would reflect Territory finances fully and accurately." However, with Treasury's help "an energetic attack is being made on this problem."

Various unofficial estimates have been attempted of whether Canberra is paying its way, through returns from auctions of leases, and the dues paid by local residents. Charges for local water supply and other services are made on property owners, as are also some payments based on land values. Recently a special tax of $10 on each lavatory in a house or dwelling has been introduced, and stamp duties on official transactions are contemplated. The authorities are clearly seeking to collect from Canberra residents some payments they think "comparable with those levied on residents of other states." Such a policy is supported by those who believe that the capital territory, without stamp duties or death duties, has offered a tax haven for skilled manipulators, and that there has been injustice in this. There is a fairly common belief, at least among citizens residing in the rest of Australia, that Canberra residents are more favourably treated and much more lightly taxed than are their fellow citizens outside the capital territory.

Many Canberra residents, of course, are likely to deny these charges of favouritism or indulgence. There is little agreement about what should be compared. Different state taxes are paid in different states. Local government dues vary with the enterprise and confidence of local councils and with the tasks performed. In no other city in Australia would local residents find as high a standard of services as in Canberra for as small a contribution. But then, say the capital's residents, these high standards of roads, streets, lighting, water supply, provision of sewerage, care in long-term planning, and so on are part of the proper responsibility of a national government in managing and developing the capital.

The departmental paper of 1967 asserts as probable that "there is a substantial Commonwealth subvention of the territory's costs of administration" and hints at increased local contribution if Canberra's community acquired some responsibilities for self-government. Critics of this paper insist that some Commonwealth subvention is and will continue to be justified to maintain high standards in the capital's services, and not only in the central capital sector.

This is not simply an argument between the "pampered" Canberra residents on one side, and on the other side, the providing government and the rest of Australia. Complaints about increased taxation for Canberra citizens, whether justified or not, are greeted with wry amusement by many other Australian citizens, but the capital's successful growth is now welcomed and even reluctantly praised. The Commonwealth government does not face serious pressure for economies and reductions in their capital development policies. A more common reaction now is to ask why the Commonwealth will not extend some of its concern for efficiency and quality in this urban area into increased assistance for the other major cities of Australia whose needs are more urgent.

The role of political parties

Since 1949 the government in the Australian Federal Parliament has been formed by a coalition of Liberal and Country party members, with the Australian Labor party in opposition. In both state and Commonwealth politics, the frequent Australian pattern is one of long terms of office for one party (or coalition) coming to an end when internal dissension opens the way for opposition success.

Though ideological differences between the two major parties would be asserted, with the Labor party claiming a socialist heritage (not Marxist) and the Liberal and Country parties emphasizing "free enterprise," they can rightly be described as parties of "interests and government" rather than parties of ideas.

It happens that the crucial decisions leading to effective development of the capital were taken by the Liberal-Country party under Prime Minister

Menzies, and that this same coalition (under two other prime ministers) has remained in power during the phase of Canberra's rapid growth. But the Labor governments of 1941-49 had accepted the necessity for this development, and it was during Chifley's (Labor) prime ministership that the Australian National University was set up, the first big move to make Canberra more than a parliamentary and administrative centre. There is considerable inter-party agreement about development plans for the capital and territory. Where open disagreements have occurred in parliament – as about the siting of a new Parliament House – the decisions cross party lines. Some Labor supporters assert that this Liberal-Country party government has been unduly favourable to private enterprise (for example, by renting major parts of private office buildings for departmental use) and too secretive and hesitant about establishing some form of self-government. But a change of Commonwealth government would be unlikely to result in many drastic changes, and would almost certainly retain the existing arrangements for long-term planning and for generous financial support.

While the Liberal-Country coalition has held confident power at the national level, the Labor party has been more active and successful in the territory itself. The present ACT representative in the House of Representatives, Jim Fraser, is a Labor member and has retained his parliamentary position since 1951. He is not likely to be defeated by a Liberal or other party candidate in the near future. The Advisory Council has commonly had more elected members associated with the Labor party than with any other groups.

The significance of this is not easy to assess. Perhaps a Canberra representative needs to play a critical role and the opposition bench suits this role best. Perhaps more academics, civil servants, and other people in Canberra sympathize with the opposition rather than with the present government parties.

The 1967 Department Paper on "Self-Government" made a passing reference to the possibility of one party having ascendancy in a future territory government, if established, while the other party had power in the Commonwealth government. But no serious worry was indicated, nor is it justified. If a territorial government were established, any Commonwealth government would be sure to retain sufficient over-riding powers to prevent serious difficulties.

PROSPECTS FOR SELF-GOVERNMENT

Local or territorial self-government was not seriously proposed for Canberra before the 1940s. Local citizens might wish for more consideration and consultation, or express dissatisfaction with failures or inadequacies of government policy concerning their city. But they did not demand self-government, nor did national governments consider this as something desirable or necessary.

In 1949 when serious consideration was at last being given to the post-war development of the capital, the same government which legislated for an elected federal member for the capital territory commissioned a report on a possible form of government for the area. This report by R.J. Cole, town clerk of Hobart, recommended a municipal council of twelve with very limited powers. But few citizens or government spokesmen thought this an appropriate arrangement, and no attempt was made to implement it.

When the Senate Select Committee reported on the development of Canberra in 1955, they concentrated on persuading the government that new and vigorous policies were urgently needed, that generous financing was essential, and that the administration of the capital should be unified and placed under strong direction of an appointed commissioner. But they spent little time on questions of self-government beyond making a brief recommendation for a legislative, instead of an advisory council.

In the same year, 1955, a study group of the Royal Institute of Public Administration produced a report on the capital's government. They proposed a National Capital Council for the whole capital territory, fully elected, exercising legislative and executive powers, subject only to the veto of a minister with a new portfolio for capital territory affairs. They rejected any municipal arrangement, as well as any purely legislative scheme. They insisted that executive functions were necessary to support and sometimes to restrain legislative proposals. Just as a parliamentary government depended on the advice and information provided by departmental officials, and on the discipline of financial responsibility to keep their proposals coherent and workable, so a capital council would need an executive-administrative arm. The functions they envisaged as possible for this capital council ranged from the ordinary housekeeping functions of local authorities to education, regulation of trades, and other matters that are, elsewhere in Australia, under state government control. They assumed a continuing Commonwealth subvention for many of these activities, but did not examine the financial implications in detail. Their main purpose was to urge the establishment of a strong multipurpose elected government devised especially for the capital and not using the model of local councils elsewhere in Australia.

The general principles of this capital council scheme have received some support, and further elaboration, especially from some academics professionally interested in government. Professor J.D.B. Miller has been one of the most vocal advocates of such a fully elected government for the territory. Apart from presenting arguments against this community remaining under paternalistic tutelage, Professor Miller and others have argued that the capital's administration should benefit from co-ordinating in one administrative unit the functions now scattered among various federal departments. This capital council scheme is not the only proposal for self-government that has appeared, but it is the most comprehensive. No proposal has resulted in anything that could be described as a public campaign. They are almost all academic exercises.

In 1957 the Department of the Interior published a booklet on *Self-Government for the Australian Capital Territory: A Preliminary Assessment*, which surveyed the existing arrangements and indicated some of the political, constitutional and financial questions that needed further examination. The report mentions the likelihood that Canberra residents will become "subject to taxes ... comparable with those levied on residents of the states," and suggests that greater taxation would justify "greater participation in government, in equity." But there is no suggestion that self-government is demanded. A popular vote, the report says, might reject any such proposal. Whether citizens especially want it or not, this report sees some greater local responsibility in community needs as a duty that should be imposed. The difficulty is in making the division between "natural" and "local" interests and especially between what the national government should and will pay for and what will come from local dues.

Both government and citizens seem alarmed at the risks of self-government. Recent public discussion in Canberra has not been enthusiastic or knowledgeable, and many alarms have been expressed about increased local dues, or possible reductions in standards. There is concern, too, among officials about the effects on their career opportunities if their jobs were transferred to the control of any self-governing body.

It is probable that some form of self-government will be established in the capital territory in the next decade. It may be a scheme for elected councils in the new residential areas, or for something more general and more imaginative. The initiative will almost certainly come from above, from the federal government, not from any strong local demand.

CONCLUSIONS

Canberra has now reached maturity. Its future is assured; its development plans moving confidently. No major problems are expected in financial provision or in the maintenance of established policies of co-ordinated physical growth. Parallel with its becoming an effective government headquarters has come fulfilment of a number of other headquarters functions associated with national capitals. It has not yet reached a position of leadership in the arts, but there are signs of vigorous development here.

Does this mean that the future of Canberra holds no problems, no possible surprises? There have been surprises before, especially in the rapid growth of recent years, and there are a great many uncertainties yet to be resolved.

The big questions for the future are related less to physical development than to social and political growth. The capital area will certainly be well supplied with parks, waterways, forests, nature reserves and places for recreation. Will this make it so much a tourist centre that any local community life will be impeded? The new satellite towns will be well-serviced and linked to the centre by good roads and even possibly by an experimental mass-transit system. But will they be good places to live in? Will they be more than dormitory areas? Will hopes for varied development be fulfilled? There will be a new Parliament House and a national gallery sometime. But when? With how much energy and imagination will the central capital project be tackled?

Self-government has been talked about recently, and predicted as inevitable in some form or other in the next decade. But the questions about self-government seem neither urgent nor clear. Government authorities treat this as a long-term possibility; many citizens would like to avoid as long as possible any major change in finance or administration; there is little agreement about what these changes might be. Will these hesitancies and alarms continue? Or will we see some enterprising experimentation in Canberra? There should be no lack of interest in the process of answering these questions.

---

[1] Before Australia's recent changeover to the dollar, one Australian £ equalled US $2.24. The Australian $ equalled about US $1.12. in 1970.

Gonzalo Martínez Corbalá MEXICO CITY

Since the foundation of the Aztec Empire, Mexico City has been the centre of Mexican political power. In 1542 the Spaniards chose the conquered capital as the seat of the Viceroyalty of New Spain. When Mexico won its independence in 1810, the city remained as capital of the newly formed nation.

The constitution of 1824 authorized the Congress of the Union to select a location to serve as the seat of the supreme powers of federation; yet, it was presupposed that the Congress would designate Mexico City as the capital. According to Article 2 of the decree of 18 November 1824, "The Federal District will comprise a circle whose centre will be the largest plaza in the capital city and whose radius will be two leagues." Under the authority of the Centralist Constitution of 1836, the District was incorporated into the Department of Mexico, but it reappeared again, in the same form as in 1824, under the constitution of 1846. The "Basis of 1853" repeated the territorial division created in 1846. On 16 February 1854, President Santa Anna increased the limits of the city and called it the District of Mexico. The 1917 constitution, signed after the revolution and still the governing law, made no changes in the legal situation and area of the Federal District, and thus its area remains the same: 1,499 square kilometres (577 sq. mi.).

Relative importance

In order to compare Mexico City with the other large cities in the country, we provide the following data based on the 1970 census: the Federal District was recorded as having approximately seven million of Mexico's fifty million inhabitants; Guadalajara, capital of the State of Jalisco and the second most important city in the republic, has 1.25 million, and Monterey, capital of the State of Nuevo León and its most important city, has a population of about one million.[1] Estimates of per capita income in the largest cities also reflect the relative importance of the federal capital: the cities of Guadalajara and Monterey show a yearly income per capita of 480 pesos, whereas the Federal District shows an income per capita of 455 pesos.[2] To ascertain the industrial importance of the capital let us compare it with the most industrialized states in Mexico: Jalisco, Nuevo León, and the State of Mexico. In 1965 the Federal District had 584,000 industrial workers; while Nuevo León had 82,000; Jalisco 164,000; and the State of Mexico 104,000.[3] It should also be mentioned that the metropolitan population of Mexico City has overflown the political limits of the Federal District on its northern side, and constitutes an important part of the adjacent State of Mexico. Thus, population density, cultural and artistic wealth, business and industrial activities, and many other aspects have made Mexico City the most important city in the republic.

Constitutional background

The Mexican republic consists of 29 states, two territories and a Federal District. In addition to having executive and judicial power, the federated states have the right to make their own constitutions. Limitations on these local constitutions are imposed by the federal constitution. Article 41 specifies that the state constitutions "shall in no case contravene the stipulations of the federal pact"; other articles of the federal constitution impose certain obligations on the states, to which these constitutions must conform.

The territories come directly under the central government. They are not states because of their lack of population and of enough resources to sustain themselves as autonomous units. However, they will probably become states when they have achieved the requisites necessary: a population of not less than 80,000 and the necessary elements, in the view of the federal Congress, to provide for and maintain their political existence. The Federal District could become a state, and it would do so automatically (as it complies with all the requirements stipulated above) if the federal authorities were transferred to another location.

Federalism is a form of decentralization, of which there are two main levels in Mexico: the municipalities, which enjoy a certain measure of administrative autonomy within the framework and under the tutelage of the states; and the states as members of the federation, which enjoy constitutional autonomy but are equally subject to the national constitution. It is customary to give the name "autonomy" to the competence which the member-states enjoy under their own legislative norms, that is, they are free and sovereign. To this degree the states are decentralized and self-governing, but their zone of self-determination is prescribed by the national constitution.

Federations which are based on the pattern of the United States, such as those of Mexico, accept the benefits of giving the federal authorities a territory of their own which guarantees their independence in the face of any of the states. The constitution of the United States took into account the necessity of designating a location exclusively for the seat of the federal authorities, and accordingly set up an area which it considered to be indispensable for the development and housing of the federal offices and officials. In Mexico, the Federal District, as the seat of the federal authorities, has always been the centre of the country's political life. Also, by reason of its size, its density of population, its artistic and architectural richness, and its economic and cultural life, it has always been incomparably superior to the other federal units.

GOVERNMENT OF THE FEDERAL DISTRICT

The Federal District is not autonomous, and this it is basically distinguished from the member-states. Its system of government emanates from the constitution of 1917, which established the three traditional powers of government for the District. Of these, two are identical with the respective federal authorities; only the judicial power has an organization separate from the corresponding federal authority.

The executive authority

The District's executive power is exercised by the president of the republic, who is elected by direct vote and holds office for a six-year term; but he exercises his control through the mayor of the Federal District (*Jefe del Departamento del Distrito Federal*), who is appointed and removed by the president. The mayor is assisted in the discharge of his functions by an appointed consultative council, by delegates and sub-delegates, and by other institutions to which the law refers.

For carrying out its administrative functions and providing its public services, the Federal District Department has the following general agencies:

1 Government Department
2 Labor and Social Welfare Department
3 Public Works Department
4 Water and Sanitation Department
5 Legal Services Department
6 Social Activities Department
7 Administrative Services Department
8 General Services Department
9 Recreation Department
10 Traffic Department
11 Police Department

12 Treasury
13 Hydraulic Works Department
14 Medical Services Department
15 Public Markets Department[4]

The legislative authority

The only legislative authority for the District is the Congress of the Union, which enjoys the power to legislate in local matters. It is a bicameral body, with a Chamber of Deputies and a Senate. The Chamber of Deputies is composed of representatives of the nation, elected every three years by Mexican citizens. One deputy is elected for each 200,000 inhabitants; and one for each fraction of more than 100,000, according to the census of the Federal District and of each state and territory. In no case can a state have less than two deputies, and a territory must have one. For each deputy, an alternate is elected. In the Federal District there are 24 electoral districts, with each district represented by a deputy and his alternate.

In addition to the directly elected deputies there are party deputies. These are provided for in five paragraphs of the constitution, the main provision being that all national political parties which receive $2\frac{1}{2}$ per cent of the total national vote in an election will have the right to have five deputies accredited from among its candidates, and one more deputy, up to a maximum of 20, for each additional $\frac{1}{2}$ per cent of the votes cast.

The Senate is made up of two members for each state and two for the Federal District, all directly elected at one time for a six-year term. As with the deputies, an alternate is chosen for each senator.

The judicial authority

Of the authorities that operate in the Federal District, the judicial one is the only one whose functions are not identified with the federal powers. The administration of justice in the Federal District is exclusively local and not common to the rest of the republic. Judicial authority is exercised by district judges and magistrates; the magistrates are appointed by the president of the republic with the approval of the Chamber of Deputies, while the judges are designated by the members of the Supreme Court of Justice, and they hold office for a six-year term.[5]

The Federal District compared with municipalities and territories

Except for the Federal District area, all cities are located within a municipality and therefore are governed by their own municipal authorities, since the constitution establishes free municipalities within the administrative and political organization of the states. Regarding the relations between the states and municipalities, it should be noted that, although there is an element of decentralization, a municipality does not have a sphere of autonomy within which it can pass its own laws. In this way it differs from a federal state, which enjoys autonomy under the constitution.

The federal territories have a different role from that of the Federal District. While the District is a fully developed political entity, the territories are in a process of development to eventually become states. However, as in the District, their legislature is the Congress of the Union; likewise, their executive is the president of the republic, but he exercises his functions through a governor appointed by him, in contrast to the situation in the Federal District where the constitution, by means of a secondary law, provides for the method by which the president's function shall be carried out.

There is a judicial power which is common for both: the attorney-general for the Federal District and territories; secondary legislation is organized in the same manner administratively and judicially in the District and territories, and the basic law for the courts is equally applicable to both.

There are only two fundamental differences between the District and the territories. The first and main difference is that the territories have municipalities with directly elected municipal governments. The other difference is that the territories are not represented in the Senate.

POLITICS AND POLITICAL PROBLEMS

Ethnic and religious differences

Neither the country nor the Federal District has ever suffered from serious ethnic or religious differences. The population is 85 per cent Roman Catholic, and ethnically the Mexican population is largely "mestiza."

Political parties

There are four registered political parties: the *Partido Revolucionario Institucional* (PRI, revolutionary); the *Partido Acción Nacional* (PAN, rightist); the *Partido Popular Socialista* (PPS, leftist) and the *Partido Auténtico de la Revolución Mexicana* (PARM). The PRI is the dominant one, but the PAN also has considerable strength. In the 1967 elections the PRI's proportion of the total vote in each of the Federal District's 24 electoral districts ranged from 56 to 75 per cent, while that of the PAN ranged from 21 to 37 per cent. Of the two minor parties the PPS showed slightly greater strength, since it obtained electoral votes ranging from 3 to 8 per cent, while the PARM ranged from 1 to 5 per cent.

Participation of federal employees in politics

Federal employees, as Mexican citizens, enjoy the same right of political participation as any other citizen. There are no legal restrictions which in any way prevent them from taking part in any legal political activity.

Recent political history

Although the president of the republic appoints the mayor, the secretary-general, and other officials of the District, they are responsible for all government acts within the District and, therefore, the inhabitants' sympathy for or opposition to the authorities depends on their acts. Accordingly, public opinion within the District for or against the federal government depends on the positiveness or negativeness of the District's administration. Since Mexico City has much the same problems of growth as any other big city, its recent political history is therefore linked to the focus which the mayor has given to the political means of resolving these problems.

One characteristic of developing countries is underemployment in the rural areas. This produces a displacement of large masses of the population. In their desire for improvement they move to the city in search of work in the industrial areas, and convert themselves into an army of underemployed. Usually they take possession, at the margin of the law, of private or national lands, and form squatter areas where they live at minimum subsistence levels in ramshackle dwellings lacking most public services. In many cases, the legal situation regarding possession of the property is not clear.

The activities of a mayor regarding this problem provide an interesting example of the impact of his activities on public opinion. The former mayor held office from 1952 to 1966. He had been reconfirmed in his appointment in 1958 and also by the president who took office in 1964, though usually public officials such as secretaries of state and governors change with the president every six years. In September 1966, by instructions of the mayor, a police guard protected a group of public employees while they broke up by forceful means a very poor colony, displacing more than 400 families. Previous circumstances and this action gave rise to a current of public opinion against the mayor. During a session in the Chamber of Deputies (13 September 1966), members from all parties backed the PRI deputies' condemnation of this negative policy and called for his resignation. The deputies set up an investigatory commission, which included representatives of the four political parties, among whom was the deputy for the district in which the colony was located. A day and a half later, the president of the republic accepted the mayor's resignation.[6] The inhabitants of the colony received clothing, food, medical attention and materials to rebuild their houses, as compensation for all the damages suffered.

The present political situation is one of great confidence on the part of the city's population in the new Federal District officials, because increasing attention is being paid to find solutions to the problems of the largest groups of the population.

FINANCES

The revenues of the Federal District arise from taxes, fees and licences, and grants, including grants from the federal government. The taxes are on land, property, industry and commerce, capital goods, liquors, slaughter of cattle, public entertainment, games, betting and lottery permits, planning works, use of water from artesian wells, transfers of title to real estate, markets, gasoline, gifts, and construction of parking lots. The fees are from the grading and control of meat, public works, installation or reconstruction of water tanks and sewers, cleaning of septic tanks, draining of private lands, vehicles, service of water, services to cemeteries, urban regulations, supervision of construction, expedition of construction licences, civil registry, public deeds and titles registry, commerce registry, general notary file, affidavit, private property registry and many others.[7] Income also derives from allowing use of public thoroughfares and several properties of the Federal District, by leasing and exploiting properties, publications, warehouse and parking services, the issuing of bonds and titles, and the establishment of different enterprises dependent upon the local government.

Grants as participation in federal taxes are also an important part of the District's revenue. In 1969 the District's total revenue was 3,500 million pesos, and its share of federal taxes was 7,802 million pesos. In setting up a system of revenue for the District, care has been taken to co-ordinate it with that of the federal government in order to avoid, as much as possible, the overlapping of taxation burdens.

The Treasury of the Federal District collects the receipts authorized by the respective legal provisions, by means of its own tax-collecting offices. There are separate collection agencies or departments for taxes on the following: trade imports, real estate, entertainments, markets, transfer of real estate, liquors, slaughter of cattle. Although the District's treasury is run separately from that of the federal government, the regulations for the imposition of taxes arise from the latter.

The authorization of expenditures consists in the approval of the estimates of the budget by the Chamber of Deputies and covers the costs of a year. The following listing of estimated expenditures for 1969 (in millions of pesos) will give the reader an idea of the services provided by the District government:[8]

General administration	28.1
Management	50.7
Legal services	12.0
Public relations	1.8
Public works	651.1
Hydraulic works	313.5
Water distribution and sewage	190.5
General services	192.5
Markets	51.9
Transit	63.8
Police	231.6
Medical services	125.8
Social activities	42.2
Sports activities	31.5
Buildings for Olympic Games activities	4.6
Administrative services	24.1
Treasury of the Federal District	149.5
Superior Justice Court for the Federal District	46.8
General Attorney's Offices for the Federal District	38.6
General expenditures	1,248.5

The main services that the federal government looks after within the District are: posts, telegraphs, electricity distribution, petroleum and combustibles, health and railway transport. The agencies and decentralized enterprises which provide these services form part of a nationwide system. It is therefore very difficult to separate, geographically, the costs of providing service for the District from those to the whole metropolitan area (Federal District plus State of Mexico).

Exemption of embassies

All foreign countries have the right to buy or rent properties for their embassies and offices, which enjoy diplomatic immunity and have the right of "extraterritoriality." Therefore they do not have to pay taxes of any kind, only for services which the municipality provides, such as water, telephone, electricity, etc. Sometimes the embassy personnel live in the embassy building or in buildings joined to it, but generally they live in nearby residences. Their incomes are exempt from all taxation by both the federal and municipal authorities, as they are foreigners. Many embassies need Mexican employees, generally people such as stenographers, chauffeurs, gardeners, and general service personnel. For local employees, who work for a monthly salary, the embassy must comply with Mexican laws on working conditions and social security.[9]

PLANNING

The following agencies are concerned with the urban planning of the Federal District:

A The Planning Commission
B The mixed Planning Commission
C The Federal District government, through its Planning Office and the Office of the Master Plan.

Although the Master Plan for the Federal District visualized and regulates the adequate use of land, population growth and rural immigration impose frequent alterations and adaptations of the plan.[10] Even though projects and pre-project plans exist for all sectors of the city and District, they have hardly been started, and the office in charge of them has done the work necessary to carry out only the most urgent projects for the city. It is true that, in order to facilitate the flow of traffic, viaducts and avenues have been built and others have been widened. The traffic plans have also generated many secondary plans. For instance, the subway system, now under construction, has provoked a reorganization of plans that will alter many previous concepts of traffic and thoroughfares. Regulations for land use and public services have also been subjected to reconsideration in view of the changing urban pattern that collective transportation systems provoke.[11] Although there are general plans for traffic and land use, schools, markets and other necessary works are being constructed at the dictates of pressing demands, and not according to an overall plan.

To carry out plans, both political and economic considerations must be taken into account. Since one can only talk relatively about the efficiency of planning, it can only be affirmed that in Mexico City the local problems of public services have not been basically solved, due to population growth and other inherent difficulties.

PROBLEMS OF GOVERNMENT

The main problem of government in the Federal District is that which is common to all big cities in the world: the population explosion which has occurred in recent years (from 4.9 million inhabitants in 1960 to 7.0 million in 1970). This automatically creates a problem in the administration of services in the planning of new public utilities. It has produced a race between the increase in urban population and the District's administration in attempting to maintain the same level of service per capita. This involves many diverse factors (dwellings, water, light, transportation, throughways, education, telephones, etc.).

The population explosion is caused by two main factors. Partly it is due to the natural growth of the existing population of the area. But the main cause is the increase of rural immigration toward the capital. This in turn is due to the fact that the capital has become a very important centre of economic growth and because of its various assets (schools, universities, medical services, public services, etc.).

The chief proposals which have been put forward recently to help solve this problem are:

1 To refuse authorizations for new subdivisions of land within the Federal District, unless the necessary public services are available.
2 To encourage industrial decentralization of the capital by means of fiscal inducements from the federal government as well as from the District government, so that new industries will be established in other states.

The mayor's annual report for 1967 indicated that needs for public services would be dealt with by priorities: firstly, a sewage system with adequate outlets for the rain water, to prevent floods; secondly, a reservoir and distribution system for drinking water to supply the needs for the population and to prevent the depletion of subsoil water; and thirdly, an efficient rapid transit system.

A proposal for structural reform

In recent years, two main proposals have been made for the modification of the Federal District's basic law, both put forward by representatives of the minority parties.[12] Only the first of these, which deals with structural reform, will be discussed here. Presented in 1965, it fundamentally consisted in proposing the popular election of a governing council, and the assurance of greater efficiency in the services provided by the District Department through decentralizing some of its functions and increasing the delegation of authority. The governing council would be substituted for the existing consultative council and would be endowed with regulatory and governing powers subject to some reasonable limitations.

The present organic law of the District concentrates power in the person of the mayor. The consultative council is merely an organ of opinion, unable to check actions of the executive authority or to analyse the effectiveness of government. The centralization of functions has converted its members into mere observers of the provision of public services and delegates of the mayor in their respective fields.

It is argued that at present the citizens of the Federal District have the least participation in the political decisions of Mexico since they intervene only in federal elections. It was therefore proposed that the government of the Federal District should be shared by the federal executive with a democratically elected council, and that the elections for this council should coincide with the federal elections in order not to increase the number of political campaigns and electoral activities. It was also argued that the system proposed would guarantee the participation of political minorities in the council, which would be constituted according to the provisions of the constitution for party deputies.

The council would have the right to nominate and to remove delegates and subdelegates, a function which is now performed by the mayor. Thus, his powers would be limited, and the efficiency of the District's government would be prevented from being conditioned by the personal qualities of the incumbent. Disagreements between the council and the mayor would be resolved by the president of the republic.

Through the decentralization of functions, allowing certain aspects of administration to be dealt with in the different precincts, the population would be better served by District authorities, and the work of public offices would be more effective. Moreover, the inhabitants would have a more direct channel to reach the uppermost authorities and, through wider contacts, to achieve their participation in the policy-making levels.

The proposal also insists that the council should have the obligation and the right to legislate; and this would be its most important function. The local regulations for the Federal District need to be more fully developed and implemented. Through this proposal, the governing council would revise current regulations and complement them or adjust them to conform with the national system of constitutional guarantees.

It should be noted that this proposal includes only the reforms considered possible to introduce in the existing political circumstances, not all those which are desirable.

The problem of social strata

The relatively recent power in the history of Mexico of the large financial and industrial corporations and consortia constitutes a force that is manifest in the "dominant" strata of the country.[13] Here we face the dual nature of modern society in the structure of its various components. Versus progress in the higher income sectors of the city stands the impoverishment of rural Mexico. This impoverishment is not only quantitative, serious as this may be in absolute terms, but, worse yet, it is qualitative, since the immigrants to the city are generally the best trained, the most ambitious, and the ones with the greatest potential. Their difficulties in finding a means of satisfaction and self-realization are aggravated by their great numbers and by the rapidly changing environment. The problems of integrating them through various cultural and educational processes designed to help them understand and assume their roles as city dwellers poses serious difficulties for individuals in transition from a rural to an urban cultural pattern. The solution of this problem introduces the immediate need for new methods of city planning, construction, and financing in Mexico City.

Immigrants to the city, and even poorer groups, were studied by Pablo González Casanova in his book *La Democracia en México* [Democracy in Mexico]. In the chapter *La Sociedad Plural* [The Pluralistic Society], he comments:

Marginality, or the condition of being bypassed by the country's progress, of not participating in its economic, social, and cultural development, and of being a member of the great mass of those who have nothing, is particularly typical of underdeveloped societies. They not only retain a very unequal distribution of wealth, income, technology, and culture in general, but frequently, as in the case of Mexico, include two or more socio-cultural complexes, a super-participating one and a super-marginal one, a dominant one and a dominated one – be it called native, Indian or indigenous.

It is this "marginal" population that initiates the process resulting in the disorganized, uneven, and unsound development of Mexico City. This development does not stem from the introduction of technology in the rural areas (or the industrialization of the farm sector), which, when managed more efficiently, frees a labour force which in turn increases potential urban manpower. It is rather an underemployment phenomenon evidenced by the shapeless mass taking refuge in the city, gathering in the centres or the city's outskirts and generating disfunction.

CONCLUSIONS

In short, Mexico City is an urban concentration that gives rise to endless problems, because not only its absolute size but its size in relation to the rest of the country make it a huge, frequently unwieldy and overly dominant entity. It is the centre of banking, finance, public service institutions, distribution services, and the most important cultural activities as well as the seat of the federal government. Such centralization in turn entails the presence of the policy-makers in all these fields. These leading groups stay in only indirect contact with the groups they lead, who constantly seek ways to join together and to obtain representation in order to assert their rights and aspirations within the framework of national culture and economic activity.

With respect to his attitude toward political problems, the citizen of the Federal District is in a unique position among the citizens of the country. Other citizens participate more directly in local government since they elect their municipal officials and, moreover, have as intermediaries between themselves and the federal government their state representatives and their state government. The citizen of the Federal District lacks these possibilities and means of representation. Between the mayor and the masses there are only the federal representatives and senators, leaving the citizens without other means of representation or channels of participation in public affairs and in the decisions that affect them.

This implies that consideration should be given to the methods of participation of the dominated sector (at the planning and decision-making levels) in order to increase satisfaction with the local government and the outputs of the political system.[14] To that end, machinery for participation, as the surest means of attaining stability, should be found and analysed. Unless suitable machinery for participation in the inputs of the system is found, dissatisfaction with the local government will ensure, notwithstanding any efforts on its part to carry out social welfare programs.

1 Dirección General de Estadística, *Censo General de Población* [General Census of Population] (Mexico City, 1979).
2 Luis Unikel, *Demografía y Economía* [Demography and Economy] (El Colegio de México, 1968). A peso is worth about eight US cents.
3 *Op. cit.*
4 *Ley Orgánica del Departamento del Distrito Federal* [Basic Law for the Federal District] (1940).
5 *Ley Orgánica del Distrito y Territorios Federales* [Basic Law for the Federal District and Territories] (1940).
6 *Diario de los Debates* [Congressional Record] (1966), 3.
7 Annual Report on Revenues of the Federal District Department (1969).
8 *Diario de los Debates* (30 December 1969), 52.
9 *Ley Federal del Trabajo* (Federal Labour Law).
10 *Publicaciones de la Dirección General de Catastro e Impuesto Predial* [Land Registrations Publications] (1967).
11 *Publicaciones de la Sociedad del Transporte Colectivo* [Publications of the Collective Transportation Society], (1969).
12 *Diario de los Debates* (1966), 36.
13 Gonzola Martínez Corbalá, "Growth Problems of Mexico City" (Institute for Environmental Studies, University of Pennsylvania, 1969), 8 pp. mimeographed.
14 Gabriel A. Almond and Sidney Verba, *The Civic Culture: Political Attitudes and Democracy in Five Nations* (Princeton, 1963), ch. 9.

5 Royce Hanson and Bernard H. Ross WASHINGTON

THE DEVELOPMENT OF THE CAPITAL[1]

By the time of the Constitutional Convention in 1787, there had been no agreement on a permanent capital for the infant American republic. Although several cities, particularly New York and Philadelphia, sought the capital, in 1790 it was agreed to establish a new Federal District, not to exceed 100 square miles in area, on the Potomac river. Virginia and Maryland ceded land on both sides of the river to form the Federal District of Columbia. In 1847, the federal government retroceded the Virginia portion, thus reducing the District to 69 square miles.

Until the Civil War, Washington, the capital city within the District, was relatively small, poorly developed, and unimportant, except for its governmental activities. It was not infrequently considered a hardship post by European diplomats. Its first period of rapid development coincided with the Civil War and the consequent burst of national government activity. Between 1860 and 1870 the population of the District increased from 75,000 to 132,000, and a rapid increase occurred in the Negro population, from 14,000 to 43,000 – about one-third of the total.

Both the Maryland and Virginia environs remained basically rural until after World War I. Since there was little industry, the capital's growth was heavily influenced by the rate of growth of the national government. Not until after 1930 did the District contain one-half million people. By 1950 the population had increased to 802,000 and was 35 per cent Negro.

By 1960 there was little change in the total population, but its character had shifted to make Washington (which is coterminous with the District) the first major American city to have a black majority. This is all the more interesting when seen in a metropolitan perspective. Since 1940 almost all population growth in the national capital region has occurred in the Virginia and Maryland suburbs. By 1960, for the first time, a majority of the population in the region lived in suburban jurisdictions, and by 1968 more than two-thirds. Race distribution is also crucial to understanding the capital's political condition. While about a fourth of the region's population has been non-white ever since 1870, the suburban ratios were relatively high until about 1930. Since then, with the movement of new white migrants to the suburbs, about 90 per cent of the area's Negroes are now concentrated in the District of Columbia.[2]

With a stable population of about 750,000 in 1970, Washington currently ranks among the ten largest cities in the USA, and it is the core city of the nation'a most rapidly growing metropolitan area. In 1960 the regional population was over two million, while in 1970 it was about three million, and recent projections for the year 2000 suggest a population of six million, with about one million living in the District of Columbia. The District is more populous than several of the fifty states which (plus the District, Puerto Rico and some smaller outlying territories) comprise the United States. But its population is rather small in relation to the country's total population of about 205 million in 1970.

Alone of the ten largest metropolitan areas. Washington has a unifunctional economy centring on the activities of the federal government. While there has been increased economic diversification with growth, government remains the largest employer in the region, and virtually serves as its "basic" industry. Though less industrialized than other metropolitan areas, the Washington area's population has a high average income. The stability of federal activity also makes the local economy less subject to cyclical fluctuations. The absence of manufacturing industry and the recent growth of suburban industry at the expense of the central city does create severe structural unemployment and subemployment problems, especially for poor blacks living in the city. The extent of federal land holdings also creates problems for local governments inasmuch as federal land is not taxable by local authorities.

THE DISTRICT'S CONSTITUTIONAL STATUS

A discussion of the government of the national capital must begin with an analysis of the most pervasive force in the region, the federal government. The myriad relationships between the federal government and the area's local governments, especially the District of Columbia, are usually lumped under the amorphous concept, "federal interest."[3] It is the principal issue of political structure in the government of the District of Columbia.

The "exclusive power" clause

Much confusion stems from divergent interpretations of paragraph 17 of the eighth section of Article I of the federal constitution. That paragraph vests in Congress the power of "exclusive legislation in all matters whatsoever" affecting the District of Columbia. The settled legal meaning and the established historical meaning of this clause sharply differ from its practical political meaning. The weight of historical evidence strongly suggests that the word "exclusive" was used by the framers of the constitution only to create a district free from control by any individual state. There is no historical indication that the framers of the constitution intended Congress actually to conduct the government or that the residents of the District would be disfranchised in either local or national elections.[4]

The courts have adhered repeatedly to this limited, historical construction of the "exclusive" power clause – that it excludes any state from control over District affairs.

While Congress cannot divest itself of its legislative powers over the District, except by retroceding the land itself to the adjoining states, it may delegate its legislative powers to local municipal authority. In delegating power to a local authority, however, Congress does not relinquish or circumscribe its own power to continue to legislate directly on any subject.[5]

The legislative power of Congress in this respect is similar to that of a state legislature over its municipal creatures in cases where there is no state constitutional limitation on legislative power. The Supreme Court of the US has held that there is no constitutional barrier to delegation by Congress to the District of Columbia of full legislative power "subject ... to the power of Congress at any time to revise, alter, or revoke the authority granted."[6]

Normally, delegations of power are made to locally chosen representatives of the municipality, councils, and mayors. This is not done in the District of Columbia. Its local officers are municipal, but they are not local. The status of the District in law is complex. It is a municipal corporation but a severely limited one. Its statutory powers restrain it from acting rather than enabling it to do so. While having some attributes of statehood, it has no attributes of sovereignty. Although the District may participate as a state in interstate compacts, it is treated as an agency of the federal government in budgetary and auditing procedures, and all general federal laws apply to the District and its agencies unless altered by special provisions.

Since no other government has jurisdiction there, the government of the District necessarily performs some functions normally vested in county or state government, such as health and welfare functions and highway development.

There is no consistent pattern for the existing allocation of functions between the federal and District governments, nor do any discernible criteria exist for the distribution or assignment of responsibilities.

FEDERAL INTEREST AND THE NATIONAL CAPITAL AREA

In 1960, the concept of regional federal interest received official recognition in the passage of the Washington Metropolitan Region Development Act which proclaimed congressional concern for regional development, planning, and inter governmental co-operation.[7] Federal interest, however, connotes something different for the District than for the remainder of the region because of the constitutional distinctions between the jurisdictions.

The boundaries of the District of Columbia, for instance, cannot be contracted except by retrocession. They cannot be extended either, by legislation or by decree. Furthermore, the federal government is limited in the types of legislation it may enact for those parts of the national capital region that lie beyond the boundaries of the Federal District. While federal administrative and proprietary interests in the Maryland and Virginia suburbs may be no less than in the District of Columbia, the ability of the national government to act is legally circumscribed by the constitutional limitations of the federal system. National legislative power in the suburbs of Washington is no greater than in other metropolitan areas in the United States. There often is, however, more interest by federal officials in the use of their powers in metropolitan Washington.

The central problem is not legal, but political; and just as there is no coherent policy expressing federal interest for the District of Columbia, there is none for the suburbs nor for the national capital area as a whole. The Washington Metropolitan Region Development Act proclaims the existence of a metropolitan-wide federal interest, but it expresses no clear policy concerning that interest, nor does it provide machinery to develop and state it.

Federal interest as financial involvement

Federal interest expressed as a financial obligation to the city has been traditionally linked with the issue of self-government for the District. The union of the two problems contributed in 1874 to the repeal of self-government in the District, when the fiscal "irresponsibility" of the territorial government led to direct federal rule.[8] Their relationship has continued to weigh heavily against re-establishment of a substantial measure of self-government.

Although a systematic formula for federal financial assistance has been repeatedly recommended for at least 30 years, the Congress has yet to adopt one, continuing instead the practice, begun in 1924, of appropriating lump sums each year to supplement District revenues. Many formulas have been suggested, but none adopted.

While the federal government's direct financial contribution to the District has not exceeded 15 per cent of the District's general fund budget since 1934, the other direct municipal-type services performed by the federal government should not be overlooked. The District, of course, is eligible to receive most of the federal grants-in-aid available to states and municipalities throughout the country. Whatever the adequacy of the federal payment, some questions could also be raised about whether the District government has made sufficient effort to raise needed revenue from local sources. When differences in levels of assessment are taken into account, the District has maintained an effective property tax rate lower than the three largest surrounding jurisdictions, whereas many central cities have higher tax rates than their adjacent suburbs.

The combination of federal fiscal and political control over the District poses a serious dilemma regarding federal responsibility in the District and in the metropolitan area. The federal government, it is asserted, has a responsibility to see that the capital of the nation is a great and beautiful city. But to what degree is local political autonomy compatible with the maintenance of active federal fiscal and operational participation in the affairs of the city? A different perspective on this question is possible when the federal interests in the suburbs, which are not under the exclusive jurisdiction of the Congress, are examined. The federal government clearly has extensive interests in the administration of its facilities and in their physical location and surroundings throughout the national capital region. Federal land holdings in the suburbs comprise an area greater than that held in the District itself, although the percentage of federal property to total land area is smaller. The distribution of the federal payroll further indicates that the economic interest of the federal government in the suburbs approaches, if it does not indeed exceed, its interest in the central city itself. Federal installations outside the District distribute a majority of the region's total federal civilian and military payroll.

In the light of these observations, one may reasonably enquire whether the constitutional distinctions between city and region should make a material difference in the federal financial responsibility for the District and the suburbs, or in the policies which recognize the impact of federal establishments on the local economy and population. The Joint Committee on Washington Metropolitan Problems argued in 1959 that the federal financial responsibility was essentially a regional one. It found little to distinguish the federal financial interests in the District from that in the suburbs. Consequently, it recommended a uniform formula for direct payments to all the jurisdictions of the region in lieu of taxes.

Federal interest as direct involvement of federal officials

Concomitant with financial assistance is political involvement in the affairs of the capital by federal officials. In addition to normal relationships which develop between federal and local officials, there exist both formal administrative activities by federal agencies and a wide array of ad hoc official interventions, not to mention informal and extra-legal involvement by federal officials seeking to achieve limited personal or agency objectives.

A large number of federal agencies are directly involved in national capital affairs, ranging from federal courts and the Department of Justice, the Corps of Engineers of the US Army, the National Park Service, the Department of Health, Education and Welfare, through the Bureau of the Budget and various members of the White House staff. In addition there are three other forms of direct federal involvement: special-purpose federal agencies performing local functions, such as the Redevelopment Land Agency and the National Capital Housing Authority;[9] ex officio representation of selected federal officials on special agencies combining local and federal functions, such as the National Capital Planning Commission; and the designation of special presidential commissions to explore particular problems of the national capital, such as the Potomac Basin Task Force, the task force on Higher Education in the District of Columbia, the Pennsylvania Avenue Commission, and the President's Commission on Crime in the District of Columbia.

If congressional involvements are added to those of the executive, the interests of federal officials may be said to run from the adjustment of parking violations (otherwise known as ticket fixing) or the location of statuary, to the general design or form of the region, and the public health and order of the city and its environs. There are few local questions too mean and none too great to entice some expression of federal interest.

Location of federal installations

The oldest direct involvement of the federal government in the affairs of the capital is in the use of land and in the physical development of the region. Starting with the first plan by Major Pierre L'Enfant, the national government has been a major force in shaping the capital and defining its character. The federal presence has always been singularly significant, but attempts to apply federal influence have been sporadic and the influence itself has been inconsistent. Congress and other federal agencies have shown considerable solicitude at various times for the park system, the highway system, or some other prominent feature of the city-scape, but neither Congress nor the executive branch has yet developed even the beginnings of a policy governing the location of federal installations. Yet they exercise a most important economic influence on the pattern of growth in the capital region.

In 1960, seven per cent of all land in the Washington metropolitan area was owned by the federal government. Adding leased buildings or lands only emphasizes the clear fact that the federal government is the region's principal land holder as well as its most important employer. Yet neither Congress nor the executive branch has a general policy on the extent or nature of agency decentralization in the capital region. Under the existing rules of the game, the key factors are the resourcefulness of the agency head who wants to move, in obtaining Budget Bureau, General Services, Administration, and National Planning Commission clearances for location, and the attitudes and interests of the members of congressional committees that authorize and appropriate funds for land acquisition and construction.

More important than a lack of a policy concerned with the extent of decentralization, is the lack of a policy for decentralization once it has been deemed advisable by the Bureau of the Budget and the Appropriations Committees of Congress for an agency to move. With impacted area assistance for schools the only exception, there is no federal statutory or administrative policy indicating recognition of, much less appreciation for, the problems incident to location of federal installations. These problems cumulatively require replanning of public works and affect local government zoning, housing, planning, education, and revenue policies. No general pattern, no general policy for the agencies can be seen in the several major cases of decentralization since 1955. In spite of the important consequences of federal location decisions, the interest of the agencies and the congressional committees has been confined almost entirely to the problems of the facility itself, without reference to its impact on the environment.

Planning, development, design

If there is no clear policy on federal location, there is ample administrative evidence of federal involvement in the planning and development of the capital. Five separate federal agencies have manifested an interest in planning, development, housing, architecture, and transportation, but each agency represents a different facet of that interest. Each was created ad hoc without relation to the others or to the local authorities they affect. Each also suggests, in its operation, the consequences of creating federal agencies to perform municipal functions, or of mixing municipal and federal responsibilities.

The National Capital Planning Commission

The agency with the most extensive mandate and, as a result, the most schizophrenic behaviour is the National Capital Planning Commission (NCPC). Its authority is extensive. The NCPC has statutory responsibility for federal planning in the entire metropolitan area, presumably including location policy, for comprehensive planning of the District of Columbia, for six-year public works planning, and for transportation planning.[10] Its structure is designed to reconcile federal officials and local citizens along with "national" representatives and a presidentially appointed chairman.

The breadth of its jurisdiction and the character of its membership may well be the key to the inability of NCPC to become a consistently effective instrument of the federal interest, or of local planning. Federal interest in the character of the capital is theoretically represented in two ways. The chairman is named by the president, who also appoints all five of the citizen members of the Commission. And four federal officials, or their alternates, sit ex officio on the Commission – the chief of the Army Corps of Engineers, the director of the National Park Service, the Federal Highway Administrator, and the commissioner of the Public Buildings Service. The sole direct representative of the DC government prior to its reorganization was the engineer commissioner, a general officer of the US Army Corps of Engineers. Under reorganization, the single mayor-commissioner or his alternate represents the city of the NCPC. Only two of the five citizen members are required to be from the metropolitan area.

Whatever its legal responsibility, the NCPC appears to combine these functions which are not fully compatible:

1 It is a group of prominent citizens to advise on the future of the national capital.
2 It is the local planning agency for the District.
3 It is a federal interagency committee to reconcile conflicting objectives in the national capital.

If the federal interest is to be rigorously defined as suggested above, the NCPC expresses it in a peculiar fashion. For all practical purposes, a majority on the Commission may be obtained only by some combination of the votes of local representatives, national representatives, the DC mayor-commissioner, and the federal agency members.

The federal interests represented on the Commission are by no means inclusive of all major capital activities of federal agencies. The National Capital Transportation Agency was represented but was not replaced by the Washington Metropolitan Area Transportation Authority when it absorbed the mass transportation functions of the former. Neither the Redevelopment Agency nor the Housing Authority had a voice on the Commission, although both were federal agencies. While the Department of the Interior, which directly operates National Capital Parks, is represented, the Department of Housing and Urban Development, which contains the greatest expertise in urban planning, has no member on the Commission. There is currently no clear rationale for the federal agency members of the Commission.

The chairman of the NCPC, though named by the president, historically has not acted as a synthesizer of the interests of federal agencies, nor as a reconciler of DC and federal interests. It is not unusual for the chairman to be diametrically opposed to the position of a majority of the representatives of the federal agencies, yet to have no power to require them to temper their views, or to reconcile differences. Historically, the chairman has tended to speak for himself and whatever clientele his views represent, but not necessarily for the federal administration or for the city. It should also be noted that federal agencies whose ambitions are thwarted by the disapproval of the NCPC are not bound to accept its decision as final, even within the administration.

The NCPC lacks the full range of agency representatives and the administrative authority to resolve location problems or to develop a location policy which will be respected by the agencies. In its first 15 years of existence, the NCPC had not developed a comprehensive plan for the District, as charged by its statute, in no small measure because its working time was occupied with federal or local project approvals and because it was not adequately linked to local agencies and citizen attitudes in the city. By 1967, a comprehensive plan had been developed by the staff, but it had not been adopted by the Commission by the end of 1968. The NCPC finally acted on a freeway system for the city late in 1968, under a mandate from Congress and the president.

While the NCPC has maintained a reasonably dedicated professional staff, it is generally cut off from both local and federal power and is saddled with a political assignment it is unlikely to be able to perform without extensive overhauling of both the commission itself and its mandate. An agency which is apparently supposed to work for everyone, federal and local alike, the NCPC often finds itself working for no one.

Other agencies

Among the other agencies concerned with planning and land use is the National Capital Housing Authority (NCHA). Federal involvement in urban renewal and housing began in 1934 when Congress passed the Alley

Dwelling Act to provide for slum clearance and public housing in the District of Columbia. The NCHA was created in 1943 by Executive Order to administer this program. In 1968 the Authority was brought under the supervision of the mayor through the reorganization plan. Public housing constructed by the NCHA must be cleared with the NCPC and the District of Columbia government. It is not uncommon for the NCHA to be in conflict with the Redevelopment Land Agency, another independent quasi-federal agency charged with general urban renewal activities and programs, which must also be approved by the NCPC and by the city council.

Another agency whose activities have consequences for land use is the Commission of Fine Arts. Composed of seven members appointed by the president, it has advisory jurisdiction over building plans for those areas of the capital distinctly "federal" in character, and also for the Georgetown area under the terms of the "old Georgetown Act" of 1950. Plans for public buildings, bridges, monuments and private structures in the areas concerned must be referred to the Commission for approval. Disapproval, however, does not necessarily doom a project, if it can obtain approval of other agencies such as the Zoning Commission, the National Park Service, the Bureau of Public Roads, the General Services Administration, the Bureau of the Budget, or perhaps the Congress or the president.

Each federal agency is virtually uninhibited in defining the federal interest from its own point of view. When the definitions differ, action usually is stalled, and the sheer number of agencies with overlapping responsibility for the federal interest in any one project tends to prevent its definition.

The two most conspicuous accomplishments representative of federal interest in the region are the parks system and the water supply system. Both are operated by federal agencies, the National Park Service and the Corps of Engineers' Washington Aqueduct, established in 1863. The federal government has not yet co-ordinated the transportation, parks, and renewal aspects of land use for either the District of the metropolitan area. In addition it has separated from the local government vital programs necessary for it to develop a co-ordinated attack on the city's environmental and social problems.

Development legislation, while of continuing interest to Congress, has been enacted on a piecemeal basis to solve immediate problems, usually by vesting particular federal interests in separate federal agencies. It must be concluded that the federal interest in the form and development of the region is thus expressed. Neither in the principal acts and agencies reviewed, nor in any separate action, nor in any series of actions together, is there a definition of the kind of capital city sought by the federal government. Finally, there is no clearly delineated process through which an authoritative determination of federal interest in the national capital, let alone a general and integrated development plan, can be developed and adopted with binding effect on the participants in the process.

The executive interest

The role of the presidency

The president nominally, and sometimes actually, is the chief of administration for the federal and municipal agencies involved in District and national capital affairs. The president's appointive power is extensive. Table 1 lists presidentially appointed officers that are directly concerned with the national capital region. A president who wishes to do so may use this power to try to mould the capital to his desires. His power in the District may also encourage him to use the city for vicarious policy – as a "model" to draw national attention to a problem – in varied fields ranging from urban beautification to combating juvenile delinquency.

TABLE 1

Presidential appointments in District of Columbia and related agencies

1 Commissioner of the District of Columbia
2 The Assistant to the Commissioner
3 Nine members of the District of Columbia Council
4 The Public Service Commission
5 Five members of the National Capital Planning Commission
   (five of the other seven ex-officio members are also presidential appointees)
6 Seven members of the Commission of Fine Arts
7 The Adjutant General of the National Guard
8 US Court of Appeals for the District of Columbia Circuit
9 US District Court for the District of Columbia
10 The DC Court of Appeals
11 The DC Superior Court
12 The Armory Board
13 US Attorney for the District of Columbia and his assistants
14 Federal members of Interstate Commission on the Potomac River Basin
15 US Marshals for the District of Columbia
16 DC Registrar of Wills
17 Board of Vocational Education of the Washington Technical Institute

Presidential involvement is far from institutional, and depends chiefly on the interests of the incumbent. Presidents Kennedy and Johnson showed more interest in the capital than any other presidents in the twentieth century. In addition to support of home rule, these two presidents, their wives, cabinet officers, assistants, and the vice-presidents occupied themselves with a wide array of projects and activities in the capital.

While presidential activity may be judged helpful, it has yet to add up to a presidential program for the capital. In part because no president can have much time for the capital, most presidents have expressed their interest in it through special projects – some of fundamental significance, others of a more vicarious quality, making use of the presidential office to stimulate a wider response in the city or the nation. The capacity of the president, as the apex of the federal executive, to "finalize" (to use the bureaucratic idiom) decisions means that one basic strategem in federal interest politics is to obtain presidential support for projects or, conversely, to attempt to prevent presidential involvement. Nor is it unusual for local interest groups to address appeals for action to the White House instead of the District Building. As agencies such as the NCPC have failed to perform adequately in expressing and reconciling federal interests in the capital area, demands for presidential involvement have increased. The incomplete and divided character of the municipal government, as well as the dismemberment of federal interests into special agencies, has forced an increasing number of municipal issues up to the level of presidential attention.

No mechanism in the White House or the Executive Office has yet been developed for the systematic co-ordination of the several national capital agencies directly responsible to the president. Co-ordination is achieved on a limited scale in budgeting; but only a few of those agencies which report directly to the president come under a common budget. The budgets for the District government and some of its related agencies are reviewed by the District commissioner and the council, but the commissioner exercises no effective fiscal or managerial power over the estimates of the federal agencies for the District. Some, such as the NCPC, are not even funded through the District's budget. Other federal agencies have direct operating programs in the District. These programs are reviewed within the respective agency or departmental budgets by the Bureau of the Budget. There is no systematic procedure for co-ordination of District and federal budgets or programs.

The President's Advisor for National Capital Affairs

From 1962 until 1967, the principal tool of presidential involvement in the District had been the President's Advisor for National Capital Affairs. In 1959, the Joint Congressional Committee on Washington Metropolitan Problems had recommended establishment of a "federal co-ordinator" in the office of the president. This official was to have responsibility for "co-ordination of all Federal activities related to land and Federal installations, but [also] such vital grants-in-aid programs of regional significance as highways, housing, urban redevelopment, and parks."[11]

Although this concept was urged on President Kennedy by some who had been associated with the Joint Committee, the advisor appointed by Kennedy and retained by President Johnson followed another course. Rather than becoming a means of co-ordinating federal agencies, the office of the advisor became a new centre of interest in its own right. The activities of the first presidential advisor became a new centre of interest in its own right. The activities of the first presidential advisor focused not on federal agencies, but on the District of Columbia itself.

The office of the advisor was retained by President Johnson until the 1967 reorganization of DC government became effective. At this time co-ordination of DC affairs in the White House was transferred to an assistant to the president who also handled other domestic problems, and the advisor's post was dropped. President Nixon assigned DC and national capital affairs to Daniel P. Moynihan, his assistant for urban affairs.

The executive agencies

Executive agencies of the federal government which have direct operating responsibilities for local services, and for other services which are both local and national in scope, not infrequently are embroiled in political conflicts springing from their particular interests. These interests are often direct, resulting from a special responsibility of functional jurisdiction imposed by statute. Not only is there a lack of central executive control over conflicts which occur between federal agencies, but these agencies frequently report to different congressional committees. Consequently, they use their separate but equal legislative basis to frustrate rival plans if they cannot achieve their objectives independently. Thus reinforced by dispersion of legislative power, agency interests often cannot be reconciled short of action by the president himself. Even this may not suffice.

The special position of the federal government in the region makes the administrators of its departments and agencies among the most important of the political groups in the metropolitan area. The high degree of specialization of federal agencies has much to do with the politics of executive interests. A second factor is their relationship to presidential and congressional power systems. Third, their regional and national clientele augment their influence in regional decision-making. Even the Bureau of the Budget may have its special institutional interests in a problem and become an advocate rather than a catalyst in a struggle for presidential and congressional approval. There is little that one federal agency can actually give another in exchange for support. Thus the political style of the federal administrator is to become an advocate of institutional interests rather than a negotiator, at least until discipline is imposed by the president. This seldom happens.

The federal administrator has a unique leadership role in Washington. Here he often replaces the businessman or the local group as the initiator of ideas and programs. Plans for Washington are largely staff plans, as contrasted with local leadership plans in some other cities. Administrators and civil servants may also find themselves the public advocates of their own expert advice, rather than just the professional rationalizers for the civic prescriptions of other groups.

Another aspect of bureaucratic politics in Washington should be noted. The federal agencies often depend more for support on their national clientele than on the area's population or political processes. In the absence of an effective local political system and of any system of effective federal administrative review, no regularly organized political means to reconcile conflicts is available, except for the ill-co-ordinated legislative processes of Congress and intermittent presidential intervention.

Congressional politics and federal interest

The committee system

Given exclusive legislative power over the District, the Congress supposedly formulates the principal components of federal interest for the District of Columbia. Congress works primarily through the committee system. The committees are themselves representative institutions, and not merely administrative task forces for the two houses of the Congress. The extent to which a committee is representative of the Congress itself is, in large part, a function of the practices surrounding selection of members for the committee, and of the "seniority rule" by which committee chairmanships are automatically given to the majority member who has served longest on his committee. Subcommittee chairs are often apportioned on a basis other than seniority, but in any event, are usually assigned at the discretion of the chairman of the full committee.

The district committees

If a scale were constructed indicating the rank of committees, according to the importance members attach to serving on them, the committees on the District of Columbia in the Senate and House of Representatives would surely rank near, if not at, the bottom. As a former House Committee member once put it, "This committee gets the dregs." Only the congressmen elected from the suburban districts adjacent to the District have a direct interest in DC affairs. Traditionally, at least one member of the House Committee is from Maryland, and another from Virginia. Similarly, at least one of the two states is normally represented on the Senate Committee. Other than these three members, no discernible criteria appear for selection to the DC committees, which is considered under the rules of the houses as "extra duty" for their members.

Many members who serve find the work unrewarding in that it consumes time they feel could be more profitably spent on other matters. In the Senate, some consideration is given to prior experience of members in asking them to serve on the District Committee. Whatever the criteria, the practices of selection have produced in the committees on the District of Columbia representative institutions dissimilar in composition and outlook.

In the House Committee, members from the southern states consistently have provided 40 per cent or more of the membership for the last twenty years. Of the Democratic members, 50 to 75 per cent have been southerners, whereas the southern states provide only 35 per cent of all Democrats in the House.

The Senate Committee has an even greater distortion in regional representation. This is mainly due to the smaller number of members on the Senate Committee.

Regional representation is essentially immaterial on a committee, unless regional interests are at stake. In the absence of such interests, or even with them, a more useful key to representation in a committee is the reflection in its members of the political attitudes of their party in the Congress. For the most part, over the past ten Congresses, District Committee members have tended to vote with the majority of their party colleagues in the House far less frequently than the average.

Briefly, then, the House Committee is not representative of the House on either a regional or a party basis. Yet it is the institution primarily charged with determination of the federal interest for the Congress. Finally, members of the House Committee have quite frequently represented rural districts rather than urban areas, thus further limiting their political rapport with the residents of the capital city.

The leadership of the House Committee in the past several congresses was centred in a few southern Democrats and one suburban Virginia Republican. What these influential members are capable of accomplishing in numbers of public laws is for most purposes less significant than what they are capable of preventing. Since 1948, seven Senate-passed bills providing some measure of local representative government for the District of Columbia have died in the House Committee. In 1965 when a self-government bill was petitioned directly to the floor by a majority of the House members, the committee's leadership succeeded in substituting a much weaker bill which the Senate would not accept. Consequently, the bill died when Congress adjourned without taking further action. Only once or twice since 1948 has the House Committee even held hearings on home-rule legislation.

The District committees share jurisdiction over the capital city with the DC subcommittees of the Appropriations Committees in each House, and with a series of other committees which regularly or occasionally handle legislation for the District and the metropolitan area. Washington is the only city in the United States where the appropriations are separated from the legislators who have surveillance over revenue and legislation. While it is true that both groups are committees of the Congress, and that city councils may operate through committees, city councils spend their full legislative time dealing with city functions.

The committees of Congress tend to deal with the governmental agencies of the District government in much the same manner as they treat the regular federal agencies, with an important difference. Federal agencies normally appear in defence of the "President's program" as it is reflected in the activities of the agency. Until the Kennedy administration there was no "President's program" for the District of Columbia, or for the Washington metropolitan area. While the District government is expected to represent the executive version of federal interest, its status before Congress is decidedly inferior to that of other federal agencies, and quite drastically inferior to the relations of a strong mayor to his council.

There is in Congress no single place where issues concerning the District or the metropolitan area can be resolved. Planning legislation may be referred to the committees on Interior and Insular Affairs. Parks legislation is sent to this committee, and appropriations for parks are considered by the Interior subcommittee of the Appropriations Committee, whose concerns encompass a far wider range of subjects than the national capital region. The judiciary committees may consider interstate compacts, and they may receive legislation dealing with the courts or with national suffrage for the District. Conceivably, they could also receive legislation on metropolitan structure.

Legislation concerned with building roads, highways, bridges, and public buildings may be referred to the committees on Public Works, except for construction in parks. Authorizations for construction may come from the subcommittee with oversight over the agency doing the construction, and different subcommittees of the same committee may handle different projects. The Corps of Engineers, which operates the District's water supply facility, the Washington Aqueduct, and conducts studies and works on the Potomac, is responsible to committees on Public Works. Projects are, of course, funded by the appropriations subcommittees. Consequently, there is no general congressional oversight over federal public works in the region. A further complication is that some matters are not referred to the same committees in the two Houses.

THE SYSTEM OF LOCAL GOVERNMENT

The role of Congress

Operating as a city council, Congress exercises greater power than any other municipal or state legislative body. While exercising plenary power to pass general laws, as may be done by a state legislature, Congress also frequently immerses itself in detailed matters concerning the administration of DC affairs. In spite of its extensive power, however, Congress has basically failed as a legislative body for the District. Too little power has been delegated. But not only has Congress retained basic power over detail, such as whether the District agencies may illustrate official reports, it has been institutionally unable to accommodate itself to the dual role as control government and local lawmaker. However well Congress may perform as a national legislature, it acts poorly as a city council for the capital city.

Representation of irrelevant interests

Public officials act in representative as well as personal capacities. The question in any representative body is the extent to which the two types of actions are weighted. It is the object of much governmental organization and procedure to accentuate the representative character of decision-making, and to diminish the personal emphasis.

We have already seen how the unrepresentative character of the committees on the District of Columbia conspires against the federal interest in the District and the interests of the District itself. Moreover, the elections which determine the tenure of committee members have little, if any, relevance to the affairs of the District, although some members receive campaign contributions from District backers. And only a few of the members have served on committees which deal with urban affairs. Most consider their other committee assignments their primary responsibility. Attendance at District committee meetings is low.

The irrelevance of the members' constituencies and the dispersion of their congressional interest tend to contribute to an irresponsible lack of local political perspective. The congressional scale of values can be weighted almost entirely toward personal prejudices or preferences in selection of the areas with which the individual members will deal, whatever the needs of the city or the desires of its citizens. Congress, insofar as it represents the District at all, does it in terms of functional civic interests or governmental bureaus, which somehow find access to well-placed members who happen to agree for some reason.

Division of access and power

Not only are the constituencies of members of the House and Senate irrelevant to the politics and problems of the District of Columbia; they are not relevant to each other. Senatorial constituencies, being broader, tend to make senators less parochial in outlook and interest than House members in responding to District problems. On the other hand, the work load of a senator is such that he can rarely give the District Committee the attention given it by a House member. This leads to quite different responses to common problems by the two committees.

Because their constituencies are so different, the members of the two committess are likely to differ on matters which would not even divide bicameral city councils, only a few of which remain in the US. In most cities the pressure of local politics tends to move the city council toward some sort of agreement. This kind of pressure is not present in the Congress regarding District affairs.

Also, it should be re-emphasized that the appropriating and legislating authority of the House is divided between two committees that have no common members. In the Senate, this division is less rigid, since by custom some DC committeemen sit with the appropriations subcommittee. The constituencies of appropriators differ from those of legislators, and neither are related to the District's politics or needs. Yet these four committees exercise most of the basic legislative power for the District.

The result of this unnatural fragmentation of legislative power has resulted in long-smouldering disagreements on matters which should be more swiftly resolved in a modern city. For six years (1955–61), the two DC committees were unable to agree to a conference report on unemployment compensation legislation. For several years they could not agree on crime control legislation, and they approached legislation to deal with parking problems quite differently, leading to an impasse that had not been resolved by 1970. The clash on these issues illustrates a fundamental problem arising from the different constituencies of the two committees. While the constituencies of both are non-District, they differ so much from each other that there frequently is little of the overlap in functional representation of local interests that one would expect to find in a more typical city government.

Congress and the city budget

Provision of adequate revenues is a persistent problem in most cities. The organization of Congress to deal with this problem is again unique, and productive of stalemate rather than accommodation. The problem is a two-fold one.

First, Congress annually appropriates a lump sum federal payment to the District of Columbia as described above. The legislative committees authorize payment, but as in other cases in Congress, the appropriations subcommittees do not regard the authorization as binding upon them. After hearing the budget requests of the District government, the subcommittees determine the size of the federal payment, as well as the appropriations for all District agencies whether financed by federal or local funds. This appropriations power may also be used to affect substantive policy in the District.

A second aspect of the revenue problem is that the District committees must recommend for congressional passage any new revenues, or increases in revenues other than property taxes. Once again the antagonism between the Houses causes the city to suffer their inability to accommodate each other's objectives or functionally represented interests. In fiscal matters, the Senate Committee has tended to favour broad taxing authority, reflecting the views of the city government, minority groups, and labour, while the House Committee, and particularly its senior members, appear more responsive to the claims of real estate, business and other large taxpayers.

Congressional dominance of the municipal executive

Unlike other major American cities, there is little or no executive pressure on Congress to make basic decisions which may be demanded of a normal city council. Whatever his decision may be, the mayor of most cities can force an issue if he so desires, by administrative or even electoral pressure and action. The president normally has far more important issues on which to expend his legislative credit than DC affairs. The mayor and council are appointed officials, and even if they were elected, their political authority and support pose no threat to most members of Congress.

The District executive's budget must be reviewed by the Congress, and it has no constituency at all, only a clientele. A mayor who clashes with Congress may lose even if his view is upheld by reason and local public opinion. The legislative strategy of the mayor, therefore, is heavily oriented toward first obtaining presidential support. It is further complicated by the mayor's need to gain executive authority and political control over the executive departments in the DC government, which under the former commission system frequently dealt directly with congressional committees.

The absence of responsibility

As has previously been pointed out, the crux of the issue of congressional control over District affairs is a lack of political responsibility for whatever action is taken. The two Houses provide no internal system of responsibility as protection against the actions or postures of members of the two committees. Indeed, the procedures and customs of Congress tend to mitigate against responsible controls over members. The seniority system, the autonomy of the committees and their chairman and the laxity of party discipline combine with the almost monumental indifference on the part of most members toward the District, to produce a stalemate or inaction in areas of vital concern to the city.

This is not to suggest that Congress never acts. It does act where matters of great urgency come to its attention, as in the case of unlicensed home repair businesses, or in providing additional policemen to meet an increasing crime rate. In such instances, in the absence of an effective (i.e. functionally represented) countervailing interest on either District committee, corrective action is taken – in some instances with dispatch.

More significant for the effect on DC legislation than the lack of internal responsibility is the lack of any effective external control on the members who legislate for the District of Columbia. In this case, Congress cannot be held accountable by the population for whom it legislates. Rather, accountability flows to constituencies for the most part ignorant of, or indifferent to, the requirements of the national capital.

In summary, Congress may be described as incredibly inept and cantankerous as a local legislature. It rarely offers any leadership. It often vetoes or stalemates vital matters which are of basic local concern, and which do not involve any higher degree of abstract federal interest than in any other American city. It often acts irresponsibly, and it is not susceptible to any form of control, internal or external, for its actions.

The 1967 reorganization of DC government

On 3 November 1967 the District of Columbia officially changed its form of government from the three-man commission which had governed it since 1874 to a commissioner (mayor)-council form of government.[12] The District was the last major city in the United States to abandon the commission form. The mayor-council form was basically the structure that had been proposed in the home rule bill which was defeated in Congress in 1965.

President Johnson decided to submit the reform proposal to Congress as a reorganization plan rather than as legislation. In this way he avoided having the bill sent to the House District Committee, since reorganization plans are under the jurisdiction of the Government Operations Committee Moreover, a reorganization plan may not be amended, and for it to be defeated a resolution of disapproval must be adopted by one of the two Houses within 60 days after the president submits it to Congress.

Within the reorganization proposal the president was particularly concerned with consolidation of executive and administrative authority in a unified municipal executive. He therefore proposed a new executive officer with power to reorganize the departments and agencies of the District government in the most effective manner possible. The president also proposed a bipartisan city council that would carry out the quasi-legislative functions formerly assigned to the District's board of commissioners.

The new government

The executive branch of District government under the reorganization plan is composed of a commissioner (also called mayor) and an assistant commissioner (deputy mayor), both nominated by the president and confirmed by the Senate. Both the mayor and the deputy mayor must have been residents of the District for three years preceding their nomination and both officials must reside in Washington during their term of office. The mayor is appointed for a four-year term which coincides with the term of the president.

The District's city council is composed of nine members nominated by the president and confirmed by the Senate. Two of them are designated as chairman and vice-chairman by the president and confirmed by the Senate. All members must have been residents of the District for three years preceding their appointment and must reside there during their term of office. No more than six may be of one political party. Councilmen hold three-year terms, three being appointed each year, and serve on a part-time basis.

Under the new organization, the president has more direct control over the District government than he had before. Since the mayor's term coincides with the president's, he is subject to reappointment as each new administration comes into office. Under the commission form of government the terms of the commissioners did not expire at the same time. The president may also remove the mayor or his deputy from office any time he desires. This affords the president the maximum amount of control over the administration of the District's government. Because the council is designated as a quasi-legislative body the president is restricted in his powers of removal. He can only remove a councilman from office for "neglect of duty or malfeasance in office or when the member has been found guilty of a felony or conduct involving moral turpitude."[13]

The executive branch

On 3 November 1967, the day the city council was sworn in, the mayor reorganized the District government by transferring several agencies to his direct control. He issued an organization order which created an Executive Office in the District government, and then transferred to it the Budget Office, the Personnel Office, the Management Office, the Office of Program Coordination, the Public Affairs Office, and the newly created Offices of the Secretariat and Public Safety Director. A short time later the newly created Manpower Administration was placed directly under the mayor's control. In 1969, a new Department of Economic Development was created, consolidating several agencies, and a series of new offices, Housing, Youth Services, Community Services, Human Resources, and Budget and Executive Management were added to the Executive Office.

President Johnson submitted two reorganization plans to Congress in 1968 which altered the structure of District government. The DC Recreation Department, which had a six-man board that supervised its policies as an independent agency, was brought under the control of the mayor. The DC Redevelopment Land Agency, the District's urban renewal agency, was not responsible to the District government but rather to a five-man board that was only partially appointed by the mayor. The Reorganization Plan (1968) provided for the mayor to appoint all the members as well as to establish the rules and regulations governing the agency's operations. The RLA, however, remains technically a federal agency.

Other agencies which have been brought under the direct control of the mayor are the Human Relations Commission, the Office of Community and Urban Renewal, the Board of (Zoning) Appeals and Review and the Contract Appeals Board.

While the 1967 Reorganization Plan separated the quasi-legislative functions of government from the administrative functions and delegated them to the council and mayor respectively, no changes were made in the overall legal authority of the city government. The council assumed the quasi-legislative functions which Congress had previously delegated to the Board of Commissioners. The mayor and the deputy mayor were made responsible for the administration of legislation enacted by Congress and by the city council.

The mayor was given virtually no new powers under the 1967 plan which had not been exercised by the Board of Commissioners. He became the chief executive with complete administrative authority for the agencies of municipal government then under the jurisdiction of the Board of Commissioners. In addition, he was made responsible for preparing the annual budget, naming the heads of departments, and organizing and managing the District government.

The significance of establishing the mayoralty is more political than legal. For the first time in almost a century, the city appeared to have an identifiable head. The mayor, as a single executive, has been able to use this moral and political authority to some advantage in negotiating with Congress, federal agencies, or the suburbs, and to increase administrative discipline within the city government itself. The absence of an electoral base remains, of course, a severe handicap for the executive in the exercise of power within the city.

The municipal budget role

The congressional role in budgeting remained unchanged. The mayor prepares the annual budget after consulting with department heads on their requests for funds. The budget is then submitted to the council for examination and approval. Once the annual budget is prepared by the mayor, the deputy mayor and the department heads hold a series of technical briefings with the council. The council then distributes the budget to interested groups and calls public hearings. Once the hearings are concluded, the council revises those parts of the budget on which it disagrees with the mayor, and returns the budget to him.

The mayor may accept the council's revisions or exercise his right of item veto. Those items which are vetoed are then returned to the council with a statement from the mayor explaining his reasons for the veto. If the council acts within five days, it may override the mayor's veto by a three-fourths vote. If the council does not approve or amend the budget within thirty days after receiving it, the budget is approved as submitted by the mayor. Once the budget has completed this process, it must be submitted to the US Bureau of the Budget for approval before it can be submitted to the Congress for final review and enactment, as described earlier.

The city council

As a result of the reorganization, the council was given over 400 specific quasi-legislative functions which formerly had been exercised by the Board of Commissioners. These included the power to: adopt city ordinances, review and revise the budget, set the real estate tax rate, approve urban renewal plans and boundaries, establish rules governing the licensing of professions, approve major thoroughfares plans, establish the level of public assistance payments, set districts and precints for the Metropolitan Police Department, and promulgate regulations for hospitals and asylums.

When an ordinance passed by the council is submitted to the mayor, he has ten calendar days in which to approve or disapprove it. If he takes no action, after the tenth day the ordinance becomes effective. If the mayor vetoes a council action within the ten-day period, he must return it to the council together with a written statement detailing the reasons for his veto. The council may override the veto by a three-fourths vote of the council members present, provided they do so within thirty days of receipt of the mayor's veto message.

While neither the mayor nor councilmen have constituencies in any normal sense, they do respond to different community interests. As the new government began to gain self-confidence, fissures began to appear in the façade of mayor-council unity. In spite of its appointed status, the council appeared to be making a strong effort to speak for community interests in city affairs, and to challenge the mayor's views or authority in a number of instances.

The quasi-legislative functions of the council are performed as they are in most other legislative bodies. Committees were formed to allow the council to focus on the functional areas of greatest concern to the citizens of the District. These committees were: Education, Youth, Housing, Health and Welfare, Manpower and Economic Development, Public Safety, Planning, Highways and Transportation, Government Operation, Personnel, and Consumer Affairs.

Not all of the committees have been active, since the council often sits as a committee of the whole when conducting hearings on matters of great importance to the community. During its first year in office the council and its committees conducted hearings on such crucial issues as the District freeway plan, gun control legislation, consumer protection, and regulations on police use of weapons.

In 1968, the council divided the District into four councilmanic districts with two councilmen assigned as each district's "representatives." This action was construed to be in accord with the 1967 plan's statement that members of the council be as broadly representative of the community as possible. Each councilmanic district had a population of approximately 200,000 people.

The city council has a small staff which aids it in the performance of its duties. The 1967 plan also provided for a secretary of the council, which appoints him and approves the staff he hires. He is in charge of all administrative and research activities of the council's staff.

The school system

Desegregation

The school system of the District of Columbia must be discussed in the context of the racial composition of the city and two major court decisions affecting the racial composition and educational practices of the public schools. In *Brown v Board of Education of Topeka*,[14] the Supreme Court of the United States stated that separate but equal facilities in the field of public education constituted segregation, which deprived the plaintiffs of equal protection of the laws under the Fourteenth Amendment. On the same day in 1954 the court also handed down its decision in *Bolling v Sharpe*,[15] which invalidated the use of racially separated educational facilities in the District of Columbia. Until this decision the District had employed a dual school system. White children and teachers were placed in Division 1, while black children and teachers were in Division 2. Both divisions were responsible to a single Board of Education and a Superintendent of Schools.

It would appear that school desegregation accelerated the migration from the city to the suburbs of large numbers of white families with school-age children. Two public opinion polls taken in Washington in June and July of 1954 showed clearly that a majority of white residents were not in favour of the Supreme Court decision ending segregation. A number of whites who remained in the District sought transfers for their children to schools with low black enrolments. Many transferred to private schools.

The track system

In 1956 the schools system embarked upon a new program – the track system – which was to have serious repercussions eleven years later. The track system, or "ability grouping" as it was sometimes known, consisted of four curriculum "tracks," the honors track, the college preparatory track, the general track, and the basic track. The objective of the track system was to allow students of similar academic achievement to work together, regardless of race. The track system was implemented in the senior high schools for all grades in 1958. Shortly thereafter it was introduced into the elementary and junior high schools.

Opposition to the track system, weak at first, grew in strength during the early 1960s. The main source of this opposition came from those who felt that the system was undemocratic and that ability grouping should be replaced by heterogeneous grouping and individualized instruction. Opposition also came from some Negro civil rights and education groups who saw in the track system a new way of reinstating racial segregation in the schools, and of providing inferior education to most black students.

Hobson v Hansen

In July 1966, Julius Hobson, a militant civil rights activist, filed suit against the Superintendent of Schools, the Board of Education, and the judges who then appointed the board. Hobson accused the defendants of unconstitutionally depriving the poor and black school children of equal educational opportunities. Hobson claimed that this inequality stemmed from adherence to the neighbourhood school policy, faculty assignments to schools, the track system, optional zones which permitted a choice of schools, to some students, inadequate public expenditures, and overcrowded neighbourhood schools.[16] There was some irony to be noted in a black civil rights activist filing a suit in which he claimed that the neighbourhood school concept deprived black and poor children of equal educational opportunity. Only thirteen short years before, the Supreme Court in *Bolling* v *Sharpe* had affirmed the concept of the neighbourhood school in an effort to eliminate the dual school system and end segregation.

In a lengthy decision, US Court of Appeals Judge J. Skelly Wright found for Hobson and against the Superintendent of Schools and the Board of Education. Judge Wright directed the Board of Education to:

1 Abolish the track system.
2 Develop a pupil assignment plan in accord with the Court's directive by 2 October 1967.
3 Provide transportation, on a volunteer basis, to children in overcrowded schools to underutilized schools.
4 Abolish the system of optional zones.
5 Develop a plan for full faculty integration in the school system.[17]

At the time of the *Hobson* v *Hansen* decision the racial composition of the District's schools was 92 per cent black and only 8 per cent white. This situation precluded any effective racial integration in most of the District's schools.

A few months after the Wright decision, the District's Board of Education released the findings of a fifteen-month study of the DC schools, conducted by Teachers College, Columbia University, under the direction of Professor A. Harry Passow.

In a section entitled "Integration in the District's Schools" Dr Passow wrote:

When a school system is more than 90 per cent pupils of one race, to speak in any ordinary sense of integration, desegregation or racial balance on a system-wide scale would be pointless. Devices that might further desegregation in other cities are now largely irrelevant in Washington. However difficult the present situation may be, the fundamental task of the District schools is the same as that for every other American school system: to provide for every child, whatever his race, education of a quality that will enable him to make the most of himself and to take his place as a free person in an open society.[18]

The elected school board

During the second session of the 90th Congress a law was passed granting the residents of the District of Columbia the right to elect their own Board of Education. As indicated above, no election for local public officials had been held in the District for almost one hundred years. The Board of Education had been appointed by the judges of the US District Court for the District of Columbia. Until the mid-1960s a majority of the board had remained white.

The new legislation provided for eight board members to be elected from wards and three members to be elected at large. Congress stipulated that the elections were to be non-partisan, although the party organizations have endorsed candidates.

The advent of this elected school board in November 1968 has been greeted with mixed feelings by observers of local politics in the District. Many have viewed it as a natural step in the fight for home rule. The opportunity to vote for elected officials had been denied for so long that the high percentage of voters who turned out at the first election must have impressed the sceptics.

On the other hand, there remained the factor of the still unsolved relationship between the elected board and the appointed city council. In its initial activities the board seemed determined to become the legitimate voice of the communities of the city in educational affairs. However, the council retains the right to review the annual budget requests of the board. Should the council make serious deletions or amendments to the budget submitted by the board, there could develop a conflict between these two bodies which might impede the operation of government in the District. This in time might have a substantial impact on the achievement and timing of self-government in Washington.

The court system

Most of the court system of the District is part of the national court system. As in many other areas of local government, the people of the District have virtually no voice in determining who the court officials will be, what compensation they will receive or the length of their term of office. The judges of all courts for the District are appointed by the president with the approval of the Senate.

Due partly to a serious backlog of criminal cases, a law was passed in July 1970 to reorganize the District's courts. The judicial power in the District is now vested in two District courts and three federal courts. The lowest District court is the new, enlarged Superior Court. Unlike the previous Court of General Sessions, which could not handle felonies or civil actions beyond $10,000, the new court has complete jurisdiction over criminal and civil matters. The second District court, the DC Court of Appeals, hears appeals not only from the Superior Court but also from decisions by the mayor, the city council and agencies of the District government. The three federal courts are, in order of ascending rank, the US District Court, the US Court of Appeals for the District, and, finally, the US Supreme Court.

US *attorney for the District*

The US attorney for the District of Columbia is appointed by the president with confirmation from the Senate, for a four-year term. There is no residence requirement for the nominee. The US attorney's jurisdiction extends to civil and criminal actions in the Superior Court as well as cases he brings before the US courts. His jurisdiction includes violations of all federal criminal laws such as income tax evasion, mail fraud, and narcotics offences. In addition, he is responsible for offences which in other cities are prosecuted by local and state officials such as homicide and robbery. The only areas not within his jurisdiction are municipal offences.

Corporation counsel of the District

Cases involving municipal offences are prosecuted by the corporation counsel, the chief legal officer of the District, who is appointed by the mayor and serves as his legal adviser. His law-enforcement activities are centered on traffic offences, but he also deals with a wide range of other violations including alcoholic beverage control, disorderly conduct, public intoxication, health, housing, and fair employment regulations. In addition, he handles many juvenile matters and serves as a legal adviser to the various agencies and departments of the DC government. There are about seventy attorneys on the counsel's staff, several of whom are usually assigned as prosecutors in the Superior Court.

Politics in the District[19]

Political parties

The absence of elections for local government officials both truncates and skews the political system of the capital city. The principal focus of partisan activity is the presidency, and since the city is overwhelmingly Democratic, the primary elections, in which delegates are chosen to the national party conventions and to city-wide party committees are of most interest and most revealing of local party currents.

These elections may have little to do with local public policy, or even officials. Rather, they may be based on national factional contests among presidential aspirants, with some heavy infusion of local personality politics.

After an amendment to the federal constitution allowed District residents to vote for president, the first such election was held in 1964. There was little competition in the primary elections of either party. In 1968, a slate of party officers and convention delegates supporting the candidacy of Robert F. Kennedy was elected in the Democratic primary. The Republican primary was not seriously contested.

The parties have not been particularly influential even in patronage matters in city government. Customarily, the party controlling the White House may expect that the president will appoint members of his own party to major city positions. While presidents normally follow these assumptions, it does not follow that he will appoint favourites of the local party committee. In recent years, Presidents Johnson and Kennedy cleared appointments with the Democratic committee, and normally consulted them, though not always. The appointment of the mayor and city council were cases in point. Only two councilmen had much previous party history. President Nixon appointed the local Republican chairman to the council, but reappointed the Democratic mayor and deputy mayor. Since the mayor and council are forbidden by law to participate in partisan political management these centrally important figures do not act as party leaders. Thus party leadership tends to be far more nominal than real, resting with the party chairmen and national committeemen, who "speak" for the party, or at least some rather indefinitely defined faction of it.

For the most part, political parties in the District of Columbia are parties in name only. They are not clear routes to power, and tend to behave more like general interest groups than party organizations.

Interest groups

Though the city has the normal variety of groups, it is far more difficult to assess their relative influence in a no-elections system than in other cities.

In general, these groups may be classified by (1) their political base – local or national, (2) their degree of specialization and the intensity of their activity, (3) the extent to which they are private groups or public officials, and (4) the arena in which they work most frequently.

Because Washington is the capital, and more directly because Congress governs it, many national interest groups involve themselves in DC affairs. The FBI director and the association of chiefs of police may become directly involved in controversies over the administration of justice in the District. By the same token, national civil rights or civil liberties organizations make DC affairs matters for considerable activity or concern. The clear implication is that proposed policies for law enforcement and many other subjects must not only have sufficient local support if they are to be realized: they must also have the support or acquiescence of the necessary combination of national groups. A local group which cannot attain its objectives alone frequently expands the conflict and brings in its nationally based allies who have either different, more, or better access to a point of decision in the governmental process.

Very few interest groups manifest both a broad range of interest and a high intensity of activity in city affairs. As in other cities, most tend to concern themselves with narrow specialties. The high-intensity "groups" tend to be composed of public officials more often than private citizens. Groups of local and federal officials, acting both as agency representatives and through professional or occupational associations, are important actors in the group politics system. In many ways, DC agencies have played the role of interest groups in dealing with the federal executive and congressional committees. This role is exaggerated because of the inability of local government officials to make final decisions on city affairs, whether it be court organization or the location of a transportation facility.

Interest group activity tends to be divided between those groups which focus their activity on the District government and those which take their cases directly to Congress or the president. Until recently civil rights and neighbourhood groups have tended to try to influence DC officials, while groups such as the Metropolitan Washington Board of Trade have been oriented toward congressional lobbying. To a large extent this situation still prevails. Because of the plurality and variety of access points in DC government, some groups undertake an appeal strategy, going to Congress if they fail to obtain their objectives at the local level.

In the last decade, and particularly after the fusion of the civil rights movement and the anti-poverty programs since 1964, racial politics has become a matter of great importance in the District. For many years the neighbourhood associations were organized into parallel white and black groups. The black group tended to be fairly middle class "homeowner" in orientation and in the issues it espoused. Groups such as the National Association for The Advancement of Colored People, The Urban League, and some Negro churches were more militant, but also fairly conventional in their political tactics.

Since 1964, many new groups have reflected the fervent and increasing militancy among the black population of the city. The Southern Christian Leadership Conference, the Student Non-Violent Coordinating Committee, the Congress of Racial Equality – all have played important roles. More important, however, have been such indigenous groups as the Model Inner City Community Organization (MICCO) which has planned an inner-city renewal program, the Black United Front, a coalition of militant and moderate leaders, and the Emergency Committee on the Transportation Crisis, an interracial group which has spearheaded the opposition to freeway programs that would disrupt black communities far more than white residential areas.

MICCO has more recently been joined by a variety of quasi-official groups, often funded wholly or partly by public funds, and involved in anti-poverty, youth, renewal and rehabilitation, or educational programs. As a result of the activities of such groups, the city government has become far more sensitive to the racial implications of its actions. Such groups have also been influential in introducing new concepts into school curricula and in improving community services or programs.

THE "UNGOVERNMENT" OF THE NATIONAL CAPITAL

The District's government is not well designed to cope with its functions as a capital city, a metropolitan centre, or a local government. To an appalling degree in a nation so sophisticated in politics as the United States, the capital city suffers from an "ungovernment" because it has no common root or base of political power or authority. The city is governed by a multiplicity of scarcely related centres of governmental activity.

The federal interest is expressed through no coherent or responsible process, but tends to emerge through accident, whimsy, occasional deliberation, or the design of some unthwarted interest. The institutions that ostensibly guard the federal interest have not yet overcome the notion that the nation's interests are identical with their own. The looseness of the political system in the exercise of political authority tends to accentuate the influence of federal officials as against local influences, but fails at the same time to provide any authoritative process for resolving conflicting assertions of federal interests.

In metropolitan affairs, the central city, as elsewhere, finds its problems growing inversely with its resources. The racial composition of the District's population adds to its normal metropolitan woes, although the suburban jurisdictions are more amenable to working with the city than most other suburbs of America's major cities. The fact that the suburbs are themselves divided between two states adds to the problem, especially when it is remembered that the District does not have representatives either in the state legislature or in the Congress to negotiate with suburban lawmakers. As a practical matter, this condition gives suburban politicians greater influence in District affairs than is normal in other American metropolises.

A principal asset of the District in its metropolitan relations may be found in the developing alliances between city officials and some federal officials in the executive branch. Here a regional assertion of federal interest could – and occasionally does – assist the city in extracting a quid pro quo in intergovernmental bargaining. Federal disorganization, however, impedes full and effective use of this resource.

The Metropolitan Washington Council of Governments, a voluntary association of local elected officials – plus DC officials – has proved to be an important instrument through which regional negotiations occur. Initiated by a DC commissioner, the new city administration began in 1968 to make some tentative steps toward using this co-operative mechanism to obtain suburban support in coping with some of its problems. In general it may be said that the suburban governments are sufficiently healthy, in a political and fiscal sense, not to be fearful of the District, which after all can hardly threaten them with annexation or consolidation, or even diversion of state revenues. This, at least, prevents all but occasional outbreaks of suburban paranoia toward the District, and makes possible constructive conversation on common problems.

The most critical test of District government is internal. No major American city can claim that it is adequately serving its population, and the District is no exception. To the normal disabilities the lack of self-government must be added. The importance of this is not that it would render the District competent in the delivery of services, but that it would make it more capable of asserting and bargaining for its own interests and those of the region, in Congress and in the executive branch.

In 1969, President Nixon proposed a constitutional amendment granting the District at least one voting member in the House of Representatives. Until this amendment is ratified, he asked Congress to provide for the election of a non-voting member. This Congress did in September 1970, and the first election was held in 1971. The President also proposed the establishment of a commission to examine how the government of the capital city might be improved and made more responsive. Their report will be issued in 1972.

1 The best historical treatment of the capital's history is Constance McLauglin Green, *Washington,* 2 vols. (Princeton: Princeton University Press, 1962). Also see Frederick Gutheim, *The Potomac.*
2 See Enice Grier, *Washington's Changing Population* (Washington: Washington Center for Metropolitan Studies, 1963).
3 A full discussion of this concept is found in Royce Hanson, *The Anatomy of the Federal Interest* (Washington: Washington Center for Metropolitan Studies, 1967).
4 See Roy P. Franchino, "The Constitutionality of Home Rule and National Representation for the District of Columbia," *The Georgetown Law Review* XLVI (Winter 1957–58, Spring 1958), 207–59, 377–417. Until 1874 the District had some form of local self-government, usually a conventional municipal government, composed of an elected mayor and council. Following the Civil War, a "territorial" government was created, composed of an elected legislative assembly and a governor nominated by the president. The resulting regime, led by Governor Shepherd, undertook an extensive and expensive public improvements program. When scandals ensued, Congress abolished the assembly and established the appointed commissioner system as a temporary expedient to end corruption and virtual bankruptcy. In 1878 the temporary system was made permanent.
5 *Thompson* v *U.S.,* 346 US 100 (1953).
6 *Ibid.,* 109.
7 P.L. 86–527, June 27, 1960, 74 *Stat. Code,* 1301–5 (1961).
8 Constance M. Green, *op. cit.,* Chapters XIV and XV, pp. 339 ff., discusses the downfall of the territorial government and the change to the commissioner system.
9 RLA and NCHA were recently reorganized to cause them to be directed by the mayor of the District, but they remain "federal" agencies located in city government.
10 The Planning Commission was first established in 1924, 43 *Stat.* 463 (1924). See Schmeckebier, *op. cit.,* 652–84, for a history of planning and zoning legislation to 1928. For a more current study of NCPC see B. Douglas Harman, *The National Capital Planning Commission and the Politics of Planning in the Nation's Capital* (Washington: Washington Center for Metropolitan Studies, 1968).
11 86th Congress, 1st Session, *Meeting the Problems of Metropolitan Growth in the National Capital Region: Final Report of the Joint Committee on Washington Metropolitan Problems.* Senate Report No. 38 (Washington: US Government Printing Office, 1959), 31.
12 *Reorganization Plan No. 3 of 1967,* 81 Stat. 948 (1967).
13 *Ibid.*
14 347 US 483 (1954).
15 347 US 497 (1954).
16 *Hobson* v *Hansen,* DC 269 *Federal Supplement* 410 (1967).
17 *Ibid.*
18 A. Harry Passow, *Summary of Findings and Recommendations of a Study of the Washington,* DC *Schools* (New York: Teacher's College, Columbia University, 1967), 13. (Mimeographed).
19 Only one major study of DC politics has been done: Martha Derthick, *City Politics in Washington,* DC (Cambridge, Massachusetts, and Washington, DC: Harvard – MIT Joint Center for Urban Studies and The Washington Center for Metropolitan Studies, 1963).

B Capitals with some self-government

BACKGROUND

Venezuela, as a federal republic, is divided into twenty states, the Federal District, two federal territories, and the federal dependencies. The latter include parts of the national territory and the islands situated in territorial waters or in the waters covering the continental shelf.

The jurisdiction of the states is limited by the constitution and the national laws. The attributions of the president of the republic include the appointment and dismissal of the governors of the Federal District, the states and the federal territories, although the constitution at present in force contemplates the possibility of the governors being popularly elected.

The capital of the republic is Caracas, situated partly in the Federal District and partly in the district of Sucre, state of Miranda. The Federal District is situated in the north-central part of the country. It covers an area of 1,930 square kilometres (745 sq. mi.) and is made up of two departments: the Libertador Department and the Vargas Department, the areas of which are 433.5 km² and 1,496 km² respectively. Each department is divided territorially into parishes.

The Libertador Department consists of the city of Caracas, which includes ten urban parishes and five outlying parishes. The Vargas Department includes seven outlying parishes.

The results of the censuses covering the period to 1961 show the following figures for the population of the Federal District:

Year	Population	Per cent of country's total population
1873	79,605	4.6
1891	113,075	5.1
1926	195,460	6.9
1936	283,418	8.4
1950	709,602	14.1
1961	1,257,515	16.7

The General Statistics Division has estimated that by 1968 the population of the Federal District rose to two million inhabitants, and the total population of the country to 10.4 million. It is estimated that the population of the metropolitan area of Caracas reached 2.2 million by 1970. Prior to 1926 the population of Venezuela and the metropolitan area grew at more or less the same rate, but as of that date, one notes the appearance of a phenomenon which is characteristic of Latin-American capitals, namely that they grow at an extraordinary rate in comparison with the country as a whole.

The importance of Caracas lies not only in its population in relation to the rest of the country, but also in its economic power. The peculiar structure of the national economy has made Caracas the centre of the country's economic activities, which, for the most part, suffer from a complete lack of organization. The important consumer market existing in Caracas has been one of the predominant factors in the localization of almost 50 per cent of the industrial activities of the country in the central region. Although there is no available quantitative indicator of the magnitude of the industrial displacement towards the central region, circumstances show that it is of considerable importance. Caracas is the scene of a great variety of commercial activities. The main banking and financial institutions of the country have their head offices in Caracas, and it is there that the largest volume of business is transacted.

Generally speaking, the metropolitan area is the economic, political and cultural centre of the nation. The seat of the national public authorities, the dynamic centre of every aspect of political life and the headquarters of the leading economic groups are all located in this area. A great number of people who live on their revenues spend their money there. The general road-transport terminus and the main junction of internal and external communications are in Caracas. The mass media used in the cultural and advertising fields also have their main installations in the capital area. It comprises the most important consumer market and the greatest human and economic concentration in the country, and it is an important centre of attraction for both the internal migratory movement and the flow of immigrants from abroad.

As mentioned previously, the growth of the city of Caracas has led to its overflowing the boundaries of the Federal District and invading a great part of the district of Sucre in the state of Miranda. But the fragmentation and diversification of the metropolis prevails not only in the political and administrative regime (since the possibilities of expansion beyond the limits of the Federal District pertain especially to the residential aspect), but also in the industrial sector. This natural orientation of the growth of the metropolitan area provides a solution to the problem of high urban concentration which, once it reaches a certain point, affects the economy adversely.

The Caracas metropolitan system has the advantage of being near the sea. La Guaira – the country's main port as far as importations are concerned – is 36 km from Caracas, to which it is connected by a first-class freeway, the length of which can be covered in half an hour at normal speed. Hence Caracas has the advantages of a seaport connected with the most important international routes. Its vicinity to the coast also provides the inhabitants of the metropolis with easily accessible bathing resorts. These recreation facilities are complemented by the nearby mountains – the Avila and the Silla. On the coast, in Maiquetia, which is less than twenty minutes from the western sector of the metropolis, is the country's main international airport, situated at one of the junctions of the great world routes.

HISTORICAL REVIEW

The Federal District was created with the federation itself. It is true that the Bases of the Federal Union of States, consecrated by the Constitution of 22 April 1864, included a commitment on the part of the states to surrender to the nation any land which it might need for the Federal District, and it was the duty of the national legislature to set up and organize the Federal District in an uninhabited area of not more than ten square miles, in which the capital of the union would be built. But the fathers of the constitution also had in mind the non-fulfilment of this provision when the additional stipulation was made that the District would temporarily be that designated by the constitutional convention, or by the national legislature. In fact, Caracas had been *de facto* and *de jure*, the capital of the republic, and no political decision could or would change this. Hence the Federal District was to be organized temporarily in the inhabited zone corresponding to the city of Caracas.

In the initial and provisional organization of the District, both a political and an administrative regime were established. In so far as the administrative regime was concerned, the public powers were divided into legislative, executive, and judicial. The legislative power was exercised for the whole District by a legislature for matters of general interest, made up of deputies elected by universal, direct, and secret ballot and empowered to legislate on all matters not pertaining to the national power. The executive power was exercised in the whole District by a governor to be freely appointed or dismissed by the president of the republic, of whom he was likewise the immediate agent. It is clear, therefore, that even before the Constitution of

1864 came into force, the intention behind the artifices of the federation was to set up a Federal District which would be the seat of the agencies of the federal power, but which would possess a distinctive feature in that its political regime would not make it completely dependent on the federal power. It was provided with a legislature empowered to legislate on those matters of general interest not reserved for the national power, with the exception of civil and criminal matters, which were governed by the national laws. In so far as the executive power was concerned, the governor was closely connected with the federal executive power, since he was not only the latter's immediate agent, but also owed strict and immediate compliance with any orders which the latter might communicate to him.

On the basis of the Constitution of 21 June 1863, the president dictated a Provisional Statute of the Federal District, in which he divided the latter's "governmental regime" into: (1) Civil and Political; (2) Administrative and Economic. According to this statute, the highest civil and political authority of the District was the president of the republic, who exercised this authority through the governor. With regard to the administrative and economic regime, the statute introduced the innovation of granting the Federal District the rank of municipality, stipulating, moreover, that it was autonomous in all matters concerning its administrative and economic regime, and that it was under the responsibility of a city council.

This statute marked the beginning of the dichotomy which was to prevail, until the law of 1927, between the civil-political and the administrative-economic regime of the District, the former being the responsibility of the governor and the latter that of the city council. This dichotomy was to lead to much confusion in the interpretation of the law enforced in 1936.

Nevertheless, the subsequent tendency was to limit the city council to deliberative and local legislative functions, whilst attributing executive and administrative functions to the governor. This situation was definitely consecrated in the organic law of the Federal District of 14 October 1936, partially reformed in its Article 62 by the law of 17 July 1937, which is at present in force. In fact, although this law continues to divide the governmental regime of the District into the two aspects, civil-political and administrative-economic, and to give the governor, as agent of the president, a series of attributions in civil and political matters, it also gives him the rank of Highest Executive Authority in administrative and economic matters, which involves a series of duties and rights. On the other hand, if one analyses the attributions granted by law to the city council, it can be seen that the latter is the highest deliberative or local legislative authority of the municipality. The law of 1936 marked a return to the original system of the decree of 8 March 1864, which clearly distinguished, in the regime of the District, between a legislative power exercised by a legislature, and an executive power attributed to a governor. The compatibility of the municipality's autonomy with the functions of the two authorities, city council and governor, is precisely determined by the law itself, in its Article 28, which reads as follows: "The municipality of the Federal District exercises its autonomy through a city council and through the governor, in his capacity as executive authority."

From this rapid analysis of the historical evolution of the regime of the Federal District, we can draw some general conclusions of interest. The criterion of the constitutionalist and the legislator has always been that of conciliating the autonomous regime of a municipality with the regime of a Federal District which is the seat of the national government and has the demands characteristic of a capital city, without reaching the point of transforming the District into a mere administrative dependency of the central power. Venezuela has succeeded in maintaining an intermediate position with regard to the Federal District, without annihilating the local regime, as is the case, for example, with the District of Columbia in the United States. In this sense, the system has a closer resemblance to that which existed in the District of Rio de Janeiro. That is why the coexistence of a legislature, or city council, elected by popular vote, and an executive authority, as agent of the national executive, has always been contemplated in the District; and why, as specified by the law in force, the municipality exercises its autonomy through both. The existence and powers of the governor are considered to be absolutely essential in a district of this kind.

In relation to this aspect, F. Albi very justly makes the following comment on the regime of Caracas and the former regime of Rio de Janeiro:

In both places we find a municipal entity with a deliberative elective body, the only reservation being that the executive agency is appointed by the president of the republic. In Rio de Janeiro, the above-mentioned entity is the normal one all over the republic, whereas in Caracas the system in operation is a presidential system, as opposed to the French one prevailing in the rest of the nation. But this is not all; both in Caracas and in Rio de Janeiro, the organic law expressly asserts the principle of municipal autonomy, in contrast to the North American Federal District system.[1]

The two authorities, city council and governor, have given rise to the division between a municipal legislative power in the hands of the council, and a municipal executive power in the hands of the governor. Thus, the law in force follows the same lines as the decree of 1864 and eliminates the confusion of attributions which existed between both entities towards the end of last century.

GOVERNMENT OF THE FEDERAL DISTRICT

When analysing the governmental regime of the Federal District and the characteristics of its political and administrative agencies, one must begin by considering the scope of the autonomy of the District municipality. Its constitutional consecration and consequent lack of similarity to the orthodox regime of a Federal District, lead us to examine first the possibility of the coexistence of an autonomous regime and the normal regime characteristic of a Federal District in which the agencies of the federal power have their headquarters, and, secondly, the scope and special characteristics of this autonomy in relation to the autonomous regimes of the other municipalities of the Republic.

In the first place, it is necessary to point out that in the regime of the Federal District it is essential that "the action of the federal power" be protected "in order to avoid any hindrance of it," although the present constitution, contrary to former ones, does not make any definite provision to this effect. This principle, therefore, "has priority over that of autonomy, since it is the very reason of the creation of the Federal District; and should a restriction of autonomy be essential for its fulfilment, this restriction would be constitutional."[2] That is why the former Federal Court and Court of Appeal declared that "the Federal District must be considered as having attributions and restrictions derived from the national constitution itself and from its own organic law, both of which define the bases of its organization and its operational limits, establishing what is perhaps an even more fundamental rule, by stipulating that 'in the special [organic] law, the political action of the Federal Power must be protected, in order to avoid any hindrance of it'."[3] There is, therefore, an element of truth in the affirmation of the court that actually "the federal system limited autonomy even more than the centralist system had done."[4]

The division of the governmental regime of the Federal District into two sections, civil-political and administrative-economic, clearly implies its mixed or hybrid nature. The civil-political regime is, as we shall see, a consequence of the very nature of the District which, as seat of the federal powers, must come under the direct "civil and political" control of the president of the republic. On the other hand, the administrative-economic regime reflects the attenuated municipal autonomy of the District. It permits the election of the city council by vote and the joint government of the District by that council, with its deliberative and normative functions, and by the governor, as the executive authority. The governor thus combines federal and municipal functions which, in view of the existence of the former, evidently attenuate the municipal autonomy of the District, in comparison with that of the other municipalities of the country.

The executive function

Within the boundaries of the Federal District, the governor exercises two clearly differentiated types of function: the governmental function, as a direct agent of the highest civil and political authority, the president of the republic; and the administrative function, as the highest executive authority in administrative and economic matters. Let us now glance at the legal implications of these two functions.

The governmental function

From the political point of view, the governor plays a preponderant role not only in the Federal District, but also in the political mechanism of the country, being authorized to attend the Council of Ministers with the right to vote on matters concerning the government of the Federal District.

As immediate agent of the president in civil and political matters, his functions can be divided into the following categories:

Functions in relation to the national power

A To countersign all the decrees and resolutions of the president of the republic.
B To comply with the national constitution, national laws and those of the Federal District, and to ensure their fulfilment in the District.
C To comply with and ensure the execution of the decrees, orders, and resolutions of the president.
D To order the publication in the press of those laws which refer particularly to the Federal District, immediately upon their enactment.
E To ensure compliance with the Electoral Law and the Law on Political Parties, Manifestations and Meetings, and provide the pertinent authorities with all the support necessary to this end; and to exercise and comply with the attributions and duties imposed upon him by these laws.
F To ensure particularly the exact and effective observance of the health laws and rules, and to communicate to the relevant ministry any data or reports received regarding the existence of epidemics, contagious diseases, foci of infection, or any other matter which might affect the public health.
G To perform in the Federal District, as far as is applicable, the functions assigned to the governors of states by the laws on the subject of uncultivated or public land, and by any others.
H To request the military authorities to hand over any officers or soldiers against whom a warrant of arrest has been issued.

Functions as highest police authority in the Federal District

A To ensure the maintenance of law and order, public morality and decency, social security, and the protection of persons and property, with authority to punish any attempt against or violation of the foregoing with a maximum imprisonment of fifteen days, or fines not in excess of 300 bolivars,[5] and the eventual prosecution of the accused.
B To request the aid of the federal police power when he deems necessary or advisable for the maintenance of law and order and the protection of persons and property.
C To give support to public officials in the exercise of their legal authority.
D To transmit to the Ministry of the Interior, when necessary, any data and information required by it in order to obtain from the Ecclesiastical authority the removal of any parish priest whose behaviour is prejudicial to law and order or to the morality or well-being of his parishioners.
E To grant or deny permits for public spectacles, and to order their closure when justified.
F To ensure the maintenance of order at public spectacles and compliance with the regulations governing them.

Functions in relation to municipal administration

A To freely appoint or dismiss the employees under his authority, with the exception of prefects.
B To submit to the president lists of candidates for each one of the posts of prefect in the Libertador and Vargas Departments and to appoint those designated by the president.
C To ensure that all officials of the Federal District fully comply with their duties, and when necessary, to apply to the competent authority for the prosecution of those guilty of infractions.
D To grant up to 30 days leave of absence to the employees under his authority.
E To control and inspect all the hospitals, charity homes and institutions of the Federal District.
F To visit the different sections of the District, either personally or by delegating commissioners, in order to become acquainted with their needs, to investigate the fulfilment of the laws and to inquire into the procedures and behaviour of the employees, at the same time lending an ear to any complaints with a view to dealing with them if he is empowered to do so, or transmitting them to the competent authorities.

Functions in relation to municipal council

To submit to the decision of the Supreme Court of Justice any ordinances, agreements or resolutions of the city council which, in the governor's opinion, conflict with the national constitution or other laws.

The administrative function

In his capacity as highest executive authority in administrative and economic matters, the governor also has a series of clearly administrative functions, which can be classified as follows:

General administrative functions

A To handle the administration of the Federal District with the assistance of the government secretary and in accordance with the provisions contained in the ordinances and resolutions of the city council.
B To represent the Federal District on all matters concerning the administration in its relations with other authorities and individuals.
C To prepare the annual budget of income and expenses and submit it to the city council for discussion and approval, with any addenda or amendments which he deems advisable.
D To comply with and exercise the duties and authority conferred upon him by the federal municipal laws.

Administrative functions in relation to the city council

A To ratify the ordinances and resolutions of the council when so required, within the eight days immediately following their receipt.
B To submit drafts of ordinances and resolutions to the council for study and discussion.
C To attend personally, when he deems advisable, or delegate the government secretary to attend the meetings of the council, with the right to take the floor. He must also appear in person before the council whenever summoned by it.
D To submit to the council, within the first fortnight of January each year, the accounts of the administration entrusted to him, together with a detailed report of all his actions during the year.

Functions in relation to the administrative offices and dependencies of the District

A To organize and manage the administrative offices of the Federal District.
B To ensure the effective operation of the municipal services, with a view to efficient organization and improvement.
C To carry out personally, or through a commissioner, together with two delegates of the city council, a monthly audit of the Revenue Administration Fund, and to transmit a copy of the corresponding report to the council.
D To establish or contract lotteries for charity purposes, with the approval of the city council, and to ensure that the funds derived from these activities are applied exclusively to their intended purposes.
E To authorize the government secretary or the directors of the different branches of the government office to expedite certain matters, when this is not contrary to the law.

Regulative functions

To dictate the regulations which he may deem necessary for the execution of the ordinances and resolutions of the city council, without altering their spirit or purpose.

Functions related to public city officials and employees

To freely appoint or dismiss the employees of the administrative offices of the Federal District, except for the Administrator of Municipal Revenue, who must be appointed from a list presented by the city council.

Administrative functions in relation to municipal contracts

To enter into contracts of interest to the municipality, but they must be submitted to and receive the approval of the city council.

Administrative functions in relation to municipal public works

To decide upon and execute municipal public works projects the individual cost of which does not exceed one hundred thousand bolivars. The previous approval of the city council must be sought for projects which exceed 100,000 bolivars, or which, when added to those already authorized, exceed the total established in the budget.

The deliberative function

In the majority of municipal systems the city councils constitute the so-called deliberative branch, but it should be made clear that although they discharge what could be described as legislative functions of a local kind, they do not constitute an equivalent, in the strict sense of the word, of state legislative power, as is commonly believed. Moreover, in all the city councils of the states of the Venezuelan federation, deliberative functions are combined with clearly administrative functions. In the case of the municipality of the Federal District, however, the administrative functions are in the hands of the governor. The law has clearly indicated that the attributions of the council "limit its autonomy to deliberative functions only." On the other hand, as Wolf points out, "in administrative matters it is the city council which operates as the legislative power, and here the governor, who has been assigned the executive function by virtue of which he acts as highest authority in administrative matters, is obliged to comply with and ensure compliance with the municipal ordinances."[6]

From the foregoing, it can be seen that the city council's main attributions are the exercise of normative autonomy and participation in a limited number of individual acts, "lacking, apart from this, any implicit power."

In accordance with the organic law of the Federal District at present in force, the deliberative functions of the city council can be classified as follows:

Normative functions

The main function of the city council is that of "dictating ordinances, agreements and resolutions which regulate the exercise of the municipality's autonomy in all the branches indicated in Chapter VI of this law." According to Article 29 of the law, and always bearing in mind that in the Federal District the autonomy is also exercised through the governor, in his capacity as executive authority, the matters in connection with which the council can apply its normative autonomy are the following:

A The police services, cemeteries, municipal embellishments, civil architecture, public lighting, waterworks, and other municipal services such as sanitary services, ways and means of communication, urban and contiguous traffic, distribution of drinking water, charity, supplies and consumption, regulation of industrial practices, arts and crafts, and the internal regime of the parishes comprising the District.
B Anti-illiteracy services, but subject to the national educational laws,

provisions and regulation. Similarly, the sanitary services are subject to
the national health laws and regulations and under the control of the
National Health Service.

C The administration of its own land and commons, which may only be
alienated for purposes of construction.

D The organization of its revenue, with the restrictions listed in Article 18
of the constitution.

In relation to all these matters, the municipality exercises its autonomy
"through a city council and through the governor, as executive authority,"
and the council exercises its normative and deliberative autonomy.

General deliberative functions

A To take cognizance of and attend without delay any petition addressed
to the council in relation to the exercise of its powers.

B To exercise and comply with all other powers and duties assigned to it
by this or any other law.

Deliberative functions in relation to the council itself

A To appoint from among its members a president and two vice-presidents.

B To dictate its internal regulations.

C To qualify its members and take decisions regarding their resignation.

D To grant up to thirty days leave of absence to its members; these leaves
of absence may not, however, exceed fifteen days without the vacancy
being filled by the respective alternate.

E To elect from among non-members of the council, in the second
fortnight of April each year, the municipal attorney and the person
who is to act as the latter's alternate during his temporary or continuing
absence.

Deliberative functions in relation to municipal administration

A Creation of Public Services. To create elementary schools and regulate
them in accordance with the national law on education.

B Financial Administration. To consider, approve or amend the draft
budget as submitted by the governor.

C Public officials. To submit to the governor, when he so requests, the
names of three candidates for the post of Administrator of Municipal
Revenue. To establish the bond required of the Administrator of Municipal
Revenue and the Collector of Revenue of the Vargas Department.

D Control of the Municipal Administration. To approve the establishment or contracting by the governor of lotteries for charity purposes. To approve those projects and investments proposed by the governor which individually exceed 100,000 bolivars. To grant or refuse approval of contracts into which the governor may enter. To examine the annual report submitted by the governor, together with the annual accounts presented to the governor by the Administrator of Municipal Revenue and the Collector of Revenue of the Vargas Department. The council must give its opinion on the report and accounts, approving or contesting them.

From the foregoing it can be seen that the autonomy of the city council is of a normative character and that the council's powers limit that autonomy to deliberative functions only.

FINANCES

With regard to the Federal District's financial and fiscal resources, it should be noted that Venezuela's constitution and laws provide the municipalities, including that of the Federal District, with a natural taxing power. Its nature is established in the text of the constitution, where the categories of income (tax-derived and non-tax-derived) which they may collect are specified, along with the taxing power of the nation and the federated states.

The main sources of revenue covered by the municipal legislation of the Federal District are the following:

Taxes: (1) on houses, other buildings and empty lots; (2) industrial and trade licences; (3) tax on motor vehicles; (4) on legal betting; (5) on spectacles; and (6) on commercial propaganda.

Tariff charges: among others can be mentioned: (1) those collected for street cleaning; (2) for the issuance of building permits; (3) for gauging of weights and measures; and (4) for copies of documents, certificates, etc.

Special taxes: the municipality has not created any special tax of a municipal character, but it can take action in the assessment for improvements as contemplated in the expropriation law.

The financial problem of the municipality lies in its decreasing share in the financing of expenses and the correlative importance which the national executive's contribution has been assuming in making up the difference between the municipality's expenses and its own income. Thus the following table shows the percentage of tax-derived income as compared with total municipal income, for the period 1950–68.

MUNICIPALITY OF THE FEDERAL DISTRICT OF VENEZUELA
Distribution of Income by Percentages for Selected Years, 1950–68

Year	National Executive's Contributions	Own Resources (total)	Taxes	Tariff Charges	Fiscal Income	Miscellaneous and Extraordinary Income	Total
1950	20.6	79.4	39.9	3.0	1.5	35.0	100
1955	27.1	72.9	46.3	1.4	0.9	24.3	100
1958	67.8	32.2	22.6	1.7	0.7	7.2	100
1960	52.0	48.0	30.0	2.8	0.1	15.1	100
1965	47.8	52.2	35.3	2.6	9.4	4.9	100
1968	51.1	50.9	36.8	2.0	5.8	4.3	100

PARTIES AND POLITICS

One of the most interesting aspects of government in the Federal District is the political composition of the municipal council. It has been characteristic during all epochs when there have been free elections in the country that the party winning the national elections has always had a very low vote in the Federal District. This has resulted in the municipal council, whose members are elected directly and secretly by universal suffrage, always being dominated by the opposition parties. The mayor, who is chosen by and is chairman of the council, is always from this majority opposition. Thus it is curious that in the capital, the seat of national authority, the influence of the party in power at the national level has not been able to influence favourably the electoral behaviour of the local citizens. Perhaps this electoral attitude of being against the government party has its origin in the fact that it is the capital city which suffers most directly from any blunders of the central authority.

One can observe this unusual political configuration from the results of the elections between 1958 and 1968. In 1958 the Democratic Action (AD) party elected the president of the republic and a majority in the national legislature. Nevertheless, it won only three of the 22 seats on the municipal council of the Federal District and only one of the seven seats on the municipal council of the adjoining district of Sucre in the state of Miranda. The 1963 elections gave a similar result. The Democratic Action party received a national total of about 958,000 votes and once again won the presidency of the republic. Despite this, of some 468,000 votes cast in the Federal District, the AD party received only about 64,000 votes, and of some 97,000 cast in the district of Sucre, only about 13,000 went to the AD party. This resulted in the AD party again winning only three of the 22 seats on the council of the Federal District and only one of the seven seats in Sucre's council. During the period 1958–68, therefore, there was a constant confrontation of political interests between the governor of The Federal District and the opposition-dominated municipal councils of the Caracas metropolitan area.

In the elections of 1968, the candidate of the Christian Socialist party (COPEI) won the presidency with some 1,067,000 votes. Again, of the 638,042 votes cast in the Federal District, COPEI won only 95,551, and of the 156,615 votes cast in Sucre, it got only 35,017. The result is that COPEI holds only four of the 24 seats on the District's council and only three of the seven seats on Sucre's council. It can therefore be assumed that in the present period there will again arise frequent clashes of interest between the governor and the municipal councils.

This phenomenon of an opposition party majority in the local governments of the Caracas metropolitan area, which at times also appeared in the old Federal District of Rio de Janeiro, results in the interests of the city being materially neglected because of a sterile political contest between the governor and the local councils. Municipal political activity virtually exhausts itself in this contest, and the major problems of the city, among them the integration of the metropolitan area, cannot be properly solved.

THE METROPOLITAN AREA

The problems of the governmental regime in the Federal District can no longer be dissociated from the more serious and far-reaching problem of the uniform and co-ordinated regime required in the whole metropolitan area of Caracas. In fact, few of the phenomena which have arisen in local administration in recent times are as important and of such general and current interest as that of the growth of large cities. According to some authors, this is the main problem of modern civilization. Actually, this phenomenon of the growth of metropolitan areas, which is now making itself felt in the regime of Caracas, exists all over the world. One must accept it as a phenomenon of our times, one which has acquired extraordinary quantitative importance. The growing number of people who group together around the large urban centres creates a series of more or less common problems fundamentally related to the administrative organization, the supply of municipal services, local finance, planning, and the participation of the citizens in the governmental regime.

From the juridico-administrative point of view, the first of these problems is the most important one, and on its solution will depend the others, to a great extent. Unfortunately, the evolution of the modern metropolis has not been accompanied by an appropriate evolution of the governmental system, or by an adequate administrative organization. The city has outgrown its primitive boundaries of territorial jurisdiction and has invaded other municipal jurisdictions. The consequent antagonism within the administrative authority, and the conflicting interests of both the neighbouring local administrations and the public authorities in different fields, have been a considerable obstacle to general planning and to the supply of services to the integrated peripheral zones. Hence the main problem to be solved in any metropolitan area is that of the transition from a normal local regime to one specifically adapted to the area in question. In other words, it is the problem of establishing an organizational structure which really corresponds to the urban population in a territorial area and to the social and economic life which evolves in that area.

Caracas, with its large metropolitan zone, is no exception to the inevitable trend towards the administrative integration of the local entities whose jurisdiction it includes. That is why the constitution has provided various juridical possibilities. In fact, Article 10 of the constitution specifically provides for agreements between the different territorial entities of the country, whereby they may surrender part of their territories. This arrangement is also applicable to the Federal District. Thus, "the modifications of boundaries, compensations or cession of territory between the Federal District, or the federal territories or dependencies and the states may be accomplished by means of agreements between the national executive and the respective states, ratified by the corresponding legislatures and by the Senate."

The first of the possible solutions aimed at achieving an integration of the metropolitan area would therefore consist of the annexation by the Federal District of the territory of the district of Sucre in the state of Miranda, by means of the type of agreement provided for in the constitution. In this fashion, the whole metropolitan area, or a large portion of it, would be integrated under one single administrative structure and a governmental regime consonant with its role as capital and seat of the federal government. Thus the Federal District would be given some sense. Caracas, as capital of a federal state, is at present divided into two urban sections, only one of which is in the Federal District. It cannot reasonably be asserted or conceived that the seat of federal power is only in the western sector of the city, for that implies the rupture of its necessary unity.

In any case, to achieve uniformity of the government of the city of Caracas as a Federal District, it would be necessary, as has already been pointed out, to reform the organic law of the Federal District, in order to provide a clear and precise definition of the District's governmental regime. Any Federal District, we insist, necessarily involves the intervention of the national power in the management of local interests. There is, therefore, a necessary attenuation of the municipal autonomy in a Federal District — and the term is used in spite of the confusion which surrounds it and the crisis which has arisen with regard to its content, as a result of the urban revolution.

In this fashion, the government of the municipality of the Federal District would be entrusted, as is now the case, to an executive authority appointed by the federal government and to a legislative authority elected by vote. In any case, it should be made clear once and for all that the city council in the Federal District has absolutely no administrative authority, its powers being limited to local legislation and administrative and political control. Thus the inhabitants of the city would retain their right to intervene in its government through the city councillors, and the intrinsic nature of the Federal District would be maintained.

An alternative solution to the problem of the administrative structure of the metropolitan area of Caracas lies in maintaining the division of the valley into two jurisdictions, but achieving co-ordination through a special law. In fact, Article 11 of the constitution, after stating that "the city of Caracas is the capital of the Republic and the permanent headquarters of the supreme agencies of the National Power," adds that "the co-ordination of the different jurisdictions existing within the metropolitan area of Caracas (mainly the municipality of the Federal District and that of the district of Sucre, state of Miranda) may be accomplished by a special law, without detriment to the municipal autonomy." In view of this rule, the Declaration of Objectives of the Constitution specifies that "in this fashion it is possible to cope with the urgent and disquieting problems arising from the growth of the city, which has outgrown the limits assigned to it when the Federal District was created." On the other hand, with reference to this same problem the constitution also points out, in establishing the municipal regime, that the municipalities may also constitute unions for certain purposes within their competence. Therefore, in view of the consecration of municipal autonomy and the small chances, at the present time, of proposing an annexation of those municipal entities with jurisdiction in the metropolitan area, the administrative integration which Caracas demands can be accomplished either through the creation, by law, of a system of co-ordination which would protect municipal autonomy, or by the constitution of municipal unions.

In fact, should the division of the metropolitan area of Caracas between the Federal District and Sucre continue, it would be necessary to contemplate compulsory procedures of overall integration. The absurdity of the supply of urban public services being limited to a certain space, and their continuity depending on the variable political position of the respective city councillors is absolutely clear. It is senseless to have two different authorities in the same city for water supply, sewage, distribution of electric energy, urban transport, street cleaning, etc.

Therefore, in order to achieve the uniformity required by the metropolitan area, it is necessary to resort to a special law which would co-ordinate the administrative activity in the city. The mechanism of co-ordination would consist of the compulsory union or federation of the two municipalities, and the establishment of a co-ordinating authority, above the existing authorities, in the administrative sector only.

In view of the fact that the city is the capital of the country, and bearing in mind the financial support which the federal treasury always gives to large-scale projects for Caracas, the co-ordinating authority should include not only representatives of the federate municipalities but also of the national government. This co-ordinating authority, which would be a council or metropolitan commission, under the presidency of the governor of the Federal District and the president of the city council of the district of Sucre, would have executive authority for the execution of its acts. In all cases involving matters within its competence, it would have the power to impose its decisions on the municipal authorities of the federate municipalities.[7]

---

1 See F. Albi, *Derecho Municipal comparado del Mundo Hispanico* [Comparative Municipal Law in the Hispanic World] (Madrid, 1955), 351 and 352.
2 See Ernesto Wolf, *Tratado de Derecho Constitucional Venezolano* [Treatise on the Constitutional Law of Venezuela], Vol. 1 (Caracas, 1945), 122.
3 See Judgement of the Politico-Administrative Division of the Federal Court on June 13, 1938, in *Memoria* (1939), Vol. I, 232; and Judgement of the Federal Court and Court of Appeal on 15 April, 1942, in *Memoria* (1943), Vol. I, 283.
4 See Judgement of the former Federal Court and Court of Appeal in its Politico-Administrative Division, on 10 August, 1938, in *Memoria* (1939), Vol. I, 269.
5 One bolivar equalled about 22 US cents in 1970.
6 *Op. cit.*, 115.
7 See A.-R. Brewer-Carías, *op. cit.*, 150.

7   L.M. Singhvi* DELHI

TRANSFER OF THE CAPITAL FROM CALCUTTA

The announcement of the transfer of the capital of the British Indian Empire from Calcutta to Delhi in 1911 was an event of momentous significance. The decision was described in official despatches as one of the most weighty decisions ever taken since the establishment of British rule in India.

The reasons for the shift were many and varied.[1] Calcutta was considered to be geographically ill-adapted; it was distant and difficult of access from the rest of India. The historical and strategic considerations which led originally to the establishment of the capital in Calcutta, a maritime city, had disappeared with the consolidation of British power throughout the country and with the growth of an extensive inland railway network. The Indian Councils Act of 1909 heralded the advent of a measure of devolution and held out the prospect of provincial autonomy. In his despatch of 25 August 1911, the governor-general-in-council foresaw the need, in course of time, to satisfy "the just demands of Indians" for a larger share in the government of the country, and was anxious to ensure this devolution of power might be conceded without impairing the supreme authority of the central government. The governor-general and his colleagues visualized some kind of imperial federalism for India, and were of the view that the only possible solution was "gradually to give the provinces a larger measure of self-government until at last India would consist of a number of administrations autonomous in all provincial affairs, with the government of India above them all, and possessing power to interfere in case of misgovernment, but ordinarily restricting their functions to matters of Imperial concern." The transfer of the capital from Calcutta, which was also the seat of a provincial government, was by implication considered essential to the prospective role of the supreme government in a quasi-federal system,

* The author requests it to be noted that this essay was originally written in 1968. Some of the proposals made have since been adopted in official and other reports. He would like to thank Lt-Governor Dr A.N. Jha and Messrs L.K. Advani, V.K. Malhotra, Hans Raj Gupta and M.R. Yardi for their suggestions.

while the co-location of the capital of the Indian Empire in the same city as the seat of one of the provincial governments was thought to be anomalous.

The real reason for the removal

The real and immediate reason for the removal of the capital from Calcutta, however, was the "uncongenial" revolutionary climate of Bengal after its partition. The bitterness of feeling towards the British raj engendered by the partition of Bengal was very widespread and unyielding. According to Lord Hardinge, the governor-general, and the members of his council, "the peculiar political situation which has arisen in Bengal since the partition makes it eminently desirable to withdraw the Government from its present provincial environment." The Marquis of Crewe, then Secretary of State for India, candidly indicated in his despatch of 1 November 1911, that the British authorities would not have ventured to contemplate and embark on such an abrupt dislocation of settled official habits by shifting the capital if they were not deeply disturbed by the political situation in Calcutta. Anxious to undo the partition of Bengal and to allay public sentiments, and keen to avoid the impression that the reunification of the five Bengali-speaking divisions was being conceded as a consequence of prolonged public agitation and unrest, the governor-general-in-council devised a package of interdependent proposals which adumbrated the shifting of the capital from Calcutta to Delhi and at the same time envisaged the revocation of the partition of Bengal. The shifting of the capital thus became a convenient cloak for conceding an insistent public demand without an ostensible retreat or compromise.

The choice of Delhi

Once the decision to remove the seat of the supreme government from Bengal was taken, the claim of Delhi as the location of the new imperial capital was strong, if not conclusive. A Site Selection Committee, constituted earlier by the British authorities for choosing a site for a separate capital where the government could stay during all seasons of the year (instead of moving to Simla, a hill station, during the summer), had recommended Saugar in the then Central Provinces (now the state of Madhya Pradesh) because of its equable climate and central location. But the antecedents of Delhi were unsurpassed and were indeed difficult to match. Although it was merely the headquarters of a division in the province of the Punjab when the decision was made in 1911 to build the new capital there, Delhi was nevertheless a name to conjure with. It ranked as one of the most ancient and historic cities of India along with Taxila, Ujjain, Varanasi, and Pataliputra.[2]

From Pandavas to Chauhans

The famous epic *Mahabharata* mentions the city of Indraprastha built along the bank of the river Yamuna and identified with Delhi through the ages. The settlement was also known under the alternative names of Yoginipura and Khandavaprastha. The Pandava Princes led by Lord Krishna reclaimed the jungles around the ruined city at this site and renamed it Indraprastha after its renovation, for it vied in beauty and splendour with the mythical city of Amravati, the heavenly capital of Indra, the king of gods. According to Cunningham, the date of occupation of Indraprastha by Yudhisthira, the Pandava king, may be assigned to the later half of the fifteenth century BC. Ptolemy, the celebrated Egyptian geographer, who visited India during the second century AD, marked "Daidale" and "Indarbara" or Indraprastha separately on his map. Another tradition attributes the name of Delhi to Raja Dhilu who preceded the Saka era, which was inaugurated 78 years before the birth of Christ.

During the periods of Maurya and Gupta kings, Delhi seems to have been an obscure settlement of little or no importance. There is reason to believe that the city of Dillika was founded or rebuilt by Tomaras or Tunvar Rajputs in the year 736 AD, when the city emerged from anonymity. Dillika, or Delhi, later came under the sway of Chauhans.

From Prithviraj Chauhan to Bahadur Shah

In 1192 AD Muhammad Shahabuddin of Ghor overthrew Prithviraj Chauhan, a great and gallant warrior, and the last Hindu King of Delhi. Mohammadan rulers adopted Delhi as the seat of their power and built several monuments, palaces, and fortifications in and around Delhi. Muhammad Tughlaq, who was the sultan of Delhi from 1325 to 1351 and who conceived many a grandiose scheme, transferred the capital from Delhi to Deogiri renamed Daulatabad (the City of Prosperity) 700 miles away in the south because of its more central situation. The move, which involved great suffering and hardship, had ultimately to be annulled and the capital was shifted back to Delhi. Later, Sikandar Lodi moved the capital to the neighbouring city of Agra where he built a new city and Agra remained the *de facto* capital for many years thereafter. In the reign of Akbar, the grand moghul, Delhi enjoyed no more than secondary importance.

It was not until the year 1638 that Shahjahan, the grandson of Akbar and the builder of the Tajmahal, laid the foundations of his capital, Shahjahanabad, at Delhi, equipped with a citadel and royal residence, and then Delhi became the premier city of the Moghul empire. Shahjahan, however, spent the last years of his life in sorrowful captivity in Agra. His son Aurangzeb, who had dethroned him, was preoccupied with his military campaigns in the south. After the death of Aurangzeb, Delhi witnessed the decline or the Moghul dynasty and its humiliation and degeneration. In the yeaf 1857, the tragic and pathetic figure of Bahadurshah, the aging Moghul emperor, was removed by the British from the throne of Delhi and sent to Rangoon.

The Delhi Durbar and the restoration

Although Delhi was not the capital of the British Indian Empire until after 1911, the three durbars (royal receptions) of 1877, 1903, and 1911 were successively held at Delhi. The third Delhi durbar, held on 12 December 1911, distinguished by the presence in person of the King-Emperor, was utilized to make the announcement regarding the transfer of the capital from Calcutta to Delhi. The British authorities saw in the shifting of the capital to Delhi "assertion of an unfaltering determination to maintain British rule in India." Concurring with the choice of Delhi as the capital of India, the Marquis of Crewe, the Secretary of State for India, observed:

Not only do the ancient walls of Delhi enshrine an Imperial tradition comparable with that of Constantinople, or with that of Rome itself, but the near neighbourhood of the existing city formed the theatre for some most notable scenes in the old-time drama of Hindu history, celebrated in the vast treasurehouse of national epic verse. To the races of India for whom the legends and the records of the past are charged with so intense a meaning, this resumption by the Paramount Power of the seat of venerable Empire should at once enforce the continuity and promise the permanency of British sovereign rule over the length and breadth of the country. Historical reasons will thus prove to be political reasons of deep importance and of real value in favour of the proposed change.[3]

Nearly half a century later, Jawaharlal Nehru, the first prime minister of free India, said:

Here we stand in Delhi city, symbol of old India and the new. ... Even the stones here whisper to our ears of the ages of long ago, and the air we breathe is full of dust and the fragrance of the past as also of the fresh and piercing winds of the present. We face the good and the bad of India in Delhi city which has been the grave of many Empires and the nursery of a republic. What a tremendous story is hers. The tradition of millennia of our history surrounds us at every step and the procession of innumerable channels passes before our eyes.

THE CHIEF COMMISSIONERSHIP OF DELHI

Except the royal proclamation in the Coronation Durbar of 1911, there appears to be no constitutional or statutory sanction for the shifting of the capital from Calcutta to Delhi. As Arthur Berriedale Keith has pointed out:

... this mode of procedure was curiously unconstitutional for a Liberal government, since it precluded the exercise by the House of Lords and the opposition in the Commons of the right of criticism of far-reaching changes in policy, involving the transfer of the capital, the reversal of the partition of Bengal, the re-establishment of the Chief Commissionership of Assam and the placing of Bihar, Chota Nagpur, and Orissa under a lieutenant-governor with a legislative council.[4]

The legal transfer of the enclave of Delhi from the lieutenant-governorship of the Punjab to the direct control of the governor-general was effected by a notification published in the *Government of India Gazette Extraordinary*, dated 17 September 1912, and issued under the authority of the Government of India Act, 1854. The notification created the chief commissionership of Delhi, with effect from 1 October 1912, but there is no instrument which specifically confers on any particular part of Delhi enclave the distinct status of India's capital. In a strict legal sense, it is difficult to say whether the city of Delhi or the municipal limits of New Delhi or the whole of what is now known as the Union Territory of Delhi comprises the capital of India.

The allocation of powers was regulated by the Delhi Laws Act (Act XIII of 1912) under which specified functions were allotted to the governor-general-in-council and the lieutenant-governor of the Punjab. The functions allotted to the governor-general-in-council were exercised by the chief commissioner of Delhi who was his own divisional and financial commissioner as also his own inspector-general of police and registration.

THE CORE OF THE CAPITAL

The chief commissionership of Delhi simultaneously had the status of a centrally administered province and the capital of India. Frequently, however, it is New Delhi which is described by official documents as the capital. The legal position is not free from anomaly and ambiguity. The definition of New Delhi, which by common consent is the core of the capital, has undergone changes from time to time. The boundaries of New Delhi, as defined in the first schedule to the Delhi Municipal Corporation Act (No. 66 of 1957), constitute the statutory limits of New Delhi Municipality, but New Delhi, as commonly understood, has no clearly defined territorial limits. New Delhi is a loose and ill-defined geographical expression which connotes an area far more widespread than the jurisdictional confines of New Delhi Municipal Committee (NDMC). The official residences of the president and the prime minister of India, the Parliament House, the Central Secretariat, the Supreme Court and the diplomatic enclave are all located within the area of 16.5 sq. miles comprising New Delhi Municipality, which for all practical purposes constitutes the official capital of India. But the memorial grounds where Mahatma Gandhi, Jawaharlal Nehru, and Lal Bahadur Shastri were cremated are in the jurisdiction of Delhi Municipal Corporation. So is the famed Red Fort, which is in old Delhi.

The difficulty is that a line of demarcation cannot really be drawn between old and new Delhi. Even in 1912 it was thought that the interests of the old city of Delhi were inextricably interlinked with those of the new city in prospect. The two parts of the city together are now "an integrated and vast metropolis." Examining the suggestion that old and new Delhi may be demarcated as distinct units under two different governments and that New Delhi alone should be regarded as the national capital over which the Union government might have full control, the States Reorganization Commission came to the conclusion in 1955 that it was not practicable to draw a line of demarcation between the two cities and to treat New Delhi exclusively as the national capital.[5] Today, the New Delhi Municipal Committee provides a separate and largely non-representative civic set-up for New Delhi, but it remains under the Delhi administration headed by the lieutenant-governor. For ceremonial purposes, it is the mayor of Delhi (New Delhi has a civil servant as chairman and has no mayor) who represents the capital and receives visiting dignitaries on behalf of the capital city.

DELHI'S POPULATION

Growth of population

The growth of Delhi's population has been substantial since it resumed its status as the capital of India in 1911, and particularly after the advent of India's independence in 1947.[6] At the time of the partition of India, Delhi alone had to accept within a period of a few months about half a million refugees who were uprooted from their homes in Pakistan and sought shelter in India. The main reason for the growth of Delhi's population after independence is that Delhi has become a major commercial and industrial centre in addition to being the administrative nerve centre of a country with large-scale planning, licensing, controls, and regulations. The following tabulation depicts the phenomenon of galloping urbanization and population growth in the Union Territory of Delhi:[7]

	1911	1931	1951	1961
Rural	181,014	188,804	306,938	299,024
Urban	232,837	447,442	1,437,134	2,359,408
Total	413,851	636,246	1,744,072	2,658,612

The Union Territory of Delhi, which has an area of 573 sq. miles comprising 0.05 per cent of India's total territory, is inhabited by 0.61 per cent of India's population. From the point of view of population, it ranks sixteenth in a list of seventeen states and ten Union territories of the Indian Union, which has a population of more than 500 million. With a population of 2.66 million in 1961, the Union Territory had the highest density of population in the whole of India and is at the top as compared with that of most countries in the world, with 4,640 persons per square mile (in 1961). According to the revised population projections made by the Town and Country Planning Organization, the Territory is expected to have a population of 3.98 million in 1971. According to these estimates, urban Delhi (or Delhi city) will have a population of 3.62 million. The annual rate of increase in the Territory during the decade 1951–61 was 5.2 per cent as compared to 2.15 per cent for the whole of India. During this period, Delhi city showed the highest percentage increase (6.2 per cent). The city (which term includes New Delhi and Delhi Cantonment), with a population of 2.36 million in 1961, ranks as the third most populous city in India. The following are the 1961 population figures (in millions) of the eight biggest cities of India:

1 Greater Bombay   4.15
2 Calcutta Town Group 2.93
3 Delhi Town Group   2.36
4 Madras Town Group   1.72
5 Hyderabad   1.25
6 Bangalore   1.21
7 Ahmedabad   1.21
8 Kanpur   0.97

The census of 1961 shows 300 villages in the Union Territory while the latest count according to the revenue authorities is 357 villages, after the urbanization of 8 villages recently handed over to the Delhi Development Authority. In 1961, the population of rural Delhi was merely 300,000 out of the total population of 2.66 million.

There is considerable immigration of population into the Territory from different parts of India and more particularly from the neighbouring states of Punjab, Haryana, Uttar Pradesh, and Rajasthan. In 1961, 36.6 per cent of the Territory's total was immigrant population; the immigrants in urban Delhi constituted 37.8 per cent of the population, while in rural Delhi they accounted for 26.7 per cent.

Characteristics of population

Most of the Territory's population are Hindus, who constituted 84.05 per cent of the total in 1961. According to available official figures, Muslims accounted for 5.85 per cent of the population, Sikhs for 7.67 per cent, Jains for 1.11 per cent, Christians for 1.10 per cent, and Buddhists for 0.21 per cent. It is interesting to note that during the decade 1951–61 the Buddhists, the Muslims, and the Christians registered increases of 18, 14, and 3 per 1,000 respectively, while the Hindus declined by 11 per 1,000 and the Sikhs and Jains, who are socially close to Hindus and are governed by the same personal laws, recorded decreases of 19 and 5 per 1,000 respectively during the same decade. The scheduled castes, the erstwhile untouchables in the traditional Hindu social fabric, account for 12.85 per cent of the total population of the Union Territory in the 1961 census figures as against the all-India percentage of 14.67. There are no scheduled tribes in Delhi.

In the growth of literacy, Delhi has outstripped all the states of the Indian Union including Kerala. With 52.7 per cent of its total population literate in 1961, Delhi had the highest percentage of literacy in the whole of India, the all-India average being 34.4 per cent. Male literacy in Delhi was 60.8 per cent. In the words of the Registrar General of India, "Delhi has moved to first rank by a long lead in 1961, not only vicariously by virtue of its being the capital which naturally attracts educated immigrants in large numbers, but also because it spends the largest amount per capita in all India on education."[8] Delhi city or Delhi town group, however, has a lower literacy rate than Madras, Calcutta, and Greater Bombay.

Occupational pattern

According to the 1961 census, the occupational categories of cultivation and agricultural labour together employ a mere 2.4 per cent of the total population of the Union Territory; manufacturing other than household industry employs 5.5 per cent; transport, storage, and communication accounts for 1.9 per cent; household industry for 0.6 per cent; and mining, quarrying, livestock, forestry, fishing, hunting, plantations, orchards, and allied activities, for 0.3 per cent. The largest single percentage (13.7) is made up of "other services" not included in the foregoing occupational categories.

All categories of workers employ a total of 32.1 per cent of the entire population, while 67.9 per cent of the population belongs to the category of non-workers. This category includes all those who are unemployed or who, like rent receivers, money lenders and dividend receivers, earn money without working. It also includes adult women engaged in household duties but doing no other productive work, as well as pensioners. Non-workers constitute 47.7 per cent of the total male population and 93.5 per cent of the female population. The Union Territory has the highest percentage of non-working females among the states and territories of India, and perhaps that is one of the highest in the world. In urban Delhi the percentage of non-working females is even higher, 95.5 per cent, and is the highest among the major cities of India except for Kanpur, where it is 96.8 per cent. The Territory also has the highest percentage of workers engaged in the industrial categories of manufacturing, trade and commerce and transport, and storage and communication, as compared with the percentage of workers in the same categories in other states and territories of India.

Pattern of life

The Union Territory of Delhi is in many ways a microcosm of the Indian nation. Besides historic traditions, it has been an area marked apart since the announcement of 1911. Though predominantly urban, the surrounding rural setting of Delhi is a constant reminder of the nature of Indian society. Socially, New Delhi has an overwhelmingly white-collar, middle-class orientation, in contrast with rural Delhi and old Delhi. Though the population of Delhi is predominantly Hindu, all the major world religions have their votaries in the capial; Hindi is the language spoken by the bulk of Delhi's population, but almost every Indian language and provincial identity is conspicuously represented in Delhi. The volume and diversity of migration into Delhi have woven a colourful and cosmopolitan pattern of life in the capital.

EVOLUTION OF DELHI'S GOVERNMENT

From Chief Commissioner's Province to Part "c" State

The evolution of administrative machinery and political institutions in Delhi has been *sui generis*. It is rooted mainly in the exigencies of administering the capital.

After the advent of independence in 1947, Delhi continued to be the capital of India and a Chief Commissioner's Province. It was taken for granted as the seat of the central government, and the Constituent Assembly, which met in Delhi from 1946 to 1949, did not consider it necessary to review the question. The constitution of India, which came into force on 26 January 1950, conferred on Delhi the status of a Part "c" State, a somewhat inferior status among the states in the federal hierarchy. But even as a Part "c" State, Delhi had an elected legislature and a council of ministers with a chief minister at its head, responsible to the legislature. The chief commissioner remained, but he was to be more of a constitutional head, like the governors in other states; the real power now vested in the chief minister and his cabinet colleagues.

From Part "c" State to Union Territory

In 1956, the states comprising the Indian Union were reorganized by parliamentary legislation. Delhi became one of the Union Territories, and the whole of the Territory came to be administered directly by the president of India, in effect meaning the central government, acting through an administrator. The legislature of Delhi was dissolved with effect from 1 November 1956. The chief commissioner as the administrator of Delhi was directly responsible to the central government and was once again in effective charge of administration. The phase of statehood for Delhi thus came to an abrupt end after a short-lived experiment.

Delhi and the States Reorganization Commission

According to the States Reorganization Commission, which submitted its report in 1955, the diarchical structure of Delhi was anomalous and had not worked smoothly.[9] The introduction of dual control in 1951 and the division of responsibility between the centre and the Delhi State government appeared to have hampered the development of the capital and had led to a "marked deterioration of administrative standards in Delhi."[10] In recommending that Delhi should be a centrally administered territory, the Commission naturally took into account the fact that Delhi, which was basically a city unit, was the seat of the Union government, and could not therefore be made part of a full-fledged state. The Commission pointed out a variety of considerations and observed: "Practice in other countries, administrative necessity and the desirability of avoiding conflicting jurisdictions, all point to the need for effective control by national governments over federal capitals."[11]

The Commission also examined the suggestion that a line of demarcation should be drawn between New Delhi and old Delhi, and that New Delhi should be regarded as the national capital over which the Union government might have full control. The Commission came to the conclusion that from the point of view of law and order, the social life of the people, trade and commerce, and common public utility service, old Delhi and New Delhi constitute one integrated unit and that it would be wholly unrealistic to draw a line between the two. The Commission did, however, suggest that the rural areas in Delhi enclave might, to the extent that they were not indispensable for the future urban expansion and development of Delhi, be retroceded to the parent state or states. Apparently, the rural areas of Delhi were not considered to be redundant for the future growth of urban Delhi, and the retrocession proposal was therefore never accorded any serious consideration.

The Commission was of the view that an autonomous municipal corporation would satisfy the requirements and aspirations of the cosmopolitan urban population of Delhi and that it would provide a model, "sound in principle and administratively workable in practice.' 'The Commission pointed out that urban problems such as slum clearance, reconstruction, city planning, recreation, transportation, and primary and secondary education all fall within the domain of municipal finance and enterprise. The denial of the paraphernalia and the benefit of popular government at the state level did not, however, constitute disenfranchisement of the people of Delhi since they were fully represented in the Union Parliament.

THE DELHI MUNICIPAL CORPORATION

The dissolution of Delhi's legislature and the assumption of the responsibility for the administration of Delhi by the central government led to a greater measure of local self-government for Delhi as recommended by the States Reorganization Commission. The Delhi Municipal Corporation Act, 1957, represents an important phase in the evolution of administrative and political institutions in Delhi. The act was designed to consolidate and amend the law relating to the municipal government of Delhi. Under the act, the functions of various municipal and notified area committees responsible for different parts of Delhi, and those of the District Board, Electricity Board, Road Transport Authority, and Joint Water and Sewage Board were taken over by the newly constituted municipal corporation. The jurisdiction of the corporation extends to the whole of the Union Territory of Delhi, including rural areas but not including New Delhi (pop. 300,000) and Delhi Cantonment. The Delhi Municipal Corporation is unique inasmuch as it includes a substantial proportion of rural area and village panchayats, which are local councils elected by villages or groups of villages. The Cantonment, like cantonments elsewhere in India, is a military-commercial-residential area governed by the military commander on the advice of a board which is mainly appointed by him but also partly elected by the residents.

Organization and functions of municipal corporation

The municipal corporation of Delhi consists of councillors and aldermen. Councillors are chosen by direct election on the basis of adult suffrage from the various wards into which Delhi is divided; aldermen are chosen by the councillors. There are at present 100 councillors, and 6 aldermen. There is statutory reservation for the scheduled castes in the same ratio to the total number of councillors as the population of the scheduled castes to the total population of Delhi. The term of office of a councillor or an alderman is four years. The mayor and deputy mayor are elected annually by members of the corporation from among themselves. The mayor is the head and the presiding officer of the corporation and is ensured full access to all of its records. He is also entitled to obtain reports from the commissioner, who is the chief of the corporation's administrative machinery, on any matter connected with the municipal government of Delhi, and from the general managers of the Delhi Electricity Supply Undertaking and the Delhi Transport Undertaking. The mayor is also the first dignitary and performs various ceremonial functions on behalf of the capital city.

The entire executive power of the corporation is vested in the commissioner, a permanent civil servant who is appointed by the central government, and who supervises and controls the acts and proceedings of all municipal officers and municipal employees except the municipal secretary and the municipal chief auditor and the officers and employees subordinate to them. The secretary and the auditor are for obvious reasons independent officers; the appointment of the chief auditor is made with the previous approval of the central government and the appointments of the municipal chief accountant and the municipal secretary are subject to confirmation by the central government. Ordinarily the executive power of the commissioner does not extend to the functions of the Delhi Electric Supply Undertaking or the Delhi Transport Undertaking, the responsibility for which is vested by the statute in the general managers of the two undertakings. The general managers are appointed by the corporation with the approval of the central government and in consultation with the Union Public Service Commission, an independent body established under the authority of the constitution and entrusted with the task of safeguarding the principle of merit and impartial selection in civil service appointments. The commissioner may, however, exercise the powers and perform the duties of the general managers in their absence or in case of failure on their part. The commissioner and the two general managers or any officer authorized by any one of them may, without being entitled to vote, take part in the meetings of the corporation or its committees.

All questions asked by members of the corporation are answered by the commissioner at meetings of the corporation unless the mayor otherwise directs. The mayor is largely an umpire in the deliberations of the corporation, with the burden of administrative and executive accountability resting squarely on the shoulders of the commissioner, who is answerable to the corporation.

Meetings of the corporation

The Municipal Corporation holds at least one meeting a month, frequently more. The agenda for such meetings is circulated at least seventy-two hours before the time fixed for the meeting. The corporation decides by the majority of the votes of the members present and voting; the voting is by show of hands except when the corporation resolves to decide any question or class of questions by ballot. The mayor, and in his absence the deputy mayor or the presiding officer elected for the purpose, is vested with the powers of maintaining order, regulating the proceedings, disallowing questions, and giving rulings.

A typical session of a corporation includes lively interpellation including short notice enquiries, and detailed, occasionally well-informed and more often acrimonious debates on the working of Delhi's municipal government. Allegations of maladministration, exposure of the lapses and the failures of the administration, and analytical discussions of policies compete for the attention of the corporation. Its deliberations are conducted in the limelight of the national press. A number of leading dailies are published from Delhi and wide coverage is given to the affairs of the capital and its municipal government.

According to the Delhi Municipal Corporation (Procedure and Conduct of Business) Regulation, 1958, the list of business of an ordinary meeting is arranged by the municipal secretary in the following order which also gives an idea of the range of the corporation's activities:

A confirmation of the minutes of the last ordinary meeting or meetings or the minutes of any special meeting or meetings since the last ordinary meeting;
B any election by the corporation;
C questions;
D petitions;
E resolutions of the Standing Committee;
F resolutions of the Delhi Electric Supply Committee, the Delhi Transport

Committee and the Delhi Water Supply and Sewage Disposal Committee;
G letters from the commissioner and business from the commissioner;
H letters from government and others;
I resolutions of the Rural Areas Committee, the Education Committee and special committees;
J reports of *ad hoc* committees; and
K notices of resolutions under the proviso to section 74, relating to matters of general public interest concerning the functions of the corporation under the act.

Questions may be asked only on the first day of an ordinary monthly meeting of the corporation. No more than half an hour is allotted for asking and answering questions at every such meeting. The questions are admitted by the mayor and answered by the commissioner. A written reply to every question in the list is supplied to the members before the reply is given orally at a meeting of the corporation. Supplementary questions are also permitted. Short notice enquiries on matters of public importance may be intimated by a member in writing to the municipal secretary two hours before the time of a meeting and the commissioner makes a statement in response to the enquiry. Interpellation in the corporation is searching, detailed, and specific. It tends often enough to be aggressive and attitudinal. Ordinarily, it deals with workaday problems of municipal administration and questions may range from education, electricity, slum clearance, or the transport system, to particular appointments or promotions in municipal jobs.

During the interpellation, as indeed in most other respects, the mayor functions as the speaker of the house with the whole paraphernalia of parliamentary procedure, while the commissioner functions as an irremovable executive. He is answerable without being really accountable. His tenure does not depend on the corporation and therefore his response to the corporation as an elective body tends to be lackadaisical. The question hour in the corporation is potentially an effective means of supervision and vigilance by the elected representatives of the people and is likely to grow in importance.

The business at the meetings of the corporation is normally transacted in Hindi, though Urdu and English are also permitted. Occasionally members speaking in the corporation may also use Punjabi. Language is not, however, a controversial issue in the proceedings of the corporation, because Hindi is commonly used and understood in Delhi and is accepted as the lingua franca.

The committees of the corporation

The committee system of the corporation is comprised of statutory committees, special committees, and *ad hoc* committees. Important statutory committees are the Delhi Electric Supply Committee, the Delhi Transport Committee, and the Delhi Water Supply and Sewage Disposal Committee, which are responsible for the conduct and management of their corresponding undertakings. Each committee consists of several members, four of whom are elected by the corporation from among its members and the remaining three members are nominated by the central government on the basis of their special knowledge and experience. The corporation has a separate Rural Areas Committee consisting of sixteen members and an Education Committee of seven members. There are several Special Zonal committees of varying size for different zones, and special committees for public works, law and general purposes, implementation of assurances, and medical relief and public health. Besides, there are *ad hoc* committees for slum clearance, for improvement and promotion and adoption of the Hindi language in municipal administration, for selection of sites for installation of statues of national leaders, for promoting urban community development and social and physical education, and for economy measures. These committees enjoy varying degrees of importance and effectiveness in the scheme of Delhi's municipal government, but there is no denying that membership on them is the most proximate source of real power for Delhi's councillors and aldermen.

By far the most pre-eminent of the committees is the Standing Committee, which consists of fourteen members elected by the councillors and aldermen from among themselves at the first meeting of the corporation after each general election. The Standing Committee renews its membership by employing the device of the annual rotational retirement of one-half of its members. The Standing Committee, which normally meets once every week, represents the authority of the corporation and transacts a great deal of supervisory and deliberative business.

Plans for reform

The impression is widespread that, during the years of its existence since 1957, Delhi Municipal Corporation has not proved equal to the tasks confided to it by the statute and that its preoccupation with trivia has sapped its capacity for purposeful supervision. There are widespread complaints of inefficiency, ineptitude, and lack of direction against the corporation, and this has tended to prompt proposals for the reform of the civic set-up in Delhi. On 18 August 1965, the government of India indicated on the floor of the Lok Sabha its intention to effect important changes in the organizational set-up of the Municipal Corporation of Delhi. These changes were embodied in a bill introduced in the Third Lok Sabha in 1966. The bill, which lapsed on the reconstitution of the Lok Sabha in 1967 (after the fourth general election), was debated and adopted in the Delhi Metropolitan Council on 8 February 1968. However, it is not likely to be enacted into law by the Parliament in the form in which it was passed by the council.

The bill would usher in several far-reaching reforms. It envisages a kind of civic cabinet in the form of a mayor-in-council consisting of the mayor and two deputy mayors, who would be appointed from among the members of the corporation by the lieutenant-governor (in his capacity as the administrator) on the advice of the mayor. The mayor-in-council would have executive functions and responsibilities and would be accountable to the corporation, which would be known thereafter by its equivalent Hindi nomenclature, Delhi *Nagar Nigam*. The diarchical diffusion of power and responsibility between the elected and appointed wings would thus come to an end and the bureaucracy headed by the commissioner would be effectively subordinated to the mayor-in-council.

Along with the move for the installation of the mayor-in-council, three other bills seeking to set up autonomous bodies for transport, electricity and water supply, and sewerage services are also on the anvil. These bodies will, according to the proposed legislation, consist of expert members and a representative each of the Municipal Corporation and the newly formed Metropolitan Council. Their governing boards are proposed to be headed by full time official chairmen and will function under the overall supervision of the lieutenant-governor of Delhi (in his capacity as the administrator). The consequence of the establishment of these autonomous corporations and boards will be to severely confine the scope and range of the functions of the corporation. While the mayor-in-council will more clearly instate the hegemony of the elected component of the corporation over the commissioner and the civil service apparatus, the establishment of these boards will introduce greater autonomy, bureaucratization and, one hopes, some professionalization and expertise in the management of essential public utilities. The problem with the institutional device of mayor-in-council, however, is that it would create another effective centre of power inevitably impinging on the authority of the Metropolitan Council and the Executive Council. That is why the government appears to have second thoughts on the idea of mayor-in-council.

Parties and politics

The Union Territory of Delhi, which is mainly urban, is highly politicized. For many years after the advent of independence, the Congress party held sway in Delhi. Within the Congress party, internecine strife has been particularly rampant in Delhi. It is safe to assert that factious intra-party feuds in the Congress party and consequent misgovernment and public disillusionment were largely responsible for the extensive electoral reverses which the Jan Sangh party inflicted on the Congress party in Delhi in 1967. Before the election in February-March 1967, the Congress party had 73 members out of the corporation's total membership of 86. Since then it has had only 42 out of the corporation's total strength of 106, whereas the Jan Sangh, which commanded a meagre strength of eight members in the corporation before the election, has moved into the seat of power, with 54 members (51 councillors and three aldermen) in February 1970. Among the remaining ten members, five belong to the Progressive group, which was formed after the elections of 1967, and three are Independents. The Right Communists (CPI) and the Left Communists (CPM) have one member each. Of 42 who belonged to the Congress party before its split into the party supporting the prime minister and the party backing the Congress Organization, as many as 36 are understood to have identified themselves with the ruling Congress led by Prime Minister, Mrs Indira Gandhi.

The mayor and the deputy mayor belong to the Jan Sangh, whose members have also won other prominent positions in the power structure of Delhi's municipal and metropolitan government. Indeed it is only in Delhi that one can see the emerging outlines of bi-partite politics; for in the rest of India, with some notable exceptions such as in the states of Tamilnadu (Madras) and Orissa, the unfavourable swing in the electoral fortunes of the Congress party has not positively brightened the prospects of polarization and a two-party system. Whether the two-party phenomenon recently evidenced in Delhi will remain stable is a question which cannot yet be answered in categorical terms, although it is reasonable to expect that political competition in Delhi will for some time be confined to the Jan Sangh and Congress parties.

The emergence of the Jan Sangh as the majority party in the corporation and the incumbency of important offices by men belonging to the Jan Sangh has lent political colour and credence to the differences between the Municipal Corporation and the central government in spite of the conciliatory, mild-mannered, and businesslike Jan Sangh Mayor, Mr Hansraj Gupta. The central government and the Municipal Corporation have had a wide range and a large number of mutual grievances since the very inception of the corporation. With the rise of Jan Sangh to power and responsibility in the Corporation, the grievances of the Corporation are more unhesitatingly and unsparingly articulated, and the responses of the central government are correspondingly less considerate and more designed to exonerate it of any direct blame. And yet because of its utter financial dependence on central subventions, the corporation is constantly in the position of a grudging but compliant supplicant.

Chronic financial stringency

The Municipal Corporation has always suffered from financial stringency. There have been many occasions when it was not in a position to pay its monthly salary bills; contractors' bills and suppliers' bills have on a number of occasions remained unpaid and had to be carried forward to the succeeding years. The Corporation's development programmes as well as its social welfare projects had frequently to be abandoned owing to want of funds. Loan instalments and debt service charges have also remained unpaid year after year. On 31 March 1968, the unpaid liabilities of the Corporation had amounted to about 86 million rupees. After taking into account the carry-over deficit of the past years, and the proposals on income and expenditure, the year 1970–71 is likely to close with a deficit of about 48 million rupees.[12]

The following table, extracted from the corporation's annual reports, shows at a glance the financial position of the Municipal Corporation (General Wing), taking the actuals of 1968–69 as the starting point:

	Accounts 1968–69	Budget Estimates 1969–70	Revised Estimates 1969–70	Budget Estimates 1970–71
Opening Balance	(−) 14.15	0.3	(−) 0.7	(−) 34.45
Income	195.34	251.77	240.85	247.72
Expenditure	182.93	251.92	273.56	261.25
Deficit on the year's working surplus	(+) 12.40	(−) 0.15	(−) 32.70	13.52
Closing Balance	(−) 1.74	0.15	(−) 34.45	(−) 47.98

The Corporation's sources of revenue are: government grants, share of assigned central taxes, municipal rates, taxes, rents, fees, fines, and other miscellaneous receipts. In 1966–67, government grants to the corporation totalled about 29 million rupees, and its share of assigned central taxes came to about 50 million rupees. Municipal rates and taxes yielded about 47 million rupees; rents, fees, and fines, about 8.4 million; and miscellaneous receipts, about 7.6 million.

On the expenditure side, the following heads and figures of expenditure delineate the contours of the corporation's activities:

	(In millions of rupees, rounded off)		
Head of account	Actuals for 1966–67	Actuals for 1968–69	Budget Estimates for 1969–70
I General Supervision and Collection of Revenue, etc.	4.1	9.8	9.8
II Water Supply	6.7	7.0	30.0
III Education	47.0	56.4	71.7
IV Libraries	0.2	0.11	0.25
V Public Health	5.0	6.1	7.1
VI Medical Relief	14.5	18.2	23.6
VII Conservancy, Street Cleaning	17.0	20.1	24.3
VIII Scavenging Drains and Sewers	0.7	0.9	0.11
IX Roads and Public Lighting	11.7	15.7	14.8
X Building, Land Acquisition, and Management	4.4	5.0	6.0
XI Fire Brigade	2.0	2.6	3.1
XII Licensing and Removal of Encroachments	0.5	0.7	0.4
XIII Gardens and Open Spaces	3.4	4.5	5.6
XIV Markets and Slaughter Houses	0.2	0.3	0.3
XV Improvement Schemes, Slum Clearance, and Schemes for Removal of Jhuggi-jhompris	2.9	2.3	10.0
XVI Miscellaneous	22.4	33.0	47.4
XVII Reserve for Unforeseen Charge	0.3	0.2	0.6

THE NEW DELHI MUNICIPAL COMMITTEE AND ITS PROBLEMS

The New Delhi Municipal Committee administers a small area (16.5 sq. miles) which is the core of the capital. The committee has a civil servant as chairman and eight nominated members. The jurisdiction of the Delhi Municipal Corporation does not extend to the areas administered by the committee and the Delhi Cantonment Board. The committee is governed by the Punjab Municipal Act. It is, however, within the jurisdictional purview of the Metropolitan Council and is accountable to the administrator-cum-lieutenant-governor, who has the authority to give directives to the committee. The financial allocations for the committee are made by the administrator and the budget of the committee is discussed (though not voted upon) by the Metropolitan Council.

The committee has to provide amenities at a qualitatively superior level for the diplomatic personnel and top government leaders and civil servants residing within its area, although it is not permitted to levy rates and charges higher than those of the Delhi Municipal Corporation. About 85 per cent of the property within the committee's area belongs to the central government or diplomatic missions. Together they pay house tax amounting to about 0.4 million rupees (in 1968), while the private owners of the remaining 15 per cent of the property pay about 0.7 million. The reason is that the central government is liable to pay taxes and rates at a lower scale and on the basis of valuation of its own making, and the diplomatic missions cannot be taxed except in accordance with the wishes of the central government. The financial allocations made to the committee are felt to be inadequate, and for many years it has strenuously represented for a more equitable deal. The problems of financial stringency and insufficient allocations were considered recently by a study group appointed by the federal Administrative Reforms Commission, who in turn submitted an interim report to the government in December 1968. There are some who feel that the New Delhi Municipal Committee would be treated with greater consideration if it had elected representatives.

TOWARDS LIMITED SELF-GOVERNMENT

The fourteenth amendment to the Indian constitution, which received the presidential assent on 28 December 1962, did not contemplate the provision of a legislature for the Union Territory of Delhi, although in Article 239A it empowered the parliament to create legislatures and councils of ministers for the Union Territories of Himachal Pradesh, Manipur, Tripura, Goa, Daman and Diu, and Pondicherry. The constitutional amendment of 1962 was invoked in 1965–66 when the Delhi Administration Bill was on the anvil, to preclude the establishment of a full-fledged legislature as well as the delegation of financial powers to the Metropolitan Council. Winding up the debate following the introduction of the bill, Mr G.L. Nanda, the then Home Minister of India, stated categorically in the Lok Sabha that the basic issue had been decided by the constitutional amendment of 1962 and that it was not a part of the government of India's policy to introduce an assembly, a council of ministers and a chief minister in Delhi. He said that the government of India was prepared to consider any other step short of full-fledged responsible government.

The Delhi Administration Bill was introduced in the Lok Sabha on 18 November 1965. The bill was referred to the Joint Select Committee which held as many as nine sittings and heard the evidence of forty witnesses in addition to the evidence of Mr M.C. Setalvad, former Attorney General of India, who appeared at the request of the Joint Committee on behalf of the Institute of Constitutional and Parliamentary Studies to opine on certain legal and constitutional questions. The main burden of the evidence of the various spokesmen from Delhi was to oppose the "denial of democratic rights" to the citizens of Delhi. Out of thirty-three members of the Joint Committee, five members, all of whom were from Delhi and belonged to the Congress party, resigned with effect from 18 April 1966, to register their protest against the main provisions of the bill. The two Communist members of the Joint Committee said in their minute of dissent that they saw "no reason whatsoever for denying Delhi's democratically elected and fully representative legislature and a Council of Ministers." Mr R.V. Bade of Jan Sangh, a member of the Joint Committee, felt that the bill failed to satisfy the aspirations of the people of Delhi. Mr H.V. Kamath, a veteran member of the Lok Sabha and a leader of the Praja Socialist party, on the other hand, expressed the view in his minute appended to the Report of the Joint Committee that it was appropriate and desirable not to repeat the earlier "unhappy experiment of a separate Legislative Assembly and Council of Ministers for the Union Territory."

The Delhi Metropolitan Council

Despite the objections, the Delhi Administration Act was passed in 1966 (No. 16 of 1966). It provides for a Metropolitan Council, consisting of 56 members elected directly from territorial constituencies and five members nominated by the central government. Among the five nominated members, two belong to the Jan Sangh party, one to each of the two Congress parties after the split in 1969, and one, an educationist, is an Independent. The Metropolitan Council has a tenure of five years. It is presided over by a chairman elected from among the members of the council. The chairman (Mr L.K. Advani) was nominated as a member of the Metropolitan Council by the central government. He is a member of the Jan Sangh party, but has not joined the Metropolitan Council's Jan Sangh party. The administrator (the lieutenant-governor) may attend and address any meeting of the Metropolitan Council and may for this purpose require the attendance of members. A person cannot be a member of both parliament and the Metropolitan Council, or of both the council and the Municipal Corporation. The Act guarantees freedom of speech in the council, and gives immunity to its members from liability in any court in respect of anything said or any vote given by them in the council or any of its committees.

The Metropolitan Council has the right to discuss and make recommendations with respect to the following matters in so far as they relate to Delhi:

A proposals for undertaking legislation with respect to any of the matters enumerated in the State List or the Concurrent (Central and State) List in the Seventh Schedule to the constitution in so far as any such matter is applicable in relation to Union territories (hereafter referred to as the State List and the Concurrent List);
B proposals for extension to Delhi of any enactment in force in a State relatable to any matter enumerated in the State List or the Concurrent List;
C proposals for legislation referred to it by the administrator with respect to any of the matters enumerated in the State List or the Concurrent List;
D the estimated receipts and expenditure pertaining to Delhi to be credited to and to be made from, the Consolidated Fund of India; and notwithstanding anything contained in the Delhi Development Act, 1957, the estimated receipts and expenditure of the Delhi Development Authority;
E matters of administration involving general policy and schemes of development in so far as they relate to matters enumerated in the State List or the Concurrent List;
F any other matter referred to it by the administrator.

The council has the inevitable question hour which operates in a somewhat unreal atmosphere. The recommendations of the council are forwarded by the administrator to the central government along with the views of the Executive Council. Since the Executive Council does not owe its appointment to the Metropolitan Council and is not responsible to or removable by the Metropolitan Council, there is no real constitutional nexus between the two. The Metropolitan Council has no financial powers; indeed the Delhi Municipal Corporation has more effective budgetary power than the Metropolitan Council. Since the Metropolitan Council has merely consultative and recommendatory functions, it has been reduced in effect to a mere debating society. This limitation on the powers of the Metropolitan Council has reduced its authority to the vanishing point and has given rise to a growing sense of frustration and futility among the members. The Delhi Administration Act has only added to the multiplicity of authorities in the capital without being able to bring about a sense of coherence and co-ordination.

The dominant majority in the Metropolitan Council belongs to the Jan Sangh. In a house of 61, including five nominated members, Jan Sangh has 35 members, and Congress has 22 (including three who belong to the Organization Congress). There are three Independents and one Republican. The strong position of the ruling Jan Sangh party ensures the smooth and expeditious functioning in the Metropolitan Council but it also strengthens the demand for the substance of power.

The Executive Council

The Executive Council consists of four members, one of whom is designated as the chief executive councillor. The stated purpose of the Executive Council is to assist and advise the administrator in the exercise of the "transferred" functions (as distinguished from those "reserved" by the central government to itself and the administrator). If there is any difference of opinion between the administrator and the members of the Executive Council on any matter in the realm of "transferred" subjects, the administrator is required by the act to refer the matter to the president and to act according to the advice given by the president (which in effect means the central government). A decision taken by a member of the Executive Council or by the Executive Council as a whole in relation to any matter concerning New Delhi is, however, subject to the concurrence of the administrator who has an unfettered discretion in the administration of New Delhi. The meetings of the Executive Council are normally presided over by the administrator and in his absence by the chief executive councillor.

The members of the Executive Council are appointed by the president (in effect, by the prime minister) and hold office during his pleasure. It is conceivable that in spite of a clear majority enjoyed by a party the president may appoint members of a different political party as executive councillors or may distribute the membership of the Executive Council among different political parties. This has not happened in actual practice, and all four executive councillors belong to Jan Sangh, which commands a clear majority. Indeed, because of the homogenous one-party character of the Executive Council the principles of collective responsibility and of the responsibility of the Executive Council to the Metropolitan Council have found a veneer of acceptance in practice.

A proposed reform

It appears to the present writer that the most desirable reform in the set-up of Delhi would be to reduce the excessive multiplicity of authorities. Towards this end, the functions of the Municipal Corporation of Delhi should be transferred to the Metropolitan Council and the Corporation should be abolished. The offices of the chairman of the Metropolitan Council and the mayor of Delhi could be merged; alternatively, the office of mayor could be retained for ceremonial purposes. The Executive Council should be led by the chief executive councillor and should be collectively responsible to the Metropolitan Council, which should, for all practical purposes, function like an assembly. The chief executive councillor, instead of the administrator, should preside over the meetings of the Executive Council.

In the sphere of transferred subjects, the autonomy of the Metropolitan Council should be safeguarded by a parliamentary resolution or even by an amendment in the act, giving real powers to the Metropolitan Council and to the Executive Council, without intervention by the administrator or the central government in the normal course.

In this scheme of things, the preservation of law and order and the control of the police force would remain the exclusive preserve of the central government. New Delhi and the Delhi Cantonment might conceivably be excluded from the jurisdiction of the Metropolitan and Executive Councils to provide for exclusive central authority in the core of the capital and in the military establishment in the cantonment area. The amalgamation of the Metropolitan Council and the Municipal Corporation would impart greater cohesion and effectiveness to the elective apparatus besides obviating pointless conflicts between the two bodies in the eventuality of their being controlled by two different political parties. The introduction of the principle of the collective responsibility of the Executive Council to the Metropolitan Council, the guarantee of full autonomy within the sphere of transferred subjects, and the conferment of the substance of the powers of a legislature without a full-fledged and regular legislature would need a parliamentary resolution or an amendment in the act. These changes would not necessarily allay the sporadically strident demands for statehood, but they would be likely to provide a practical and viable administrative and political framework, and would help to reconcile the contending claims for the democratic rights of self-government and for control by the central government over its own capital.

---

1 See *Proceedings of the Home Department*, Nos. 8, 9 and 10 of 1911 (December 1911).
2 See D.C. Sircar, *Studies in the Geography of Ancient and Mediaeval India; The History and Culture of the Indian People*, Vol. 5, Bharatiya Vidya Bhavan. Also Cunningham, *Archeological Survey of India*, Vol. I (1862–63).
3 *Proceedings of the Home Department*, No. 9 or 1911 (December 1911), 12–13.
4 *A Constitutional History of India* (second edition, reprinted, Allahabad, 1961), 35.
5 *Report of the States Reorganization Commission*, 160.
6 Figures in the discussions which follow on demographic trends, religious composition, occupational patterns, literacy, etc., are culled from *The Census of India* Vol. XIX, Delhi, Part I, *General Report*.
7 *Ibid.*, 62.
8 *Ibid.*, 205.
9 *Report of the States Reorganization Commission 1955*, 157.
10 *Ibid.*, 158.
11 *Ibid.*, 160–1.
12 One rupee was worth about 13 US cents in 1970.

Part II   **Capitals not in federal districts**

A Capitals as states

8 Annmarie Hauck Walsh and Samuel Humes LAGOS

Lagos is the economic and political capital of Nigeria. Both before and after national independence, it proved a powerful magnet to migrants from all regions and ethnic groups of the country, increasingly encompassing a cosmopolitan cross-section of Nigerian society, which elsewhere remained relatively segmented. This development was halted, however, when mutually reinforcing political, economic, and ethnic rivalries burst into civil war in 1967. These tensions also underlay the frequent changes in the constitutional status of the capital over two decades.

At independence in 1960, nearly two-thirds of the population of metropolitan Lagos had been born elsewhere, and two years later the census indicated that the central city population had surpassed that of Ibadan, Lagos becoming the largest city in a nation of over 55 million. Experiencing rapid growth of about four or five per cent per year, the city was estimated to include nearly 800,000 residents by 1969.

More important, Lagos encompassed a lion's share of Nigeria's developed human and economic resources. In the early 1960s its literacy rate was five times that of the nation as a whole and Lagos contained well over one-third of industrial employment, half of domestic electricity consumption, and the headquarters of most periodicals. Even with renewed development of ports, oil, and other natural resources in the strife-torn East, Lagos is likely to continue to capture a large share of the benefits of Nigeria's development, as its port facilities are superior and it stands astride ground transportation routes. Moreover an important governmental role in economic development gives the administrative capital enormous advantages as a headquarters site.

While these growth factors reflect the capital's strength, they also signal its problems. The influx of primary school graduates has been far greater than the job market of Lagos could absorb, producing swelling ranks of unemployed in the region, estimated at over 100,000 in 1964.[1] Demands upon urban housing, sewerage, water supply, and health services severely strained the governmental apparatus and have resulted in deteriorating standards. As a result, pressing problems of public service and urban infrastructure have been a second source of tension underlying the shifting status of the capital.

CONSTITUTIONAL HISTORY

Geography and colonial history were determinant influences in the selection of Lagos as the nation's capital. Lagos was the first and major point of colonial contact in Nigeria. Lagos Island, the seat of a traditional Yoruba town conquered by Benin invaders, became a prominent West African port of call in the slave trade. British attempts to secure the port for legitimate trade and to halt the by-then illegal slaving resulted in the use of force to obtain the treaty of 1861, which put Lagos under direct colonial rule. British penetration of the Nigerian interior and organization of various patterns of indirect rule proceeded from 1885 to 1920. Colonial power, and later modernizing forces fanned out from Lagos into the rest of Nigeria. From 1862 until 1951, however, Lagos Colony had separate status as a unit of colonial administration, with its own governor or otherwise titled official.

By 1913, all the territory which was in 1967 to become Lagos State was encompassed by the Lagos Colony, subject to direct British rule. Within Lagos Colony, the town of Lagos was given legal status in 1917, together with its own council, on which the proportion of representative members grew gradually over the years. In 1950, the council no longer included appointed officials, and the town of Lagos was endowed with a mayor. This arrangement was short-lived, however, since the mayor exercised active political leadership in competition with the traditional chiefs of indigenous Lagos, as well as with colonial officials.

By 1950, the various groups, parties, and regions of Nigeria had begun jockeying for position as governmental power was being devolved by Britain. Party competition, rather than colonial power, became the central factor in shaping Lagos' legal structure. The creation of the Action Group party in 1951, drawing its major support from Western Nigeria and its Yoruba tribal groups, marked the growing regionalization of Nigerian politics. The National Council of Nigeria and the Cameroons (or NCNC, which later stood for the National Council of Nigerian Citizens) had been the major nationalist party, forming a national front that attempted to draw support from all groups. After creation of the Yoruba-based Action Group, the NCNC became more and more predominantly linked to Eastern Nigeria, and particularly to support from people of Ibo origin.

During the constitutional discussions of 1950–51, the NCNC and its leader Dr Nnamdi Azikiwe, argued for a unitary form of national government, but the constitution of 1951 devolved some power to three regional governments. Moreover, it abolished the separate status of Lagos, incorporating it into the Western Region, reflecting a victory for those of the Lagos Yoruba elite seeking to end the dominance of Azikiwe and the NCNC in the capital. The 1951 elections confirmed the NCNC's fears that regionalization of political parties would shrink its own support in the North, the West, and the Yoruba sections of Lagos.

In the 1953 constitutional conference, however, a full-fledged federal system for Nigeria based on the existing three regions was agreed upon. Those discussions had nearly foundered on controversy over Lagos, which split an NCNC-Action Group alliance. The British secretary of state for the colonies ultimately handed down a compromise solution. The town of Lagos (not the whole of the former Lagos Colony which encompassed Yoruba-Action Group strongholds, but an area of only 27 square miles), was excised from the Western Region and thereafter administered as a federal territory directly under the control of the federal government. The city of Lagos remained a federal territory through Nigerian independence in 1960, until 1967. The debates – which had been central to preindependence politics – over whether Nigeria should have a unitary government, continue the federation of the existing regions, or be a federation of more numerous states, came again to a head in 1967. The military government turned to the third alternative. Twelve states to replace the regions were formally established. One of these was Lagos State, its boundaries stretched beyond the federal territory to encompass the jurisdiction of the former Lagos Colony.

Into 1970, Lagos and Nigeria remained under a military administration that was designated temporary to meet the exigencies of the "military emergency" – the continuing civil war in the East triggered by the 1967 secession of Biafra. The legislatures of the nation, the states, and the city had been suspended since 1966. Lagos State was administered by a military governor, acting as chairman of its executive council, which also included one other representative of the armed forces, a commissioner of police, and civilian commissioners chosen by the governor. Within Lagos State, the city of Lagos was run by an appointed committee of management, and outside city boundaries, divisional administrators exercised the duties normally devolving upon local councils.

The city of Lagos remained the capital of Nigeria but became an integral part of the new state, and responsibility for local government within it was transferred from the federal to the state government in May of 1967. Hence, in two decades, the Lagos region had been a distinct colonial entity, part of Nigeria's Western Region, a federal territory, and, finally, a full-fledged state.

POLITICAL BACKGROUND

The constitutional structure of the capital has thus been inextricably bound up in Nigeria's ethnic-political tensions. Although peopled by many village, clan, and linguistic groupings, large and small, Nigeria has been dominated since 1950 by a three-way territorial-ethnic cleavage intensified by a corresponding party system. Prior to introduction of British forms of government, Nigerians tended to identify with small local and sub-tribal units. It was during the devolution of colonial power and organization for elections that the three largest ethnic categories – Yoruba of the West, Ibo of the East, and Hausa-Fulani of the North – took on major political significance. The three major political parties formed by the time of independence included the Action Group, the NCNC, and the Northern People's Congress (NPC), each of which found its largest core of support in one of the three large tribal groupings. Hence, these three parties controlled the governments of the Western, Eastern, and Northern Regions, respectively. The Moslem North, while less developed than the other regions, was much more populous, so that the electoral mechanics of the constitution that was devised in 1960 ensured a federal government dominated by the northern party in shifting coalition.

Lagos has long been in an ambiguous position in this competitive pattern. It was not, like Washington, DC, carved out of the mud to serve as national capital, but rather had a sizeable indigenous population of largely Yoruba groups, well organized in traditional urban fashion. Extended family compounds, descendants of settling clans recognizing a common chief, and, finally, the Oba or paramount chief over all of central Lagos represented three levels of traditional authority in Lagosian urban society.

To the descendants of original settlers were added to Lagos society the migrants from Liberia, Sierra Leone, and Brazil, who came in the 19th century. These included peoples of Yoruba origins who had been displaced by several generations of slavery and returned to their homeland to establish prominent families with some Western orientations. One member of such a family was Herbert Macaulay, who in 1923 founded the Democratic party, which built up firm support among Yoruba Lagosians. His party joined with that of Ibo leader Azikiwe in 1945 to form the NCNC, which for six years drew together both Yoruba and non-Yoruba sectors of the Lagos population in the early nationalist movement. The 1951 creation of the Action Group out of Yoruba cultural associations, however, again split Lagos politics between the "Lagosians" and the immigrants from other parts of Nigeria.

Traditional Lagosian organizations, such as the market women's association and various clans and tribal associations, have actively resisted incursions of higher government power since the 1860s (when they raised a storm over cession of Lagos to the British by King Docemo), into the 1960s (when they objected to destruction of traditional compounds by urban renewal). Several organized groups specifically espoused separate state status for Lagos. The Lagos State Movement and the Egbe Omo Eko, for example, argued that the status of federal territory deprived Lagosians of their political rights. As the non-Yoruba population of the city of Lagos passed 40 per cent in the 1960s, these Yoruba groups became increasingly concerned with creation of a larger Lagos State which would incorporate the Yoruba settlements in the city's hinterland.

The federal government, dominated by the Northern People's Congress, was willing to consider extension of Lagos boundaries, but only if it remained a federal territory. The Western Region, however, vigorously defended its right to the Lagos hinterland, where it had placed investments in housing and industrial estates at Ikeja. Another piece of the Western Region had been carved out to create the midwest Region in 1963, increasing its resistance to further loss of the Lagos "suburbs." When a faction within the Action Group split from it and, with support of the federal government, gained control of the Western Region, it nevertheless continued the Action Group's policy in opposition to further federalization around Lagos, in spite of its alliance with the Northern People's Congress and federal officials. The realignment of election coalitions of 1964 ended the threat of extended boundaries for the Lagos Federal Territory, because each of the parties which had previously supported such extension – the NCNC and the NPC – was now in alliance with a Western party – the Action Group and NNDP respectively – which opposed it.

Local elections in Lagos, taking place in 1963, had been dominated by the issue of the trial of the Yoruba leader, Chief Obafemi Awolowo, by federal authorities. Although the Action Group was at this time immobilized as a formal organization, its supporters won a substantial majority in the Lagos city council. The NCNC nevertheless drew support from the newer migrant settlements in the federal territory. For the federal elections of 1964, those two parties joined in alliance against the governing Northern People's Congress. At the end of an election campaign marked by sporadic violence, that alliance called for a boycott; no polling whatever took place in Lagos. Local government in the capital reached a high point of political opposition to its federal master.

Military government and constitutional talks

There were two successive coups in 1966. In the first, the government of Nigeria passed into Ibo army officers' hands. Following the second, a middle-belt Northerner, Lt-Col Yakubu Gowon, became supreme commander. When he called for constitutional talks to reframe Nigeria, the internal cohesion of the Ibo, Hausa-Fulani, and Yoruba groups hardened. The delegations from Lagos and from the Western Region submitted a joint memorandum calling for creation of a non-federal Lagos State with extended boundaries similar to those surrounding old Lagos Colony. In order to gain allies in its opposition to the bid for a strengthened central government, the Western Region was willing to concede the Lagos hinterland to its fellow Yoruba neighbours.[2]

Lagos was even willing to give up its status as national capital to gain its operating autonomy. "For strategic reasons," the joint memorandum argued, "the capital of the Commonwealth should not be located in the present vulnerable position of Lagos and should be removed to a far more central, more easily accessible and more secure place like Lokoja." Growing ethnic and political tensions were reflected in the assertion that "It is a misconception to say that 'Lagos belongs to all of us.' The truth is that Lagos belongs to the Lagosians." However, the memorandum went on to state:

The Western and Lagos delegations are willing to agree that Lagos should continue to be Federal Capital provided this is not used as an argument for continuing to deprive the people of Lagos of a status equal in all respects to the status of people in the Regions. In the considered view of those delegations neither the creation of a Lagos State nor the inclusion of Lagos in Western Nigeria endangers the position of the federal capital.[3]

In the event that Nigeria was not divided into new states, the memorandum proposed that Lagos once more become part of the Western Region.

The economic strength of Lagos provided ample evidence of its viability as a prospective state, even in comparison to the large regions of pre-1967 Nigeria. Revenues to the federal government from the federal territory that would be transferable to a state government would provide it with a budget over twice the size of that of the midwest Region and only slightly under that of the Western Region.

The Western and Lagos delegations to the 1966 constitutional talks further argued that federal government rights could be adequately safeguarded if the capital became a state. They proposed that a Federal Capital Commission be established to control federal properties in Lagos, including the port facilities in Apapa. That commission would be authorized to acquire land for central government purposes and to pay grants to the Lagos city council in lieu of local or state taxes on federal properties.

In November of 1966, the head of the federal military government,

Lt-Col Yakubu Gowon, declared the constitutional talks indefinitely adjourned, with no agreement in sight. Confronted six months later with the threat of Biafra's secession, the central government, with firm backing from the Northern Region, sought support from the Western Region and above all, from Lagos, to deal effectively with civil war in the East. The creation of 12 states, including one for Lagos (but otherwise leaving the Western Region intact), met the major demands of the Lagos and Western delegations, demands which had not been acceptable to the central government the year before. Major questions concerning the division of powers between the federal and state governments, and the replacement of the city's appointed management committee by an elected city government, were held in abeyance during the persistent struggle in the East.

DEVELOPMENT PROBLEMS

The rapid growth of the Lagos region has had an impact on the issue of the capital's status. On the outskirts of the city, swelling settlements of badly housed newcomers, without the urban social bonds found in central Lagos, presented needs for new governmental services and added to the political volatility of the capital. The sheer growth in numbers of residents, of businesses and of trips to work confronted the government with an enormous task, if only to extend public services and infrastructure to keep pace with growth and stave off deteriorating levels of output. The fact that the metropolis had spilled well over the boundaries of the federal territory aggravated some developmental problems.

In 1962, 30 per cent of the population and 60 per cent of the land of the metropolitan area of Lagos was within the jurisdiction of the Western Region.[4] Practical operating relationships between federal and regional authorities relating to developments in metropolitan Lagos were rough and minimal. When the federal government called a meeting in 1964 to discuss proposals for governmental reorganization in the area, the Western Region delegation did not attend.

While the federal government was the major source of public investment in the region, its projects were kept within the boundaries of the federal territory. Yet increasingly the most severe service deficiencies were in the Western Region portion of the urban area. There were no housing projects in Mushin and Ajegunle where they were most needed and where land was available at relatively low cost. Federal housing projects were concentrated in the federal territory where the price of land was considerably higher than across the regional boundary. Ajegunle, a settlement with a population approaching 20,000, received neither water supply nor bus services. Schools and roads in the fringes were inadequate. In 1963, 95 per cent of eligible school children in the federal territory were enrolled in elementary school; the comparable figure for the Western Region portion of the urban area was 80 per cent.

The interrelated problems and imbalanced resources of the city and its hinterland nevertheless stimulated manifold *ad hoc* relationships between federal and regional jurisdictions. The city bus service extended its routes along the main thoroughfares into the Western Region as far as Ikeja. (But running battles continued over city attempts to regulate taxis and lorries licensed by the region and operating in the city.) Co-operative arrangements were worked out by federal and regional police and firefighting units. Lagos Water Supply Agency, an office of the federal Ministry of Works and Housing, drew its supply from the city's hinterland and serviced some distribution points in the Western Region. However, while some 90 per cent of residents of the city-federal territory were reached by the water supply, many of them by public taps, only half of the population of the urban area outside city boundaries was so served, and a dual structure of water charges resulted in the consumer in the suburbs paying far higher prices for water than the taxpayer in the city.[5]

Practical problems as well as political ambitions therefore underlay proposals for extension of the boundaries of Lagos. Hence, before the events that were to lead to the creation of Lagos State, there was a political stalemate as to whether an enlarged unit should continue to be a federal territory, become a local government, or be some combination of federal and regional government. Proposed solutions were, as a result, highly complex.

The technical assistance team provided by the United Nations studied the problem under the auspices of the federal Ministry of Lagos Affairs in 1964. After assessing a wide range of social and economic problems related to the growth of the Lagos urban area, the team concluded that Lagos should have a metropolitan administration to plan and carry out development projects. It proposed the creation of a Metropolitan Development Authority (MDA) whose jurisdiction would span both the federal territory and the urban fringe in the Western Region. The MDA would have been jointly responsible to the federal and regional governments (how this joint responsibility could in fact be effectuated was not spelled out). The federal government, however, would have had ultimate control. The prime minister would have appointed the governing board of the authority and federal grants and loans would have dominated its capital financing. The authority would have taken over major responsibilities from city, federal, and regional agencies in the fields of housing, planning, zoning and land control, transportation, water supply, and waste disposal. Its proposed budgeting and borrowing powers were greater than those of existing local governments.

Another attempt to bridge the gap was proposed by a team of British consultants working under the auspices of the Lagos city council, who – not surprisingly – recommended extensions of the jurisdiction of local government.[6] An elected Greater Lagos Council would have spanned both federal and regional portions of the urban area. For non-municipal purposes, the residents of the regional portion would have remained subjects and taxpayers of the Western Region. The proposal implied that the federal government would be the supervising authority over the council. However, the main issue in contention – that of the relationship and boundary between federal and regional jurisdictions – was again not confronted head-on by the proposal.

The two conflicting proposals were accepted in principle by the Ministry of Lagos Affairs and the Lagos city council, respectively. Their fundamental differences were striking. The metropolitan development authority alternative would have weakened local councils in the capital region and concentrated planning and operating powers in an appointed agency, with a strong executive structure. The Greater Lagos Council would, on the other hand, have relied upon an elected council without a chief executive, patterned on British local government, to take on some of the jobs being performed by federal authorities, together with the tasks of existing local government.

The suspension of the city council and the abolition of the Ministry of Lagos Affairs by the military government in 1966 changed the context of the debate. With competing political parties and elected legislatures immobilized, the government could use the power of decree to bring about more far-reaching changes than either of the two technical assistance proposals contemplated. We have seen that this resulted in the creation of Lagos State, which encompassed the urbanized area together with a sizeable hinterland.

GOVERNMENT OF LAGOS AS A FEDERAL TERRITORY

From 1954 through 1966, the city of Lagos was a federal territory in which governing roles were divided between an elected city council and federal ministries. The city of Lagos also elected representatives to four seats in the federal House of Representatives, and four seats in the Senate.

Many functions were directly performed within the city by the federal ministries themselves. The Ministry of Lagos Affairs was in charge of supervising the city government, co-ordinating the activities of other national agencies operating in Lagos and taking direct responsibility for land development, housing, and planning. These last functions were largely carried out, however, by the Lagos Executive Development Board appointed by the ministry. And its efforts to co-ordinate sister ministries met with very limited success. The minister did operate, however, in some ways as surrogate executive of the city by use of his powers of control over the city council. In 1966, the functions of this ministry were scattered: land and housing to a Ministry of Works and Housing; local government supervision to the Ministry of Internal Affairs.

The other ministries operated in Lagos with considerable *de facto* independence. The Ministry of Works built major roads and public buildings, and within it was the Lagos Water Supply Agency. The Ministry of Commerce and Industry undertook some licensing functions and industrial site approval. The Ministry of Transport and Aviation managed the Lagos airport and inland waterways, and supervised the port and railroad. The Ministry of Education supervised all schools and provided the city council with grants by which operating school expenses in the city were subsidized. Hospital facilities and preventative health programs were provided by the Ministry of Health, while the Ministry of Labour maintained the city's labour exchange and regulated trade unions. Port management, railroad service, and electricity in the capital were provided by public corporations with national jurisdiction that were formally under the authority of ministries. They had independent operating budgets, however, and investigations sponsored by successive governments spotlighted alleged corruption and mismanagement in the corporations.

Powers in each of these major functional areas were to some extent shared with elected local government in Lagos. Under the Lagos Local Government Act of 1959, the city council consisted of forty-two elected members and five traditional chiefs. The Oba, or traditional major chief of Lagos, served as president of the council. Elections to the city council were held every three years on the basis of universal adult suffrage. Single-member wards varied in size from 1,000 to 36,000 residents. The council operated through a series of committees composed of its own members. These included committees on finance; public health; education and libraries; personnel; property and general purposes; markets, parks, and cemeteries; contracts; and roads, drains, and plans. The municipal transport service was organized like a public corporation directed by a special board which was appointed by the Minister of Lagos Affairs but on which the city councilmen had a majority. Each of six regular departments of city government supervised by the committees was managed by a professional civil service officer.

Formally, the responsibility of the city council was to manage the resources entrusted to it by national law and to carry out the policies of the federal government in Lagos. It functioned as both a local government and an administrative agent of the ministries. Responsibilities assigned to the council included road maintenance, day-to-day supervision of primary schools, traffic regulation, libraries, sewage and garbage disposal, some preventative public health services, operation of maternity care centres, and regulation of markets and buildings.

About 5,000 employees served the city government, including bus drivers, street sweepers, and nightsoil collectors. The civil service personnel were organized in a separate city cadre, for which the national government nevertheless established general regulations. Appointments to posts carrying maximum salaries of 900 pounds[7] or more (that is, the upper executive, and professional personnel) required ministerial approval. Recruitment and training of other personnel did not require review of decisions exercised by the city establishment (personnel) officer. Many department heads in city government were well qualified, some of them trained in Britain, but councilmen themselves frequently became involved in the details of contracting, purchasing, hiring, and employee discipline, not infrequently for purposes of private profit, according to the findings of an official inquiry in 1968.

The allocation of functions

Perhaps the system of shared functions between the city council and the federal ministries in the Federal Territory of Lagos can best be understood by describing its operation in particular fields. Housing and land development in Lagos, for example, were legally the full responsibility of the federal government. Housing problems were, however, of deep concern to city councilmen and their constituents.

The Lagos Executive Development Board (LEDB) was designated as the operating authority for housing and land-use planning. A statutory corporation which predated Nigerian independence, its board of thirteen members was directly responsible to the Minister of Lagos Affairs. The board included, however, the city clerk and city engineer (department heads working for the city council) and two elected members of the city council. Headed by a chief administrative officer, the LEDB staff was divided into several divisions, including town planning, land survey, housing development (estate) management, and housing finance. The LEDB undertook several clearance and housing construction schemes. Its capitalization was derived from the federal government but it had sought external loans.

The city council maintained records showing the inadequacy of housing efforts. It maintained that there was an average of eleven persons per dwelling unit in Lagos, over 500 persons per acre in some areas with only one-storey structures. Yet the LEDB's central Lagos slum clearance scheme, which the federal government took over from colonial authorities, actually reduced the housing supply in the city. Initially designed to make room for downtown development, the project was protested by indigenous Lagosian groups whose housing and social organization were to be uprooted. This pressure resulted in the residents being given a legal option to repurchase their original plots at 120 per cent of the public acquisition costs. The legal obstacles that this arrangement entailed in addition to shortages of funds, resulted in the scheme remaining incomplete fifteen years after its commencement. In 1969 construction of a shopping centre on the central Lagos clearance site was under consideration. A hotel and office buildings had risen there, but vacant land remained.

In 1969 the Lagos Executive Development Board was also working on several construction and site-preparation projects scattered throughout the city. In Apapa, both industrial and residential estates were being developed by it and another industrial estate was under way at Iganmu. A resettlement project was being undertaken to rehouse those displaced by construction of the second bridge to the mainland, and a southwest development scheme was providing residential lots.

Disposal of sewage was the responsibility of the city council. This was carried out through contracts for nightsoil collection. The growth of Lagos made this system grossly inadequate, but the establishment of a piped sewerage system was beyond the resources and capacities of the council. For years it unsuccessfully exhorted federal authorities to finance a sewerage system. In principle, the project was endorsed by the National Development Plan, but federal financing of what was considered the legal responsibility of the city was not forthcoming. As of 1966, the federal government had not even financed construction of pipes to connect existing pumps and septic tanks in the city. Yet a technical study had concluded that a comprehensive metropolitan sewerage project would require 178 million pounds over a thirty-five-year period.[8] In the meantime, the council struggled to expand pail collections and septic tank installation in a city approaching three-quarters of a million persons.

Urban transportation was also assigned to the city government. The Lagos Transport Service, which provided urban bus services, was directly responsible to the city council until 1964, when a supervising board was created by central authorities. This transport board included one businessman and the city council members appointed by the Minister of Lagos Affairs. Legally, however, the service remained a city agency. The city increased the size of the bus fleet more than five times between 1958 and 1966. This expansion was financed by the agency's own earnings, but profits dropped rapidly while ridership increased during the 1960s. Any capital expenditure which was not provided out of profits would have to come out of the city budget. As the possibility of a needed subsidy became more imminent, the continuation of the existing arrangement became problematical.

In the meantime, any major improvement in the capital's transportation routes in effect depended upon action by the federal government. Central Lagos is an island which until 1969 had only one bridge connection to the mainland. Because the railroad terminated at Apapa, a section of the city on the mainland coast, vehicular bridge traffic was a crucial link in the urban network. Construction of a second bridge was begun by the federal Ministry of Works with aid from the West German government. Real improvement of bus services in the capital depended upon this and other major road, highway and traffic improvements.

Most transportation experts who have worked in Lagos agree, however, that some form of rail transit will be required to give the capital region a viable system of movement. The United Nations survey proposed an elaborate monorail system with a feeder network of buses and hydrofoil boats. A similar plan was suggested by West German technical assistants. In either case, it was clear that if the serious deficiencies of transportation in Lagos were to be eased, federal government commitment of enormous financial investment, provided with foreign assistance, would have to be forthcoming.

The implications of these examples are that the developmental tasks in the capital of Nigeria inevitably required commitments from the federal government and that the relationships between city and federal authorities were crucial components in development administration for Lagos. Under the federal territory-city arrangement, local-federal politicalt ensions had a significant impact on every important aspect of governing the city.

Finance

In spite of Lagos being a federal territory, local government in Lagos was in many ways stronger than in any other town in Nigeria. The Lagos city council, for example, was the only major local council with an established system of property taxes providing its primary source of revenue. The local government budget in Lagos exceeded the sum of all local budgets in Western Nigeria. The Lagos council's total revenues (including grants) increased by about 325 per cent between 1959 and 1964 (from 0.9 to 3.8 million pounds). In the same period, the net revenues retained by the national government increased by only about 60 per cent. By 1967–68, the city budget had grown to 4.8 million pounds. About half was derived from property taxes.

The property tax rates were based on the annual rental value of dwelling houses and the depreciated capital value of properties owned by public utility corporations. Assessments were made by the Ministry of Lagos Affairs. Exempted from the property taxes were dwellings with an annual rental value of six pounds or less, those owned by the federal or local government, schools, places of worship, and parks. The council could collect the rates only after federal approval of budget estimates, and taxpayers in default had to be prosecuted through the courts. Numerous bottlenecks in this system, together with limited registration of land titles, accounted for large arrears.

Other city council taxes included a flat rate on bicycles; vehicle, liquor, and gasoline licences; and entertainment taxes. In addition, earmarked grants from the federal government were extended as specified percentages of city expenditures in each field. These were enumerated in the Lagos Local Government Act of 1959 as follows:

	Percentage of grant	
Service	Ordinary expenditure	Capital expenditure
Health	50	50
Roads Maintenance – Trunk	100	—
Maintenance – Specialist List	50	—
Improvement and alteration	50	—
Traffic lights	75	100
Street lighting	50	50
Welfare	50	50
Education	70	100
Parks	50	50

In computing these grants to the city council, the total expenditure on which the percentage was based excluded income accrued to the service – for example, user charges. The grant rates were statutory and stable. Delays were frequently encountered in the receipt of grant payments from the federal treasury, however. For example, the grant of 70 per cent for teachers' salaries was commonly six to eight months behind salary payments. As a result, the council ceased paying full salaries, giving the teachers only 30 per cent in each month and thereby forcing federal authorities to make current payments of the remaining 70 per cent.

In the water supply function, these city and federal financial roles were reversed: the city contributed to the costs but disbursements were made by a federal ministry through its Lagos Water Supply Agency. The city council paid to the agency an aggregate sum, agreed upon in advance. This amount was generally well below costs of water production and distribution. On the other hand, the city council collected water taxes within the city in an amount that only partially compensated for its outlay. Hence, it neither bought nor sold water at an economic rate. This subsidized distribution covered by the city water taxes was to domestic consumers within the federal territory. The Lagos Water Supply Agency distributed water directly to industrial users who were, for the most part, metered. The agency also charged consumers outside the boundaries of the federal territory direct fees for excess consumption over a specified minimum level and sold water by the gallon at stations in Ikeja and Agege (in the Western Region portion of the metropolis).

In general, the legal responsibilities of the Lagos city council exceeded its financial resources, as was illustrated with respect to transportation and sewerage. Several advisers proposed new city taxes, such as a city income tax on both residents and commuters. (Local authorities in the Western Region and in post-1967 states received a share of state income taxes.)

The inexorable pressure on available funds for *capital investment* was the crucial problem, however, and on this a small local income tax rate could have only limited effect. The city council made annual charges against revenues for small capital projects. Legally, the council could borrow through bond issues on the open market with federal government approval (or, after 1967, with state approval), but it had not done so through 1969. The capital market was very limited, and all major development projects in the metropolis would depend upon higher government grants and foreign loans for some time to come.

Central government controls

The major technique of federal operating controls over city government in Lagos was the requirement of prior approval for council action. Approval was required by the Minister of Lagos Affairs (or by another minister in case of aided services) for the council's operating and capital budgets, tax rates, specific grant projects (such as trunk road improvements), loans, by-laws, compulsory purchase orders, and senior appointments. Actually, the pattern of detailed approvals did little to prevent irregularities, as the subsequent investigations sponsored by the military government revealed, but it did slow down administrative processes considerably.

The budget power was the key one for control of policy directions. The Minister of Lagos Affairs could require that the budget of the Lagos city council be altered in whole or part. Once the budget was approved the city could only reallocate funds among budget heads as long as such changes did not increase the expenditure of any one department more than 25 per cent or 5,000 pounds (whichever was smaller). Post-audit was also carried out by federal treasury authorities.

The federal authorities also retained fundamental regulatory powers together with control of the police. Federal regulations were controlling with respect to public service standards, land use, criminal and civil offences, sanitation, etc., and city by-laws in these areas were approved only if consistent with them. Finally, the government had general supervisory powers which allowed it the right of access to all records and accounts or enabled it to suspend the council. The military government took both of these actions in 1966, launching a commission of inquiry into city government and appointing a committee of management to take over from the council.

The coexistence of detailed central controls, continued irregularities, and problems of interservice co-ordination was notable. The city council was given roles which brought it considerable power over the distribution of monetary benefits (including jobs and contracts), but it had little real influence over general policies or the pace of urban development. At the same time the Ministry of Lagos Affairs was involved in the day-to-day business of the city government. Both the UN and the British teams in Lagos in the early 1960s recommended that the ministry relax some of its requirements for the approval of minor matters. Also, it had failed to co-ordinate the activities of other ministries having a major impact on local services (for example, on school construction, water extension, road improvement, and job development).

Planning

There was no master plan for the Lagos Federal Territory. By virtue of its status as a federal territory, however, the capital was the subject of special attention in the federal chapter of the National Development Plan of Nigeria (1962–68). Each of the existing three regions in turn had their own chapters as well. For the most part, this plan outlined forecasts and goals for the allocation of investment capital. It did not spell out operational programs, intergovernmental relationships for carrying them out, or priorities among investments, given the scarcity of capital funds.

The Lagos portion of the plan was prepared by the Economic Planning Unit of the federal Ministry of Economic Development. Its small staff was aided by foreign assistants. Its tasks included preparing the overall federal program and reconciling with it the three regional plans prepared by the states. Shortages of trained staff, equipment, and, above all, of reliable statistics put a tight limit on the depth that the planning processes could plumb. The planning unit simply analysed project proposals forwarded to it by the various ministries in terms of some general guidelines from the Council of Ministers. The National Economic Council, which included ministers of finance and economic planning from the federal and state governments, was the mechanism for negotiating differences among the units in the federal system. Lagos itself was not represented on that council.

Investments for metropolitan Lagos were actually scattered throughout two chapters of the plan – the federal program and the Western Region program. The total capital expenditure for projects listed in the federal program was slightly over 400 million pounds. Of that amount, nearly six per cent was devoted to "town and country planning." That category applied entirely to the Federal Territory of Lagos. It included the following:

	Million Pounds
Lagos Executive Development Board, housing, land planning industrial parks, highway clover leaf	15.03
African Staff Housing Fund, housing in Lagos	1.83
Nigerian Building Society housing loans	1.50
Additional federal contribution to housing in Lagos	1.34
Lagos sewerage system	1.57
Lagos City Council projects (markets, streets, one bridge, drainage, abattoir)	1.84
Victoria Beach Protection Survey	0.05
Total	23.16

Other sections of the federal program contained Lagos projects as well. Nearly 2 million pounds were planned to expand the metropolitan water supply capacity. Port facility expansion and construction of the second mainland bridge were also listed. The program of the Ministry of Education included 7 million pounds for school construction and teacher training in Lagos, together with 5.5 million pounds for the University of Lagos. Over 7 of the 10 million pounds in the Ministry of Health capital program were allocated to facilities primarily serving Lagos. Other projects for Lagos included investment in fire fighting equipment, a sports stadium, a financial institution to aid co-operatives, and initiation of youth and welfare programs. In total, well over 10 per cent of the total investment called for by the federal program was related to the physical and social infrastructure of the capital territory.

Theoretically, the federal government, in exercising its approval authority over budgetary plans of the city council, the Lagos Executive Development Board and the public corporations, was to measure their activities against the goals of the National Development Plan. The six-year period did not see the planned investments substantially implemented, however. Political crises followed by civil war were the overwhelming obstacles. But in some cases the plan had not been entirely realistic. It assumed, for example, that the central Lagos slum clearance project would be self-financing. Actually returns from sales of cleared land were well below costs.

Although ambitious in relation to accomplishments, the targets of the plan for Lagos were modest when measured against needs. In terms of water supply, for example, a far more ambitious plan was submitted to the federal government by the United States Agency for International Development. That plan was designed to meet the demands of an urban population of two million by 1975, while increasing per capita daily consumption to at least forty gallons.

The United Nations survey of 1964 provided a more thorough plan for Lagos in the sense that it outlined priority projects and operational targets. Subsequent ministry plans also changed targets for Lagos. Under pressure of a general strike, a new Ministry of Housing prepared a housing plan in 1965 calling for large-scale construction of low-income housing in the capital region, and this scheme was approved by the military government in 1966.

Physical town planning for Lagos was the responsibility of the Lagos Executive Development Board. Rather than prepare a master plan, it concentrated its scarce staff and technical resources on planning for specific development areas (its housing and industrial estates). There were only three trained town planners in the agency, and the board was responsible for zoning maps and building permit checks, as well as for project planning. It did publish, however, *Planning Standards for the City of Lagos*, which suggested minimum standards for schools, housing, and population density.

GOVERNMENT OF LAGOS AS A STATE

With the creation of Lagos State as one of twelve units in a new federal structure in 1967, the city ceased to be a federal territory. It became legally a local government jurisdiction within a state, the state itself approximating an urban region centred on the capital. The city is the capital of both the federation and the state.

The state encompasses the city of Lagos, and the Ikeja, Epe, and Badagry Divisions of the former Western Region, an area of 1,381 square miles. The population of that expanse was 1.4 million according to the 1962 census, of which nearly half was within the city. People of Yoruba origin dominate the state.

Legally, the state took over all the powers of the federal government and the Western Region with respect to supervision of local government in Lagos, and established a state ministry of local government to exercise them. Through the end of the civil war in January 1970, however, the state was ruled by a military governor, and local administration was provided by a management committee for the city and by appointed administrators in other localities. Federal and regional ministries continued to act as agents of Lagos State, performing transferred functions while preparations were being made for civil service transfers to the new state.

Legislation for Lagos State into 1970 was promulgated by edict of the military governor after consultation with the appointed executive council. The commissioner of Lagos Affairs, appointed by the state governor, had wide discretionary powers over the city, including the making of regulations for maintenance of grant-aided services, and budget control. Former legislation governing local government remained technically in effect, however, with powers transferred to the new state unit.

Local government in portions of Lagos State other than the central city had consisted of eighteen councils. In some portions of the region these had been organized in two tiers. For example, in the Epe Division was a divisional council under which were ranged six "district councils." In Ikeja and Badagry were found only all-purpose district councils. The elected councils in all of these localities were replaced by appointed management committees in 1963. In 1966 all of these committees were replaced by appointed administrators who became the divisional officers of the state Ministry of Local Government. The existing local staffs were retained.

The senior staffs of the local councils in the Western Region had been appointed, assigned, and transferred by a single Local Government Service Board for the whole region. Junior staff and employees were recruited by the councils themselves. The size of local staffs varied from 2 to 205. Teachers dominated the staffs of the councils that had been designated local education authorities. The council units received portions of the state income tax, and local authorities were used as collecting agents for taxes on incomes not exceeding 300 pounds per year of self-employed persons.

At the end of the civil war the form that the local government system of Lagos State would ultimately take was not clear. At that point in time, the city of Lagos was receiving large grants from the state to reimburse it for services elsewhere performed directly by the state government. City officials found grant payments by the state prompter than they had been by federal authorities. For the most part, the governing legislation has remained the same as before. Hence, if the local councils were to be restored, the formal controls exercised by the state government over the city council would be somewhat less than those exercised over the local councils that had been in the Western Region. New systems had to be forged for the state which encompassed different school systems, tax systems, and local government powers. Gradually, changes were being made to give the state uniform patterns. The Lagos Education Act was revoked, for example, and replaced by the education law of the former Western Region.

The fate of the capital is clearly bound up with the fate of the nation. The future constitutional structure of Lagos will undoubtedly depend upon the future constitutional structure of the Nigerian federation. At the end of the civil war, the ultimate relationship between federal and state governments in a non-military regime remained an open question within which Lagos would be an important bargaining point, but for which the settlement between the federal authorities and Biafra would be determinant. There seems little prospect of undoing the creation of Lagos State, however, to restore the federal territory. The failure of the federal territory approach in Lagos was due partly to its restricted boundaries vis-à-vis urbanization and partly to the ethnic and political rivalries between those groups in control of the federal government and those predominant within Lagos. Change in the status quo was difficult to effect, however, under a parliamentary system paralysed by conflict, and came only with exercise of extraordinary powers.

The prospects of the city-state framework for development of the capital in peace time also remain problematical. If the past can be taken as a guide, special attention by federal authorities and in national plans, together with foreign financial assistance, will be required to improve conditions of living and commerce in Lagos and the suburbs. Although endowed with more political influence and governmental authority than the city had as a federal district Lagos State might want for the financial weight of the federal government.

1 Otto Koenigsberger, Charles Abrams, Susumu Kobe, Maurice Shapiro and Michael Wheeler, *Metropolitan Lagos* (United Nations Commissioner for Technical Assistance, 1964).
2 Prior to independence, leaders of Nigeria's North opposed a strong central government, for they feared dominance by the more developed and educated southern regions. In 1966, however, northerners favoured central power, having experienced their own ability to capture it.
3 Memorandum of the West Lagos Delegations, reprinted in full in the *Daily Times* (Lagos, 30 November 1966).

4 The "metropolitan area" was delineated by the UN study team in Koenigsberger, *et al., op. cit.,* 1964.
5 Babatunde A. Williams and Annmarie Hauck Walsh, *Urban Government for Metropolitan Lagos* (NY, 1968).
6 G.C. Jones and B. Keith Lucas, *Report on the Administration of the Lagos Town Council* (Lagos Town Council, 1963).
7 One Nigerian pound was worth US $2.80 in 1970.
8 Cited in Alhaji H.A.B. Fasinro (Lagos Town Clerk), "Governing a Metropolis: The Problems of Administering the Federal Territory of Lagos," *Administration* (Quarterly Review of the Institute of Administration, University of Ife, April 1969).

Herbert Haller **VIENNA**

Austria is a federal republic consisting of nine provinces with a total population well over seven million in 1970 and an area of 84,000 square kilometres. Until 1918 its territory had been part of the Austro-Hungarian Empire, which covered the successor states of Czechoslovakia, Hungary, Yugoslavia, and parts of Poland, the USSR, Roumania, and Italy. The Empire encompassed 600,000 km² and a population of more than 50 million. After the break-up of Austria-Hungary, Vienna, which had been the imperial capital and residence, became the capital of the Austrian republic. Although geographically it was no longer in the centre of the state it governed, it was nevertheless regarded as the natural centre of the republic. Considering Vienna's history and size, as well as its political and cultural life, there was no other choice for a capital.

HISTORY

Vienna is situated at the crossing of two important trade routes, one of them leading from the North Sea to the Adriatic and the other from the West to the East, following the course of the Danube. This geographical position formed the natural basis for Vienna's rise from a Roman stronghold to a medieval trading centre and finally to one of the foremost cities of Europe. The development of the city can only be understood, however, in view of its role as the residence of the Austrian princes, a position it occupied, with only short intermissions, from the twelfth to the twentieth centuries. In the middle of the twelfth century the Austrian margraves of the house of Babenberg were raised to dukes, and about the same time they moved their headquarters to Vienna. The Babenbergs were succeeded by the Habsburgs, who also resided in Vienna, and who in the fourteenth century assumed the title of archdukes of Austria and finally, in 1804, took the title of Austrian emperors. From 1438 onwards the Austrian rulers were at the same time emperors of the Holy Roman Empire. In 1526 the Habsburgs also inherited the kingdoms of Bohemia and Hungary.

As the place of residence of the Austrian rulers Vienna was hardly able to pursue its own politics. It enjoyed little autonomy, especially from the sixteenth century onwards. Only in the first decades of the nineteenth century, a time of economic prosperity which saw the rise of the middle classes, the citizens came to claim their share in the political life of the city. The demand for self-government was voiced repeatedly. In this respect the revolution of 1848 brought a partial success as Vienna was to elect a city council, and in 1862 self-government was realized. As to its position within the State, Vienna was subordinated to the governor and the parliament of the province of Lower Austria (then still called *Erzherzogtum unter der Enns*). The provincial parliament controlled the matters within Vienna's competence and the provincial governor supervised them. The Viennese government was only the executing organ.

Direct control by the central parliament and the government had been discussed, but even in the city had been favoured by a minority only. There was, however, a change of public opinion when it became evident that this state of affairs – the provincial parliament having to approve of all important matters, in particular the budget – gave an overpowering influence to a body in which the middle classes and as a consequence of this, Vienna, were unequally represented. Among those who advocated exemption from the provincial authorities was Dr Karl Lueger, the Christian Socialist Lord Mayor of Vienna (1879–1910), under whom the city prospered greatly. The program of the Social Democratic party of 1914, too, contained the demand of extended autonomy for Vienna and separation from Lower Austria.

The 1919 elections for the first parliament of the new republic, which was to decide upon a constitution, yielded the following results. Of the two major parties, the Social Democrats won 72 seats and the Christian Socialists 69. In constitutional matters the Social Democrats advocated a centralized and uniform state, while the constitutional proposals of the Christian Socialists were based upon federal principles. Their attitude was a question of doctrine, but, at the same time, it was also inspired by practical considerations. The Social Democrats, which were the strongest party, had gained half of their votes in Vienna. It is easily understood from this that they worked for a strong centralized government to be located in Vienna because this would best serve their interests. The Christian Socialists, on the other hand, upheld federalism. As they had been the strongest party in most of the provinces, this was more to their advantage. When, finally, a moderate federalism had been agreed upon, the future status of Vienna was still a major constitutional problem.

If Vienna, which in 1918 had a population of 1.87 million, had remained part of Lower Austria, it would have made this province's population total 3.3 million. Such a number would then, however, have been quite out of proportion since at that time the whole of Austria had no more than 6.4 million inhabitants. A special problem would have arisen in the Federal Assembly (*Bundesrat*), the second chamber of Parliament, in which the Austrian provinces were to be represented according to the number of inhabitants. A Lower Austria that included Vienna would gain the overall majority thereby overriding all the other provinces.

Three main solutions to this problem were offered: to put Vienna under the direct control of the central government, to establish Vienna as a province in its own right, or to split Lower Austria into two districts, each with its own curia, or assembly. The political parties were at variance among themselves and hesitant to embrace one or the other of these possibilities. Where they were in the minority – the Social Democrats in Lower Austria excluding Vienna, the Christian Socialists in the city – they dreaded the majority of the other party and wished for a compromise that would guarantee an approximate balance of votes. On the other hand, the respective majority party advocated complete separation, which would ensure its advantage over the minority party. In the ensuing discussions the menace of a Socialist Vienna on the one hand and the unwillingness of the Socialists to lose their overall majority in the city on the other hand, were two of the main motivating forces.

The constitution of 1920 finally settled that the province of Lower Austria was to be divided into two parts. The parliament of the province was to consist of two curiae, namely Lower Austria Rural District and Lower Austria City District, each with the number of seats that corresponded to its population. There were only a few matters which the constitution of the province marked off as common, to be decided jointly by both curiae. In all other respects each of the two parts had the position of an autonomous province, as was the case in regarding representation in the Federal Assembly.

At the same time, the constitution offered the possibility of a complete separation if both curiae in agreement passed a law to this effect. After difficult negotiations especially over financial problems, the separation was enacted. Since 1922 each of the two parts of Lower Austria has thus been a province in its own right. By this separation the province of Lower Austria lost its capital, but an amendment to the constitution provided that its government should remain in Vienna, which it has done to the present day.

The separation of the city from the rural parts of the surrounding province proved to be a success, and all of the following temporary changes in the constitution of Austria have respected this state of affairs. The authoritarian constitution of 1934, which was based on the corporate system, declared Vienna a town under the immediate control of the central government without greatly changing its actual legal status. In 1938 Vienna inclusive of some of the surrounding municipalities was made a separate province (*Gau*) of the German *Reich*. After World War II the constitution of 1920 was restored in its 1929 version, and Vienna too regained its former status.

The following survey of Vienna's constitutional position will discuss the situation as it has existed since 1945, and especially since the Municipality Act of 1962, by which the rights of the municipalities were extended. The Municipality Act involved a complete revision of the passages in the constitution that refer to the municipalities and thus cleared up a somewhat complicated state of affairs.

THE LEGAL SITUATION

Austria

Although Austria is a federal state, it is nevertheless highly centralized. The judicial branch as a whole falls within the competence of the central government, which also assumes direct responsibility for most of the important matters in legislation and execution.

Legislation within the province is a function of the provincial parliaments, which are elected by equal, direct and secret ballot. The provincial parliaments are furthermore in a position to exert some influence upon federal legislation. They elect the members of the Federal Assembly (*Bundesrat*), the second chamber of the federal parliament, which has a suspensive veto power over legislation passed by the directly elected National Assembly (*Nationalrat*).

Executive power in the provinces is in the hands of the provincial governments, which are elected by the provincial parliaments. For administrative matters within provincial competence, these governments are the second and last stage of appeal. The first stage of appeal is generally the district governor (*Bezirkshauptmann*), who is appointed by the provincial government.

Besides administering their own affairs, the provinces have a share in federal administration. The constitution decrees that in many matters the executive power of the central government shall be exercised by the elected provincial premier, in some other matters it may be transferred to him. This is called indirect federal administration (*mittelbare Bundesverwaltung*), and in these matters the provincial premier is required to follow the directions of the federal ministers. Thus there are three stages of appeal, the district governor, the provincial premier and finally the federal minister.

Within the framework of shared powers some matters of local interest and importance are assigned to the municipalities in their own right, though under the general control of either central or provincial government (depending on whether it is a matter normally falling within the jurisdiction of the central or provincial government). This control, however, does not entail directions; as self-governing bodies the municipalities are autonomous. In addition are other matters that may be transferred to their administration, a practice comparable to that of indirect federal administration. In this case the municipalities receive instructions since they act as the first stage in federal or provincial administration.

The organization of the provinces is to a large extent regulated by the constitution, as supplemented by the provincial constitutions. With the municipalities the situation is similar. Their function is also defined by the federal constitution and the respective provincial constitution. Further regulations for all municipalities of an individual province are provided by simple provincial law, the so-called *Gemeindeordnung*. The organs of the municipality according to the federal constitution are the municipal council (*Gemeinderat*), the municipal government (*Gemeindevorstand*) and the mayor. Their position corresponds to that of the provincial organs. The municipal council is elected as the local representative body according to the electoral system of proportional representation, as is the provincial parliament. It has to decide upon all important matters. The municipal council also elects the municipal government and the mayor, whose position may be compared to that of the provincial premier.

Vienna

The federal constitution lays down that Vienna is the federal capital and the seat of the supreme federal authorities. Only for the period of an emergency may the president, upon the recommendation of the government, give permission that parliament, the seat of the president, the ministers, the federal government, and the three supreme courts be moved to some other place within the republic's territory. This is all the constitution says about Vienna in its capacity as capital. It contains, however, further passages that establish the exceptional position of Vienna as a municipality and province at the same time.

Before it was raised to a province in its own right, Vienna as a whole was administered as one municipality. To split it up into several municipalities after the model of the other provinces when it became a province itself would not have been feasible. The problems of a modern metropolis are such that they can only be dealt with adequately by a centralized administration. Vienna is therefore a single, large municipality covering the whole of the province.

One paragraph of the constitution is restricted to the special regulations made necessary by the double function of Vienna as a municipality and a province. It rules that in regard to the capital as a province the municipal authorities should also assume the functions of provincial authorities. Further regulations are laid down in the constitution of the city of Vienna. This consists of two parts: the first, a simple province law, forms the *Gemeindeordnung* and is concerned with Vienna as a municipality; the second, titled "Vienna as a province," contains the provincial constitution.

Vienna as a municipality

All matters of primary or exclusive interest to the municipalities fall under their autonomous jurisdiction as far as they are able to attend to them within their boundaries and with their own resources. As the average municipality, apart from a few larger towns, is a community of 100 to 2,000 inhabitants, the power thus granted to the municipalities is in effect rather small. The constitution quotes as examples of matters that are to be delegated to the municipalities the appointment of municipal employees, service regulations concerning such employees, local safety police, and building inspection. The municipalities are moreover entitled to own and to acquire property and to engage in economic enterprises. It is through this circumstance that larger cities like Vienna may exert additional influence, and this influence is steadily gaining in importance.

The double function of Vienna as a municipality and a province rules out delegated provincial functions for the municipality, but it entails delegated administrative powers. These, however, are of minor importance, and are the sole responsibility of the mayor.

Vienna has a city council (*Gemeinderat*) of 100 members, elected every five years. There are no restrictions for soldiers, civil servants or municipal employees on their right to vote or to seek election. For its term of office the city council elects the mayor (*Bürgermeister*), the executive board (*Stadtsenat* corresponding to the *Gemeindevorstand* of smaller municipalities), and the department heads (*amtsführende Stadträte*), who all may, but need not, be members of the city council; from among its members it also elects special administrative committees. As in all Austrian municipalities the parties represented in the city council are entitled to proportional representation on the executive board.

The city council takes the final decisions and supervises the management of municipal affairs. It is responsible for the internal organization of municipal administration and decides upon important issues such as the budget and all contracts that involve value exceeding a certain established amount.

The second important authority in municipal affairs is the mayor. He acts as the ceremonial head of the city, directs and conducts the city administration and presides over the executive board. He also controls the department heads and the prefects of the city districts as well as municipal employees, who are all subject to his directions. Finally, it is his duty and privilege to annul any decision of the executive board, the district councils or the administrative committees that he considers illegal or detrimental to the interests of the city.

The executive board consists of the mayor as chairman and, including the two vice-mayors, thirteen members. Among other duties it prepares agenda for the council sessions, attends to all questions in connection with the city's personnel and constitutes the final appeal body on the legality of the municipality's administrative acts. From among its members the board selects the candidates to be proposed as department heads to the city council.

The municipal board (*Magistrat*) consists of the mayor, the department heads, the magistrate-in-chief (*Magistratsdirektor*), and the necessary bureaucracy. In constitutes the first level of appeal in administrative matters, carries on the bureaucratic affairs of the municipality and is its executive organ. Finally, it also manages municipal property. The board is split into departments, each of which is presided over by its department head. The department head is at the same time a member of the council committee that, as a rule, corresponds to the department.

Vienna consists of 23 districts. When elections for the city council are held, district councils of 30 members each are also elected. These attend to some minor matters of local interest that are specially delegated to them. They can make regulations on such matters, but have no civil service of their own. The districts are headed by district prefects, who take a seat in the city council and are thereby in a position to defend the interests of their district. However, these districts should not be confused with the administrative districts that constitute the first level of provincial administration. There is no such first level in Vienna. Like some other Austrian cities (14 in all), Vienna is a city with a special charter, which means that it takes these functions upon itself, and it is the municipal board that attends to them.

The workings of this complicated organization, here only outlined, are reasonably direct and effective in practice. As a rule, the chairman of the Socialist majority party is elected mayor as well. Because of the strict party discipline customary in Austria, in addition to the mayor's already very strong legal position, he controls his party friends in the city council as well as in the other city organs, where they usually hold the majority. As the bureaucracy is also absolutely loyal, city administration must be regarded from the party aspect. It is from party politics that it receives its most decisive impulses. The diversity of organs is thus counter-balanced by the unifying element of the party-line of the majority party (alone or in conjunction with that of the second party).

Vienna as a province

The constitution provides a different set of regulations for the provinces and the municipalities. This presents a difficult problem because of Vienna's double function. Regulations that concern only the municipalities necessarily affect the province of Vienna as well. On the other hand, there is always the question whether a special regulation affecting the provinces should be: (1) not at all applicable to Vienna, (2) applicable only in regard to its function as a province, or (3) for the municipality as well.

For conducting the affairs of the province of Vienna the city council is specially summoned to act as the provincial parliament. In these sessions municipal matters may not be discussed. The mayor, who is the chairman of the city council, does not assume the same function in the provincial Parliament. In accordance with the principle of the balance of power, another chairman has to be elected who is not at the same time a member of the provincial government like the mayor who acts also as provincial premier (*Landeshauptmann*). According to the constitution, civil servants and soldiers are to be allowed sufficient time off to enable them to run for a seat in the provincial parliament and attend to their functions there. In Vienna this applies also to the city council, and personal immunity is guaranteed to its members.

In administration, too, provincial and municipal matters must be kept apart. The executive board signs decrees as the provincial government of Vienna and the mayor does the same as the provincial premier. Vienna is the only province whose administration is, by constitutional regulation, run by a coalition government, as this is required in the composition of the municipal executive board. By supplying Vienna with two extra governmental boards for taxation and building, the constitution already provides for helping to relieve the Vienna government from the heavy burden of its double function.

As the territory of the province of Vienna is small, there is no need for decentralization. This and the wish for rationalization made it advisable to dispense with the usual three stages of appeal for delegated federal functions, so there are only two, the provincial premier and the federal minister. In the case of Vienna the federal right of supervision over municipalities would also affect the organs of the province. The right of supervision was therefore substituted by the possibility of impeachment proceedings before the constitutional court. The federal government is entitled to take action and charge breach of law against officials of the municipality of Vienna. In minor cases this may end in a mere statement of the unlawfulness of a procedure; otherwise, the guilty official loses his office. On the whole, these impeachment actions are of little practical importance. The federal government may, by the way, take the same action against provincial premiers regarding their delegated federal functions, and the provincial parliaments may also take impeachment proceedings against the provincial governments.

Vienna's finances

The Austrian system of public finance has its constitutional basis in the "Constitutional Law of Public Finance" (*Finanzverfassungsgesetz*) of 1948, which has since been amended several times. It provides for the distribution of public income among the federation, the provinces, and the municipalities. Its basic idea is that every local community should itself cover the expenses necessary for fulfilling its tasks. It therefore distinguishes various types of tax according to where the money goes, i.e. federal, provincial, and municipal taxes, or taxes divided in various ways between two or all three levels of government. This general frame is filled out by federal laws regulating what taxes belong to which type of tax and giving the ratio of distribution where necessary. Besides, both provinces and municipalities have the right to create new taxes, which, however, must not interfere with the federal tax laws. This system is made even more flexible by the institution of general grants as well as subsidies for specific purposes.

There is only one Vienna budget for both province and municipality. In 1968 it amounted to nearly twelve billion Austrian schillings which made it rank second after the federal budget of 85 billion schillings.[1] The budgets of the other provinces taken together added to about 15 billion, and those of the municipalities other than Vienna to about 16 billion. Vienna's budget thus amounted to nearly one-third of the sum total of all Austrian provincial and municipal budgets.

Of Vienna's income, 37.4 per cent consists of its share of common taxes against 16.9 per cent from municipal taxes. Administration fees and charges for the use of municipal facilities make up 12.5 per cent and the contributions of municipal departments to each other 9.4 per cent. The remaining 23.8 per cent is mainly composed of the gains from the city's own property and various federal subsidies.

Of Vienna's expenditures, 29.7 per cent were handed out for wages in 1966. The city employs about 35,000 persons and has to pay pensions to 17,500 retired employees. During recent years the share for wages has shown a rising tendency, as have the costs for maintenance and purchases, which in 1966 made up 35.9 per cent of expenditures. The disposable funds for investments have decreased and were 26.2 per cent in 1966.

The following table gives a summary of the principal tasks of the Vienna government and at the same time shows where the emphasis is laid financially. The figures are for 1968, classed according to departments.

	Income	Expenditures
	(in millions of Austrian schillings)	
I Personnel and administrative reforms	286.1	850.2
II Finance	8,195.3	2,668.8
III Cultural activities and education	44.8	623.0
IV Welfare	278.9	1,058.3
V Sanitation and public health	805.1	1,744.8
VI Building	355.1	2,085.9
VII Building inspection and technical matters	115.4	239.1
VIII Public services	640.2	1,105.8
IX Housing	527.0	604.8
X Economic matters	125.2	242.0
XI General administration	85.7	511.4
Total	11,458.8	11,734.1

Department number XII, *Wiener Stadtwerke*, has a budget of its own. It covers the electrical and gas companies, which are managed like private undertakings, public transport, cemeteries and funerals, and the agricultural undertakings of the city. For 1968 the total turnover of this budget was an estimated 4.8 billion schillings.

The soundness of the city's economy is controlled by the independent Court of Audit (*Rechnungshof*). The report of the Court of Audit on its examinations of federal and provincial undertakings is always widely noticed, and quite often it gives rise to political discussions. Also, the constitution of Vienna provides for its own auditing board, which is responsible to the mayor. At least once a year it must report to the city council on its most important findings.

THE POLITICAL SITUATION

The Austrian political scene is dominated by three parties. But as a consequence of a strong tendency towards a two-party system, the third one, the Freedom (liberal) party, has declined in recent years. It now remains as merely a small opposition effective only in some fields. The fourth party, the Austrian Communist party, is hardly of any importance in federal politics. It never gained more than 5.5 per cent of votes, and with the elections of 1959 lost its quota of three seats in parliament. In the 1966 elections, the 165 seats of the Austrian National Assembly were distributed among the parties as follows: People's party (the catholic, conservative party), 85, which thereby gained the overall majority; Socialist party, 74; Freedom party, 6.

The history of the first Austrian republic began with a short coalition government of the Social Democrats (now Socialist party) with the Christian Socialists party (now People's party). But in 1920 the Christian Socialists, who had gained the majority in the elections of that year, took over on their own, only at times collaborating with groups from the third party. The economic crisis of the late twenties and the early thirties made interparty political tension grow rapidly. Armed units were formed which operated in close contact with the parties, and government authority dwindled. Also, the 1929 amendment to the constitution, which was passed with the votes of the Socialist opposition, did not improve the situation. Through the inconsiderate abdication of the president of the National Assembly in 1933, parliament suspended itself. Though the parliamentary crisis might have been overcome easily, the government availed itself of the opportunity to seize the entire control of the state through a breach of the constitution. The National Socialist party and, following fighting and conditions verging on civil war in February 1934, the Socialist party were suppressed. A new constitution was adopted, based on the corporate system. Austria became a Christian Federal State, but it was none the more able to cope with internal disorder or difficulties from without. In the spring of 1938 Austria was occupied by National Socialist Germany.

After Austrian independence had been restored in 1945, the People's party and the Socialists formed coalition governments (at first together with the Communists). It was the necessities of the day that forced the coalition upon the Socialists, in spite of the resentment that had accumulated during the first republic. Notwithstanding smouldering ill-will among the coalition partners, these governments quite successfully managed post-war problems. Only after Austria had regained its full autonomy with the Austrian State Treaty of 1955, did the coalition become less efficient and workable. Instead of mutual co-operation, each partner tended to obstruct the actions of the other. Another undesirable practice was the equal division of all important government posts between the two parties. The elections of 1966 made a renewal of Austrian political life possible. As the People's party succeeded in winning an overall majority, it formed a government on its own with the Socialists constituting a strong and healthy opposition in Parliament.

In Vienna the situation is entirely different. Since the times of the first Republic the Socialists have been the dominating party in the city. In 1968 they had a large majority in the city council, where they occupied 60 seats, as well as in the executive body where the mayor and eight of the department heads were Socialist. The People's party had 35 seats in the city council and had appointed four department heads. Two more parties were represented in the city council, the Freedom party with three members and the Communists with two.[2] The People's party draws its supporters mainly from the inner city, where it holds the majority, and from those districts in which small trade is concentrated. The Socialist party, on the other hand, surpasses the People's party in the typical working-class districts, getting an average of votes that is two or three times that of the People's party; it is in these districts that the Communists, too, win their votes.

The People's party is made up of three unions (*Bünde*). Of these, the Farmer's Union (*Bauernbund*) is not represented in Vienna though it has a strong influence elsewhere. In 1966, 32 of the 85 seats of the People's party in the federal Parliament were filled by men of the Farmers' Union. The Vienna section of the People's party co-ordinates only the interests of the Industrialists' Union (*Wirtschaftsbund*) and the Workers' and Employees' Union (*Arbeiter- und Angestelltenbund*). The Industrialists' Union has the fewest members of the three, but as it contributes heavily to party finances it has considerable influence upon the party line, especially as to economic policy. In 1968 it held 15 of the 35 seats of the People's party in Vienna (22 in the National Assembly). The Workers' and Employees' Union advocates welfare politics that mark it off as the left wing of the People's party, and it is thus one of the three unions that comes nearest to the Socialists. It is also the most dynamic group, with rising membership numbers. In 1968 it held 20 seats in Vienna (31 in the National Assembly).

The Socialist party is basically centralized in its organization. It is a membership party to a much greater extent than the People's party and is also well backed by the trade unions. As to party doctrine it is rather more to the left than most Socialist parties in Western Europe. This holds true especially for the Vienna section. It plays the leading role within the Austrian Socialist party. This is only natural if we consider its advantage over the other provinces as to membership numbers. Its influence has been declining a little, however, as a consequence of the party's gaining strength in the provinces. Frictions that resulted from this development made the Vienna party bureau start its own newspaper in the spring of 1968, which now competes with the *Arbeiterzeitung,* the official organ of the whole party, in its main market, Vienna. All presidents of the second Austrian republic, which are elected by direct and general elections, were Socialists. The leading role of the Vienna Socialists is revealed by the fact that the last three presidents held the post of the capital's mayor at the time of their election.

The results of an investigation of Vienna's city council in 1964 may further illustrate the make-up of the political parties in Vienna. It was found that the council members represented their party supporters as to social status and trade. Of the members of the People's party, 26 per cent were self-employed and belonged to the Industrialists' Union. Only five per cent of the Socialist members were self-employed, while 53 per cent gave their original occupation as workmen. The People's party had a much higher percentage of university graduates, namely 51 per cent against nine per cent for the Socialist members. The average age of People's party members was 44 years, which was considerably below that of the Socialists. This was 51, but also here the leading members were rather younger than the average. Of the Socialist members, 19 per cent were women, while only 14 per cent of the People's party were women. While 55 per cent of the Socialist members did not profess any religious creed, there was no unbeliever among the former Christian Socialists.

In accordance with Vienna's constitution, the two large parties are proportionally represented on the executive board. Moreover, they form a coalition, as without this the size of the executive board might be increased until it were possible for the Socialist majority to elect all department heads, who must be elected from among the executive board members. The Socialists might also abolish proportional representation in the executive board altogether, by amending Vienna's constitution, which is a simple provincial law. By the coalition agreement the People's party was allotted four departments, among them two important ones, sanitation and public services. In spite of this, Vienna is regarded as Socialist. This view is justified because of the strong position of the Socialists in the city and also because of the antagonism (which was much stronger formerly) between Vienna and Lower Austria, which has a People's party majority, and between Vienna and the federation. Since 1954 the People's party has always been the stronger partner in the federal coalition, and has appointed the federal chancellor (prime minister). Since 1966 it has been strong enough to form a one-party government.

In many ways Vienna is linked with Lower Austria by common interests, though there are purely metropolitan or purely rural concerns that may conflict at times. Lower Austria is dependent upon Vienna, and also makes use of the city's public institutions, such as hospitals. Every day a large number of employees that live in the surrounding municipalities come to work in the capital. Moreover there are some 80,000 inhabitants of Lower Austria and the Burgenland employed in the city who return home at greater intervals. This influx of labour, as well as the problems in connection with the greenbelt of Vienna and the water-supply for the city demand mutual co-operation, which sometimes proves difficult though the situation has been improving.

Besides being the capital city, Vienna is also the only major city of Austria. Its problems are therefore in a way unique. The special circumstances of Vienna also create difficulties for the local party organizations of both Socialist and People's party. While the Socialists have to face charges from their members in the provinces of pursuing egoistical metropolitan politics, the People's party is likely to be found guilty of a lack of loyalty towards the federal government. As the actual tasks of the Vienna government sometimes leave little room for basically different attitudes, the two local parties very often agree. In Vienna their coalition has therefore survived the breakup of the federal coalition, a situation which is to the advantage of both groups. The Socialists, by showing their readiness to co-operate, thus demonstrate to the People's party how it should deal with the weaker party at the federal level. Besides, they have a partner who shares the blame for unpopular measures in Vienna such as a rise of municipal taxes. The People's party gains the right to participate in the city government and by this gets a better chance to stand the test in the eyes of the voters.

In this connection it should be noted that in Vienna the People's party as a rule gains fewer votes at elections for the city council than at those for the National Assembly. The fact that the Vienna voters favour the Socialists rather than the People's party at elections for the city council shows that they conceive the juxtaposition of Vienna and the federation also in terms of Socialists versus People's party. This may be explained historically. The Socialists, who were primarily centralistic in their outlook, later showed federalist leanings for the sake of their only major stronghold in the province of Vienna. Thus on the occasion of the 1929 amendment they prevented the Christian Socialists from giving Vienna a status below that of the other provinces. The Socialists also on other occasions know how to take good advantage of provincial privileges and rights, for example when they contest federal bills or decrees before the Constitutional Court. On several occasions Vienna successfully contested the federal budget; these challenges however, were answered by equally successful challenges of Vienna's own budget. In Vienna, the Socialists, who at the federal level were the weaker party, found their own sphere of activity where they could put their political skills to the test. This is a sphere of considerable scale and importance and therefore well suited to build up the Socialists' image of a modern party. It is here that they also try to challenge the People's party's reputation of being the party that is more versed and successful in dealing with economic problems. Political differences are therefore revealed openly to the voters. Finally, Vienna as the capital city offers to its ruling party international contacts which may be useful for political propaganda.

On the whole, political antagonism is never so strong that the opposing orces will not work together. It rather enlivens political life and gives new impulses or shows new ways in the interplay between the parties, federation, the provinces, and the capital.

THE FUNCTIONS AND PROBLEMS OF VIENNA

In area, Vienna is the smallest of the Austrian provinces (415 km^2 or 160 sq. mi.), but it is also the most populous (1.63 million inhabitants in 1961). In both respects Vienna heads the 4,000 Austrian municipalities. The second-largest town, Graz, had a population of only 240,000 in 1961, which is about one-seventh of Vienna's population. The town that was fifth in size had a population of only about 70,000.

During World War II Vienna was severely bombed, and for ten days fighting raged in its streets. Afterwards the condition of Vienna was pitiful. Gas, water, and electricity mains as well as bridges and streets had been badly damaged, transport was virtually non-existent, and 21 per cent of the houses were partially or completely damaged. All of these war damages have since been made up for, but there is one consequence of the war that could not be overcome and still constitutes a great problem for the city. Already after World War I the city had suffered from being deprived of the great empire whose capital it had been. A well-functioning economic unity had been cut into pieces. After World War II the Iron Curtain made almost all traffic and commerce with Austria's neighbours to the east come to an end. Vienna thus became more aware of its eccentric position within the state: it is situated only 60 km from Austria's eastern boundaries, but 800 km from Austria's most western point. Neutral Austria as well as Vienna have therefore aimed their efforts at a relaxation of the Iron Curtain, which makes a circuit around the whole of Eastern Austria. Vienna's cultural and sports contracts marked a beginning in this direction. Now the tourist traffic and economic and political relations are also becoming more intense. In 1965 the annual European panel organized by the Vienna government was dedicated to the general theme of "European Unity – Idea and Task." It is on the strength of age-old political ties, new common interests and the confidence in Austria's neutrality that Vienna is the town where this idea of unity in respect to Eastern Europe is still alive and again reviving.

Economy

In 1945 Austria was divided into four zones among the four occupying powers. The same happened to the capital, which was cut up into five sections, the fifth being the inner city, which was common territory. As traffic restrictions between the Russian zone and the zones occupied by the Western Powers were removed, the economy recovered though it prospered at a different pace in the two parts; traces of this state of affairs are left even today. Business enterprises in the Western-occupied parts were aided through the Marshall plan. The Russian part, however, contained four-fifths of all the Viennese business enterprises and nobody wanted to invest in them. Some of these firms moved to the western provinces, as there was the danger of the Iron Curtain going down along the border line of the Russian zone, isolating Vienna like Berlin. Luckily this did not happen in Austria. Thus during the eight years following the Austrian State Treaty of 1955, the industrial production of Vienna increased by 60 per cent, and the average income in Vienna is now 35 per cent above the Austrian average.

Vienna is primarily a centre of finance, commerce, and administration. It is the seat of large state-owned banks, which possess 75 per cent of the Austrian share capital. The Vienna fair which takes place in autumn and spring is among the leading fairs of Europe. Besides being the natural centre of Austrian federal administration, Vienna is attracting more and more the headquarters of international organizations.

A little more than half of the working population of Vienna hold jobs in industry, and they produce one-fourth of all industrial goods manufactured in Austria. The most important industries in Vienna are food-processing, chemical, and electrical industries. The latter two especially are expanding and developing. In spite of some tendency towards concentration, the structure of the individual undertakings is still unprofitable. There are about 3,000 small or middle-sized firms against a mere 20 that employ more than 1,000 persons.

That Austria's economy shows a steady upward tendency and unemployment never rises above two per cent is partly due to the economic policy of the authorities, among which the Vienna government plays a considerable role. Its possibilities of influence are not adequately rendered by the figures and headings of the budget. It owns or participates in undertakings of all sorts on a large scale. These include a hotel agency, factories for china, building materials, as well as the greatest insurance firm of Austria and one of the two major Vienna banks. The insurance and banking firms are booming because of their close co-operation with the city, while, on the other hand, they use their weight to assist communal measures. The great variety of city undertakings does not allow for too much generalization. A considerable number of them are by necessity run by the city itself. These constitute a major controversial point between the Socialists and the People's party. The People's party opposes the expansion of the influence of the city government into spheres which can be covered by private enterprise (cf. the film production of the city, which was stopped). It considers this clandestine nationalization process dangerous, especially since it evolves without the legal control that is normally imposed upon state activities.

Building and town planning

In the time of the Austro-Hungarian monarchy it was expected that the population of Vienna would surge to the four million mark, and plans for the future were made accordingly. As a consequence of the decline in population after 1918 – figures sank from the culmination point of 2.2 million to 1.6 million, and there has been only a slight increase during the last years – the world-wide metropolitan problems of housing and traffic did not assume dangerous proportions in Vienna. They are nevertheless among the foremost problems of the city.

Now that war damages have been made up for – mostly by means of interest-free loans from a federal fund – the demand for flats in Vienna is rather in regard to quality than quantity. Most of the old houses are no longer adequate by modern living standards, but adapting them was made virtually impossible through rent regulations that out of social considerations had been decreed by the state after World War I. Only in 1968 did the federation take steps to relax these regulations. However, just as with the reorganization of federal support for housing projects, this relaxation was strongly criticized by the Vienna government. The statistical data are that Vienna raises 46 per cent of all the funds available for housing in Austria and that 35 per cent of these funds are again shared out to Vienna, which means to 23 per cent of the Austrian population. These figures have a double aspect and have been used both ways for political propaganda.

As during the first Republic, the city of Vienna still builds flats on a large scale. The blocks of flats it has erected since 1919 house more than half a million, and the communal housing programme still projects 5,000 new flats per year. Though these flats are fairly small they are otherwise well equipped with all modern conveniences. In order to be able to realize its building projects the city acquired the majority of shares of a new company for pre-fabricated buildings units, which annually erects 1,000 flats for the city. To raise more money for building the city has started to change over to the profit system with communal flats. Rents that had been very low were somewhat raised. Since 1968 it makes new tenants pay 20 per cent of the costs of their flats, and only needy applicants are considered for a financial aid.

By means of its own extensive building activity and by supporting other housing schemes to the amount of some 7,000 flats per year the city is in a position to realize its own planning concepts. These provide for moving people from the densely populated central districts to the outskirts, where residential areas surrounded by parks are built. Vienna is thus becoming a city interspersed with public gardens, parks and gardens covering an area of 4.2 km². The federation is responsible for the former imperial gardens while the city tends the new gardens. Parts of the Vienna Woods, which stretch from the north-west to the south-west of Vienna, are within the territory of the city. They are to be preserved as a recreation area for the Vienna population and may not be used as building land.

The expansion of the town which results from this building activity and the breaking up of the central districts is subject to the town planning concept approved by the city council in 1961. This was prepared for several years in the town planning offices of the city, which continue to record all relevant cartographical and statistical data and try out town planning measures in miniature models. The spreading of the town is directed mainly towards the south, though because of fiscal considerations the boundaries of the city are observed. It is also increasingly directed towards the east, on the left bank of the Danube. This is placing the river again in the centre of the town. It is in this part that pre-fab blocks of flats are being erected.

To a great extent the city may rely on its own landed property (it owns 182 km² in Vienna), but it still spends enormous sums on the purchase of land. The building of the necessary streets and the costs for canalization, water supply, etc., are also a heavy drain on the city's resources and sometimes overdraw them, resulting in the slow progress of various projects. The scarcity of available funds is partly due to unjustified social benefits (such as almost free communal flats) and the unwillingness to resort to unpopular measures (such as raising the fees for water and gas or adopting rationalization measures in the offices and undertakings of the city). This, of course, has political reasons. But since Vienna's population tends to demand that the city authorities should act and, at the same time, is ready to criticize any measure taken, the city's position is indeed a difficult one.

Besides erecting flats the city also builds for other purposes. For instance it erected a new town hall with facilities for various sports (hand-ball, rowing, skating), for special sporting events (such as riding competitions), and for political and other meetings. The city is also partly responsible for the building of new schools and has distinguished itself in this field. A still greater financial burden is the upkeep of the 21 communal hospitals, which bed more than 15,000 patients. The rebuilding of the General Hospital, a pressing need, has begun but will take years to complete.

Public transport and public services

The street plan of Vienna, with its good radial streets and its two circular roads, the first around the inner city following the old fortifications, and the second around the former suburbs, has stood the test of growing motorization. Traffic conditions in Vienna are still tolerable. Since there is only limited room for private traffic in some parts of the city, the municipality has directed its efforts towards the creation of efficient and thereby attractive public transport, but at the same time providing for better private traffic.

As a first step it concentrated on crucial crossings where it built new traffic facilities, disentangling the traffic jam by splitting it into several levels. A next step was that in some streets the tram was moved underground and in others it was replaced by buses which are more flexible. The federal railway also introduced speedy trains which connect the outskirts of the town and facilitate commuting to the new residential areas across the river. Plans for an underground railway for Vienna are ready but financial difficulties have so far delayed a realization of them.

About 60 per cent of the working population of Vienna use public transport to go to work, while only 16 per cent use their own vehicles and 24 per cent walk. In spite of high passenger figures, Vienna transport regularly shows a considerable deficit. The reasons for this are rising labour costs and necessary investments, but also the high percentage of retired employees who receive pensions, some of them still dating from past political upheavals. Rationalization measures that were introduced could not compensate for this deficit, which is therefore paid for with the profits of the city's electrical and gas companies. These companies are thus deprived of valuable means for investments.

Besides these public services the municipality also provides such services as canalization, garbage removal, and communal baths. Among these the water works should be mentioned separately as a Vienna speciality. The greater part of the water supply for the city, which is famous for its excellent drinking water, is spring water and comes from two aqueducts whose headwaters are in mountain massifs south-west of Vienna and which span a distance of 118 and 200 km respectively. These being no longer adequate for the rapidly increasing demand, the municipality had to resort to various measures. It makes use of ground water and also built several new reservoirs. A third aqueduct for Vienna is also near completion.

As to public health and welfare, the municipality lays particular emphasis upon prophylactic measures. It has established medical care in the schools, maternity welfare centres, and centres for the early diagnosis of cancer. The authorities are furthermore concerned about fighting noise and air pollution in the city. The 24 per cent of citizens over 60 years of age constitute a special problem for communal welfare politics. Besides giving financial aid to those in need the city provides old-age homes and founded more than 100 clubs for the retired, measures by which it tries to assist those not living with a family to cope with the major problem of old age, loneliness.

CULTURAL AFFAIRS

Vienna has world-wide renown as a centre of music, theatre, and the arts. It offers a rich program in all of these fields, with the Vienna Opera, the Philharmonic Orchestra, and the Museum of Fine Arts, to mention only three of the most famous institutions.

Besides the famous state-owned theatres – the Opera, the *Burgtheater*, the *Volksoper*, and the *Akademietheater* – Vienna has some excellent private theatres, such as the *Theater in der Josefstadt*. Taken, together Vienna's 20 theatres count more than 3 million spectators per season. Vienna's two most famous orchestras are the Philharmonic and the Symphonic Orchestras, and its interesting musical season records more than 1,000 concert performances. As to what is performed, the theatre and concert programs offer a good cross section of world literature and the principal composers. In addition, Austrian authors and composers, such as Grillparzer and Mozart, are paid special attention, and the typical Vienna folk plays of Nestroy and Raimund, as well as the operettas of Strauss, Léhar, and Millöcker, are an indispensable part of the Vienna repertory.

The Vienna Festival is held during four weeks in summer. The tradition was started in 1950, and by now is well established in the cultural life of the town. Since the times of the Vienna Congress (1814–15) the Viennese have taken pleasure in balls. Today the Vienna carnival offers many splendid balls in the imperial palace, the opera house, and the concert hall besides several smaller but exquisite balls in Vienna palaces.

As the Habsburgs had dynastic connections with the Netherlands and Spain, and were connoisseurs themselves, they were able to bring together at Vienna unique art collections. Most famous are the galleries of the Museum of Fine Arts and the Belvedere and the graphic collection of the Albertina. Apart from these principal attractions there are many minor ones, such as the Imperial Treasury where the crown of the Holy Roman Empire is kept, the Museum of Applied Arts, the charming collection of old watches and clocks, and the Museum of 20th Century Art.

Vienna itself is in some parts a large open air museum. Amidst rows of old houses rises the tower of St Stephen's Cathedral, the most famous landmark in Vienna. The inner city is encircled by the *Ringstrasse*, which was planned on a large scale in place of the old fortifications and along which the splendid buildings of the university, parliament, the opera, and other representative edifices are arranged. Though it is the baroque style that dominates the city, with its numerous churches and palaces, Vienna also boasts of buildings in all other European styles, from Roman remains to buildings that were erected around the turn of the present century, when Vienna was one of the centres of *art nouveau*.

The federation maintains the state theatres and most of the Vienna museums, Vienna being the only place where it runs such institutions. It also subsidizes the private theatres of Vienna, and for this purpose spends the same amount as for all other Austrian theatres taken together. In the cultural affairs of Vienna, the federation, as well as the municipality, usually comes in as patron. The municipality for its part also spends large sums on the private theatres by arranging a competition among them and awarding a prize every month for the most successful performance. It also maintains many local museums and memorials, such as for Beethoven and Schubert, and runs its own representative museum. The Museum of the City of Vienna offers a well documented survey of Vienna's history and art.

The care of public monuments falls within the competence of the federation. The city, however, is very much interested in the preservation of historic buildings and whole areas. An example of the municipality's activity in this field is the saving of some medieval quarters in the vicinity of St Stephen's Cathedral. The city had to work together with and under the control of the federal authorities, but it bought the houses in question and advanced the necessary means for their adaptation. To preserve the atmosphere of the neighbourhood the exteriors of the houses were left untouched but inside they were furnished with all modern conveniences to serve as flats or shops.

It will be evident from the above that the city does not bear the main financial burden, but comes in with considerable sums to supplement federal measures where it thinks necessary. Many of its efforts are made for the tourist traffic, as was the introduction of the Vienna Festival, the costs of which it shares with the federation but itself paying two-thirds.

Another important aspect of the city's cultural policy is its endeavour to let the entire population profit from it. This means a lot of small-scale activity besides the more spectacular cultural projects. Thus the city encourages young artists and experimental work and gives assistance to various local undertakings. During the Vienna Festival it organizes local district festivals which are very popular. It maintains public libraries in all parts of Vienna and instituted adult colleges which offer courses or lectures in all fields of knowledge. The adult colleges are very successful and participation shows a rising tendency. In 1964–65, for example, 8,400 lectures were held with one million participants, and 4,800 courses with 110,000 students.

There are more than 25 scientific libraries in Vienna, the most famous being the National Library and the university library, with large and valuable collections. There are also eight universities and colleges among which, of course, the University of Vienna is the most prominent, as it is the oldest German university still in existence. In 1965 it celebrated the 600th anniversary of its foundation, while in the same year the Technical College commemorated its 150th anniversary. The universities and most of the libraries are federal, but the municipality also gives subsidies, and on the occasion of their jubilees generously endowed the university and the Technical College. The city also maintains its own scientific library. Among the 30,000 students in Vienna, 5,000 are foreigners, most of them studying in the School of Arts or the Medical School of the University or at the Technical College. The great number of foreign students, and the fact that Vienna attracts many foreign professors and has its own called to all parts of the world, gives proof of the great tradition of Vienna's colleges as well as their high standards and open-mindedness.

A great many tourists come to Vienna every year, attracted by its famous sights, cultural events and the beautiful surroundings of the Vienna Woods and the Danube. Vienna has also won renown as a centre for congresses. In 1967 more than 250 congresses were held in the city, and 1968 set a new record in this respect with three UN conferences. Vienna also accommodates the headquarters of several international organizations, among them the International Atomic Energy Agency (since 1956) and the Organization of the Petroleum Exporting Countries (since 1965). In 1967 the economic committee of the United Nations agreed to establish the United Nations Industrial Development Organization in Vienna. Their decision was prompted by a generous offer of the city, which promised to take care of the temporary accommodation of the organization and, furthermore, for a permanent residence supplied a beautiful park-land site near the Danube within easy reach of the city. The necessary buildings are to be erected jointly by the federation (which will pay 65 per cent of the costs) and by the city. A congress centre and several other facilities are planned for the same site, which covers twelve hectares, as an attraction for other organizations that might be prompted to settle in Vienna.

CONCLUSION

With the former imperial capital of Vienna, the Austrian Republic took over a precious heritage. The federal government tries to preserve and develop this heritage at all costs. The city for its part does its best to assist these endeavours. As for the legal status of the city, there are at present no serious proposals for a reform of the existing situation that would go beyond rationalization measures in administration.

The political scene is characterized by a rather lively competition between the capital and the federation, enhanced by the rivalry of the two great Austrian parties. Vienna is tied to the other provinces by common federal interests, but more often than not these are outweighed by specific interests. As the only Austrian metropolis and the capital city housing the federal authorities, Vienna's case is unique. This brings considerable advantages over the other provinces and municipalities: rich revenues, a high living standard, cultural leadership, and above all the special attention of the federation.

1 One Austrian schilling was worth about four US cents in 1970.
2 *Author's note:* Party representation in the city council changed somewhat after this essay was written, as a result of an election in April 1969. The Socialist party gained three seats and the People's party lost five, while the Communist party lost its two seats and the new Democratic Progressive party won three. As a result, the People's party lost the right to name one vice-mayor. Though it is still represented in the city's executive board with four department heads, the board has gained two more members. Despite this loss, the coalition was renewed. The Socialists' reason was that they did not wish to bear alone all the responsibility for unpopular measures. The People's party rejoined the coalition because otherwise its executive board members would not be elected as department heads.

In the elections of March 1970 to the Austrian national assembly, the Socialists gained the position of the strongest party. Nevertheless, in some cases, their cabinet was overruled by the opposition parties, which together held the majority. To clarify this situation new elections were held in October 1971. The Socialist party got 93 of the now 183 seats and with this the absolute majority (People's party 80, Freedom party 10 seats). This political change has brought hard competition: the Socialists try to establish themselves in their unprecedented position while the People's party is struggling to regain its old one or at least break the Socialists' majority.

As to Vienna, the number of Socialist voters increased less than elsewhere in Austria. A press campaign incriminating the mayor has hurt the image of the local Socialist party. Another handicap for Vienna's Socialists may be the fact that the federal government—although also socialistic—is not able or willing to fulfil all of Vienna's wishes. These factors have encouraged the Viennese People's party for the next city elections, due in 1973.

B Capitals in relatively centralized federations

Miodrag Jovicic **BELGRADE**

The capital of Yugoslavia, Belgrade, was the capital of the Serbian medieval state for a time in the fifteenth century, and after the formation of the new Serbia at the beginning of the nineteenth century it became her capital. Belgrade was also the capital of the unitary state of Yugoslavia from 1918 until her collapse in the Second World War. Today, it is the capital of the new, socialist Yugoslavia, which is organized as a federation of six member states. Thus, the choice of Belgrade as the capital of Yugoslavia has been strongly influenced by history. Not once in the life of Yugoslavia has the selection of another city as the capital been considered seriously.

Belgrade's characteristics

Belgrade is the largest city in Yugoslavia. The city proper has an area of 187 km². At the end of 1965 it had 697,000 inhabitants, and by the end of 1967 had 745,000. In population size it is followed by Zagreb (503,000), Skopje (228,000), Sarajevo (227,000), Ljubljana (182,000), Novi Sad (126,000), Rijeka (116,000) and Split (114,000).[1]

Besides being the largest administrative centre as the seat of federal organs and of a series of federal institutions, as well as of the organs of the member state of Serbia, Belgrade represents the largest scientific and cultural centre in the country. This is owing to a large system of scientific and cultural institutions and to a considerable concentration in Belgrade of scientific and cultural workers from the whole of Serbia, and even Yugoslavia.

Belgrade is not a typical industrial town, yet it has a considerable number of industrial enterprises (involving processing and light industries), and is a large commercial centre which includes a considerable number of foreign trade corporations, banks, insurance companies, representatives of foreign firms, etc. Some idea about the nature of Belgrade as an urban agglomeration can be gained from figures on the structure of employment in the city area. At the end of 1967 the total employment figure was 293,565, which was distributed as follows: industry 82,505, transport 26,277, construction 39,399, trade, hotel catering and tourist industries 48,694, crafts 21,476, farming 3,024, housing and communal activities 6,069, forestry 237, cultural and social activities 43,358, state organs and services 22,256.

NATURE OF THE FEDERATION

The Socialist Federal Republic of Yugoslavia is composed of six member states termed socialist republics: Bosnia and Herzegovina, Montenegro, Croatia, Macedonia, Slovenia, and Serbia.[2] Each socialist republic has its own constitution and its own legislation and authorities.

The 25-year history of the Yugoslav federation shows a constant evolution toward the strengthening of the federative principle. This evolution is reflected, first of all, in the constitutional achievements themselves. Comparing the first Constitution of socialist Yugoslavia (1946) with the Fundamental Law on the Bases of the Social and Political Organization (1953), the Constitution of 1963 and the latest Constitutional Amendments (1967), the federative principle is seen to have been increasingly implemented in the Yugoslav federation, i.e. the rights of its member states have increased constantly. However, even more important than the constitutional texts has been their practical application and the real functioning of the federative system. Centralistic tendencies have always receded in favour of decentralization.

Ethnic differences

Yugoslavia represents a multinational state comprising, besides the Yugoslav peoples, numerous national minorities. According to the last census (1961), Yugoslavia had 18,549,000 inhabitants (the figure rose to over 20,000,000 in 1967), including 7,806,000 Serbians, 4,294,000 Croatians, 1,589,000 Slovenians, 1,046,000 Macedonians, 514,000 Montenegrins, 973,000 Moslems (ethnic determination), and 317,000 nationally undetermined Yugoslavs. It is in fact such an ethnic structure of Yugoslav that led to the formation of a federation constituted by six member states wherein each Yugoslav people accounts for the great majority of the population. Only one of the member states – Bosnia and Herzegovina, which has a mixed population (1,406,000 Serbians, 842,000 Moslems, 712,000 Croatians, 276,000 nationally undetermined Yugoslavs, and so on) – lacks a distinct ethnic personality.

The languages of the Yugoslav peoples are three: Serbo-Croatian or Croato-Serbian, which is spoken by Serbians, Croatians, Moslems and Montenegrins; Slovenian; and Macedonian. All these languages, together with Bulgarian, make up the group of South-Slav languages. Two equal-status alphabets are used in Yugoslavia – the Cyrillic, used in Serbia, Macedonia, Montenegro, and parts of Bosnia and Herzegovina, and the Latin, used in Croatia, Slovenia and parts of Bosnia and Herzegovina.

As for the religion of the population, for which there are no recent official statistics, over one-half of the inhabitants of Yugoslavia (including, in the main, Serbians, Macedonians, and Montenegrins) are Orthodox and less than one-half are Catholic (to which persuasion mostly Croatians and Slovenians belong), Protestant, Mohammedan, and so on.

Thus, Yugoslavia is seen to be characterized by a complicated ethnic pattern, with differences in language, religion, etc., as its concomitants. Evidently, though, differences of a religious nature today have a relatively secondary importance while the ethnic and linguistic differences are not such as to jeopardize allegiance to the common Yugoslav state.

Political organizations

Yugoslavia today has no political parties in the conventional sense. In 1952 the Communist party of Yugoslavia – the only political party existing in post-war Yugoslavia – was converted into the League of Communists of Yugoslavia, as "the organized leading force of the working class and the working people in the buildup of socialism and the realization of the solidarity of the working people and the brotherhood and unity of the people" (The Constitution of the Socialist Federal Republic of Yugoslavia of 1963, Basic Principles, VI). The League of Communists of Yugoslavia represents a form of political organization which corresponds to the contemporary Yugoslav society, founded on the principles of self-government and direct socialist democracy. In 1966, the League of Communists of Yugoslavia had slightly over a million members.

However, the most massive political organization in the country is the Socialist Alliance of the Working People of Yugoslavia. Originating from the old People's Front, the Socialist Alliance represents "the widest platform of social-political activity and social self-government of the working people" (The Constitution of the Socialist Federal Republic of Yugoslavia, Basic Principles, V). Membership of the Socialist Alliance can be individual or collective (collective members include the social-political organizations, the League of Communists among them). Actually, the Socialist Alliance represents a kind of all-nation parliament, a unique free and open social forum, around whose socialist platform today (1968) are rallied over 8,000,000 members.

There are no obstacles in Yugoslavia to the full participation of employees in political activities. Like all other citizens employees are free to take part in political life, to belong to the League of Communists and to the Socialist

Alliance, or not to belong to them. In view of the application of the principle of self-government each citizen and, even more so, each employee, is expected to be an active participant in the process of self-government, to be interested in tracing and implementing policies. The political sympathies of the inhabitants of Belgrade reflect no significant differences compared with the inhabitants of other towns and generally with the rest of the population.

Local government

For an understanding of the position and organization of Belgrade, it is important to have some knowledge of Yugoslav local government in general.

The unit of local government is represented by the commune. In the Yugoslav system of what are termed social-political communities the commune represents "the basic social-political community," other social-political communities being the republics and the Federation.[3] According to the Yugoslav concept of local government, the commune exercises all those functions of the social community which are not expressly established by the constitution as the rights and duties of a republic or of the federation. To be able to discharge such functions a commune has to be large and strong. As a result of such a conception, at the beginning of 1968 Yugoslavia had only 509 communes, larger, on the average, than the communes found in other countries.

Save in the largest cities, Yugoslav communes consist of a number of separate urban and rural agglomerations. In other words, a great majority of Yugoslav communes have a mixed, urban-rural character. Hence, there is no need to distinguish between urban and rural local government, and in principle, all communes have the same status, organization, and powers.

This conception of the Yugoslav commune distinctly contrasts that of "one agglomeration – one commune" which still prevails in a majority of countries. However, in observance of the social reality, and so as to satisfy the needs of the citizens within the framework of the neighbourhoods where they are resident, local communities are established in the territory of communes. They do not represent a kind of micro-commune, that is, they have no organs with the attributes of authority, but the inhabitants themselves exercise direct self-government in the activities whereby certain joint needs are served. The existence of local communities, and particularly their activities (true, not especially great as yet) should assist the elimination of the basic deficiency of the communes: their remoteness from the citizenry.

The territorial division of the republics into communes is governed by republican law. The republican constitutions provide a possibility for the largest cities to be divided into several communes. This is explained by the need to find special solutions for large cities which are difficult to organize within the framework of a single commune. Since it is left to the republics to regulate this, considerable differences appear in this respect between cities, which otherwise are similar in size and potential. For example, Zagreb, the largest city in Yugoslavia after Belgrade, which previously contained several communes, has been constituted as a single commune since the beginning of 1967.

By Yugoslav standards, a major city is one with over 100,000 inhabitants, and there are several such cities in Yugoslavia. Basically their organization can be of three types depending upon the solution adopted by the republic concerned. First, some of these cities, such as Zagreb, Novi Sad, and Rijeka, constitute a single large integrated commune. In other words, the territory of the city as a social agglomeration, and the territory of the commune as a social-political community, coincide. Second, several of the major cities, including Skopje, Sarajevo, and Ljubljana, consist of a number of smaller-scale communes, and for attendance to tasks of common interest for the city as a whole separate city councils are established to which the communes from the territory of the town delegate some of their powers. Belgrade presents an exceptional case. The territory of the city as a social-political community is constituted by the territories of thirteen communes, of which nine are urban and four are suburban. The number of inhabitants of the urban communes ranges between 68,000 and 131,000, while the suburban communes, though larger in area, have fewer inhabitants.

In its conception, the whole Yugoslav system of local government is highly original, although it is not implied that the system represents a brand new invention and that in the course of its build-up no resort has been made to the experiences that comparative studies afford. The same also holds fully for Belgrade. A very important point is that the organizational formulae for the administration of the Yugoslav capital have constantly evolved in a ceaseless quest for superior solutions, better adapted to the needs of the capital. The resultant frequent changes cannot but render scientific research difficult and its results tentative. On the other hand the changes have the advantage of making for an increasingly apposite organizing of self-government in the capital.

THE GOVERNMENT OF BELGRADE

Belgrade is the capital both of the Socialist Federal Republic of Yugoslavia and of one of its six member states, Serbia. The Constitution of Yugoslavia, (Article 5) names Belgrade as the capital of Yugoslavia and the Constitution of Serbia (Article 10) establishes it as the capital of Serbia. The federal constitution contains no provision which directly relates to Belgrade. This conforms to the conception of the Yugoslav social-political system whereby all communes, both urban and rural, have the same status in the system, and basically indentical rights and duties. However, Article 102 of the federal constitution does provide the possibility for individual cities to consist of several communes. It lays down that in such a city a self-governing body may be constituted for attending to tasks of common interest to the city as a whole under the statute of the city and in conformity with the constitution and law of the relevant member state. The provisions of the said article are the only ones that affect Belgrade, if indirectly. The constitution of Serbia elaborates this provision of the federal constitution in its Articles 114–117. The provisions of Article 117 were abrogated on the entry into force of a special Serbian Fundamental Law on the Exercise of Rights and Discharge of Duties by Communes in the City of Belgrade, enacted on 28 December 1966.

Besides the mentioned constitutional texts, the basic law relating to the administration of Belgrade is the Statute of the City of Belgrade. Each commune has its own statute, which it enacts independently. A communal statute is known popularly as a "little communal constitution," because of the range of the subject matter covered. Belgrade's statute was enacted in March 1964. But in view of the provisions of the above-mentioned Fundamental Law, as well as those of the coincidentally enacted Fundamental Law on Abolition of Districts in the Socialist Republic of Serbia (28 December 1966), it became necessary to harmonize Belgrade's existing statute with the newly-created constitutional situation. This was done by adopting a new Statute of the City of Belgrade, on 16 May 1968.

Belgrade's two-tier system

As previously explained, Belgrade consists of thirteen communes, nine of which constitute the urban area proper while four have a suburban character. Thus, the city represents a unique social-political community. It is a community partly exercising the rights and discharging the duties of a commune as the basic social-political community of the Yugoslav system and partly performing tasks of common interest for the communes constituting it. By virtue of this singular character of Belgrade, its communes inevitably differ from other communes in Yugoslavia in the matter of rights and duties: in other words, Belgrade's constituent communes are also unique.

The communes forming the urban area proper exhibit the following specific features. In Yugoslavia generally, the boundaries of communes are established by the legislation of the member states (subject to consultation with and/or agreement of the communes themselves). Such, too, is the case with the four suburban communes of Belgrade. However, the boundaries of Belgrade's nine urban communes are established by the Statute of the City of Belgrade. In other words, the City Assembly, as the top authority in the area, effects the division of the urban territory proper into communes. This demonstrates the unique nature of the communes forming the urban territory proper.

By virtue of the unquestionable differences that exist between the nine communes within the urban territory proper and the remaining four communes, the rights and duties of the city in particular domains relative to these two groups of communes also differ. Actually, the city leaves some of its rights and duties in the four communes to the communes themselves. That is to say, these four suburban communes have a status more like that of the country's communes in general than do the nine urban communes.

Basically Belgrade has two kinds of functions. On the one hand, it has specified rights and duties as a commune, and, on the other, it has functions as a city constituted by an aggregate of communes. Thus, the city discharges all functions of a commune involving the planning and orienting of the social-economic, regional, urban, and demographic development of the city as a whole. The city government adopts plans and programs for the city's social, economic, regional, and urban development; it regulates all the more important relations in different domains of life, including the issuing of by-laws on taxes, duties, and other revenues, on public order and peace, and on communal sanitation; it attends to the establishment and promotion of services and organizations serving the town as a whole, and to meeting the common material, cultural, social, and other needs of the inhabitants and working organizations; and it creates the general conditions needed for economic development and the promotion of social activities.

The jurisdiction of the city as a community of communes covers, among others, the following services of integral importance to the city: water supply, heat, electricity, and other power supplies; the construction and maintenance of streets, roads, and other communications; the maintenance of public hygiene; the organization of public transport; and the development and utilization of urban land.

In addition, the communes perform the usual communal tasks under the system. They are directly responsible for the establishment and functioning of different institutions and services intended for satisfying the needs of the inhabitants in various districts of the town – primary schools, centres of culture, libraries, day nurseries, health centres, smaller-sized catering establishments, etc. The communes also perform a series of tasks derived from the jurisdiction of the organs of administration. This facilitates contacts between the inhabitants and the administration (incident to obtaining various attestations, certificates, licences, etc.).

The fact that Belgrade has the combined rights and duties of a commune and of the aggregate of communes within its territory makes it necessary for the assemblies of these communes to participate in the adoption of specified acts by the City Assembly. Thus, the agreement of a majority of the assemblies of the communes is required for the following acts of the City Assembly: (1) the regional development plan; (2) the general town development plan; (3) the program of the city's economic and social development; (4) the regulations on development of land; and (5) decisions on the distribution of the joint funds of the city and the communes. In the case of certain other acts (the decision to introduce public imposts, the determination of the types and amounts of revenues, the town budget), consulting with the assemblies of the communes is obligatory. The same holds for the domain in which the city and the communes perform specified tasks jointly. Other acts are issued by the City Assembly independently, yet this does not exclude the right of the communes to give their opinions and proposals in respect of matters regulated by such acts.

The City Assembly

As in all other communes, the top body of local government in Belgrade is the Assembly of the City of Belgrade. The Assembly consists of a City Chamber (100 councillors) and four chambers of working communities: the Economic Chamber (80 councillors), the Chamber of Culture and Education (50 councillors), the Chamber of Social Security and Health Protection (50 councillors), and the Chamber of Public Services (40 councillors).[4] In the case of all these chambers, their members are elected in the corresponding electoral units, those of the City Chamber being elected by all individuals enjoying suffrage and those of the other chambers by individuals employed in the relevant fields of social activity. The term of office of a councillor is four years, and one-half of the total number of councillors are elected every two years.

In spite of its five-house structure, as a rule the City Assembly performs its tasks through decision-making on a basis of equality, by two of the chambers only – the City Chamber (invariably) and the competent chamber of the working communities. Besides, the City Assembly deals with some matters at a joint meeting of all the chambers. And lastly, each chamber separately deals with certain matters within its own sphere of action.

The City Assembly has a president and several vice-presidents, elected from among the councillors for an official term of four years. The president is not an executive organ, and has no executive powers of his own. The president and the vice-presidents are salaried officers. Each chamber of the City Assembly also has its president. The Assembly and its chambers appoint standing and ad hoc commissions for the performance of specified duties, the preparation of proposals, and the execution of other tasks from the jurisdiction of the Assembly.

The political-executive bodies of the City Assembly for specified domains or branches of activity are councils, composed of members elected by the Assembly from among the councillors and other citizens. Each council has its own president and 14 members, elected for four years. There are councils for such matters as economy, planning and finance, urban development, housing and communal activities, internal affairs, and national defence. Finally, the organizational pattern of the city government includes organs of administration such as secretaries, institutes, and boards. The work of these organs is directed by the secretary of the City Assembly.

In keeping with the principle of rule by Assembly, which is applied to the organizations of authority on all levels, both the political-executive and the administrative organs are responsible to the Assembly of the city, which may remove from office the members of a council or the heads of the administrative bodies at any time. In other words, local executives are subordinated and answerable to the local parliament.

The pattern and character of the bodies in charge of the government of the capital is basically the same as in all other Yugoslav communes, with the following two major exceptions. First, as against the Belgrade City Assembly's five chambers, a majority of Yugoslav communes have only two chambers – the Communal Chamber and one unified Chamber of Working Communities (instead of four chambers of working communities as in Belgrade). This is a normal consequence of the under-developed nature of some domains of social activity in particular communes, as a result of which there would be no point in establishing special chambers. Second, in view of the considerably inferior number and complexity of the problems facing the governments of the smaller or less-developed communes it is natural that they should have fewer councils and commissions than has the City Assembly of Belgrade.

Control by higher authorities

The nature and range of the control exercised by the higher authorities of the federation and of the state of Serbia over local authorities on the territory of the capital is the same as in the case of any other local authority.

Basically, this control is two-fold. First, there is control of the constitutionality and legality of the by-laws issued by the local authorities, specifically by the City Assembly and its duly authorized organs. This control is exercised by the Constitutional Court of Yugoslavia, or by the Constitutional Court of Serbia, depending on whether it is a question of the conformity of these local prescriptions to federal or state laws. Second, there is control of the legality (in terms of administrative procedure but not the appropriateness) of decisions issued by local administrative authorities. The appropriate republican organs of administration consider appeals against such decisions.

Besides, if the local organs are failing to enforce the laws and regulations for which they are responsible, the organs of the member states – in this case Serbia – may directly ensure their enforcement through its own organs.

At all events, it is pertinent to emphasize that the local authorities of Belgrade are in no way subject to greater controls than other local authorities in the country.

FINANCES

We have already mentioned that Yugoslavia's system of social-political communities is made up of communes, member states, and the federation. The financing of all of them is governed by the federal Law on the Financing of Social-political Communities, which is applicable to Belgrade the same as to any other commune. Thus Belgrade does not enjoy any special status in respect of financing. In principle it has the same sources of revenue as the rest of the communes.

The sources of communal revenue are three: contributions, taxes, and duties. Contributions include those from personal income derived from employment, from agricultural activities, from independent exercise of craft, and other economic activities (self-employment), from independent provision of intellectual services, from copyright, patents and technical improvements, and the *contribution for use of town land (communal land tax)*. Taxes include the sales tax on goods and services and those levied on *income from buildings*, on *income from property and ownership rights*, on *implements for agricultural production work*, and on *income derived from the engagement of outside labour*. Duties include administrative duties, *communal duties*, and court duties. Among these revenues only those in italics represent exclusively communal revenues while the rest are joint revenues of the commune, the member state, and the federation, collected by the commune.

Of all these revenues two are by far the most important, viz., the contribution from personal income derived from employment and the sales tax on goods and services. Under the Budget of the City of Belgrade for 1968 (total revenue 351.5 million new dinars),[5] the first of these items accounts for 115 million (32.8 per cent) and the second for 142.2 million (40.5 per cent), which leaves 92.3 million (26.7 per cent) for all the rest combined.

All persons in employment within the city pay income tax in a percentage of their gross personal income. The percentage is mainly determined by the prescriptions of the member state, leaving certain minimal possibilities for the commune to change, i.e. increase, the tax rate to a slight extent in accordance with its needs. The greater part of the state-local share of this contribution goes to the member state. Thus in 1968, from the 26.2 per cent tax on gross personal income the state took 14.9 per cent and the city itself 11.3 per cent. The fact that a very large number of persons in Belgrade pay the contribution from personal income derived from employment therefore loses considerable impact. In other words, Belgrade does not have as much revenue from the large number of people who are employed by federal and state institutions as it would were it in a position to collect more of this contribution.

A similar situation exists in connection with the other most important revenue of the city, that derived from sales tax. It is a tax shared, in specified percentages, by the federation, the state, and the city. Once the federation and the state have fixed in advance the percentages which will be theirs, the city is left with no possibility to specify a major percentage as its share of the sales tax, or else the prices of goods and services would inevitably be caused to go up by an economically unjustified margin.

In dealing with the financial problems of Belgrade, it is pertinent to note two points. First is the position of Yugoslav communes in general. Under the terms of the constitution, the communes are the basic social-political communities with a series of rights and duties of essential interest for the social community as a whole. The constitution also lays down the right of the communes to establish their revenues and to allocate them. However, de facto the communes basically are financed persuant to the decisions of the higher levels of government and not to the decisions of the communes' own inhabitants, the communal authorities. This is because, in establishing their revenues, the communes are restricted by the detailed provisions of the revenue laws at the higher levels, and because the rates of the most important contributions and taxes, which make up by far the greatest part of the communal revenues, are restricted by the prescriptions of the federation and the respective member state. In other words, the material position of communes in Yugoslavia is generally unsatisfactory, and it has been causing them to demand – especially through their organization the Permanent Conference of Towns of Yugoslavia – an improvement of the system for financing communes and generally of their material position.

Second is the position of Belgrade itself. The generally unsatisfactory position of communes becomes only worse in the case of Belgrade. It is self-evident that the needs of Belgrade, as the capital both of Serbia and the federation, are far greater than those of other communes. Yet its possibilities to satisfy these needs remain basically the same as the others – inadequate. As a result, increasing demands have been raised to make an exception of Belgrade by adopting one of these alternatives: (a) that Serbia and the federation take less from the revenues of Belgrade, or (b) that they allocate extra funds to Belgrade for functions directly connected with its status as capital. For the time being, though, the problem remains unsettled and the material situation of Belgrade unsatisfactory.

ECONOMIC AND SOCIAL PLANNING

Belgrade has a City Institute for Social Planning, which is a special organ of the administration. It drafts programs and plans for adoption by the City Assembly. The most general plan of this type now in force is the Programme of Economic and Social Development of Belgrade 1966–70. On the basis of this programme different specific plans and programs are adopted, including the regional development plan, the general town plan, and the development plans for social services. At the end of each year the City Institute for Social Planning presents its analyses of the development of economic and other activities which the City Assembly uses, inter alia, to improve the planning for the succeeding year. Notwithstanding certain problems with which the capital is grappling, the development plans and programs of Belgrade are, in the main, being fulfilled.

Problems of growth

One of Belgrade's basic problems is the rapid growth of its population; more rapid, in fact, than that of a majority of other Yugoslav towns. From 320,000 in 1940, and 313,000 immediately after the Second World War, in 1945, the population of Belgrade (the city area proper) increased to 484,000 in 1955 and 730,000 in 1966. It is self-evident that such a quick rate of population increase resulting mainly from new-arrivals and much less from natural increase, has been causing a host of various problems which are difficult to settle quickly or effectively, problems whose solution calls for substantial financial resources. It is to be noted that this rapid population increase is owed most largely to Belgrade's being the capital of Yugoslavia and the seat of federal authorities as well as of a series of institutions and organizations whose proper place is in the capital. In other words, the problems being experienced as a result of the rapid population increase either would not exist or would be more readily solvable if Belgrade were not the capital of the country.

A FEDERAL DISTRICT?

As noted, the status and organization of Belgrade are governed by the laws of Serbia and by those of the city itself. We believe that the question of Belgrade as a Federal District cannot be considered seriously in Yugoslavia, and for three main reasons.

First, such a solution would be incompatible with the Yugoslav concept of federalism as a system with considerable and increasing powers of the member states. In Yugoslavia each state reserves the right to organize the system of authority on its territory, and surely so does Serbia in relation to Belgrade.

Second, the system of local government rests on certain premises of principle which are contained in the federal constitution, and while the states can adapt these premises to their conditions and needs, they cannot change them. Consequently the existing system of government for Belgrade probably represents the maximum adaptation of the unified conception of the Yugoslav commune to the specific conditions of the capital that the constitution will allow, a maximum beyond which it is impossible to go.

And third, the introduction of a special Federal District would be likely to be defied by memories of what was termed the Administration of the City of Belgrade, which existed in pre-war Yugoslavia during the 1931–41 period. With a status and organization different from the existing normal system of local government in the country and a considerably inferior degree of self-government, it served the then regime to "keep a stronger grip" on such a neuralgic point as a capital often represents.

1 Figures for the other cities are for the end of 1965.
2 The population of these republics was as follows about the middle of 1966: Serbia, 8,048,000; Croatia, 4,314,000; Bosnia and Herzegovina, 3,667,000; Slovenia, 1,662,000; Macedonia, 1,530,000; and Montenegro, 520,000.
3 The Republic of Serbia incorporates two autonomous provinces, Vojvodina and Kosovo. Established for specific purposes, primarily on account of being largely inhabited by national minorities, the provinces represent a cross between a commune and a republic. Until recently the Yugoslav system of authority included also districts as social-political communities, larger than the communes. However, in accordance with the needs of the republics, in 1957 districts began to be abolished and by the beginning of 1967 they had disappeared in all the republics.
4 Analogous chambers exist in the Federal Assembly and in the republican assemblies.
5 One new dinar was worth about eight US cents in 1970.

Muhammad Swaleh ISLAMABAD*

HISTORICAL BACKGROUND

After several decades of political see-saw, in the final phase, measures for the division of India were taken in bewildering haste. On 3 June 1947, His Majesty's government announced the plan under which two separate constituent assemblies could be formed for framing the constitution of two new states, Pakistan and India, the one consisting of areas having a preponderant Muslim population, and the other of the remaining parts of old India. The plan anticipated the actual transfer of power to the successor states by June 1948, or "at an even earlier date." But nobody then foresaw that it could be as early as the middle of August 1947. Reasons for this haste are not relevant to our subject, but the fact itself cannot be ignored, for, obviously enough, it greatly aggravated the complexity of the problems concerning the establishment of Pakistan's government. Not the least among them was the choice of a capital which could even temporarily house the new government without too much inconvenience.

Choice of Karachi

There is no record to show that the question of selecting the seat of the government was discussed among the leaders of the Muslim League party at any great length. It might not have been possible to do so, for at that moment the speed of decisions mattered more than the just balancing of their merits. All we know is that Karachi was chosen as the capital of Pakistan. Perhaps that was the only possible choice. Peshawar and Chittagong were too far at the extremities; Dacca had to accommodate the government and legislature of the province of East Bengal; Lahore was too near the Indian border; Rawalpindi had to house the headquarters of the Pakistan army. Perhaps a sentimental factor in favour of Karachi was that

---

* Since this essay was written, West Pakistan was divided into its four former provinces in April 1970, and early in 1971 Pakistan was plunged into a civil war and then rent asunder. The impact of these events upon the former legal status of Islamabad as the executive capital, and of Dacca as the legislative capital, is not yet clear.

it was the birth-place of the founder of the new state, Mohammad Ali Jinnah, popularly called the Quaid-e-Azam (great leader). It was, however, clear that the choice was only temporary, and the matter would receive fuller consideration at some later day.

From the 14th day of August, 1947, when Lord Louis Mountbatten gave over charge of the office of governor-general in respect of the territories comprising Pakistan to the Quaid-e-Azam, Karachi formally became the capital of the new state. After a few months of frantic effort at building hutments, procuring furniture and stationery, reconstructing records, reorganizing offices, and various improvisations, the government machine started functioning in a tolerably effective manner. Karachi was then a port city within the province of Sind and was also the capital of that province. Under the provisional constitution of Pakistan as contained in the Indian Independence Act, 1947 (10 & 11 Geo. 6, Ch. 30), the Government of India Act, 1935 (26 Geo. 5, Ch. 2), as adapted and modified by the Pakistan (Provisional Constitution) Order, 1947 (Governor-General's Order of 14 August 1947), Sind was an autonomous province within a federal scheme, and had its own government and legislature. Location of the federal capital in a city under the administrative and legislative jurisdiction of a province caused some uneasiness in the federal circles, partly because they soon anticipated and experienced conflicts between the federal and provincial interests, and partly because the example of centrally administered Delhi was too recent in their memories.

Confirmation of Karachi as capital

There was no point in losing time and waiting for serious frictions to appear. Moreover, Karachi was till then only a temporary capital and needed formal declaration for placing it on a permanent basis. On the 22nd of May 1948, Khwaja Shahabuddin moved the following resolution in the Constituent Assembly:

This Assembly resolves:

A that the capital of Pakistan shall be located at Karachi;
B that all executive and administrative authority in respect of Karachi and such neighbouring areas which in the opinion of the central government may be required for the purposes of the capital of Pakistan shall vest in and shall be exercised by or on behalf of the government of Pakistan, and the legislative power shall vest in the federal legislature; and
C that notwithstanding anything in any law for the time being in force, the government of Pakistan shall proceed forthwith to take such steps and adopt such measures as may be necessary to give effect to the purposes of this motion.

The debate on that motion is interesting and instructive. Nobody seriously opposed the continuance of the capital in Karachi, though several hinted that being a provincial capital and a fast-growing centre of commerce and industry, and for strategic and climatic reasons, it was not an ideal place for the country's capital. Comparative advantages and practical considerations weighed so heavily in favour of Karachi that there was no earnest search for another place. Still, two of the members, in a passing reference, suggested that the ideal place lay somewhere in the neighbourhood of Taxila, the seat of the Zoroastrian, Buddhist, and Greek empires in the centuries before the birth of Christ. Their passing suggestions proved prophetic, for it is in those very surroundings that Islamabad has been built.

It was the second clause of the resolution that raised the bitterest controversy and the mover of the resolution knew that it would. "It is regrettable," he said in the very beginning of his speech, "that in the past this question got mixed up with sentiment, prejudice and other extraneous factors leading to unpleasant controversy." In their provincial patriotism, members from Sind were strongly opposed to the severance of Karachi from that province, but all others favoured transfer of its executive and legislative control to the centre.

In their arguments against separation of Karachi, members from Sind largely relied upon the federal principle. According to them, the people of Sind were opposed to the separation of Karachi from their province. The Legislative Assembly of the province and the Council of the Sind Provincial Muslim League had both passed resolutions strongly opposing the move. There was no instance of a federal government having taken over a provincial capital without ascertaining the wishes of the people or legislature of the province. Karachi being the most important city of Sind and in fact of the whole of Pakistan, and a big and growing port, its loss would mean loss of revenue and opportunities to the province, which was already close to being a deficit province. The question of regular subvention of revenue from the centre to the province was also raised. The buildings taken over by the central government were estimated to cost about five hundred million rupees, and adequate compensation was demanded for them. The difficulties of retaining the provincial capital in Karachi after its control and jurisdiction had passed on to the centre were pointed out, and it was urged to be unavoidably necessary to build a new capital for the province, the cost of which would be met from the compensation demanded of the centre. And, if a new capital were to be built for the province, why should not the federal government make a new capital for itself? Besides, the buildings taken over from the provincial government were too small and inadequate for the purposes of the centre, and the latter would have to make their own capital ultimately; this would involve a very expensive duplication. It was also argued that continuance of Karachi within provincial jurisdiction after becoming capital of the country was not incompatible with the federal principle. While Delhi was an example of a centrally-administered capital, Calcutta had been the capital of the central provincial governments, while under the jurisdiction of the province.

Those who favoured the transfer of Karachi to the control of the centre regarded continuance of provincial jurisdiction over the city as subordination of the central government in many respects to provincial control, and therefore regarded it as inconsistent with the federal principle. They referred to the various kinds of conflict that provincial control might give rise to. They argued subordination of provincial interests to national interests and referred to the immense benefits that would accrue to the people of Sind in the fields of commerce and industry and government employment, if the capital remained in Karachi. Such benefits had accrued to the province of Bengal when Calcutta was the capital of India and later to the province of the Punjab when it shifted to Delhi. Members from every other province would welcome any move to shift the capital of Pakistan to their province. There was no attempt to advance positive arguments in support of transferring the control of Karachi to the federal government, perhaps because the position was too clear to need any arguments. As the Prime Minister, Liaquat Ali Khan, said, "If once you decide that Karachi should be the capital of Pakistan, then it is but natural that the administration of Karachi should be in the hands and under the control of the federal government."

Provisions for Karachi as capital

The resolution was adopted without division. Soon thereafter constitutional powers necessary for demarcating the area of the "capital of the federation" and securing its administration in the hands of the federal government were acquired by inserting Section 290-A in the Government of India Act, 1935 (26 Geo. 5, Ch. 2), by means of Governor-General's Order No. 22 of 1948 (22 July). That section read as follows:

Establishment of the Capital of the Federation
1 Notwithstanding anything contained in the preceding section, the Governor-General may by order demarcate, for purposes of the Capital of the Federation, an area forming part of a Province, and thereupon so much of the area as may be specified in the said order shall cease to form part of that Province.
2 The Governor-General may by order make, in respect of the area demarcated for purposes of the Capital of the Federation, such provisions
A for its government and administration;

B for varying the composition of the Legislature of the Province affected thereby and the representation in the Federal Legislature of that Province;
C with respect to the laws which are to be in force in the area;
D with respect to the jurisdiction, expenses or revenues of any court theretofore exercising the jurisdiction of a High Court in the area;
E with respect to appointments and adjustments of and in respect of, assets and liabilities; and
F with respect to other supplemental, incidental and consequential matters; as he may deem necessary or proper.

3 Any provision with respect to the jurisdiction of a High Court contained in an order made under this section shall be subject to the provisions of Chapter II of Part IX of this Act, except that the provisions of sub-section 1 of Section 230 and of sub-section 2 of Section 231 thereof shall not apply.

4 The Governor-General may by an order alter, amend or modify any order made under this section.

5 The executive authority of the Federation extends to the Capital of the Federation and any order made under this sub-section may be cancelled or superseded by an Act of the Federal Legislature.

6 An order made under this section may authorize expenditure from the revenues of the Federation.

[Sub-sections 5 and 6 of that section were added by the Government of India (Second Amendment) Act, 1950, with retrospective effect from July 22, 1948.]

The next day (23 July), the Pakistan (Establishment of the Federal Capital) Order, 1948 (G.G.O. No. 15) was made. In its preamble it invoked the resolution of the Constituent Assembly and Section 290-A of the Government of India Act, 1935. It provided for the demarcation of the area of the federal capital, and for the appointment of an administrator of Karachi by the governor-general to exercise executive authority on his behalf. This authority extended to matters contained in the provincial list in the Government of India Act, 1935 (26 Geo. 5, Ch. 2). That order continued in force for all enactments and laws and all notifications, orders, schemes, rules, forms or by-laws which were already in force in the demarcated area. It also provided for the apportionment of assets and liabilities between the federal government and the government of Sind. Karachi thus became the federal territory, or "the capital of the federation" as it was usually called. Thenceforward legislative authority in respect of it was vested exclusively in the federal legislature, and the executive authority continued to be exercised by the governor-general through his officers, till it ceased to be the capital of Pakistan. But the Chief Court of Sind continued to be the High Court for Karachi.

The Establishment of West Pakistan Act, 1955, passed by the Constituent

Assembly on 3 October 1955, which merged all the provinces and acceding states in the Western Zone into a single province named West Pakistan, expressly retained the special status and character of the capital of the federation. Section 2 (2) of that Act provided for its being "administered in accordance with the provisions of Section 290-A of the Government of India Act, 1935." However that act empowered the governor-general to establish, by order, a single high court for the new province by merging the High Court in Lahore, the Chief Court of Sind, and the Courts of Judicial Commissioners in the north-west frontier province and in Baluchistan. In the exercise of that power, the governor-general made the High Court of West Pakistan (Establishment) Order, 1955 (G.G.O. No. 19) on 8 October 1955. By that order, the Chief Court of Sind was merged in the newly established High Court of West Pakistan. The new high court was to sit at Lahore, but the high court was to have benches at Karachi and Peshawar and circuit courts at other places within the province of West Pakistan, consisting of such of the judges as were from time to time nominated by the chief justice. The chief judge and the other judges of the Chief Court of Sind became judges of the new high court. Besides the appellate, original, and other jurisdiction exercisable by the new high court, the bench at Karachi "shall have the same original civil jurisdiction for the civil district of Karachi and the same criminal jurisdiction and powers of the court of session for the sessions division of Karachi" as were formerly exercisable by the Chief Court of Sind. Thus very little substantial change was made in the administration of justice by the formation of the new province of West Pakistan or by the establishment of the new High Court of West Pakistan.

On the 23rd day of March, 1956, the Constitution of the Islamic Republic of Pakistan made by the Constituent Assembly came into force. Section 211 of that constitution relating to the federal capital read as follows:

211. *Federal Capital*
1 Parliament shall by law provide for the determination of the area of the Federal Capital, and until such a law is passed the area which immediately before the Constitution Day was comprised in the Capital of the Federation shall continue to be the Federal Capital.
2 The administration of the Federal Capital shall vest in the President who may, by Order, make such provision as he may deem necessary or proper
A for its government and administration;
B with respect to the laws which are to be in force therein;
C with respect to the jurisdiction, expenses or revenues of any court exercising the jurisdiction of a High Court therein;

D with respect to apportionments and adjustments of, and in respect of, assets and liabilities;
E for authorizing expenditure from the revenues of the Federation; and
F with respect to other supplemental, incidental and consequential matters.
3 Notwithstanding anything in the Constitution, Parliament shall have power to make laws for the Federal Capital with respect to matters enumerated in the Provincial List and matters not enumerated in any list in the Fifth Schedule, other than matters relating to the High Court.

Under sub-section (3) of that section, all legislative power for the capital, excluding matters relating to the High Court, was conferred on the Parliament. But sub-section (2) of that section was also interpreted as conferring full legislative power on the president in respect of the federal capital. And in exercise of that power the president did actually make several important laws named president's Orders. Among these were: the Karachi Courts Order, 1956 (P.O. No. 2 of 1956), which made provision for the establishment of a district court in Karachi and for appointment by the central government of the district judge and subordinate judges having jurisdiction in the capital; the Federal Capital (Essential Supplies) Order, 1956 (P.O. No. 3 of 1956), which provided for the control of the production, storage, supply, distribution of and trade and commerce in certain specified commodities; the Hoarding and Black-market Order, 1956 (P.O. No. 14 of 1956), which re-enacted in relation to the federal capital the expired Hoarding and Black-market Act, 1948 (XXIX of 1948); and the Karachi Development Authority Order, 1957 (P.O. No. 5 of 1957), which created an autonomous authority for the development and improvement of certain areas in the federal territory of Karachi. All these were in substance and form full-fledged laws. Thus while the 1956 Constitution remained in force the president exercised in relation to the federal capital legislative power concurrent and co-extensive with the power of the Parliament. The orders made by the president did not need ratification or re-enactment by the Parliament.

Article 224 of the 1956 Constitution had continued in force all laws (including ordinances, orders, rules and regulations), which were in force immediately before the commencement of that constitution, as far as applicable; and by virtue of this article the laws applicable to Karachi continued in force.

On the 7th day of October, 1958, Proclamation of Martial Law abrogated the 1956 Constitution. However, the Laws (Continuance in Force) Order, 1958, dated October 10, provided that notwithstanding the abrogation of the constitution by the proclamation and subject to any order of the president, or regulation made by the chief administrator of martial law, the republic to be known henceforward as Pakistan was to be governed as nearly as may be in accordance with the late constitution. Article 4 of that order continued in force (with the exceptions of the constitution and certain specified laws) all laws in force immediately before the abrogation of the constitution. The laws applicable to Karachi also continued in force. During the period of martial law the president exercised legislative power in relation to the federal territory and he made a few ordinances to apply in the Federal territory, like Control of Orphanages (Karachi Division) Ordinances 1958, and the University of Karachi Ordinance, 1962. But there was little change in the administrative system of the territory.

THE NEW CAPITAL

The idea of building a new capital had been in the minds of the successive governments since independence. A few locations were considered, one or two even selected, but there was no progress beyond that, partly due to want of agreement on the site of the new capital and partly due to the instability and indecision of the governments. In 1958, when President Ayub took over power, all plans for development and economic progress received an acceleration, and the plan to erect a capital was no exception. The desire to have a proper capital for the country was in the heart of the people, and President Ayub shared that feeling with full passion. Conscious of the rich heritage of the people, and determined to shape a respectable present and a prosperous future, he was eager to build a city which would not only provide an adequate seat of government, but also reflect the nation's identity and cultural distinction. "The capital of a country," he said, "has to encompass much bigger vistas and provide light and direction to the efforts of the people. It must be located in the best possible surroundings."

In 1959 a Site Selection Commission was appointed to consider whether Karachi was suitable as a capital from the point of view of location, climate, availability of adequate supply of food and water, communications, and defence and, if Karachi were found unsuitable, to recommend another site for the capital. After a thorough examination of all aspects of the question, the commission unanimously recommended the terraced table-land of the Potwar plateau, near Rawalpindi, as the site for the new capital. In June 1959 the central government accepted the recommendations of the commission and took the momentous decision to build the national capital, which was later named Islamabad.

In September 1959 the Federal Capital Commission was formed and entrusted with the task of preparing a master plan, which it did by October 1960. The master plan fixed the location of the site, the successive stages of development and its relations with the surrounding areas. It divided the entire area of the site into various sectors.

The Capital Development Authority

In June 1960 an ordinance (XXIII of 1960) was promulgated to establish a Capital Development Authority for the planning and development of Islamabad within the framework of a regional development plan. In September of that year the authority was created and entrusted with the gigantic task of building up the new capital. The authority is a body corporate. The general direction and administration of its affairs vest in a board consisting of not less than three members appointed by the central government. In the discharge of its functions, the board is required to act on sound principles of development, town planning, and housing. On questions of policy it is to be guided by the directions of the central government.

In the schedule of the ordinance, the limits of the capital site and of the "specified areas" to which the capital site may ultimately extend are provided. In these areas the authority can acquire property on payment of compensation. A special procedure has been laid down in the ordinance for expeditious determination of the compensation and for the disposal of appeals in this connection.

The authority is empowered to make a master plan for the development of the capital site and similar plans for the rest of the specified areas. These plans must, however, be submitted to the central government for approval. The authority is also empowered to call upon any local body or agency operating in the specified areas to prepare, in consultation with the authority, a scheme in respect of any of the following matters:

A land use, zoning, and land reservation;
B public buildings;
C industry;
D transportation and communications; highways, roads, streets, railways, and aerodromes;
E tele-communications, including wireless, television, radio, and telephone;
F utilization of water, power, and other natural resources;
G community planning, housing, slum clearance, and amelioration;
H community facilities, including water supply, sewerage, drainage, sewage disposal, electricity supply, gas supply, and other public utilities;
I preservation of objects or places of historical or scientific interest or natural beauty.

The central government may alter the aforesaid list or add to it by means of a notification published in the official Gazette. The expenditure incurred on the preparation of any such scheme is to be apportioned between the authority and the local body or agency according to their mutual agreement. In the event of disagreement between them the matter is to be referred to the central government for decision. No planning or development scheme can be prepared by any person or by any local body or agency except with the concurrence of the authority. The authority may also prepare schemes relating to the aforesaid matters. These schemes should, however, follow the master programme.

All the necessary powers for the development of the capital site and for construction of the capital have been vested in the authority. In particular it has the power to acquire land, to incur any expenditure, procure plant, machinery, instruments, and materials, enter into contracts and cause studies, surveys, and technical researches to be made.

The authority may appoint such officers, servants, experts, and consultants as it may consider necessary for the performance of its functions. In the case of higher appointments, however, approval of the central government is needed.

Finances for the construction of the capital and other activities of the authority are supplied by the Capital Development Authority Fund. The fund consists of:

A grants made by the central government;
B loans obtained from the central government;
C grants made by local bodies;
D sale proceeds of movable and immovable property, and receipts for services rendered;
E loans obtained by the authority with the special or general sanction of the central government;
F foreign aid and loans obtained from the International Bank for Reconstruction and Development or from any other source outside Pakistan, with the sanction of, and on such terms as may be approved by, the central government; and
G all other sums receivable by the authority.

The authority is required to submit each year to the central government for approval a statement of the estimated receipts and expenditure in Pakistan rupees. Likewise a statement of the estimated receipts and expenditures in foreign currencies must also be submitted. All schemes costing more than two and a half million rupees require the government's specific sanction. Accounts of the authority were audited by auditors appointed by the central government in consultation with the comptroller and auditor general of Pakistan.

Progress of construction

The development and construction of Islamabad actually began in 1961. By the middle of 1968, the following progress had been made: more than 43,000 acres of land had been acquired; eight office blocks had been completed and occupied by the central ministries; more than 7,000 houses had been built; over 125 miles of roads had been completed and 125 bridges had been constructed; water supply of more than ten million gallons daily had been provided; Hotel Shehrzad (275 rooms) and Government Hostel (168 rooms) had been built; eight shopping centres had begun to function; and several schools, colleges and hospitals had begun to run. The population at that time was about 60,000 and growing very rapidly; it may reach 500,000 by 1980.

Municipal functions

With the sudden increase in population the question of municipal functions became important. The Capital Development Authority Ordinance of 1960 had to be amended in 1966, in order to confer upon the authority all powers and functions which are exercised and performed by a municipal committee elsewhere under the Municipal Administration Ordinance of 1960. The central government was to be the controlling authority in relation to the municipal functions entrusted to the authority. This is, however, a purely transitional arrangement. While rapid development and construction is apace all over the area and the population of the town is constantly on the increase, it is not feasible to create a properly representative elective municipal body; nor is it desirable in the interest of co-ordinated activity to entrust the control of the municipal functions to any individual or organization other than the Capital Development Authority itself. Sub-section 1 of Section 15A of the ordinance by which these functions were conferred upon the authority reads as follows:

Municipal functions. During such period and for such areas within the Islamabad Capital Territory as the Central Government may, by notification in the official Gazette, specify, the Authority may, notwithstanding anything contained in any other law for the time being in force, exercise, and perform such powers and functions as a Municipal Committee may exercise and perform in relation to a municipality under the Municipal Administration Ordinance, 1960 (x of 1960).

This clearly implies that the arrangement is purely temporary and that local self-government will ultimately devolve upon the inhabitants of Islamabad, as it does elsewhere in Pakistan.

Constitutional foundation

In June 1962, when the Constitution of the Islamic Republic of Pakistan came into force, the federal capital was given a constitutional foundation. Under this constitution Pakistan continued to be a federation of two provinces, West and East Pakistan, which are geographically far apart. Of the country's total population, 93.7 million in 1961, 42.9 million lived in West Pakistan and 50.8 million in East Pakistan. Article 211 of the constitution reads as follows:

The Capitals
1 The Capital of the Republic shall be Islamabad situated in the district of Rawalpindi in the Province of West Pakistan at the site selected for the Capital of Pakistan before the enactment of this Constitution.
2 The area of the Capital (in this Constitution referred to as "the Islamabad Capital Territory") shall be determined by the Central Legislature, but shall not be less than two hundred square miles.
3 There shall be a second Capital of the Republic at Dacca in the Province of East Pakistan.
4 The area of the second Capital (in this Constitution referred to as "the Dacca Capital Territory") shall be determined by the Central Legislature.
5 The principal seat of the National Assembly shall be at Dacca.
6 The principal seat of the Central Government shall, subject to clause 7 of this Article, be at Islamabad.
7 Until provision is made for establishing the Central Government at Islamabad, the principal seat of that Government shall be at Rawalpindi in the Province of West Pakistan.

Under clause 2 of this Article, the Capital of the Republic (Determination of Area) Ordinance, 1963 (IV of 1963), which was promulgated on 26 October 1963, demarcated a total area of 350 square miles within the District of Rawalpindi as the area of the Capital of the Republic.

The legislative power in respect of the Islamabad Capital Territory and the Dacca Capital Territory was conferred upon the central legislature by clause 4 of Article 131 of the constitution. This was, however, not an exclusive power. West Pakistan can also legislate for the Islamabad Capital Territory and East Pakistan for the Dacca Capital Territory in the provincial field, that is to say on subjects not covered by the central legislative list contained in the Third Schedule of the constitution. In the case of inconsistency between a central law and a provincial law, the central law would prevail and the provincial law would, to the extent of the inconsistency, be invalid. By the middle of 1968, no central law, with the exception of the Islamabad (Preservation of Landscape) Ordinance, 1966 (III of 1966), and the University of Islamabad Act, 1967 (XIV of 1967), had been made exclusively for the Islamabad Capital Territory, and all laws, both central and provincial, in force in the district of Rawalpindi applied to the Territory. Civil and criminal law, and laws relating to the judiciary, police, labour, education, and health were the same as in force in the rest of West Pakistan, and the courts and executive authorities concerned with these subjects were also under provincial control. There seems to be little likelihood of the centre at any time resorting to large-scale legislation for the administration of the capital territory except in so far as may be necessary to resolve conflicts between the centre and the province.

THE SECOND CAPITAL

A word should be added about the legislative capital of Pakistan, the principal seat of the National Assembly. It is a township adjacent to Dacca, the provincial capital, and is named Ayub Nagar. It, too, is under rapid construction. By the middle of 1968, a hostel for the members of the National Assembly and residential houses for the staff of the National Assembly Secretariat had been built. Substantial progress had been made on the works relating to the National Assembly building, residences for the speaker and deputy speaker, and hostels for officers. The municipal functions of the Dacca capital territory continue to be performed by the Dacca Municipal Corporation. All the central and provincial laws in force in Dacca apply to the Dacca Capital Territory and no special laws have been made for that territory.

David Harner KUALA LUMPUR

Kuala Lumpur, capital of the Federation of Malaysia, is located near the west coast of Malaya at the confluence of the Gombak and Klang rivers, some twenty-five miles inland from the Straits of Malacca. The first permanent settlement was established at this site about 1857. It was established as the supply point for the many developing tin mines inland. Apparently this was the highest point at which supplies could be conveniently landed by boat.

THE CAPITAL AND THE NATION

By an 1874 treaty between the British government of the Straits Settlements and the Sultan of Selangor, a British resident went to Selangor with broad protectorate authority. His residence was in Klang (seventeen miles west of Kuala Lumpur), the long-time capital of Selangor. The State of Selangor named Kuala Lumpur its capital in 1880. When four of the states of Malaya were constituted a federation (the Federated Malay States) in 1895, with a British resident general, Kuala Lumpur became the capital. This continued until 1942 when Malaya was occupied by Japan during World War II. After the war, the British proposed to establish a Malayan Union to replace the Sultanates and to take the reins of government from the British Military Administration (set up in September 1945 after the Japanese surrender). The Union had a short existence from 1946–48 (due primarily to Malay opposition) with Kuala Lumpur continuing as capital. The Federation of Malaya, with Kuala Lumpur still the capital, was the successor to the Malayan Union.

The federation's first elections to the Federal Legislative Council were held in 1955. An independent Constitutional Commission was appointed in March 1956. The commission, headed by Lord Reid, included British, Australian, Pakistani and Indian members. Its report, on which the new Malaysian constitution was ultimately based, was published in February 1957. The Reid Report proposed that Kuala Lumpur remain the capital. It further proposed that the development and administration of the capital be under the control of the federal government. Malaya's independence from Great Britain, and the new constitution, took effect on 31 August 1957.

Kuala Lumpur became capital of still another political unit on 16 September 1963. At that time, a new federation called Malaysia came into existence from a merger of the colonies of North Borneo (now Sabah) and Sarawak and the State of Singapore with the existing states of Malaya. Singapore later separated from Malaysia under the Independence of Singapore Agreement concluded between the two countries on 9 August 1965. After this, Malaysia was made up of thirteen states, which had a total population of about 10.5 million in 1970.

The federation is an elective monarchy. The sovereign, the *Yang Di-Pertuan Agong* (Malay for "the Supreme Ruler"), is elected by and from among the Malay Rulers (known as the Conference of Rulers) for a term of five years. But the parliamentary system is in effect. Although executive authority is formally vested in the Yang Di-Pertuan Agong, for all practical purposes this authority is in the hands of a prime minister and his cabinet, who are responsible to the legislature – a system of government largely patterned after that of Great Britain. The states have a similar system, in which the ruler (or governor) is only the formal executive.

The state legislatures are unicameral, while the federal legislature is bicameral. The upper house, the Senate, consists of 58 appointed members while members of the House of Representatives are directly elected from single-member constituencies. The legislative assembly of each state chooses two senators, and the Yang Di-Pertuan Agong appoints the other 32. Principal legislative powers are vested in the House of Representatives. The Senate can debate and delay, but cannot prevent, legislation.

Three legislative lists are appended to the constitution as the "Ninth Schedule." These are a "Federal List," a "State List," and a "Concurrent List." Subjects on the last-mentioned list can be dealt with on a federal and/or a state basis. All other matters are reserved to the government listed. When a state law is inconsistent with a federal law the state law is void but only to the extent of that inconsistency.

Early local government

Kuala Lumpur's first formal status as a local government came in 1890, when it acquired a Sanitary Board. The formal name was later changed to Town Board. In March 1948, Kuala Lumpur was elevated to the status of a Municipal Commission, the third municipality in Malaya, under the provisions of the Straits Settlement Municipal Ordinance. Under this ordinance, Kuala Lumpur became, for the first time, financially autonomous.

Even so, the municipal commissioners were all appointed by the Ruler of the State of Selangor.

The Local Authorities Elections Ordinance of 1950 provided that the majority of councillors should be elected in cities which had municipal councils (then only two in number). In the case of other local governing bodies, election was provided as a possibility open to the discretion of each state. No local government officials had been elected in Malaya from 1913 until 1951. Although there is evidence that some communities had some form of election prior to 1913, these apparently involved small segments of the population. After 1951, the majority of local government officials were still appointed although elected ones replaced appointed ones in many local governments.

Kuala Lumpur was given a constitution providing for twelve elected and six nominated members to start its operation as a Municipal Council in 1952. Elected members were to serve overlapping three-year terms with elections to be held annually. The city therefore had seven elections from 1952 to 1958. The most significant one was that of 1952, which witnessed the birth of the alliance. Two national parties formed an "alliance" to contest the municipal elections. Success (all local seats were won by the Alliance) encouraged it to aim higher. Before the 1969-70 elections the Alliance (by then including three parties) held 89 out of 104 federal seats and 240 out of 282 state seats.

Local elections throughout the country were suspended by the federal government in 1959. This was preparatory to parliamentary action on a new Local Government Elections Act. The act, approved in 1960, transferred responsibility for local elections from the states to the Elections Commission and established uniform qualifications for voting. Previously there had been varied qualifications for local election registration. Nationally, the right to vote exists for all resident citizens.

The suspension of local elections in the capital became permanent when the federal government assumed administrative control of the capital on 1 April 1961. This resulted from the Federal Capital Act of 1960, which dissolved the municipal council, and placed Kuala Lumpur under the control of a minister and a federally appointed commissioner. Although opposition party members had been elected to the council, majority control of the council was still firmly in the hands of the Alliance at the time of the Act.

Economic significance

The economic significance of Kuala Lumpur and its metropolitan region is difficult to assess in precise terms. Statistical economic information is rather limited and not available on an area basis. Certainly the west coast of Malaya is more highly developed and has a higher income than the east coast. Nearly 80 per cent of the cities and towns over 10,000 in population are located in the western coastal plain. The important sea ports (including one very near Kuala Lumpur), rubber plantations, tin mines, oil palm and rice cultivation, and factories are concentrated there.

Kuala Lumpur and its metropolitan area is growing at a more rapid rate than any of the other Malaysian population centres. The city's population increased from 46,700 in 1911 to 176,000 in 1946, and to 316,200 in 1957. Population estimates for 1968 (in the absence of a census since 1957), varied from 400,000 to 525,000. Estimates for the total metropolitan area ranged from 600,000 to 800,000.

Malaysia's second largest city, Georgetown (250 miles north of Kuala Lumpur and commonly known as Penang), had a 1968 population of about 300,000 within its boundaries. Next in size, Ipoh (130 miles north of the capital), had a 1968 population of some 150,000. On the other hand, the city-state of Singapore had a population nearing two million. Although not a part of Malaysia, Singapore adjoins Malaysia and is only 250 miles from the capital.

These figures help to show that Kuala Lumpur is not a primate city. It is not super-eminent in size and influence, and it does not dominate the business, political, and intellectual life of the country. It is, however, quite important in the life of Malaysia, and this importance is increasing. Besides being a governmental centre, the metropolitan region is a national centre for education and research. It is also the most important national site for finance, commerce, and industry.

It could be argued that the city's economic growth and importance resulted from many years as capital of the federation. Without doubt, major economic benefits have resulted from this factor. Still, Kuala Lumpur was first established as a business centre. It is near the geographical centre of the heavily populated areas of the country, is the centre of land and air transportation facilities and has a large port within the metropolitan region. These factors afford considerable attraction to business.

THE FEDERAL CAPITAL ACT OF 1960

Provisions of the act

In 1960 the Minister of the Interior, Dato Suleiman bin Dato Abdul Rahman, presented to the Federal House of Representatives a bill titled, "An Act to provide for the Local Government of the Federal Capital and for matters incidental thereto." Generally, the act provided for the federal government to assume administrative control of the capital. However, the act did not establish a Federal District or territory. That is, land ownership, until alienated (transferred from state control by some legal means), remained with the Sultan of Selangor. This meant, in effect, that the land was held by the State of Selangor in its corporate capacity.

Although the act provided that the municipal council be dissolved, Kuala Lumpur remained a municipality, and its corporate powers were not markedly changed. Most of these powers were entrusted to the commissioner of the federal capital, who reports to a federal minister. At first this was the Minister of the Interior, who was then responsible for local government, and after 1964 the new Minister of Local Government and Housing. The minister has powers to issue general instructions, and is responsible to Parliament on federal capital matters. The commissioner is selected by the cabinet and formally appointed by the supreme ruler for a term of five years (subject to removal at any time by the appointing authority). He is assisted by an Advisory Board of eleven, five of whom are appointed as above. In addition to those appointed, six federal civil servants are ex-officio members of the board. The commissioner is not required to accept the advice of the board, but he must record his reasons in the municipality minutes if the advice tendered is rejected.

The parliamentary debate

During introduction of the bill for debate, Dato Suleiman said:[1]

At the April [1960] meeting of this House, Article 154 of the Constitution underwent a major amendment which when brought into force will result in the transfer of the legislative and executive authority over the Federal Capital to the Federal Government. I think everyone in this House agrees that Kuala Lumpur has progressed rapidly during the last decade and the more so since Independence. Its population has grown, by leaps and bounds, from a population of approximately 225,000 in 1950 to an estimated total of 360,000 in 1960. Further, with the active participation of the Federation in international affairs, the Federal Capital has increased in importance and prestige. A number of international conferences has been held here, and a number of state visits by foreign dignitaries have been made. Indeed, the Federal Capital has become the centre of our national pride, and the cynosure of all eyes, at least in South-east Asia. Its further progress has become not merely the concern of the local government of Kuala Lumpur or even of the State of Selangor, but of the nation as a whole.

Noting the magnitude of problems to be faced as a result of rapid population increases together with increases in importance and prestige, the minister continued:

The Federal Government with its many technical officers and resources is in a better position to control the development of this growing town than the state government.

He called attention to the 1956 report of the Reid Commission (the independent Constitutional Commission), and quoted from this report the following:

We do not think it practicable to make Kuala Lumpur federal territory and we have no presentation that this should be done. But we think that the federation ought to be able to control the development and administration of its capital and seat of government. We therefore recommend that the federation and not the State of Selangor should have the power to legislate with regard to local government and town planning of Kuala Lumpur, and that for administration that municipality should be directly under the federation.

Later, other speakers for the bill argued that extra expenditures are required in a federal capital. These expenditures could only be made through taxes paid by all the taxpayers in the whole country. Therefore, everyone in the country should have a voice in running the capital through administration by federal rather than local government. Other nations having a federally governed capital were pointed to as examples. It was stated that both the United States and Australia have found this system most satisfactory and have retained it over many years.

Debate on the bill lasted for a number of hours, extending well into the second day. Members of the Alliance (a coalition of political parties with a strong majority in Parliament) spoke for the bill. Most of the time of opposing speakers was used by members of the Socialist Front. Representatives of other parties also appeared to oppose the bill.

Those speaking against the bill based their principal objection on the loss of voting rights by citizens of Kuala Lumpur insofar as municipal elections were concerned. Among other things, the opening Opposition speaker, Mr K. Karam Singh, said:

We find that the Honourable Minister has brought in a lot of high sounding words and talked a lot about local government; he also talked about different local governments and propagated local government in our land. However, here in this case he comes in wielding an axe on the strongest seat of local government in our country.

Later, Mr Singh said:

... now we have two elected councillors in the elected Municipal Council and they are causing enough sleepless nights to the Alliance, and what would be their discomfiture, what would be their panic if the whole council in Kuala Lumpur, or at least a greater part of it, is filled by Socialist Front councillors? That, Mr Speaker, Sir, is the guiding and motivating factor in bringing up this Bill. I submit that this Bill is cowardly in its purpose, and it is motivated by political fears.

Another speaker, Mr V. David, presented a rather different charge:

The Bill itself has embodied the various provisions and explains by itself that it is nothing but a mouthpiece of the Alliance Government, for these provisions would enable the Minister of the Interior to assume the role of sole dictator. . . . The Commissioner is appointed to serve the interests of the Minister, and the Members of the Board are appointed to serve the interests of the Commissioner.

Later, Mr David said:

The powers of the Kuala Lumpur Municipality will not any more rest in the hands of properly and constitutionally constituted Members elected by the People of Kuala Lumpur, but the powers and the destiny of Kuala Lumpur town will rest in the office of the Honourable Minister of the Interior. Sir, as we all know, all powers are corrupt and absolute powers corrupt absolutely. The whole thing, according to this Bill, will be tackled and handled by a single person without any consideration for the aspirations and views of the taxpayers of the Kuala Lumpur town. Sir, centuries ago, we heard and read that people in the various parts of the world had been fighting for representation in the various Legislatures and a cry had been heard that "no taxation without representation," but Kuala Lumpur today is going to be facing the same fate, where there is not going to be any representation while taxation is on.

Mr David then referred to the suspension of local elections in 1959:

The moment the Alliance knew, Sir, that they can no more hoodwink the people of Kuala Lumpur, who are civic conscious and who are conscious of what is going on in Kuala Lumpur, and that they will not return the Alliance Members to the Council, a sudden and surprising stop was put to Elections in Kuala Lumpur as well as all over the Federation with a lame excuse that the Electoral Rolls were not in order.

Finally Mr D.R. Seenivasagam called attention to clause 15(4), which reads:

The Yang Di-Pertuan Agong may by notification in the Gazette from time to time divide the municipality into districts or other subdivisions and exempt from the operation of this Act or of any written law affecting the municipality such place or places within the boundaries of the municipality as may be specified in such notification.

Referring to this sub-clause, Mr Seenivasagam said,

Surely, then, one must infer from these peculiar clauses in this Bill, I say, wrongful motives on the part of the Government to take over the Municipality of Kuala Lumpur.

Enactment and review

After various other charges and counter-charges, the House resolved itself into a committee on the bill. The committee reported the bill with one minor amendment (changing the title of the commissioner as written in Malay). After that time, on 13 September 1960, the bill was read the third time and passed.

It seems clear that fear of the possibility of partisan actions of an extreme nature, by some future municipal council of Kuala Lumpur was an important reason for passage of the act. However, contrary to the inferences and statements of the Opposition, this did not appear to be a simple fear of loss of face if a municipal election were lost in the capital. Rather, it was based on the delicate political situation prevailing in the country. It was generally feared that an extremist council with Communist or racist leanings might some time be elected. If this happened, municipal officials and powers could be used to embarrass the federal government, foreign dignitaries, and other official visitors to the capital. This might, for example, take the form of encouragement of unruly demonstrations or closing of streets just before their planned use by a cavalcade.

LOCAL GOVERNMENT IN MALAYSIA

Municipal councils and other forms

The powers and responsibilities of Kuala Lumpur, as the Municipality of the Federal Capital, can be fully understood only as compared with the powers and responsibilities generally available to local governments in Malaysia. The most realistic comparison would be with those having municipal councils. This was the Kuala Lumpur status immediately prior to the Federal Capital Act. Many authorities still place Kuala Lumpur with the municipal councils for purposes of classification.

There are several levels of local government in urban areas of Malaysia. These range from units which are little more than departments of the state governments through several variations to relatively autonomous units. In the former, all governing officials are appointed by the ruler of the state, which in effect means by the state premier and his cabinet. All tax rates and most other local charges are set by the state legislature, expenditures can only be made with state approval, employees are state officers, seconded from the state or state appointed, and powers and services are few in number.

There are two municipal councils in Malaysia. In addition, one city (Georgetown) has a city council with identical powers. Municipal councils are financially autonomous statutory corporations whose membership is elected. They are more independent of services rendered by the federal and state governments than other local authorities. They employ their own staff, set their own budgets and tax rates, and are largely self-contained entities, operating within a rather wide range of powers conferred on them by national legislation. Their activities include public works, public housing (for which federal funds are distributed by the states), cultural activities, certain health services (such as sanitation inspections and abatement of nuisances), refuse collection and disposal, sanitary sewerage, parks and recreation, town planning, and building and zoning controls. This list expands for individual municipalities. For instance, Georgetown provides public transport (transit), electrical generation and distribution, water supply and distribution, and pre-natal, post-natal, and child care.

The role of higher governments

The activities of municipal councils are relatively unrestricted within the limits of their finances. They are usually dependent upon the states for fire protection, water supply and distribution, public transport, land for municipal use, and certain minor aids and controls. The federal government is responsible for electrical service (through a statutory board), health care, police protection, education, training and advice for the fire authorities (the states), some welfare services, and loan funds to local authorities.

The federal department of Town and Country Planning, within the portfolio of the Minister of Local Government and Housing, provides an advisory service to the federal and state governments and local authorities on all planning matters. Also, this department is responsible for planning advice to the Municipality of Kuala Lumpur and for the preparation of master plans.

KUALA LUMPUR UNDER FEDERAL CONTROL

Although the Federal Capital Act abolished Kuala Lumpur's elected governing council, the residents continue to elect representatives to the higher levels of government. One federal constituency is wholly within the city limits and three others are partially within the city. Unlike in a Federal District, the residents also elect members to the legislature of the state. There are seven state constituencies of concern, of which two are located wholly within the city limits.

The Federal Capital Act did not result in major changes of municipal personnel or services. The former municipal staff remained in the civic service with the same rights and privileges. Acceptance of responsibility for fire prevention and control resulted in the immediate establishment of a fire brigade. There is no special nation-wide municipal service and therefore very little mobility. In spite of this, Kuala Lumpur appears to have attracted essentially capable people to fill municipal positions. As a consequence, promotion opportunities are few and promotion tends to be slow. The city salary structure partly explains the ability to attract capable personnel. A limited survey of salaries indicates that municipal salaries at the higher administrative level exceed state and federal salaries at comparable levels.

The town planning section was integrated with the federal Department of Town and Country Planning in 1956. Staff salaries and other expenses are still an obligation of the municipality, but the commissioner of Town and Country Planning was assigned administrative responsibility for these personnel. The State of Selangor also has a planning section. The highest officers in this section are federal civil servants.

Elimination of the intervening layer of the state with respect to housing has increased city powers in the development of low-cost housing projects. Kuala Lumpur completed 3,055 low-cost residential units and 93 low-cost shops from 1956 through 1965. Of these, 2,156 residential units and 20 shops were completed since adoption of the act. Total cost of all these projects was M$16.3 million.[2] As in other municipalities, these costs were borne by the federal government.

The State of Selangor provides water to the residents of Kuala Lumpur. It also maintains, at federal expense, a few miles of state roads within the city. These roads were constructed prior to the act. Most important, Selangor retains ownership and control over the sale or leasing of all unalienated land within the city. Certain state services are still provided within the city, but generally municipal boundaries are strictly observed in determining where state services begin and end. After passage of the act, a future state capital was chosen for Selangor. This is the new town of Sungei Rengan, about 8 miles from Kuala Lumpur. Actual construction of legislative and administrative buildings had not taken place by mid-1972. These were still located within Kuala Lumpur. The residence of the ruler is in the old capital, Klang.

The 36-square-mile limit of Kuala Lumpur was in existence at the time of the act. The act provides that existing boundaries may be amended by enabling the Yang Di-Pertuan Agong, with the approval of the Ruler of the State of Selangor, by order, to alter the boundaries of the capital. The population of the metropolitan area extends far beyond these boundaries. In recent years a large new town, Petaling Jaya, has been built just outside the city's western border and the new University of Malaya is on this border, located partly in Kuala Lumpur and partly in Petaling Jaya. Although some key city and federal officials would like to see the boundaries extended, the state is in firm opposition, and no substantial change of boundaries had occurred by 1972.

FUTURE PROBLEMS

Most of the problems of Kuala Lumpur are inseparable from those of the total metropolitan area. These fall into three categories. The city faces the basic challenge that would exist regardless of the form of city government. This is not to say that all forms of government are equal in their ability to develop solutions. Some of the potential conflicts are partly caused by the manner of distribution of legal powers among federal, state, and city governments. It should be noted that most of these potential conflicts are equally present in municipal councils. They are not unique to Kuala Lumpur. Finally, the Federal Capital Act has certain intrinsic weaknesses which are not present in the law governing the other municipalities.

Urban planning

With the metropolitan area expected to double in population within twenty-five years, an obvious need exists for regional planning. This is not only a basic problem and need. It is, in fact, an opportunity. Many cities of the world can lament, with considerable accuracy, that it is too late – too late to plan, too late to prepare, too late to control. Not so in Kuala Lumpur. Mistakes have been made in the development of the city, and these mistakes are not all small ones. But none of these mistakes represents a really major obstacle. The sixty square miles of greatest population is expected to grow from approximately 550,000 in 1967 to 1,400,000 by 1990. This is an opportunity with few parallels in the world today.

The three elements of a good plan – economic, social, and physical – are all needed in Kuala Lumpur. To 1970 at least, urban planning had largely been limited to the physical element. Planning efforts do exist. A Kuala Lumpur and Klang Valley Regional Committee has advisory responsibility for planning within the urban growth area. Chairman of the committee is the state secretary of Selangor, and the federal commissioner of Town and Country Planning is secretary. Little progress has been made beyond the paper plan stage. Probably the most important cause for slow progress has been lack of power to implement.

The federal government will make a final decision on the future of the Kuala Lumpur metropolitan area within the next few years. Only a little time remains before similar decisions must be made on other urban growth areas. To 1970, the decision was for minimal short-range expenditure and minimal control. With relatively insignificant increases in expenditures and in controls, serious and predictable problems could be avoided in such fields as transportation, health, housing, and public safety. Metropolitan growth is an area where centralized control offers distinct advantages. One advantage is that vested interests are not in a position to block metropolitan improvement and progress – as they are in the United States and other countries.

Only the federal and state governments possess the powers to qualify as contenders for primacy in developing a framework for urban planning and control. Although the states may have the greatest desire for a primary position, they generally have less planning and administrative competence. It is doubtful that either state or federal decision-makers have the necessary action commitment. While time remains for action, there is still hope that Malaysia will face up to urban planning and control needs.

Housing

Housing remains a major problem in spite of the many low-cost housing units constructed since independence. This need is shown by the presence of the squatter – the man who illegally occupies land and builds his home on it. One 1954 estimate placed the number of squatters in Kuala Lumpur at 140,000. Since this was one-half, or more, of the total population at the time, it is probable that this estimate was overstated. A 1961 estimate set the squatter population at 100,000. This represented approximately 25 per cent of the population. Such a percentage is in the range of other estimates for Kuala Lumpur. In 1968 the commissioner estimated squatters to number 117,000 on state land and 20,000 on private land.

Probably the most significant cause for increases in squatter numbers is continuing immigration to Kuala Lumpur from rural and village areas. These immigrants usually have housing and employment problems as they arrive. It is common for a man to remain a squatter after he has found suitable employment. The Japanese occupation apparently stimulated squatters. Shortage of food during that period caused some to move to the outer edges of the city where they could have garden plots. Usually, the move was to land not owned by the new occupant. For a substantial time after the Japanese defeat, the government was struggling to re-establish operations. There was no time to worry about squatters. Abandoned mining land is frequently the site for substantial squatter settlements. Now, squatters present social and economic burdens to the community and are an obstacle in the way of physical planning. They are also, most assuredly, a major political problem. An informative review of this subject (with reference to Kuala Lumpur and other cities) appears in T.G. McGee's *The Southeast Asia City* (London, G. Bell and Sons, 1967).

Possibly the biggest obstacle in the path of professionally planned and administered development of the Klang Valley (the Kuala Lumpur metropolitan area) is the placement of urban development very low in the national priority scale. Though a Ministry of Local Government and Housing has been established, this ministry has a small budget and staff. National focus has been on rural development for a number of reasons far too complex to discuss here.

Potential conflict areas

Land administration is a very strong candidate as a potential conflict area because of the roles played by each government. Though the State of Selangor owns all unalienated land in the state, the constitution provides that the federal government may require the state government to grant land for a federal purpose. The federal government has been reluctant to use this power. It would be possible for the state to veto certain city projects through failure to make unalienated land available. On the other hand, the city controls land use and building construction and use. The city could, through these powers, halt sale of state land to a private purchaser.

Overlaps are quite obvious in considering the squatter problem. The squatter has a home on state owned land. The only government with real power to move him is the state. The state, understandably, is reluctant to move a squatter unless adequate housing (usually low-cost housing) is available. Funds for constructing low-cost housing are federal. Along with the funds go certain requirements and certain advice. Usually, these funds are apportioned by the state, and low-cost housing projects may then be state and/or local. In the case of Kuala Lumpur, federal funds come directly to the city. Welfare, another possible resource for squatters, is partly state handled and partly federal. It is apparent that positive and timely action by each jurisdiction is needed for an attack on the squatter problem to have any hope of success.

The lack of locally elected representatives has caused extra pressures to be brought to bear against the state and federal representatives elected by the residents of the capital. Service problems must be raised in a question to the minister in Parliament. As might be expected, an appointed city government tends to place more emphasis on efficiency, or other goals, than on responding to public pressures.

Since there are interlocking memberships and responsibilities among the three units doing planning in the area, co-ordination of efforts might be expected to be the common rule. Unfortunately co-ordinating problems exist. During hearings in 1967 of a board of inquiry headed by the commissioner, on a proposed "Draft Town Plan" (a commercial centre plan primarily concerning land use), it was revealed that neither the municipal architect nor the municipal engineer was included in the team which drew up the plan.

Weaknesses of the Act

The Act contains certain built-in problems in addition to the problems caused by the lack of local representation. There is the possibility of conflict between the minister of local government and the commissioner of the capital. Admittedly, this is not likely to develop when the commissioner is a federal civil servant, and the first three commissioners have been civil servants. It is clear that the commissioner is to report to the minister and that the minister has the power to issue general instructions. But the specific language leaves the real meaning and intent of the act open to debate with reference to the ultimate authority. The act has placed great powers (both of legislation and execution) in the hands of a single official. A strong-minded commissioner might decide to exercise them too fully.

Also, the composition of the Advisory Board is questionable. The board consists of the secretaries to the Treasury and the Ministries of Local Government and Housing, Health, Education, and the Ministry of Works Posts and Tele-communications; and the Principal Establishment officer, together with five unofficial members. The six official members have extremely heavy responsibilities of their own. For most of the six, the problems of Kuala Lumpur have no close relationship to problems of their ministry. Although these are top-level civil servants with years of government experience, it does not follow that they can be expected to be seriously interested in and dedicated to city problems or give them the necessary attention and care. Further, the ex officio members are representative neither of citizens' interests nor of specific governmental interests. In fact, they can send alternates to the meetings and frequently do. The unofficial members are often prominent residents who are not actively involved in politics. This helps to ensure sound government but further reduces the probability of any real representation of interests. Even if the Advisory Board included such representation, it has no real power.

Suggestions for the future

What might be done to cope with the problems facing Kuala Lumpur? Most important would be to revise the order of national priorities. It would not be necessary to slow the pace of the other development efforts. The urban development needs are manpower (to develop and administer solutions), laws (to put the solutions into effect), and modest increases in expenditures (to avoid really major problems and expenditures a few years hence).

The first step should be to strengthen substantially the Ministry of Local Government and Housing. More staff is needed – capable individuals who are trained and experienced at attacking urban problems. Training capacity is equally necessary to help the cities develop their own personnel and their own systems and procedures. Also, a system for controlling regional development by cutting across narrow jurisdictional lines would be an acceptance of the opportunities that lie ahead. A workable growth planning and control system must be developed. The system must be acceptable to state and federal officials. Kuala Lumpur is already a beautiful city. The whole Klang Valley could become an outstanding metropolis.

Regarding the Federal Capital Act, the principal purpose – to avoid improper partisan use of municipal employees and powers – could still be satisfied with a few basic changes. To eliminate the valid objections to the Act's passage, legislative power should be vested in an elected body. Placing administrative power in the hands of a highly qualified professional commissioner, selected in accordance with the Act, would achieve its objective. Additional safeguards could be provided through a waiting period, with provision for veto, before new local ordinances become effective. Responsibility for the review of these ordinances, and the veto power, could be given to the Minister for Local Government and Housing.

---

1 *Parliamentary Debates, Official Report*, Vol. II, No. 22, and Vol. II, No. 23 (Kuala Lumpur, The Government Press, 1961).
2 A Malaysian dollar is worth about 33 US cents.

Maurice Hookham **MOSCOW**

The status of Moscow as the federal capital of the Soviet Union is in many respects peculiar. The constitutional form of the Soviet Union is federal and some of the constituent republics are themselves federal in form. Moscow is both the federal capital and the capital of the largest constituent republic. The system of government in practice is, however, highly unified. This unification is expressed most clearly in the existence of a single political party and in the comprehensive economic plan which unifies the whole economy of the Soviet Union. Both in form and in practice there is a combination of a hierarchy, with emphasis on unity and centralized control, together with democratically elected councils or soviets at all levels of the hierarchy as the main generating centres of local initiative. This is held to be the essence of the principle of democratic centralism characteristic of the political system.

Moscow is both the apex of the hierarchy, housing the main instruments of central control, and a city with an elaborate system of democratically elected soviets which serve as a model for the whole country for the expression of local initiative. The common aim is the creation and development of a communist society and the means by which this is to be achieved is a locally based initiative mobilized in the elected soviets.

These factors make it difficult to discuss the position of Moscow in terms of federalism and local-central relations as these are understood in western countries. At the same time, many aspects of Moscow's political status arise from its present existence as a great metropolis and from its history as the cultural and economic centre of the country.

LOCATION AND HISTORY

The famous Russian geographer, R.P. Semyonov-Tyan-Shansky, was the first to point to the importance of the location of Moscow in the centre of the geological basin. "Just as Paris, London and Vienna lie in the central parts of geological basins ... so Moscow lies in the heart of a vast geological basin known as the Moscow basin of the carboniferous formation." At the place where the various circular and semi-circular layers emerge to the surface a variety of geological resources is made available and provides raw materials for industry. Moscow is also situated on the border between coniferous forest and swamp, which offers poor conditions for agriculture, and a broad-leafed forest belt which gradually gives way to forest and steppe-land much more suitable for farming. A division of labour arose between the localities engaged mainly in trade, industry, and agriculture. This area is also the centre of a mass of waterways which provided a network of communications in all directions.

F.V. Kotlov published a pioneering work in 1962, entitled *Man-made Changes in the Natural Conditions in the Territory of Moscow and their Significance for Civil Engineering and Geography*. One of the changes to which Kotlov refers is the sinking of bore holes and artesian wells into the various water layers under Moscow. One of these layers is more than half a mile thick and provides brine water which was used as a source of table salt during the war and is used in winter to be sprayed on to roadways to keep them clear from snow and ice.

In the twelfth and thirteenth centuries, Moscow was a relatively obscure village compared with the neighbouring towns of Vladimir, Suzdal, and Pereyaslavl, which were located in the rich agricultural Opolye plain and were the main centres in the large area between the Volga and Oka rivers. The reasons why Moscow developed to a much greater importance than these other towns are complicated. Those which are clearly of significance were the growing importance of handicrafts and trade, which arose out of the diversity of local conditions, and the relative safety provided by the geographical location from attacks by the Tartars and Baltic peoples. The people engaged in handicrafts and trade in particular sought shelter there and later contributed to the forces which ultimately defeated the Tartar threats. By the end of the fifteenth century, Moscow had united the scattered Russian areas into a unified state and had become its capital. Substantial settlements of people from other nations (Greeks, Poles, Lithuanians, Serbs, Bulgarians, and Germans) were formed in Moscow. The good natural routes for which Moscow was the centre served to develop trade once there was an ordered, political authority. By the seventeenth century, Moscow had become the centre of trade for the whole of European Russia. In the 1630s, there were over 2,000 craftsmen in Moscow, practising a variety of crafts. By the end of the 1720s, there were more than 8,500 craftsmen (in more than 150 workshops) and a number of state and privately owned factories, employing altogether about 14,000 people.

The two capitals

It was at this time that Peter the Great transferred the capital of Russia from Moscow to Petersburg, where it remained for 200 years. Pushkin remarked in his travel notes, *Voyage from Moscow to Petersburg* (1833-35), that there was "once a period of rivalry between the two cities. Moscow's decline is the inevitable consequence of Petersburg's rise. Just as no human body can have two hearts, so no country can have two equally flourishing capitals." Pushkin also pointed out that the Moscow gentry had become impoverished and the large estates around it had been broken up. Belinsky wrote in 1844 that "Russia suddenly seems to have two capitals – the old and the new – Moscow and Petersburg. Little by little, Moscow is becoming a city of commerce, industry, and manufacture, clothing all of Russia with its cotton goods. Its suburbs and outskirts are studded with factories, large and small; in this respect, Petersburg is in no position to compete with it, for by its very location in the heart of Russia, Moscow is destined to be the centre of the home of industry."

In 1814 Moscow had 253 enterprises employing 27,000 people, 94 per cent in textiles, in spite of the destruction caused by the Napoleonic war. It had 400 enterprises by 1843, employing 16 or more workers each, with a total labour force of 38,000 people. About half those gainfully employed worked in industry. In the 1850s, the construction of the first railways was followed by an upturn in industry and trade. The rivalry between Moscow and Petersburg continued, however, and in 1900 the commercial and industrial turnover of the latter slightly exceeded that of Moscow (1,250 million roubles compared with 1,172 million roubles).

Pushkin wrote that "Moscow was once the home of wealthy and idle boyars, erstwhile court grandees, complacent and independent people highly given to harmless gossip and cheap hospitality. Once the meeting place of the whole Russian gentry who came from all over the provinces to winter there ... Moscow today seems humble and subdued, as the great mansions stand silent and forlorn. ... Whilst it has lost its aristocratic sparkle, Moscow is flourishing in other respects; its highly patronized industry is spreading and developing with unprecedented vigour. The merchants are growing richer and are moving into the spacious mansions vacated by the gentry."

The census in 1897 recorded a population in Moscow of 978,500 (1,038,000 including the suburbs) whereas the population of Petersburg was 1,130,400 (1,265,000 including the suburbs). The main influx of population to Moscow was peasants who had moved in from the three neighbouring south-eastern regions. At the time of the revolution, in 1917, it was a large industrial city with a population of two million. The collapse of industry after the revolution and the civil war led to a sharp fall in the population, which was only recovered by 1926. It rose to 4.1 million in 1939, 6.0 million in 1959, and 7.0 million in 1970. Moscow had triumphed over its old rival, Petersburg, mainly for the reason Belinsky had noted. In 1970 the population of the latter was 3.9 million. Many people regarded the transfer of the capital back to Moscow in 1918 as the restoration to the city of the position it had always occupied. Petersburg (renamed Petrograd and later Leningrad) still retained much of its cultural eminence, which had come from the founding of the Russian Academy of Sciences there in 1725 by Catherine the Great. It was not until 1935, some years after the revolution, that the Academy was transferred to Moscow and renamed the Soviet Academy of Sciences. The two cities, between them, house the majority of the leading figures of Soviet learning and culture.

Moscow's central role

The historical traditions of Moscow are preserved in the beautiful churches, palaces, and fifteenth-century walls of the Kremlim; in the severely classical buildings of the eighteenth century; and in the "Empire" style mansions erected after the Napoleonic war. Their preservation and the outstanding quality of the theatres, museums, and libraries make Moscow the show place and cultural centre of the whole Soviet Union. Leningrad is the only city that even approaches Moscow's population. The eight other cities in the Soviet Union with a population of over one million in 1970 were: Kiev, the capital of the Ukraine, with 1.6 million; Baku and Tashkent, with 1.3 million; Gorky, Kharkov, and Novosibirsk, with 1.2 million; and Kuibishev and Sverdlovsk, with a million.

Moscow is the capital not only of the Soviet Union, but also of the largest of the fifteen constituent republics, the Russian Socialist Federative Soviet Republic. This had a population in 1970 of 130 million people of whom 83 per cent were of Russian stock. Its area is 6,500,000 square miles, stretching from the Baltic to the Pacific and from the Arctic Ocean to the deserts of central Asia. Of the remaining 14 republics, the largest are the Ukraine, with a population of 46 million and an area of 230,000 square miles, and Kazakhstan with a population of 12 million and an area of 1,200,000 square miles.

After the introduction of the first five year plan for the development of heavy industry in 1928, there was a tendency toward highly centralized control of the whole Soviet Union from Moscow. It is difficult to assess how rigorous this centralized control was in practice. There were strong vestiges of resistance to direction from the centre, stemming from the experience of Tsarist autocracy, the radical traditions of the exiles in Siberia, nationalism in the Ukraine, and the limited means of control and communication available to the central government.

MOSCOW'S LOCAL GOVERNMENT

The beginning of local self-government in Moscow, as in other cities in Russia, was the grant of letters patent in 1785 by Catherine II. The Tsarist government issued urban regulations in 1862 setting up town dumas (councils) and fixing the franchise for their election. This was twice extended later but, up to the revolution in 1917, there were never more than half of one per cent of the population in Moscow who were entitled to vote at local elections. The council elected in 1912 was composed of 146 members, of which 63 were manufacturers and bankers, 32 merchants, 24 property owners, and 27 members of the professions (especially lawyers and stock brokers). The provincial governor, appointed by the Tsar, had the right and effective power to annul the election of councillors and to veto decisions of the council. Most of the public utility services were privately owned (including electricity, water supply, sewerage, and tramways).

In the February 1917 revolution, the duma met in its building (now the Lenin Museum), along with representatives of various emergency wartime organizations and welfare bodies, to form a provisional revolutionary committee. The leadership of this committee quickly passed into the hands of the bolshevik, menshevik, and socialist revolutionary organizations. On 1 March 1917, the elected representatives from 52 different workplaces in Moscow, numbering about 625 in all, established themselves as the Moscow soviet. The president of the provisional revolutionary committee opened the meeting by handing over power formally to the soviet, and an executive committee of 44 members was elected to exercise this power. Although fresh duma elections were held in June, the soviet effectively replaced the duma after the October revolution as the government of Moscow. The models on which it was based were the soviets which had arisen in the 1905 revolution, and the Petrograd soviet which was the first revival of these earlier models in the February 1917 revolution. In 1931 both Moscow and Leningrad were given special status in the hierarchy of local soviets, being placed directly under the republic soviet independent of the provincial soviets. This superior position in the formal machinery of government was duplicated in the hierarchy of the political party organization.

During the first fifty years of its rule the Moscow soviet effected the following improvements (compared with the position in 1917): central heating of buildings 95.5 per cent (22); water supply 95 per cent (45); drainage 94.3 per cent (37); gas supply 96.5 per cent (3); bathrooms 78 per cent (11); school population nearly 1 million (140,000); crèches 400,000 (819); hospital beds 91,000 (10,600). Its boundaries have twice been substantially extended (in 1960 and 1967), and it now covers an area of 342 square miles (five times the size it was in 1917).

A local soviet in the Soviet Union differs considerably in its powers and functions from a local authority in a country with privately owned industry. The Moscow soviet, like all the other soviets, is a local organ of state power; it is the representative of the national government within Moscow and, as such, has the general responsibility for carrying out all the functions of the Soviet state. There are no specific limitations on the powers of the Moscow soviet other than the fact that it is subordinate to the higher authorities and must conform with their directives. The powers of the soviets are generally defined in Article 97 of the Union constitution: "The Soviets of Working People's Deputies direct the work of the organs of administration subordinate to them, ensure the maintenance of public order, the observance of the laws, protect the rights of citizens, direct local economic and cultural affairs and draw up and approve local budgets." The Moscow soviet is responsible for administering the range of services normally to be found under local government anywhere. These include public health, education, housing, roads, bridges, water supply, drainage, sewerage, street lighting, town planning, parks and open spaces, police, fire services, and the welfare of children and old people. It also administers passenger transport, the distribution of electricity and gas, libraries, museums, and art galleries. The unusual local government responsibilities it has include a wide range of local industries, wholesale and retail trade, public restaurants, and cultural institutions such as theatres and cinemas.

The government of Moscow is organized on a two-tier system. The Moscow city soviet exercises authority throughout the city and there are 29 district soviets within the city boundary proper, which contains an area of 34 square miles. Beyond this there are five suburban districts within the green belt area and one city settlement soviet (Zelenograd) which is an experimental satellite town orginally planned for a population of 70,000, to take some of Moscow's overspill. There is no constitutional principle governing the division of functions between the city and the districts. Each service is planned and administered for the whole city by the city soviet and by each district soviet on a district scale. Divisions are made by agreement from time to time within particular services. Housing, for example, may be erected and administered by both the city and district soviets. The district soviets are responsible for supervising the proper administration of city soviet institutions within their district just as the city soviet is responsible for surveillance of the proper administration of union and republic institutions within the city area. The city soviet has the power to direct the district soviets in all matters with a right of appeal by the latter to the republic or union soviet.

Article 99 of the Union constitution provides that the executive and administrative organ of a city soviet is the executive committee elected by it, consisting of a chairman, vice-chairman, secretary, and members. There were 60 members of the Moscow soviet's executive in 1967 (there are only 25 in other towns). It is primarily responsible for the preparation of annual, quarterly, and monthly plans for the whole work of the soviet and for the detailed scrutiny of the day to day fulfilment of the plans. It issues a printed bulletin every two months setting out the decisions it has taken, which is circulated to all members of the city and district soviets and their departments, and to republic ministries. Shorter statements of its decisions are printed in the local press.

The chairman of the Moscow soviet and of its executive committee, who performs many of the functions of a mayor and a city manager, has usually been a well-known public figure. The first chairman, elected in November 1917, was the well-known Russian historian, Professor M.N. Pokrovskii.

Democratic centralism

The relation between higher and lower soviets is governed by the principle of democratic centralism, which is defined in Article 101 of the Union constitution: "The executive organs of the Soviets of Working People's Deputies are directly accountable both to the Soviets of Working People's Deputies which elected them and to the executive organ of the superior Soviet of Working People's Deputies." Thus the executive committee of the Moscow soviet is responsible to the soviet which elected it and to the Council of Ministers of the Russian Republic; and the executive committee of a district soviet is responsible to the district soviet that elected it and to the executive committee of the city soviet.

The explanation usually offered as to why conflicts do not arise in this dual responsibility is that every soviet, from the lowest to the highest, has been directly elected by the people and is inspired with the common aim of creating a communist society in which there are no conflicts of interest. A concerted effort was made to reinforce this common aim after 1958 with the extensive operation of groups meeting regularly together in wards, combining members of the soviets of the Republic, city, and district. Such groups had existed in the 1920s and 1930s. In the Pervomaiskii district of Moscow these groups were united in 1961 into councils for whole neighbourhood areas, based on the offices which had been set up to administer consolidated blocks of housing. Each of these offices covers three or four constituencies for the city soviet and upwards of ten for the district soviet. The experiment in this district was quickly extended elsewhere and in 1967 there were 440 of these councils in Moscow, engaged mainly in the investigation of complaints and in their submission to the appropriate authorities for remedy. In January 1965 the city executive committee reviewed the procedure for dealing with complaints and reported that the improvements which had been effected had produced a fall in the number of complaints addressed to the town soviet administration of over 23,000 in the three years 1962 to 1965. The executive committee had drawn up a set of model regulations for these councils in 1964, and thereby gave them a legal status. The decision to base the councils on the offices of the housing administration (which is mainly concerned with the allocation of housing) was, no doubt, because allocation had been the most common basis for complaints in an earlier period when there was still a very serious shortage of housing and no unified administration to control its allocation.

A major factor which contributes to the absence of serious conflict among the different units of local government and other public bodies is the existence of one political party which is omnipresent, with its representatives playing a leading role in all the institutions. The high standard of political skill in the leadership of the Moscow Communist party is frequently noted in the Soviet press as a significant reason for the high measure of harmony which is attained between the various institutions involved in the government of the town and its districts. There is in practice an overlap of membership in the Republic, city, and district governments.

In March 1966 the city soviet called upon its executive committee and those of the district soviets to improve the publicity given to the work of the soviets, with organized public meetings to explain the decisions which had been taken, and to mobilize support from the electorate for the implementation of the decisions. The agenda for the sessions of the soviets are published in the local press and circulated to officers of the trade unions, housing administrations, and social organizations in the area. At the same session of the city soviet, there was a lengthy discussion of proposals for further improvement in the role of councillors and volunteer activists in the work of the soviet.

The standing and other committees

The city soviet meets four times a year for a one or two day session at which there is usually a review of a major area of the work of the soviet. These sessions take the form of a public meeting, addressed by the leading councillors and staff in the particular field of work under discussion. Representatives of social organizations connected with this work are usually invited to be present and to take part in the discussion. The main report delivered will have been prepared earlier by the officers of the standing committee of the soviet which is primarily concerned, and by groups of volunteer activists who assist in this work. There were 17 standing committees of the city soviet in 1967, covering all spheres of the economic and cultural life. There were also about a dozen standing committees in each district. The total membership of these city and district committees came to about 4,000 councillors and nearly 7,000 co-opted volunteer activists.

In May 1962 the city soviet empowered its standing committees (which meet monthly or bimonthly) to issue orders to directors of organizations to carry out the decisions of the city soviet and its executive committee (so long as these orders did not involve any change in the current plan, budget, or allocation of material resources). The standing committees (or groups of its members) at this time were developing the practice of holding formal meetings on the premises of the organization concerned, with the staff of the organization present, so that questions could be examined on the spot. In December 1965 and 1966, all the standing committees prepared reports on the relevant aspects of the annual plan and budget for the following years. In 1966 alone, the standing committees of the town and district soviets prepared and submitted over 700 reports to meetings of the soviets or of their executive committees.

The city soviet standing committee on socialist legality (law enforcement) held a meeting in 1966 at one of the taxi garages to discuss the extent to which the drivers were observing the traffic regulations. More than 100 of the taxi drivers took part in the meeting. This and other examples of such work are given prominence in press reports as a desirable way out of not only finding solutions to problems of local government but also ensuring that a wide circle of the population is persuaded to co-operate enthusiastically in carrying out the soviet's decisions by active involvement in the process of reaching them.

Throughout 1965 and 1966, the dominant theme in discussions of the work on the soviets was the development of even greater involvement of the population in self-government. In 1967, there were in operation nearly 4,000 committees for neighbourhood groups of housing, on which more than 45,000 volunteer members served; there were 3,000 parents' committees at schools and kindergartens composed of 15,000 members; libraries, clubs and other cultural centres were supervised by committees containing in all about 5,000 members. There were more than 3,000 people's brigades of part-time volunteer patrols to help the militia (police) in the campaign against disorderly behaviour in public places, on which 240,000 volunteers served. Informal (comradely) courts, numbering altogether about 5,000, operate in housing blocks and work places, composed of about 47,000 volunteer members, who relieve the regular courts by dealing with minor offences or holding preliminary investigations into more serious ones. In January 1964 the executive committee of the city soviet, with the collaboration of the city trade union council, decided to set up district councils to assist in the comradely courts in propaganda and mass educational work to prevent law breaking and anti-social behaviour. A review of the first two years of the working of these district councils showed that they had been very successful in their work, and they were accepted as a desirable and necessary adjunct to the district government institutions.

The distinction between the staff employed, the elected councillors and volunteer activists is not easy to establish. There were over 17,000 unpaid officials and inspectors in the administrative departments of the city and district executive committees in 1967. The general practice has been for the mayor and seven deputy mayors to be full-time salaried officials who have been elected as councillors, but each district executive committee has a number of deputy mayors who are unpaid. In 1967 there were about half a million volunteer activists involved in the administration of both the city and district soviets. City and district councillors are entitled to travel free on local transport, and when engaged on soviet business receive the rate of pay they would obtain at their regular employment.

Local elections

The electoral law does not limit the number of candidates standing in the biennial elections but it has been the invariable practice for only one candidate to be nominated for each constituency. Potential candidates are selected at meetings held at institutions where large numbers of people are employed in the constituency, such as a factory or a hospital. At these meetings representatives are also elected to serve on the local electoral commission which then selects from those proposed a single candidate for the constituency. At the meetings to propose candidates it is the practice to put forward propositions for action by the candidates when elected, called mandates. During the 1965 elections to the city and district soviets in Moscow, the electors put forward about 400 separate mandates to the city soviet and over 1,000 to the district soviets. The executive committees are expected to report to the electorate periodically after the elections on the actions which have been taken to implement these mandates.

At the elections of the city soviet in 1965 there were 1,104 councillors elected. These included 632 members of the Communist party and 87 members of the youth section of the party (Komsomols). There were 488 workers, 62 employees of Soviet institutions, 67 employees in the party and trade union administrations, 120 scientific specialists, 38 teachers, 41 doctors, 27 employees of cultural and educational institutions, 21 employees in housing and public utilities administration, and 14 employees in trade and restaurant services.

Although the Moscow city soviet is formally independent of the Moscow regional soviet there are a number of matters in which collaboration between the two has been in evidence. In 1967 they shared the same offices in Moscow and the same telephone number served for inquiries to the regional and town executive committees. There is a single economic council for the region and city to plan economic development. There were 15 cities within the region in 1967 with a population of over 50,000, and the region covers an area of 17,250 square miles with a total population of over 4 million excluding Moscow. The common economic plan, which applied to the area as a whole, helped to minimize any conflict over the two major extensions of the cities' boundaries, which brought under Moscow's control a number of regional cities and a considerable amount of industry.

A Moscow district

There have been several changes in the district subdivision of Moscow. The number of districts was increased from six to ten in 1931, to 23 in 1936, and to 25 in 1941. In 1960, in line with the general policy to amalgamate the local soviets generally, the districts were rearranged into 17 (four within the inner ring around the Kremlin, and 13 radial districts). In 1965 the town of Zelenograd in the greenbelt, with its own city soviet, was put under the control of the Moscow city soviet. On 3 December 1968, the Moscow city soviet approved a new pattern of districts, which had been decreed by the presidium of the Supreme Soviet of the Russian Republic. An extensive development of new housing had produced a shift of population out of the central area (in eight years it had fallen from 970,000 to 520,000 and was continuing to fall), and the administration of the 13 radial districts had become excessively complicated. The new pattern, which came into operation on 6 January 1969, has 29 districts based on the main radial thoroughfares, but in two belts. The inner belt has 13 districts and the outer one, extending to the 86-mile outer ring motorway that forms the city boundary, has 16. They range in population from 200,000 to 300,000.

Moskvoretskii district soviet may be taken as an example of the 17 districts that existed in Moscow prior to the rearrangement in 1969. It had a population of 495,000 in 1967, and occupied a narrow wedge-shaped area running from the inner core of the city 14 miles out to the city's boundary. It was governed by a soviet of 250 members, elected every two years at the same time as the city soviet. In the 1963–65 soviet, just over half of them were industrial workers and the same proportion were members of the Communist party. Women members numbered 123. It met once every two months and usually had only one or two major items on the agenda. It elected an executive committee of 11 members, of whom six were full-time paid employees of the district (the mayor as chairman, the secretary and four departmental heads). The executive committee met weekly. There were 12 standing committees, which met monthly (health, housing, education, planning and open spaces, finance, social welfare, trade and public catering, construction of new buildings, cultural activities, communications and transport, central heating stations, and personal services – tailoring, shoe repairs, furniture repairs, hairdressing, and depots for the hire of labour-saving domestic appliances). The administration was divided into 30 departments, employing 26,000 staff. There were many examples of the sharing of services between the city and district administration such as the bakeries, which were staffed by the city soviet but the district soviet appointed the manager of the bakery in its district.

The councils in the district numbered 18, one for each residential ward, and included 296 city and district councillors. Their duty was to see that decisions of the city soviet were carried out by the housing management, offices, shops, restaurants, and welfare, cultural, health, and educational institutions within the district. There were altogether about 40,000 volunteers serving as assistants in the work of the soviet. Many of these served from time to time as inspectors, investigating complaints and visiting the various institutions to ensure that they were being run efficiently, that the sanitary and other regulations were being observed, and that authorized prices were being charged.

Members of the Moscow executive committee and senior officials of its departments are expected to help the district soviet in its work, to attend meetings of its full sessions and of its executive and standing committees, and report to meetings of the district electorate on future plans and current progress of the city soviet's work. In the 1960s the city soviet transferred to the district soviets a number of additional powers in the fields of planning, finance, construction of new buildings, welfare and cultural matters. This trend was being encouraged in 1968 by the increasing initiative and resources of the district soviets.

Relations between soviets and citizens

The principal features of the relationship between the municipal authorities in Moscow and its inhabitants may be summarized as follows:

1 The ubiquitous unifying force of the single Communist party eliminates the possibility of organized political conflict.
2 The full session of the soviets serves a very different purpose from that

of the typical municipal council in the western world, to which committees have to report before action can be taken. The full power of the executive committee facilitates rapid action and the sessions of the soviet are devoted to a thorough review and public criticism of particular aspects of the work of the executive committee.

3 The active interest of the citizens of Moscow is mobilized by an election every two years and continuously maintained by the active participation of volunteers and representatives from all public organizations, places of employment, and residential apartments, in every aspect of the work of the soviets.

4 There is no restriction on the election of members of the staff of the soviet from serving as elected councillors, other than the requirement set out in the Communist party program that there should be a turnover of elected councillors of about one-third every two years.

5 There has been a high and increasingly prominent part played by women in the municipal government of Moscow.

FINANCES

The budget of the city soviet forms part of the Republic's budget and is fixed only after the latter has been approved. It has been increasing steadily during the 1960s and in 1967 amounted to 1,334 million roubles. The Moscow city budget for 1967 was, in millions of roubles:[1]

Revenue		Expenditure	
Turnover tax	495	On national economy	742
Profits	619	including	
Income tax from		industry	7
co-operatives and public		trade	15
undertakings	15	housing	499
State personal tax	77	communal economy	201
State excise duties,		Social and educational	533
entertainment taxes,		including	
local taxes and excise duties	32	education	237
Fees and various non-tax		health	281
incomes	16	social security	15
Lotteries	6	Miscellaneous	54
Miscellaneous	74	Excess of income over	
		expenditure	5
Total	1,334	Total	1,334

After mid-1965, industrial undertakings were steadily transferred to the new system of economic management whereby they were given greater incentives to achieve a profit. In 1970, of the 324 major enterprises in the city, 301 of them, responsible for 96 per cent of the economic production, were operating on this new system. This applies also to the municipal enterprises, and the income to the budget from them in 1968 was planned to be 811 million roubles, which was 20 per cent more than in 1967, together with 363 million roubles profit, which was 15 per cent more than in 1967.[a] There was to be an increase of 11 per cent in production between these two years. Income from communal services, housing and transport were set in the budget at 270 million roubles, which was 41.5 per cent higher than in 1967. Sales of goods from municipal shops and restaurants were budgeted to provide a profit of 218 million roubles in 1968.

The rapid growth in the sales of consumer goods, industrial goods and foodstuffs was calculated to provide a turnover tax (sales tax) of 390 million roubles, from which the city budget would receive 271 million roubles. The relatively much smaller element of direct taxation was set at 87 million roubles. Personal taxes include income tax (paid monthly, and graduated according to income between 0.7 and 13 per cent, with a 30 per cent income allowance for more than three dependents) and a bachelor tax, paid by men between the ages of 20 and 50. There are also excise duties on all forms of transport and livestock, and a variety of stamp duties on legal documents and certificates.

The 1968 budget allotted 603 million roubles to capital investment, to which the various municipal undertakings were to contribute out of their own funds an additional 84 million roubles. The budget allotted 161 million roubles for the financing of all branches of the municipal economy, which included 48.8 million roubles for repairs, the operation of the various municipal installations, maintenance of roads, street lighting, and open spaces. There was an allotment of 106 million roubles for the financing of district housing, capital and current housing repairs, with an additional allotment of 35.4 million roubles by non-municipal undertakings for housing and house repairs.

The provision of cultural and social services was covered by an item of 487.2 million roubles. Of this, education received 159.7 million roubles (general education schools for 781,000 pupils were allotted 70.2 million roubles, and for the education of a further 117,500 children in sanatoria and boarding schools were allotted 25 million roubles). The education of 185,000 children in kindergartens was budgeted to cost 58 million roubles. The annual cost of maintaining a child in a kindergarten was estimated to average 440 roubles, for which the budget provided 329 roubles and the parents paid 111 roubles, whereas the average cost per child in a crèche was calculated to be 489 roubles, to which the parents contributed 88 roubles. The maintenance of 50,000 children in homes and crèches was calculated to cost 21.4 million roubles. The allotment for free and subsidized feeding of 110,000 children in various kinds of schools and children's homes was fixed at 3.2 million roubles. There was also allotted 270.8 million roubles for health services, 15.5 million for social security and 5 million for the housing of over 7,000 old people and invalids. Cultural and educational establishments, such as libraries, clubs, music schools, parks and theatres, were allotted seven million roubles.

It was pointed out in the presentation of the budget for 1968 that a reduction in expenditure by undertakings under the control of the Moscow city soviet of 0.5 per cent would provide a saving in a year of 18 million roubles. The financial inspectors of the city finance department, the principal tax collecting authority, audit the accounts of all undertakings in Moscow to ensure that the accounts are properly kept and that the undertakings are run efficiently.

The district budgets for 1968 together totalled 528 million roubles, which was 11 million roubles higher than in 1967, but their total was less than half that of the city budget. The budget for Moskvoretskii district soviet in 1963 contained the following major items, in thousands of roubles:

Revenue		Expenditure	
Turnover tax	13,734	Trade	223
Taxed profits of		Housing	4,339
municipal enterprises	3,451	Municipal enterprise	642
Income tax on enterprises		Education	9,118
and organizations	164	Health	7,448
State taxes on population	1,924	Social welfare	229
Excise, stamp duty and		Administration	226
entertainment duty	1,118		
Market fees	548		
Miscellaneous	59		
Rents from land used for			
privately built housing	1,227		
Totals	22,225		22,225

PLANNING

The first five year plan came into operation in 1928. By 1931 there had been a considerable construction of new factories, and the population of Moscow had increased by over a million compared with 1917. The central committee of the Communist party took note of the "great deficiencies in the working of the Moscow municipal services." There had been "blunders in the tramway system, shortcomings in housing, poor execution of street and underground work" and the sanitary condition of the town was admitted to be "extremely unsatisfactory." The small, single storeyed, wooden houses which provided the bulk of residential accommodation had earned Moscow the title of "the big village." The majority of the streets were too narrow to permit the development of communications. Instructions were given therefore for the "elaboration of a serious, scientifically developed plan for the building of Moscow." Two projects were begun immediately; these were the building of an underground railway (the Metro) and the linking of the Moscow and Volga rivers by canal, which went a long way toward solving the water problem.

By 1935 a detailed plan, the General Plan for the Reconstruction of Moscow, had been prepared, covering the entire municipal economy. The main features of this plan were the fixing of a ceiling on the town population of five million, with a gradual extension of the town boundary as new buildings were erected (all new construction work being placed under the control of the city soviet); the creation of a greenbelt, ten kilometres wide, outside the planned expansion of the city boundary, "as a reservoir of fresh air for the city and a place of recreation for its inhabitants;" the straightening and widening of the main thoroughfares within the city to 30–40 yards and the construction of two new ring roads; the erection of new residential areas of tall apartment houses to secure an even density of population of 160 persons per acre; the existing irregular distribution of industry to remain so that people would be able to reside close to their work; a ten-year expansion program for all the municipal services, including the provision of new department stores, warehouses and cold-storage plants, grain elevators, bakeries, cinemas, and other cultural amenities.

Before the outbreak of war considerable progress had been made with the realization of the plan, although the pace declined with the diversion of resources to defence purposes. During the war, destruction by enemy action and by the ravages of the severe climate while maintenance and repairs were neglected, caused a delay in the resumption of the planned reconstruction until 1947, when the wartime dilapidation had been made good. The general reconstruction was resumed with a five year plan for 1946 to 1950, in which the dominant features were an intensification of house building, the construction of a large central heating network and the bringing of natural gas from Saratov by pipe line over a distance of 525 miles. In the post-war years it became impossible to keep the population down to five million in spite of a decline in the average housing space per person to about four square metres.[3] The pressure to expand industrial output proved too great to prevent the extension of existing industrial buildings and the erection of new ones within the town, in spite of repeated injunctions against this by the government and the party.

By 1966 a tremendous improvement had been made in the development of the municipal services, far in advance of that outlined in the 1935 and 1946 plans. In the previous four years nearly 14 million square metres of housing space had been erected (far more than the total housing area of Moscow in 1917) enabling 1½ million inhabitants to move into new accommodation. Also, 171 new schools had been built; the rapid expansion of the school population after the war had meant that most of the schools for a time operated on a two-shift basis, but this had been reduced by 1966 to 20 per cent of the school population. New hospitals provided an additional 11,876 beds. There had been a considerable improvement in the city transport system, with extensions to the underground (33 kilometres), trolleybus lines (200 kilometres) and bus routes, which enabled the public transport system to carry 11½ million passengers a day. A multiplicity of separate building construction units was consolidated into a Moscow Construction Trust, under the direction of the city soviet, which employed over 200,000 workers.

The many experiments which had been made in the decentralization of control over the economy had led to the transfer for a short period of some industrial undertakings, which had been under the control of the city soviet, to the regional economic council. These were handed back in 1965. By the end of 1966 it was decided by the Union government that the time had come for a new long-term plan to be adopted for the city. The city soviet, in October 1966, adopted an outline of key indices for the future development of the city and called for the preparation of a detailed plan up to 1980 by the end of 1968. These indices specified in particular, once again, that there would be no further expansion of the industrial plant in Moscow; the existing plant could be modernized to provide a constantly increasing output. It was planned to increase the volume of housing accommodation by almost 100 per cent by 1980, to provide an optimum norm of 12 to 15 square metres per person (so that each family will have a separate apartment on the scale of one person per living room). By mid-1967, the average was nine square metres. Improvements in the city transport, together with the rehousing of population, could reduce the average journey from home to work from 50–70 minutes to 30–40 minutes. The plan provided for a rapid expansion of recreational facilities, especially in the greenbelt area, to cater to up to two million people a day. This plan was awaiting the resolution of some minor details before final approval by the government in January 1970.

Moscow's daily per capita water supply increased from 163 litres in 1935 to over 520 litres in 1964, with a planned production of 1,000 litres in 1970.[4] This was estimated to cover residential use 40 per cent, commercial and communal use 24 per cent, and industrial use 36 per cent. The water is supplied from four main filtering stations drawn almost entirely from the

Moscow river and the Moscow-Volga canal (providing 3½ million cubic metres a day in 1964).[5] The bulk of the city sewage is treated in large biological purification plants operating on the aeration principle. The capacity of these plants was increased from 275,000 in 1935 to 1,550,000 cubic metres a day in 1962. During this period an increased volume of 800,000 cubic metres of sewage a day had to be dealt with and for a time some of this had to be pumped into the Moscow river untreated. The capacity had been increased in 1967 to 2.7 million cubic metres a day. In 1962 the collection of solid refuse amounted to 3½ million cubic metres. Solid refuse has in the past been very poorly utilized. Eight refuse disposal plants have been erected about 25 miles outside of Moscow.

The residential planning unit used in earlier plans had been a neighbourhood unit of 6,000 to 12,000 people. This was changed to one of a residential district of 30,000 to 70,000 people, complete with all basic amenities, grouped to form administrative districts of 200,000 to 350,000 people. In order to achieve adequate housing for everyone, in 1966 it was decided to build by 1980 40 to 50 million square metres of housing space (compared with 75 million square metres built since 1917 – half in the previous 7 years) in tall apartment houses of 9, 12, 17, and even 25 or 27 storeys. The total residential area was planned to cover 60,500 acres, industry and office buildings 34,500 acres, and the remainder to be preserved as open space. Particular attention had been paid to the prevention of atmospheric pollution. It was planned to move out of the city 200 factories which presented dangers of polluting the atmosphere or fire hazards, and by mid-1967, 3,700 air purification plants had been installed in factories within the city. It had been for some time the policy to retain and extend trolleybus lines and to use only petrol-driven buses, as against diesel, in order to keep the atmosphere cleaner.

At a conference of architects in Moscow in February 1968, there was some evidence of a dispute about the planned development of the centre of the city. This was represented as an argument between a central city and a city centre. The inner area around the Kremlin had become increasingly a zone of administrative and cultural buildings, with a falling residential population. At the same time a rival centre was being developed around the Moscow University buildings on the Lenin hills to the south-west. The Kremlin area is predominantly the Union and Republic capital area. The presence there of the Lenin mausoleum and the tomb of the unknown soldier, which enshrines the heroic saga of the defence of Moscow in the second world war, heightens the sense of the inner area as the capital of the Union.

The great strides made in city planning in Moscow, and in other Soviet cities, are usually attributed to three particular factors. The common ownership of all the land, with the absence of private landlords and high land values, meant that the cost of reconstruction was reduced to the cost of demolition of old buildings and the erection of new ones. Common ownership also has encouraged popular enthusiasm and considerable voluntary labour for maintaining and improving the open spaces. Second, the social ownership of industry and all other resources has made it easier to plan the total economy of the town. Third, the concentration of all building work into a single organization has meant both an economy of use in building resources and a harmony in the overall design.

INTERGOVERNMENTAL RELATIONS

This essay began with a recognition of the difficulty of analysing the status of Moscow in terms of federalism as it is understood in the west. When Professor W.A. Robson attempted in 1937 to characterize the relation of Moscow to the central government he gave as his general impression that "the centre of gravity" was in the town hall and "the main initiating impulse comes from Mossoviet, although central approval is continually required..." "The government, we were assured, never hampers the initiative of Mossoviet. It is concerned to foster energetic action rather than to restrict it." He was writing at a time when the present relationships were first taking shape; since then there have been many formal changes in the organs of government and their relations. The allocation of executive powers to federal ministries, to federal and republic ministries jointly, and to republic ministries has been changed many times. The city of Moscow has throughout usually retained a special relationship with the federal government and the republic government and has benefited from the general trend towards a greater measure of decentralization of powers. This overall trend may be seen in the increasing proportion of the state budget allocated to the republics and local soviets: in 1956 this was 23.5 per cent; in 1959 it was 47.5 per cent: and in 1962 it was 55.7 per cent.

The trend toward decentralization might conceivably have led to a reduction in the status of Moscow as the apex of the federal hierarchy. It remains nevertheless as the great metropolis with the leading role in the political, economic, and cultural life of the country. The movement of population from the rural areas to the cities has made it impossible to prevent Moscow's growth beyond the population limit of five million set in 1935. Town planners in the Soviet Union increasingly talk of the need to develop the republic capitals and regional cities, with accompanying satellite cities, to relieve some of the pressure on the metropolis. The improvement of the amenities, and especially the standards of the educational and cultural institutions, of the major provincial cities has lessened both the attraction of Moscow to the young intellectuals of the provinces and also the sense of jealousy which was felt in the provincial centres.

It is difficult to forecast what effect these social changes will have in terms of any formal constitutional changes in the status of Moscow. There were confident rumours in 1968 of the likelihood of a new federal constitution to be promulgated in 1970. It is possible that the decreasing significance of the separate national identity of the republics may lead to a change in the form of the federal constitution. Fourteen of the fifteen republics (i.e. excluding the Russian republic) retain their "embassies" in Moscow with strong sentimental bases in tradition. The Armenian "embassy", for example, is located on Armenian Street in the district which was a long-established Armenian settlement in the capital.

Sentiment and tradition may ensure that the status of Moscow remains much as it is in spite of the trend toward a levelling up of the provincial centres and a reduction of the central apparatus of government. The reduction of socio-economic differences in the society at large makes also for a unification of the society, in which one centre, Moscow, is likely to be especially significant. Such speculation about the future is, however, made the more difficult by the inability to be certain about current intergovernmental relations. These present especially difficult problems of understanding to those who live outside the USSR, for the evidence on which one can base judgments is very slender.

---

1 Source: *Moscow in Figures During the Years of Soviet Power, A Short Statistical Handbook* (Moscow, Statistical Publishing House, 1967), 20–1. A rouble was worth about US $1.11 in 1970.
2 V. E. Mikheev, "Moscow Budget," *Gorodskoi Khozyaistvo Moskvy* (February, 1968), 14–15.
3 A square metre equals about 1.2 square yards.
4 A litre is about equal to a US quart, or one-quarter of a US gallon.
5 A cubic metre equals about 1.3 cubic yards.

H.N.A. Enonchong YAOUNDÉ

As the capital of a federal nation,[1] Yaoundé seems to occupy a hybrid position. It is not only capital of the Federal Republic of Cameroon but also of the federated state of East Cameroon. At the same time, as the most important town in the Central-South administrative region, it has a resident Inspector of Federal Administration.

HISTORY AND BACKGROUND

The name "Yaoundé" is a German mutilation of the word "Ewondo" (the original inhabitants of the area). The name was adopted after the Germans occupied and extended their political and commercial activities in Cameroon as an integral part of the "Scramble for Africa" preceding the Berlin Conference of 1885. But Yaoundé did not become the Cameroon capital until 1921, after the victory of the allied powers, in the first world war. German forces in Cameroon were defeated in 1916. After a Franco-British military occupation, Germany, whose capital in Cameroon had been Douala, a seaside city accessible to ocean transport, ceded her interests in Cameroon to Britain and France under Article 119 of the Treaty of Versailles in June 1919. In March 1916, the two allied powers had de facto partitioned the country into what later became known as British and French Cameroon, and Article 22 of the League of Nations Covenant conferred on the two territories mandatory status within the international legal order. The article decreed, in part, that to ex-enemy countries inhabited by "people not yet able to stand by themselves under the strenuous conditions of the modern world" should be applied the principle "that the well-being and development of such peoples form a sacred trust of civilisation." The territories were thus entrusted to the Mandatory Powers, Britain and France, which were exhorted "to promote to the utmost the material and moral well-being and social progress of the inhabitants." This required France, as the administering power of "French Cameroon" with Douala as capital, to submit annual reports to the Permanent Mandate Commission sitting in Geneva.

France agreed that the continued maintenance of a military government in Douala was inconsistent with the spirit and terms of the mandatory agreement. Furthermore, from the viewpoint of conventional military strategy Douala was vulnerable to enemy surprise attacks by sea. Besides, the Douala natives had, in the historical past, demonstrated their vigorous resistance to direct foreign rule. The French reckoned that a joint confrontation of the Douala people and the enemy would deprive them of their territorial foothold. Faced with the desirability of protecting their newly acquired interests, French administrators decided to choose Yaoundé as the new capital. Its annual average temperature of 23 degrees centrigrade provided an extraordinarily equable climate within an equatorial region, although this climatic condition is characterized by dry and rainy seasons. It rains for a total of about 143 days, within a precipitation of 1,500 to 2,000 mm (60 to 80 inches) a year.

Another reason for moving the capital to Yaoundé was the menace of the mosquitoes which were predominant in Douala. Malaria had converted Douala and its immediately outlying areas into the "white man's grave" while Yaoundé, "*La ville au sept collines*," with a distance of 280 kilometres from the coastal areas and an altitude of about 1,400 metres (5,000 feet), was relatively easy to drain and rid of mosquito infestations, constituted a centre of attraction for the French resident administrators, who continued to occupy Yaoundé until the first Republic of Cameroon was established on 1 January 1960. Malaria is still regarded as an endemic disease in the Douala region.

On 1 October 1961 the Federal Republic of Cameroon was "formed ... of the Territory of the Republic of Cameroon, henceforth called East Cameroon, and the Territory of the Southern Cameroons, formerly under United Kingdom administration, henceforth called West Cameroon" (under Article 1 (1) of the Cameroon federal constitution). Article 1 (3) of the Constitution provided that "the official languages of the Federal Republic of Cameroon shall be French and English." Article 1 (6) expressly stated that "the seat of the national institutions shall be Yaoundé." Although both the federal constitution and the East Cameroon Constitution of November 1961 were silent on the question of state capitals, Yaoundé continued to serve as the capital of East Cameroon while Buea, a town located around the Cameroon Mountain with an estimated altitude of 13,350 feet above sea level, remained the capital of West Cameroon, as it has been as far back as 1916.

Various serious studies to carve out Yaoundé and convert it into a federal district like the District of Columbia in the United States generated no political enthusiasm from either the anglophone politicians in West Cameroon or from the francophones. It was economical, convenient, and prudent to employ buildings and materials left over by the First Cameroon

Republic for the newly created federal governmental apparatus in 1961. That this might be a derogation of the principle of federalism which required the separate and independent utilization of the different powers allocated between the federal and state authorities, was not even considered. It is normal for the same officer, for example a prefect, to function in a dual capacity for both the federal and state governments, without fear of conflicts of power, so exercised. Indeed the federal constitution itself contained special transitional provisions wherein the president of the Republic of Cameroon, resident in Yaoundé, became president of the Federal Republic, while the prime minister of West Cameroon, resident in Buea, was vested with the powers of vice-president of the Federal Republic, but made visits to Yaoundé as occasion and responsibilities demanded. The West Cameroonians, whose ascendency to independence and reunification was shrouded in bleak financial circumstances, generally accepted the new apparently imposing federal capital as a welcome relief. This is not to minimize the restrained resentment and embarrassment that was discernible among the arch-federalists, who perceived the multiple governmental role of Yaoundé as an adulteration of the principle of federalism.

Experience since then, however, has proved beyond doubt that the choice of Yaoundé as federal capital was a counsel of wisdom even in the estimation of sceptics. It has stoutly withstood political and ethnological vicissitudes since it is situated in the Central region, which is more centrally located than the other five administrative regions (North, East, Coast, West, and West Cameroon). There is no visible hostility to the Yaoundé inhabitants, for although the Ewondo ethnic group is the orginal tribe of the city, there has been, within the last few years, an influx of people from the many neighbouring tribes, and also West Cameroonians, thus giving it a special cosmopolitan character. Yaoundé has an orderly and even sometimes almost serene atmosphere in contrast with Douala, a large commercial city.

Situated in the Mefou Division, Département de la Méfou, Youndé is accessible by either paved or dirt roads from Obala, Mbalmayo, Douala, Akonolinga, Makak, and West Cameroon; and by railway and air from Kribi port, a suitable holiday seaside resort, and Waza, an attractive wild animal reserve area way north. Two main industries, a cigarette factory and a beer brewery, as well as hotels and tourist industries, are notable. The recently constructed Mont Fébé Palace hotel, with 250 rooms, has a comparable quality in grandeur and service to any modern hotel in the world.

Yaoundé is also an intellectual centre. It has the country's only university, the Cameroon Federal University, in which teaching and learning are undertaken in both English and French. The university has four faculties,

Law and Economics, Science, Arts, and Medicine, with two attached institutes, the École Normale Supérieure (higher normal school), and the École Fédérale Supérieure d'Agriculture (Higher Federal School of Agriculture) at Nkolbisson. It is politically fashionable to describe the University as a genuine "laboratory" for national unity because of its apparent reflections of the bilingual and bicultural policies designated for it. Although it has a semi-autonomous public status (établissement public), it is rigorously under the control of the federal government, with the Minister of National Education, Youth and Culture, as its ex officio chancellor.

THE CONSTITUTIONAL SETTING

What is the national constitutional setting in which Yaoundé functions as capital?

The Cameroon federal constitution confers, separates, and limits powers. Besides conferring express, implied and inherent executive powers on the federal president, it stipulates that the vice-president cannot be elected from the same state as the president, a device originally intended to constitute one of several checks and balances in the constitution. There are also express powers vested in a fifty-member unicameral legislature, the National Assembly, and to a certain extent in the judiciary. Thus at the federal level, each of the tripartite branches of government is vested with specific functions. The National Assembly exercised exclusive enumerated legislative powers under Article 24 of the constitution until in 1969, when the president was empowered by a constitutional amendment to share these powers with the National Assembly under his ordinance-making powers, notwithstanding his exercise of separate and independent plenary regulatory powers under Article 12 of the constitution.

Judicial functions are vested in federal courts in a judicial pyramid in which the Federal Court of Justice, a common supreme court for both states, is at the apex. Judicial independence is secured by a Federal Judicial Council and by Article 1 (4) of Decree No. 66-DF-205 of April 1966; "members of the Bench shall be irremovable. In carrying out their jurisdictional duties, they shall only be responsible to the law and their conscience." The administration of justice is an exclusively federal matter outside the ambit and control of the two states, save in respect of the West Cameroon customary courts which have been, for historical reasons, reserved to the state. The Federal Court of Justice is endowed with powers to review both legislative and administrative action. The English constitutional maxim, "the King can do no wrong", is anathema in Cameroon jurisprudence.

The concept of federalism contained in the constitution is power-limiting. The vesting of express enumerated powers in the federal government under Articles 5 and 6, and the reserving of residual powers to the states, under Article 38, is somewhat similar to the allocation of powers under the American constitution. Federalism supplies the restraint between the Cameroon national state governments, which are each sovereign within their own spheres. The powers of the federal authorities include nationality, the status of aliens, regulation concerning conflict of laws, national defence, foreign affairs, development and planning, the monetary system, higher education, information services, postal telecommunications, criminal law, and all other such subjects as inspire national unity. Article 38 expressly states: "Any subject not listed in Articles 5 and 6, and whose regulation is not specifically entrusted by this constitution to a federal law shall be of the exclusive jurisdiction of the federated states, which, within those limits, may adopt their own constitutions." Thus, among subjects not specifically entrusted to federal law by the constitution are primary education, public services of the federated states, local agriculture, the West Cameroon customary courts,and particularly local government in the Anglo-Saxon sense. This means that the regulation and control of local government bodies, both urban and rural, is within the competence of the state legislatures. The West Cameroon legislature is bicameral, the House of Assembly with a membership of 37, and the House of Chiefs, is a relic of British parliamentary organization. The East Cameroon legislature, however, is unicameral and, among other things, regulates and controls local authorities, including the Yaoundé municipal council.

In law, there are two distinct categories of local authorities in East Cameroon, the autonomous municipal authorities (*les communes de pleine exercice*) and the non-autonomous or semi-autonomous local authorities (*communes de moyen exercice ou communes mixtes urbaines*). Those in the former category – for Douala, Yaoundé and Nkongsamba – created by a French municipal law of 18 November 1955, and their general functioning is based on the French municipal government pattern. The non-autonomous and semi-autonomous councils are mainly creations of state legislation vesting in them powers compatible with their ability and size to wield them.

THE MUNICIPALITY OF YAOUNDÉ

The nature and political composition of the Yaoundé municipal authority (*Commune municipal de Yaoundé*) are of considerable interest. The municipality has a council of 37 members, each elected for six years by secret ballot from a single list under a system of universal adult suffrage, with eligibility for re-election. The electoral constituency is a named *quartier* (quarter), and any legally existing political party may present a list consisting of as many candidates as there are seats to be filled in the council. The list obtaining the largest number of votes lawfully cast must be proclaimed elected. This procedure is remarkably similar to that adopted in national elections.

At the moment there is only one legally recognized political party in the municipality as well as in the rest of the country. The party, the Cameroon National Union (CNU), is a resultant of a voluntary merger on 1 September 1966 of a multiplicity of rather antagonistic political parties, in response to President Ahidjo's call for a single "unified party" to create unity out of the diversity of the country's ethnic groups. The president successfully convinced the other parties that only in this way could Cameroonians mobilize and direct their energies to the economic and social development of the country, and also that democracy could be preserved within a single political party. This does not in theory imply the legal proscription of any other party or parties. In fact, the federal constitution permits the operation of a multi-party system. Article 3 states: "The political parties and groups play a part in the expression of the suffrage. They shall be free to form and to carry on their activities within the limits established by law and regulations." But the degree of tenacity and vivacity with which the Cameroon masses have so far embraced the advent of the CNU is proof positive of the present popularity of the one-party system. How long this will last is beyond anybody's prediction. The truth is that the new party has introduced a general air of confidence and unity in the people, with an attendant feeling of governmental stability in Yaoundé and the rest of the country.

The national organization of the party is tripartite; the CNU itself, and its appendages, the youth wing and the women's wing of the party. The organs of the party are the cells, branches, subsections, sections, and a political bureau. Each member of the CNU or its two wings must register with the cell of his or her place of residence. The cell, as the basic organ, elects representatives to the branch which in turn elects representatives to form the subsections. In Yaoundé, the subsection is the highest organ. It sends representatives to the section, the highest organ within the Méfou Division. The highest party authority at the sectional level is the party congress, which meets every three years to elect the National Political Bureau. So, the party can be perceived as a vertical pyramid with the cell at the base and the Political Bureau at the apex. The headquarters of the party are located in the heart of the city of Yaoundé.

Freedom of constructive internal dissent within the party is not merely a democratic platitude; it is a healthy reality, the continuation of which will combine a flexible toleration of individual opinion with a sense of national unity. Evidence of the support given to the CNU during its formative years in Yaoundé and the close relationship of the municipal government and the CNU, is that the *délégué du gouvernement* of Yaoundé since 1958, Mr André Fouda, has been not only an elected member of the Federal National Assembly but also the president of the section of the CNU in the Central-South region.

Before 1967 elected members of the Yaoundé municipal council could elect a mayor (*le maire*). But under Law No. 67–2–COR of 1 March 1967 the functions of the mayor were transferred to the *délégué du gouvernement*, who is appointed by the East Cameroon government and has the powers of a liaison officer between the vice-prime minister of East Cameroon and the municipal council. After 1967 the council elected a chairman and two vice-chairmen from among its members. The chairman was vested with powers to summon meetings of the council upon request of the *délégué du gouvernement*.

Yaoundé's municipal government must be contrasted with the eleven semi-autonomous local authorities in East Cameroon, where the administrative head still is an elected mayor who is appointed from the local council by the East Cameroon Cabinet. The mayor is assisted by two deputy mayors appointed from among the elected councillors by the Secretary of State for Internal Affairs. In these councils (*communes*) the prefect is the immediate permanent representative of the Secretary of State for Internal Affairs. A decree of 2 November 1960 vests the prefect with rule-making powers for supervision and control of such communes and he is enjoined to approve all their budgets if they fall below 30 million francs cfa.[2] But a decree of 17 July 1967 requires that if the sum involved is 30 million francs cfa or more, the prefect must within thirty days compile a detailed report on the budget, which must be submitted to the Secretary of State for Internal Affairs for scrutiny and approval.

The municipality of Yaoundé undertakes such services as road construction, street-lighting, registration of deaths and births, the collection of revenue through the granting of building and driving permits, building of of markets stalls, and street cleaning. Its most important recent preoccupation has been a slum-clearance scheme designed to overhaul and modernize the city. As could be expected, this scheme has not captured the immediate popularity of the individual land owners or tenants affected by it, although the overwhelming majority of Yaoundé inhabitants welcome it as a concerted attempt to rid the city of dilapidated and unsanitary structures unfit for human habitation. To offset any homelessness by the dispossessed owners or tenants, the municipal authority, in close co-operation with the federal and state authorities, is being assisted by the Société Immobliere du Cameroun, a public corporation, to carry out a progressive, inexpensive small-house building scheme for resettlement of the ejected persons. But whether the building construction is fast enough to meet the demand, is quite another matter. The question of the scarcity of accommodation in Yaoundé has been a matter of concern to the federal government. The president recently issued a decree appointing a special board of competent civil servants and technicians to study the entire problem and to submit a report with recommendations for government consideration and action.

The dimension of the housing demand cannot be overemphasized because it is the creation of not only the dispossessed in the municipal slum-clearance scheme but also the high birth rate of the inhabitants and the movement into the municipality of rural population in search of work, fortune and adventure. Indeed, a demographic study of Yaoundé indicates an increase in population between 1959 and 1969 from 60,000 to 150,000, which represents about 150 per cent increase during a single decade. The high demand for land in the city has caused an increase of rents and prices. The average cost of land in residential areas is 1,000 francs cfa per square metre and about 2,000 francs cfa per square metre in commercial areas. It is predictable that the current governmental studies of the present municipal situation will generate some legislation and control.

The discussion and approval of the municipal budget is another function that engages the responsibility of Yaoundé's municipal council. Under a French overseas law of 1884 and the decree of November 1960, the municipal council has a duty to deliberate on and regulate all matters of the municipality that come within its competence. On the other hand, under the same law and decree, as amended by the law of 1 March 1967, the *délégué du gouvernement* is solely responsible for the proper administration of the municipality. To this extent there is an element of the separation of powers within the municipality similar to that within the federal and state governments. In budgetary practice, however, the *délégué du gouvernement* collects the requisite financial information from each chief of service of the municipality and prepares a draft budget which he submits to a finance committee chosen by the council. The committee is not a decision-making body but examines and prepares a report for the plenary assembly of the council, after giving the *délégué du gouvernement* every opportunity to explain the draft budget item by item. The report is presented to the council by the committee's *rapporteur*. The council may not approve the budget unless revenues at least balance expenditures. But above all it must ultimately be ratified by the vice-prime minister of East Cameroon, who is in charge of Internal Affairs, including local government bodies.

The annual totals of revenue and expenditure for the municipality from 1962 to 1968 were as follows (in millions of francs cfa):

Financial Year	Revenue	Expenditure
1962–63	305	269
1963–64	329	272
1964–65	364	322
1965–66	518	430
1966–67	481	421
1967–68	480	378
1968–69	574	381

CONTROL OF THE MUNICIPALITY

Control of the municipality is exerciseable in four ways. First is control by the council itself, in plenary assemblies and committees. This is really internal control. Second, the East Cameroon legislature, as already indicated, is empowered to regulate any matter concerning local government. For instance, it was a law of this legislature that abolished the title *maire* and introduced the new title *délégué du gouvernement* with somewhat enhanced responsibilities. Third, there is control by the East Cameroon executive through the prime minister's power to issue *décret-loi* or executive decrees under the law of November 1961, establishing the East Cameroon constitution. Furthermore, all administrative decisions are guided by administrative circulars and directives issued by the East Cameroon Ministry of Internal Affairs. Fourth, the municipality is a corporate entity and can sue and be sued in law. Its actions are governed by the principles of administrative and judicial legality. That is to say, under Cameroon law, the municipality is governed by the principles of administrative law (*droit administratif*), if as a corporate person it commits some acts through its agents, whereas it is governed by the ordinary law in other acts. Under Federal Law 69-LP-1 passed in June 1969, only the Federal Court of Justice has jurisdiction where the act of a local authority comes within the scope of administrative matters defined therein. This law also provides (Sec. 14, para. 3) that "the ordinary courts shall have jurisdiction over any other claim or dispute in accordance with the ordinary law." So, all acts of Yaoundé's municipal government are subject to judicial review.

Yaoundé is simultaneously the federal capital, the capital of East Cameroon, the seat of the Inspector of Federal Administration in the Central-South Region, and the capital of the Méfou Division with a resident prefect, thus involving an apparent conglomeration of administrative hierarchy. Yet the intranational and state comity that has persisted over the years since independence and reunification has avoided conflicts between the various governmental organs. After all, the president of the federal republic appoints the East Cameroon state government and would not appoint a government likely to be hostile to the interests of the federal government in Yaoundé as the federal capital. The president has a right to dissolve any East Cameroon government whose hostility to the federal government becomes evident; and this is a deterrent to the exercise of independent action by the East Cameroon Secretary of State for the Interior or the East Cameroon legislature in their control of the affairs of the municipality. The harmony and co-operation that exists between the federal, state, and municipal authorities in the administration of Yaoundé tends to give the impression of a fusion of multiple governmental action. This is partly attributable to the strong centralization of the national government and partly to the fact that one of the two component states of the federation, East Cameroon, much richer than West Cameroon and with some four-fifths of the nation's total population (about 5.4 million in 1970), tends to dictate the trends of constitutional and political events.

SOCIAL CHARACTERISTICS

The foregoing thesis also affords an explanation for the bicultural and bilingual imbalance in the federal capital. For, although English and French are equal official languages, English is still treated, in practice, as a secondary language since it is only spoken by a small minority in the city. Official documents are often drafted first in French and then later translated into English. Neither the gazettes of the East Cameroon government nor documents of the municipality are translated into English. At the federal level, however, a linguistic service attached to the office of the president is responsible for translating official federal documents.

It must be stated that the kind of bilingual-bicultural clash that exists in Ottawa is non-existent in Yaoundé, because Cameroonians have their own native cultural and linguistic backgrounds and they are generally enthusiastic to learn both English and French to facilitate communication of ideas at the administrative level. There is, for example, no open clarion call by the Cameroon anglophones or francophones to remain English or French. The general sentiment is in favour of acquiring an effective knowledge of both English and French not only as a means of internal communication of ideas but as foreign languages with international repute. There is no visible resentment to either of the two languages or their cultural heritages so long as their preservation and dissemination is identified with the Cameroon national policy content. This is not to minimize the interaction and the multicultural blend in a country where customary principles vary substantially from ethnic group to ethnic group; and even within an ethnic group there are apt to be agreements only on broad principles, partly because customs are changing with contemporary circumstances.

The social stratification of Yaoundé is much the same as can be found in the capitals of other developing countries. Civil servants of the higher cadre own one or two cars as a status symbol, while the rest go and return from work in buses donated some years ago by the West German government.

Foreign diplomatic hegemony is hardly a real menace. No diplomat has been branded persona non grata during the last five years, which is indicative of the amicable rapport between foreign government representatives and the Cameroon government. The Ministry of Foreign Affairs in Yaoundé, however, requires for its own security advance information of the movement of any diplomat from Yaoundé. Otherwise diplomats enjoy diplomatic immunity and have freedom of action within the framework of Cameroon municipal laws.

There are no religious conflicts in the city because Cameroon is, by constitutional enactments, a secular state. This means that there is absolute separation of church and state. In a country with a multiplicity of religious denominations, already faced with many social, economic and administrative difficulties, it was considered prudent to avoid further problems that might arise from adopting an established religion. Yaoundé therefore conveniently accommodates Roman Catholic churches, Cameroon Baptist, Presbyterian, the Sudan United Mission, Moslem, and other religious sects. The Jehovah Witness sect has, however, been banned.

FUTURE PROSPECTS

Any forecast of Yaoundé's continued existence as a federal capital must be limited. At the opening of the Foumban Constitutional Conference, which preceded the reunification of the country, President Ahidjo, as leader of the First Cameroon Republic delegation, had this to say about the nature of the federation:

You know that, in our meetings with Mr Foncha (leader of the British Cameroon delegation) and before and after the referendum, we had chosen a federal structure for our future state. Why this formula? Because of the existing linguistic, administrative, and economic disparities we cannot seriously and reasonably envisage a unitary centralised state; because, on the other hand a very loose federal system would not permit the specific reconciliations and close links which we want.[3]

There have been specific reconciliations and close links since reunification; for there has been a realization of harmony in the economic, social, and political fields through the formulation of common policies and legislative enactments covering the entire federation. For instance, there have been the Federal Labour Code, Criminal Code, Investment Code, similar principles governing administrative legality, and the introduction of bilingual institutions all over the country as an attempt to close up the linguistic and cultural barriers. The emphasis in political orientation is gradually moving from federalism to assimilation and uniformity. The original linguistic, administrative, and economic disparities which constituted the basis for federation are perceptibly disappearing. It is therefore natural to expect the folding up of the Cameroon federation and the conversion of Yaoundé into the capital of a unitary state before many years. The idea of creating a unitary system is gathering momentum from proponents in both states who consider its achievement true national consolidation and unity.

1 Since this essay has been written, events have proved my concluding prediction on future prospects to be right: on 20 May 1972, at the request of the President of the Federal Republic, Cameroonians voted at a referendum and approved by an overwhelming majority a draft constitution having the effect of converting the present federal republic into a unitary state, to be styled "the United Republic of Cameroon." The new constitution is expected to come into force during 1972. The two federated legislatures and their governments will then disappear, and Yaoundé will become the capital of a unitary state.
2 Cameroon franks. One frank cfa was in 1970 worth about 0.4 of a us cent.
3 Henri Cazalou, Director of Judicial Affairs, "Note relative à des difficultés d'application de la Constitution fédéral du Cameroun" [Notes on Difficulties of Applying the Federal Constitution of Cameroon], mimeographed sheet (Yaoundé, 1964).

C Capitals in decentralized federations

Hermann Boeschenstein **BERN**

Though certainly a well-organized, independent state, Switzerland has no real capital. Bern is the capital of the canton (state) of Bern, but to Switzerland it is only the Federal City, the seat of the federal parliament and administration, and of the foreign diplomatic missions in Switzerland. The word "capital" sounds in Swiss ears like the centre of a centralized state. The Swiss prefer to stick to the traditional *federalisme*, the Swiss Confederation being the final result of a very old alliance among sovereign states, the cantons (of which there are now 25). Yet it must be admitted that since the two world wars the trend toward a centralized state has been strong.

THE SEAT OF GOVERNMENT IN HISTORY

According to the loose confederation created after the Napoleonic wars in 1815, the small federal administration, with all its archives and papers, moved every second year from Zurich to Bern and from Bern to Lucerne, the respective cantonal government taking over the leadership of the common Swiss affairs. The president of the cantonal government currently providing the seat for this nucleus of an administration, was also president of the Swiss confederation.

The first experiment of creating a real united Switzerland goes back to the years 1832 and 1833. In 1832 some people thought it the best solution to create a federal territory for the seat of government, like the District of Columbia in the United States, and one well-known politician who was a forester even proposed that a new capital should be built on one of those beautiful Swiss hills which are covered by woods. Finally, Lucerne was proposed as the seat of government, but this proposal never became law, there being no majority of the sovereign cantons.

The choosing of Bern

The modern Swiss confederation goes back to the year 1848, famous for the European revolutionary movement and its failures except in Switzerland.

In that year there was a strong competition between Bern and Zurich as to which should become the federal seat. Heavy polemics opposed one city to the other. But the committee charged with elaborating the constitution of the new state was from the very beginning against any constitutional rule concerning the choice. The constitution says simply that it should be a matter of federal legislation to designate the seat of the new federal authorities. The legislation was also to enumerate the accommodation the Federal City would be required to offer to these federal authorities.

The old system of moving the seat of government again got some support, but the political satirists made a great mockery of the "federal coach" transporting the new state from one town to another. The opposition against Bern was partly against the Radical party, which the left-wing of James Staempfli and his friends had taken over in 1846. It was also partly a matter of jealousy. Finally, it was argued that Bern had a bad climate, with much fog in the winter, and was a boring town – a remark variously repeated in the letters of Count Gobineau as Secretary of the French Embassy to his famous friend Alexis de Tocqueville. On the other side it was said that since Bern was not exactly gay Paris, the members of Parliament would do more serious work.

When the first Swiss Parliament met in the autumn of 1848, both chambers had to decide where the new authorities should take their seat. In the National Council, the people's chamber, Bern got 58 votes; Zurich, 35; Lucerne, 6; and the small district town of Zofingen, one. The Council of the States, the upper chamber, took the following vote: 21 for Bern, 13 for Zurich, and 3 for Lucerne. But the matter was not yet settled.

The conditions of the choice

The next thing to be done was to establish the conditions the future Federal City had to fulfil. This was done by the newly elected federal Parliament, but it needed the agreement of the citizens of Bern. The Federal City was required to provide the necessary buildings for both parliamentary chambers, for the Federal Council (the cabinet of seven members), the seven departments, the federal chancery, the administration, the archives, and the federal mint, without any financial compensation. In December of 1848, a meeting of the Bernese citizens considered the municipal council's proposals, which involved expenses amounting to 300,000 old Swiss francs (450,000 new francs, or roughly US $100,000, 1970 value).[1] Since Bern was a town of only 26,000 inhabitants, the sum was a heavy one. It is therefore understandable that the citizens were not at all enthusiastic about this burden. After a long and stormy debate the conditions were finally agreed to, by 419 votes to 313.

The city provided various old buildings which could provisionally house the new authorities. The National Council got the "Casino," a music hall built in 1821, on the spot of the existing Federal Palace. The Council of the States got a patrician club-house, while the cabinet and the chancery were given the Palais d'Erlach, which was a beautiful town house of the 18th century belonging to the wealthy von Erlach family. It now belongs to the municipal administration and is still a jewel of the old town. The canton offered a house for the mint, and one for the first postal administration, as well as offices for the then meagre archives.

From the very beginning of the federation of Bernese authorities became aware of the urgent need to build a Federal Palace. The Federal Council was asked about the necessary rooms and replied that 96 offices would be suitable. An architectural competition was opened, and in September 1851 the plans of the prize winner, the well-known Bernese architect Frederic Studer, were approved by the municipality. The total expenses were estimated to be 1,660,000 new francs. In addition to floating two public loans of 400,000 francs each, the municipality levied a special tax, which was opposed by a group of the new federal civil servants. The total costs to the municipality were finally 2,145,000 new francs (about half a million US 1970 dollars). By the summer of 1857 the Parliament, cabinet and other federal authorities could officially enter the Palace. Today it is still one of the three big buildings on the so-called Federal Terrace, overlooking the river and the glorious landscape with a tremendous view of the snow-covered Alps—in fine weather of course.

The cost of expansion

The Swiss constitution was the object of a total revision in 1874, the main idea being a further development of the central state and thus of the federal administration. The slogan was "*one* people *one* army, and *one* civil and penal law." Some figures will illustrate this development. The total expenses of the federal government were 4.6 million francs in 1850, 8 million in 1860 and 19.4 million in 1875. (Today the total expenses are about 7,000 million!) In 1849, the first year of the activity of the new administration, it counted 80 civil servants, without of course the public services like post and telegraph and the army factories for ammunition, gun-powder, etc. The number of civil servants in the seven departments was 338 in 1875 and 2,942 by 1900. The figure for the end of 1967 was 28,307, nearly half of the civil servants being in the civil departments and the other half in the Army Department. In addition there were 47,000 in the Department of Posts, Telegraphs, and Telephones and 41,000 in the federal railways.

After the revision of 1874 the citizens of Bern got quite a fright when the federal government informed the town council that in view of the new tasks of the federal administration much more office space must be placed at the disposal of the confederation. The government's letter sounded like an ultimatum. In distress, the city turned to the cantonal government for assistance. The canton proved to be a strong supporter of the city. Both took the view that Bern had already fulfilled its conditions, which were based on the constitution of 1848 and not of that of 1874. Negotiations started, and finally the federal government agreed to take over the Federal Palace which was still owned by the city. Bern had to pay a lump sum of 500,000 francs in order to be freed from any further obligations and had to offer the necessary land at a cheap price for a second Federal Palace in the immediate neighbourhood of the existing Palace. An agreement was signed and later ratified by Parliament, and the canton of Bern voluntarily offered to pay 200,000 francs to the city. The Federal Council was at once able to open a new competition for a second Federal Palace, which was finished in 1892. The impressive front of the two palaces was crowned by a new Parliament building in 1902.

The federal government in a "foreign country"

The federal state was created in a "foreign country" insofar as the canton of Bern was up to 1848 an independent and sovereign state. At first the rulers of the canton were Radicals (left-wing Liberals), and on the whole friendly to the federal state. But, in 1850 this government was overthrown by a Conservative majority, and then the federal government and even Parliament did not feel completely safe in Bern. What would happen if the cantonal Conservative government would one day (or night) arrest the members of the cabinet and simply close Parliament? Who would then defend the federal state? It was fairly weak, without a police of its own and without an army independent of the canton.

In 1851 Parliament elaborated a law creating the necessary guarantees against this possibility. The seven Federal Councillors and the federal chancellor (secretary of the cabinet as well as head of the Parliamentary chancery) were to keep their domicile in their respective cantons, and the civil servants were freed from any requirement to live in Bern. The canton of Bern was explicitly declared fully responsible for the confederation's property, which was to be entirely tax free. In the case of internal troubles the Federal Council was entitled to call Parliament to meet out of Bern, even outside the canton of Bern. Should the cabinet be prevented from exercising this power, the speaker of Parliament or his deputy could exercise it. Finally, this very important law of 1851 was declared valid from 1848.

But in 1854 the Bernese cantonal elections showed a near balance between

Conservatives and Radicals, and they formed a coalition government. Since then, there has never been a real danger to the federal government, for the Bernese Conservatives, though opposing the federal Radical-Liberal government in many things, firmly supported the federal constitution. The Conservative feelings may have been hostile, but this did not mean illegal action. Up to now the members of the Federal Council and the chancellor have been treated like foreign diplomats, with great respect. There has never been any real difficulty except perhaps for the three days of the general strike in November 1918, when the Federal Council moved to the nearby Palace Hotel where the army had its headquarters.

THE LOCAL GOVERNMENT

The city's legislative body is a council of 80 members elected every fourth year. The party distribution after the 1967 election was: 33 Labour, 16 Radical Liberal, 11 Independent, 8 Conservative, 5 "Young Bern," 5 Christian Democrat, and 2 Protestant Christian. Before the introduction of full political rights for women within the commune in 1970, there were 45,000 men entitled to take part in the elections. Of these, 57 per cent voted in the election of 1967.

The city's executive body is a council of seven members, each of them being the head of a department: economics, finance, police, welfare services, education, industrial enterprises (such as water, gas, electricity, and public transport), and public works (such as roads, and bridges). The chairman of the executive council is the mayor of the city. He is head of the department of economics, and also directs the town planning office as well as the public gardens. Before becoming members of the executive, three of the councillors were lawyers, one was a chief editor, one a medical doctor, one a protestant clergyman, and one a headmaster.

The city's budget estimates for 1970 showed expenses of 246 million Swiss francs and revenues of 240 million. Though this indicates a deficit of six million, usually the final result is better than the estimate. On the revenue side, direct taxes were expected to bring in 136 million francs; industrial enterprises, 20 million; income from the city's estates, 21 million; and subsidies and direct taxes about 50 million.

PRESENT FEDERAL–CITY RELATIONS

At present the federal and the cantonal governments are on very friendly terms, and the relations between the Federal Council and the mayor and aldermen of Bern are a model of mutual comprehension. A great many problems are dealt with by the federal government in agreement with the local municipal police. Examples are the policing of new federal buildings and of federal ceremonies like troop parades and receptions of foreign heads of state, and the protection of the Federal Palace in case of demonstrations in Parliament Square. This is a place often used by demonstrators, as is London's Trafalgar Square, for instance by the farmers' union and for the workers' May-day parade.

Federal-City co-operation is greatly facilitated by the fact that the present mayor of Bern is also a member of the federal lower house of Parliament, the National Council. Each newly elected Parliament is usually invited by the Bernese authorities to a dinner party. Switzerland is a small country and everybody seems to know everybody else. There are a great many possibilities of getting to know one another, through common interests of political life, the compulsory army service and the universities. There may often be passionate debates in Parliament and press between political parties and their supporters, but afterwards they sit peacefully together in Bern's hotels and pubs, having a friendly conversation or a game of cards.

Though the population of Switzerland was about six million in 1970, Bern was still a town of only about 175,000 inhabitants. However, the population of the metropolitan area was about 270,000. The suburbs are also used as seats of the federal administration. When the Office of Topography was built in 1938 in a nearby village, a well-known professor of constitutional law claimed that this was a violation of the law designating Bern as the seat of the government. The town, however, did not protest, and because of the overcrowding since then, has been quite pleased to support this geographic extension of the federal administration.

When Bern was chosen in 1848 it was understood that other places would one day have a chance to get federal establishments. In 1874 the Federal High Court chose Lausanne as its seat, and the much larger Zurich was consoled by the fact that it got the Federal Institute of Technology, the only federal school of higher education, and the National Museum. It was originally intended that the central government would create a federal university in Zurich, but this plan was never realized. Now a second Federal Institute of Technology is to be created in Lausanne.

The character of Bern has, of course, been greatly alerted by becoming the seat of government. But architecturally, the old medieval town has been well preserved, the federal buildings being outside this area. Bern has often been called a town of civil servants, lacking big industry and banking like Zurich. On the other hand, Bern has a stately tradition and strong links with the federal element. Since 1848 there has always been one politician from the canton of Bern amongst the seven members of the federal cabinet. Out of the ten Bernese Federal Councillors since 1848, seven had been members of the Bernese cantonal government before entering the cabinet and one had been mayor of Bern. This former mayor served in the cabinet from 1895 to 1919.

Parliament meets usually four times per year, each session lasting from 2–3 weeks and the members staying in the Bernese hotels from Monday evening to Thursday afternoon. Nearly two-thirds of the parliamentary committees meet in Bern, but others meet in mountain resorts like St Moritz, Zermatt, or the Italian-speaking area, Lugano or Locarno, together with one member of the cabinet and leading officials dealing with the matter at hand.

No Swiss civil servant is allowed to be a member of the federal Parliament, but permission is always given to them by the Federal Council if they want to become a member of the cantonal Parliament or the city council. A considerable number of federal civil servants are members of one of these bodies. Dr Reynold Tschaeppaet, formerly a deputy director in the Federal Home Office, became acting mayor of Bern and speaker of the cantonal Parliament when he was a federal official. He is now mayor of Bern as well as a member of the National Council. The acting director of the Federal Office for the Conservation of Energy is a leading member of Bern's municipal council, and the acting Swiss Consul General in Amsterdam had a seat in Bern's cantonal Parliament whilst he was a member of the Swiss Foreign Office. Thus federal, cantonal, and municipal authorities are strongly bound together.

POLITICAL PROBLEMS

The language problem

One problem affecting Bern as the seat of government is the fact that the federal state is tri-lingual. The federal administration needs several thousand French-speaking and a number of Italian-speaking officials, but schooling is mainly a matter for the canton and the city. Following the territorial principle, the German-speaking city of Bern has German-speaking schools. The French- and Italian-speaking officials therefore were concerned. What about their children's future if they were one day to return to their original canton? First the French-speaking people in Bern founded a French school, and later the federal government began to pay subsidies to the school for the children of French-speaking officials. The University of Bern is cantonal, and the canton of Bern is bilingual; though most of the lectures are given in German, the law teachers, historians, philosophers, and of course linguists are trained in both of the leading national languages.

In 1848 French-speaking members of both chambers voted for Bern and against Zurich or Lucerne. Today they may often criticize the typical Bernese mentality, but they also fully recognize the great advantages of a bilingual canton, with a population speaking mainly German but also a considerable number speaking French. Any customer of a federal railway or post office is entitled to be answered in German, French, or Italian. Parliamentary debates are translated into French or German simultaneously, and all official documents are published in both languages, with the important drafts and laws being also published in Italian.

The metropolitan problem

Bern has an area of 5154 ha (1 ha = 10,000 m²), while the area of the suburbs is 30,536 ha. Most of the suburbs surrounding Bern are independent communes with municipal councils of their own. After the first world war one commune was incorporated into Bern, but since then these suburbs have firmly maintained their autonomy. Some of them are financially strong, for any commune has the right to levy taxes upon the inhabitants, and some suburbs have wealthy inhabitants. People pay taxes where they live, not where they work. However, the compensation for Bern, economically speaking, is the fact that the inhabitants of the suburbs go to town for their purchases, concert and theatre performances, etc., and spend a good deal of their earnings in the shops and pubs of Bern.

There are of course a great many problems which can only be dealt with by a sincere collaboration between the city and the suburbs, not only of transportation, but also of sewerage, roads, bridges, schooling, fire brigades, etc. In all of these cases both partners, the city and the suburban communes, try to reach an agreement. There is a growing understanding for solving common problems in a way that is called the "regional spirit" – a strong sense of an extended region or area which includes the suburbs as well as the city.

Police administration presents no serious metropolitan problems because the police are cantonal. A very important exception is that all matters concerning criminal and traffic police are entrusted to the city. However, Bern has a well-trained police force which collaborates loyally with the cantonal police.

Reasonable town planning is certainly made more difficult by the existence of various independent communes in a single urban agglomeration, and very often long negotiations are needed before an agreement can be reached. On the other hand, many members of the municipal councils, especially the mayors, are members of the cantonal Parliament, and everybody knows everybody else well enough to maintain friendly relations. Common interests are emphasized by the double existence of a great many citizens: they work in the city and live in a suburban commune, thus being interested in a fruitful development of mutual understanding.

CONCLUSION

The fact that the national government has never had a territory of its own has not been felt as a weakness. Most retiring members of the federal cabinet stay on in Bern and do not go back to the canton from which they started their political career. The Federal City offers opportunities for an agreeable life, first-class musical performances, a municipal opera house, various theatres, and a vivid social life amid the seventy embassies of foreign countries. It is interesting to note that the descendants of those who voted against Bern in 1848, or objected to the federation not having its own territory for its seat of government, now without exception agree to the solution the newly born confederation adopted in 1848.

[1] One new Swiss franc was worth about 23 US cents in 1970.

Raimund Beck **BONN**

Unlike most capitals of the world, Bonn does not and never did hold any special place among the cities of that part of Germany which forms the federal republic. The only natural fact which contributed to its final selection as the federal capital is that it is approximately in the middle of a north-east axis in Western Germany and consequently can be reached fairly well from all parts of the republic's eleven states (including West Berlin). Until its selection as capital, Bonn had not played an important role in German history. The times of the ancient archbishops and electors of Cologne have passed. What they left in Bonn are a few old churches and villas and the calm way of life of many former German residences. This fits with the academic life of the university, which was founded in 1818. Though many famous scientists worked and do work at Bonn, the university is more a place of academic research than a seedbed of revolutionary political thought. The situation of Bonn on the river Rhine, and especially at the beginning of its beautiful, romantic part with castles and vineyards, has contributed to the calm atmosphere of the town. For a century tourists have been visiting the town, and pensioners and persons with independent means have liked to settle there. Their villas and luxurious houses are still characteristic of the town, though nearly a third of its houses had been destroyed during the second world war.

Like some other federal capitals, Bonn is an artificially made capital. While capitals such as Canberra, Brasilia and Islamabad were newly planned and constructed from the beginning, the artificial element of Bonn consists in the fact that a very old, small and calm university town on the romantic river Rhine was changed into the capital of one of the most important industrial nations, a country whose population exceeded sixty million in 1970. This transformation process has not yet been completed, over twenty years after the selection of Bonn as capital of West Germany. The reason is that Bonn is not only an artificial capital but also a provisional capital. After the breakdown of the German "Reich" in the second world war, the German "states," which had been created by the American, British, and French forces in their occupied zones of Germany, united into a federation under the constitution of 1949, the so-called Basic Law. This proclaims in its preamble that it will be in effect only for a period of transition, until the German people may accomplish by their own free will the unity and liberty of Germany, that is to say, until the people of the Federal Republic can be reunited with those of the German Democratic Republic, which developed in the Russian occupied zone of the former Middle-Germany. This "reunification" is the outspoken goal of all West German governments. Berlin, the capital of the former "Reich," is now an enclave surrounded by the territory of the German Democratic Republic. The German desire for reunification implies that Berlin will be the capital of a reunified Germany, and this means that Bonn will be a capital only for a provisional period. Both these elements, the artificial one and the provisional one, are at the bottom of all the difficulties of the administration of Bonn.

THE GERMAN CAPITAL IN HISTORY

Up to the foundation of the second German empire, the "Reich" of 1871, Germany had never had an official capital. In the times of the ancient "Sanctum Imperium Romanum Germanae Nationis" the emperor had his residence at Vienna, but he received the crown at Frankfurt. The "Reichstag," the assembly of the princes and towns, met at Regensburg while the Supreme Court was situated in Wetzlar. The "Deutsche Bund" of 1815, the alliance of sovereign German princes and towns, proclaimed Frankfurt as Federal Town, where its assembly would meet. But Frankfurt was not yet a real capital, for it was only the meeting place of a conference of diplomats. The German states still held their sovereignty. After the revolution of 1848, the German constituent assembly met at Frankfurt. The resulting constitution, however, did not decide the capital question. Consequently Frankfurt could only achieve a certain importance as a symbol and as the spiritual capital of a liberal and democratic Germany.

It was only in the year 1871 that Germany got a capital for a long period. After the victory over France, Prussia and its allied German states (without Austria) founded the Second German Reich, and it was decided in the constitution that Berlin, the capital of the hegemonial power, Prussia, should be the capital of the federation (Art. 71). But there was opposition to the choice. To the protagonists of the idea of a "Great-Germany," Berlin was the symbol of the Reich which excluded Austria. Also, in the southern part of Germany, with its liberal and democratic traditions, Berlin was the incarnation of the abhorred Prussian authoritarian ideas. To the protagonists of the federal idea, like Konstantin Frantz, this capital was the symbol of the wrongly constructed federation of the Reich, which was not at all based on the principle of the equality of the individual states but on the predominance of the overwhelming power, Prussia.[1] Consequently, Berlin had to wait many years before it was generally accepted as the German capital. But the concentration of culture and science in the years up to 1932, the heroic struggle of Berlin against the blockade by the Russians in 1947, and the attempts of annexation made by the German Democratic Republic, ensured that today Berlin is the symbol of the German desire for reunification.

Berlin as the former capital

Under the constitution of 1871 Berlin had no special status except for the fact that it was named as the capital of the Reich. Claims that the Reich as a federation should have a federal territory for its capital, like the American District of Columbia, had no echo. The idea of a capital which is related on equal terms to all states of the federation did not correspond to the constitution, which was based on the principle of Prussia's predominance. Even within the framework of Prussia's constitutional law, Berlin did not hold a much different position from that of the other Prussian towns. The Prussian Local Government Law of 1853 included Berlin too up to the end of the first world war. Only in the context of the general administration of Prussia could there be found a few special laws which took account of the size and importance of the city. In 1875, for instance, Berlin left the province of Brandenburg and became an administrative province of its own. The state supervision of the city was then executed not – as in the case of the other Prussian towns – by a district governor (Regierungspräsident) but by a provincial governor (Oberpräsident) who was immediately responsible to the Prussian Minister of the Interior. Police matters were administered, as in all Prussian towns, by an organ of the state, the "Police-president."

Apart from this, Berlin and all other Prussian towns had been governed since Baron von Stein's famous Town Ordinance of 1808, under a regime of locally elected government. An elected body of councillors chose the persons for an executive body, the "Magistrat." This right of local self-government was restricted only by a few laws which had regard to Berlin's status as capital of Prussia and the Reich, for instance, laws on the erection of public monuments or on town planning.

After the revolution of 1918, Germany remained a federation under the constitution of Weimar, with Berlin as its capital. Berlin's constitutional status continued as before with the only exception that the constitution did not mention Berlin as capital of the Reich. Over against this, the form of local government of the city underwent a thorough change.[2] This change, however, referred only to the fact that the population of the city had grown considerably and that the seat of government affected not only Berlin but also many surrounding local communities. The Prussian law of 1920 on the formation of a new community for Berlin did not refer to the special situation of Berlin as capital of the Reich and did not neven mention the term "capital" (Reichshauptstadt).

According to the new law Berlin was united with seven other towns and 59 rural communities into the new city of "Great Berlin." Most of the affected municipalities had already been collaborating since 1911, pursuant to a Prussian law, in a local administrative union for the execution of common interests. Another aspect of this reform bill was the decentralization of Berlin's administration, which still characterizes its system of local government. The territory of the city was divided into twenty districts, which possessed their own administrative organs – an elected assembly and an executive board chosen by (but not necessarily from) the assembly. The division of administrative tasks between "Great Berlin" and its districts originated many disputes about competence. The final issue was that the district bodies were to handle their own matters but in accordance with general instructions given by the city council.

In 1934 the government of Berlin was changed according to National Socialist principles. The parliamentary system was abolished and superseded by the so-called "leader principle." The latter meant that the leading civil servants were appointed not by the city council but by the supervising state department, the Prussian Ministry of the Interior. The generally elected city council and the assemblies of district deputies were superseded by a single council of appointed members. These honorary posts were the only remainder of the former self-government. The new Prussian law took the special situation of Berlin as capital into account and transferred important powers of the city's administration directly to the Minister of the Interior.

After the second world war the West-German Federal Republic had to abandon its desire to institute Berlin as its capital because of the Four-Power occupation of the city. In 1948 the Russian occupied part of the city had built up its own administrative and political system. The full membership of West Berlin as part of the West German Federal Republic is still opposed not only by the Russians. The US, Great Britain and France, the occupying powers, base their presence in Berlin on the Four-Power Agreement of 1944. They do not want to endanger the validity of this agreement by granting the incorporation of West Berlin into West Germany, though the Russians have allowed the German Democratic Republic to institute East Berlin as its capital. West Berlin's Constitution of 1 September 1950 proclaims in its preamble the desire of Berlin "to remain the capital of a United Germany" and says in Article 1 (2) that Berlin is a state of the federal republic. But according to Article 87, the execution of Article

1 (2) had to be suspended for the above-mentioned reasons "until the validity of West Germany's Constitution will no longer be restricted in Berlin."

At present West Berlin is under a Parliamentary regime. There is an elected city council, or House of Deputies, which chooses an executive organ, the "Senat." The House has 200 members, while the Senate consists of the "Reigning Lord Mayor" (Regierende Burgermeister), a mayor, and not more than 16 "senators." The 12 districts of West Berlin are administered, according to the already-mentioned system of 1920, by elected assemblies of 45 deputies and executive boards of not more than nine members.

The selection of Bonn

Since it was impossible to institute Berlin as the seat of government for West Germany, the organs of the federation had to decide in 1949 which of the West German cities should be the future capital.[3] There were huge cities like Hamburg or Cologne; the cultural capital of Germany, Munich; or the ancient city of the emperors, Frankfurt. But finally none of these great cities, not even one of the second-class cities like Stuttgart or Düsseldorf, was chosen, but the little university town, Bonn. This town had no special characteristic apart from the fact that within its walls the famous composer Beethoven had been born – a fact that had perfectly satisfied the ambitions of the city.

Why was this town selected as the capital? There was a certain precedent. The foreseeing government of the State of North Rhine Westphalia (NRW) had proposed that the constitution-drafting body for the West German federation – the "Parliamentary Council" – should meet on the territory of NRW at Bonn. This proposal was accepted. A different and very human reason is said to have been the preference of the first president of the Parliamentary Council. This was Dr Adenauer, leader of the Christian Democrats and later Federal Chancellor. Dr Adenauer's villa was only a few kilometres from Bonn and it is evident that the selection of Bonn as capital corresponded to his personal interests.[4]

In the midst of the "battle of the sites," there were also important political interests. Among these, federal rivalries – apart from the mentioned ambitions of NRW – played a very small role. At that time the majority, the Christian Democrats, had a marked tendency toward federalism, and unconsciously they might have preferred Bonn to a city like Frankfurt which was more associated with the idea of German unity. Another factor was that Bonn was in an area of Christian Democratic strength. The official reasoning, however, was that the selection of a small town like Bonn was the best guarantee for a provisional capital, leaving Berlin unrivalled as the permanent capital of a united Germany.

As candidates for becoming provisional capital, there were, in addition to Bonn, the cities of Frankfurt, Kassel, and Stuttgart. The Parliamentary Council had set up a committee to examine the possibilities. This committee had asked the candidate cities to report only on the question of the expenses necessary for the construction of 22,000 square metres of office space and for the housing of 2,000 civil servants. It did not want to disturb the German public by the idea of an immense federal bureaucracy. Nevertheless, it knew that in future the federation would have to construct a considerable number of public buildings. It finally recommended in favour of either Bonn or Frankfurt, and in May 1949 the Parliamentary Council decided, with 33 votes against 29 votes, that Bonn should be the capital.

But the battle of the sites was not yet over. The very day of the first meeting of the Parliament, the leader of the main opposition party brought forward a motion that the provisional seat of government be Frankfurt, and the first parliamentary committee to be set up was the "capital committee." After a thorough inspection of the two cities, the committee submitted a report. It did not give a definite recommendation, but its tendency was friendly towards Frankfurt. However, it dealt only with the financial and practical aspects of the problem and did not take into account the judicial and political aspects, and in November 1949 the lower house, the Bundestag, voted 200 for Bonn against 176 for Frankfurt. The reasons for the decision of the Christian Democrats in favour of Bonn have already been indicated. A reason many Socialists and Liberals opposed Bonn was because it was predominantly of Roman Catholic population and to them meant a government under more clerical influence. The Social Democratic leader spoke of the Federal Republic as having been "engendered at Rome and born in Bonn." Also, the location of Bonn on the left bank of the Rhine is associated with the idea of partition, which disturbed German political life after both world wars. Chancellor Adenauer was very often attacked for having supported partition after the first world war and for renewing this policy by his orientation to the western powers after the second world war. To the opposition, Frankfurt was regarded as a symbol of German democratic and liberal traditions and of the desire for German unity.

The influence of the choice of Bonn

It is difficult to decide whether the fears and hopes which determined the attitudes of the political parties on the capital question have been justified. However, there is a general feeling that the policies made in Bonn have developed in the direction which had been feared by the Social Democrats and Liberals. The "Länder," the states of the federation, have become of great political importance. Especially in the field of culture, the Länder possess nearly exclusive competence. As in other centuries of German history, this fact has originated and fomented a fruitful variety of cultural life. On the other hand, there has been a considerable lack of centrally concentrated planning, financing, and execution of cultural and especially scientific tasks, which today must be undertaken on a large scale. Evidently this would not have happened to such an extent if the capital had attracted the cultural elite of the nation. Apart from this, the spirit of provincialism which in comparison with Berlin reigns at Bonn and consequently in the whole republic, had led to an influence of the churches on public life which has not been known in Germany for a long period.

In the field of foreign policy, the government in Bonn has declared German reunification to be a supreme aim. But its policy of exclusive orientation toward the west has been widely criticized. The reunification slogan has been suspected to be a mere subterfuge of those who like to be in Bonn and who dislike Berlin and its Prussian mentality. On the other hand, one undeniable advantage of policy born at Bonn has been Germany's reconciliation with its ancient enemy, France. It can be supposed that this political result would not have been achieved by a government in Berlin, which would have adopted a more eastern oriented policy.

To what extent these and other aspects of policy have been determined by the political atmosphere of Bonn must be left to future research. It will have to take into account the sociology of the recently developed leading class of politicians and civil servants at Bonn. There are many hints that the style of government has been greatly influenced by the atmosphere of the capital and by the characteristics of its society.

Without anticipating the results of such research, we can present some sociologically relevant facts which must have influenced government policy. In recent history there might have been a few new states which did not choose their cultural centre as capital. But otherwise the identity of the cultural and intellectual centre of a country and of its political capital is virtually the rule all over the world. Consequently, one could have predicted easily that the choice of a little university town as capital of one of the world's greatest industrial nations would lead to difficulties for the creation of an active and effective leading class of politicians and civil servants. It can justly be affirmed that great ideas may be born in small huts. On the other hand, it must be stated that the optimal functioning of a huge government is only possible on an adequate territory which provides for a community with the necessary dimensions of social communication and integration.

The formation of such a community has not been possible in Bonn for the simple reason of lack of space. The old town, with its winding streets and its territory of only 32 square kilometres (12.3 sq. mi.), was filled up by its own population and the students and employees of the university. There did not exist possibilities for the acceptance and integration of the great influx of federal politicians and civil servants. As the city could not offer lodgings for the newcomers, the government had to build the needed quarters. The effect was that the autochthonous people of Bonn and the new population had very few opportunities for contact and integration. The civil servants and the politicians, living in not very comfortable "civil service ghettos," developed a special, frustrated ghetto mentality.[5] This mentality was favoured by the fact that the native people of Bonn consciously ignored the presence of the federal government and its civil servants. According to the views of the natives, the busy activity of the federal administration did not fit in with the calm way of life of the university town. A more intensive integration of the Bonn community could have a psychologically releasing function for the civil servant sector of the population.

But even if this difficulty did not exist, Bonn would not be capable of creating the intellectual atmosphere of a real capital. According to a "Bonnmot" of an American, Bonn is only half as large as Chicago's cemetery, but is twice as dead. This indicates the tendency not only of Bonn's night life, but also its intellectual atmosphere. Bonn's university and theatre are far from being national centres of intellectual life and public opinion, and no great supraregional newspaper is published at Bonn. This situation was the more depressing for the first generation of Bonn's politicians and civil servants, and originated a frustrating feeling of being exiled, as most of them had known and worked in Berlin during the "golden twenties." The subsequent resignation, and the lack of contact with an active public opinion and with new and provocative ideas, have been characteristics of post-war German policy.

Apart from the relative lack of cultural life, there is a considerable shortage of social places such as clubs and restaurants where people of the town, the university, the administration and the Parliament can meet and relax. Under these circumstances it is not surprising that Bonn is regarded by most MP's and high civil servants as a mere working place, as a "garrison town" which is to be left as fast as possible after the end of the five-day week. The way of thinking and policy-making which corresponds to this way of life results in a more improvised and often incoherent policy, a defect for which the Bonn administration has often been reproached. Another aspect of this situation is that though the states cannot offer quite as high a salary to civil servants, state capitals such as Munich, Hamburg, Stuttgart and Düsseldorf offer a larger, better integrated and more highly developed community, and thus many advantages of social and cultural life. Consequently, it was difficult to get the elite of the civil servants to come to Bonn, and some of the states were administered better than the federation itself.

THE CAPITAL IN THE FRAMEWORK OF THE CONSTITUTION

That Bonn should be only the provisional capital is not expressly stated in the constitution but is indicated by the fact that the constitution says nothing regarding the site of the capital. While the self-consciousness of other nations crystallizes in the awareness of their capital as the centre of the nation, and a corresponding constitutional provision, the silence of the Basic Law over this point is an indication of the broken self-consciousness of the German nation, which lacks the feeling of having found its final area, identity and constitutional organization.

When the Bundestag declared Bonn to be the capital it was exercising a competence of *rei naturae*. The consequence is that theoretically it could change the seat of government without any constitutional difficulties. It follows that Bonn does not have that special constitutional status which is characteristic of federal capital districts. The idea of a federal district has never had many protagonists in Germany.[6] Insofar as the idea is supported by the intention of securing the absolute equality of every state against a possible hegemony of one of them, this fear was of very little importance at the time of the founding of the federation. At that time the impression of the lost war and the need for national reconstruction and unification were the overwhelming facts. If the conception of a federal district is based on the idea of protecting the federal government against the possible pressures of the surrounding state government or of the town administration, the fathers of the Basic Law did not take into account such a possibility. The maintenance of security and order in the capital seldom had been difficult in this country of efficient administration.

In principle Bonn's status is no different from that of any other West German city. It is true that from 1949 to 1955, from the founding of the federal republic to the acquisition of its full sovereignty, Bonn had a certain special status. The city and a few surrounding local communities formed an enclave which was free from occupation by the allied forces. It is also true that federal law contains some provisions regarding the seat of government. However, these do not concern the whole city but only a small zone, the Bannmeile, and are designed to protect the meetings of the Bundestag and the Bundesrat (upper house). In this zone demonstrations and meetings are allowed only if the federal Minister of the Interior has given his assent. Apart from this, federal law does not provide for any possibility of institutionalized influence of federal authorities on the administration of the capital. The federal government gives financial subsidies to Bonn from time to time, and these may, of course, influence the local administration. But as they are not institutionalized, the intensity of the federal influence is difficult to measure.

Any attempt to alter this independent situation of the capital in the constitutional framework of the federation would meet with serious difficulties. Article 28 of the Basic Law guarantees the right of self-government to the local communities, according to which they possess the right "to settle all matters of local concern according to law but on their own responsibility." A form of restricted local government for Bonn would be violating this principle. Moreover, the organization of Bonn as a federal district would require an alteration of the constitution, which does not provide for federal territories. To achieve such an alteration would have been politically possible in 1969 when the coalition of Christian and Social Democrats was in control of more than two-thirds of the legislature. However, though discussions on reorganizing the capital's administration have been very lively, the idea has not yet become popular that Bonn needs a special constitutional status. There have been some suggestions in the German press to give Bonn the status of a federal district,[7] but these have not yet been the object of serious discussions. Whether this will happen one day is to be doubted. The constitutional difficulties and the old traditions of German local government will prove to be serious difficulties. And the causes of organizing federal districts – jealousy among the states and the need to protect the federal government – are not likely to grow up in West Germany to the extent which requires corresponding political action.

The fact of Bonn being the federal capital has not influenced the status of the city within the constitution of North Rhine Westphalia. The guarantee of local government in the federal constitution has been followed in the state Constitution of 1950 (Article 78), which must not be in contradiction to the federal constitution. Consequently, Bonn is related to the state in the same way as all the cities of this state which do not belong to a county (Landkreis). This means that the organization and operation of its government are regulated by NRW's Local Community Act of 1952, which corresponds to the requirements of the federal constitution. Article 28 of the Basic Law says that the local communities must have a representative body elected by free, direct, general, equal, and secret vote, that their self-government is guaranteed, and that they are in principle competent to deal with all of their own matters. So long as these principles are obeyed the states are free in the way they organize local government. Therefore, among the states, different types of local administration are possible and have developed due to the fact that in the years after the war the occupation forces in their respective zones influenced the shaping of local administration. The type of local government possessed by Bonn is therefore typical only in the states of NRW and Lower Saxony. It is the so-called "North German council" type. Its main characteristic is that in addition to the city council there is a chief committee of councillors, which has both deciding and executing functions.

While the Local Community Act regulates the organization and operation of a city's administration in general, the individual acts of the administration are submitted to state supervision. Regarding matters of mere local concern, the state of NRW supervises only the legality of the acts. However, regarding the so-called "duty tasks" (Pflichtaufgaben) – which are matters of state competence but charged for execution upon the city – the state supervises both the legality and the expediency of the local acts. In these cases the supervising authority may give individual instructions in accordance with the law to the local authorities.

THE LOCAL GOVERNMENT[8]

Bonn had in 1969 a large governing council of 51 members elected for five years. Since the principle of the separation of powers is not strictly realized in German local administration, the council acts as both a legislative and executive organ. Candidates for the elections are mainly presented by the national parties, though the Local Community Act, in contrast with the Basic Law, does not mention political parties. While in the cities of southern Germany local political groups, or "town hall parties," have had considerable success, in Bonn the "independents" have received but few votes and had no seats in the council in 1969. Normally the majority consists of Christian Democrats (28 seats in 1969, with 19 seats held by the Social Democrats and four by the Liberals).

Except for its executive functions, the local council has the position of a democratic representative organ. The councillors, however, do not enjoy parliamentary immunity. An individual councillor cannot demand information about matters of administration and look into the files. A quarter of the members of the council, however, may demand that this access be granted to one of them. The council must constitute a chief committee, and committees for finance, for audit, and for public enterprises. Members of these committees are not only the councillors but also a number of expert citizens. Apart from the committees prescribed by the Local Community Act, Bonn's council has constituted the following committees: on town planning, parks, traffic, sports, public health, the promotion of industry, and a special committee on the reorganization of the Bonn region. No committee on co-operation with federal agencies or with the surrounding local communities has been formed.

The lord mayor is the president of the chief committee and of the local council and is elected by its members for a period of five years. He represents the community but more in a political than in a legal sense. Vis-à-vis the administration he is entitled to get full information about any matter or plan. But he lacks the right of looking into individual files. There is also a chief administrative officer of the city (Oberstadtdirektor), who is elected by the council for a period of twelve years. He must have special experience and knowledge which qualifies him for this job. This means that, in effect, he must be a jurist. His job is to execute the resolutions of the local council and to head the city's administration, which until 1969 had a staff of about 3,500 (500 civil servants, 1,000 white-collar employees and 2,000 manual workers).

PROBLEMS OF THE CAPITAL AREA

Until 1969 the area of the federal capital presented two main problems detrimental to the work of both the local and federal administrations. The first one was a lack of space and money, preventing the city of Bonn from providing for all the necessities of a great capital. The second was a lack of co-ordination between the work of the city administration and that of the county and its communities.

Problems of space and planning

In 1887 Bonn was released from the surrounding county, and its permanent policy of extending its boundaries did not succeed in satisfying its later needs as a capital. The city contained only 32 square kilometres. Scarcity of space made Bonn the most densely populated city of West Germany, with an average of 45 persons per hectare (2.47 acres). If we accept the recommended limit of 30 persons per hectare the town was by far overpopulated. Between 1949 and 1960 the population of the town increased from 110,500 to 144,100, that is to say, by 33 per cent.[9] During this time the religious composition of the population underwent a thorough change, owing to the influx of federal functionaries and politicians. While in 1950 the population of the town, situated in the Roman Catholic "Rhineland", included only 29,000 Protestants, in 1961 there were about 49,000,[10] more than a third of the population.

Beginning with the year 1960, there began a process of reduction in Bonn's population, which had 1,186 fewer persons in 1963. This was a consequence of the transformation of the inner town into a mere centre of business and public administration buildings. The emigrating people settled in the surrounding county, and came to town only for shopping and for work – especially in the federal administration, where 23,000 persons were employed in 1966. Thus the links between Bonn and its surroundings have grown to a very high degree, giving rise to many traffic problems. The integration of town and county has been further augmented by the fact that many ministries, foreign embassies, and national associations had to settle outside the town because of the scarcity of space. Altogether, there is an area of about 472 km^2, with a population of about 364,000 persons in 1965, affected by the presence of the federal government, called the Bonn Area (Raum Bonn). This region is administered not by one administrative authority but by many local communities. In the economic structure of the outer area, farming still prevails. In comparison with the Cologne area and its contiguous industrial Ruhr region to the north, there is little industry in the Bonn area. In 1960 only 16,000 people were working in the industry of the county of Bonn. Consequently the gross national product of the county was only 63 per cent of the average for the state. Because of this situation the modernization of the administrative infrastructure of the whole Bonn area became one of the main problems of the town and its region.

Until the creation of Greater Bonn in 1969, the largest administrative unit in the Bonn Area was the county, which is situated on both sides of the Rhine, though primarily on the left bank surrounding Bonn. Until 1969 it contained about 441 km^2, and in 1965 it had a population of about 227,000 (while Bonn had about 41,000).[11] Its representative organ is the county council, the members of which are directly elected for a period of five years by all the inhabitants of the county. It also has an executive committee elected by the council from among its members. The president of the council and its executive committee is called the "Landrat." There is also a chief administrative officer (Oberkreisdirektor), who carries out the resolutions of the council. Until 1969 he directed a staff of about 450 civil servants and office employees and about 50 manual workers. The number of manual workers was small because most manual work was done at the community level.

Until 1969 the county contained 48 rural communities and four towns. The most important town was Bad Godesberg, adjoining Bonn to the south, with about 70,000 inhabitants. It contained so many ministries and embassies that it was a rival of the capital city. The towns were administered by the same type of local government as Bonn. Only matters of common interest to all communities of the county (which excludes Bonn) are managed by the county administration, as for instance, road construction, water supply, sewerage, high schools, and hospitals. No organ existed for co-ordinating the work of the city and the county; and the state, which exercises only supervisory functions, had not required the co-operation of the local units.

While the selection of Bonn as capital originated these problems of the capital area, the fact that it was regarded as only a provisional capital had defeated their solution. Until recently political leaders feared that a thoroughgoing solution of the problems of the federal capital would demonstrate that Bonn was regarded as the permanent capital and that reunification was far from being achieved. Any politician who suggested such a solution would have taken the risk of being denounced by his opponents as a traitor in the great national task of reunification, or at least as a man who wished that Bonn and not Berlin should be the German capital. Consequently, it can be said that Bonn and its area have been among the main victims of a divided Germany.

This situation has especially influenced the territorial distribution of federal buildings in Bonn. A bold planning of buildings in a government quarter was not possible for a long time. Consequently every ministry sought its lodgings where they could be found. The requirements of quick and easy communication between offices, the traffic and transport situation and the housing problems of the federal civil servants were not taken into account. The federal government became a tenant in or bought all kinds of existing buildings. The ministry of defence, for instance, worked for many years in a former barracks, and Parliament still meets in a rebuilt former teacher-training school. The dispersion of the offices, in particular, proved to be very detrimental. Only about half of the ministries were located in Bonn and only a few of the main ones were found there. In addition, only a third of the foreign diplomatic missions had their offices in Bonn, and only 14 of 91 ambassadors actually lived there.

The consequence of the lack of a plan for the federal government's building activity was that neither the city nor the county could elaborate a corresponding plan for traffic and supply. It was also impossible for the local authorities to retain enough land for the eventual use of the federal government. With the beginning of the sixties the federal government made up its mind to construct a certain number of federal buildings, and in 1966, began construction of a few ministries and a high office building for the MP's on an open space within the southern border of Bonn that extended into Godesberg. But this location does not have space enough for an adequate government quarter. The lack of a plan for federal buildings is not only detrimental to the work of the government. It is the main cause of the difficulties in planning the whole capital area. If in the first years after the founding of the federation a comprehensive plan had been elaborated, the later years could have been used for developing a corresponding infrastructure in the whole area.

Financial problems

It is clear that the settling of the federal government in Bonn caused many new capital expenditures by the town and the county. New public institutions, schools, parks, supply installations, roads, etc., have been constructed, which otherwise would not have been needed at all or not to such an extent. In 1967 a new bridge over the Rhine was finished. This was necessary to provide for the immensely grown traffic, which has made Bonn the second densest motorized city of the federal republic. Moreover, the city has built a new theatre and a large festival hall. Since these undertakings were considered as belonging to matters of local concern, they were financed primarily by the local community. The city has stated that from 1948 to 1964 it had to spend for investments caused by the presence of the federal government 384 million marks (about US $96 million, 1970 value).[12] Apart from this, the city claims that its yearly additional expenditure for special branches of the administration is 27 million marks or about 25 per cent of its current budget. Under these circumstances the budget remained balanced only up to the year 1964. In 1965 the deficit was 6.7 million, and in 1966 an estimated 7.4 million, as shown by the following tabulation (in millions of marks):[13]

Year	Revenue	Expenses	Surplus	Deficit
1961	98.5	93.5	4.8	—
1962	100.3	98.1	2.3	—
1963	99.7	100.7	—	1.0
1964	99.4	99.5	—	0.1
1965	96.5	103.2	—	6.7
1966 (estimated)	104.5	111.9	—	7.4

Because of its high capital expenditures Bonn is one of the most indebted cities of West Germany. In 1950 the indebtedness of the town per capita was only 12 marks while by 1967 it was 1,189 in spite of the considerable growth of the population. Yet many public investments remain to be undertaken, as the town in this respect has acted very cautiously. It estimates that about 250 million marks, amounting to more than two annual budgets, must be spent for these purposes. Only investments on such a scale can alter the face of the "federal village" into that of a representative capital city.

In spite of the special financial burdens by the presence of the federal government, until very recently the communities of the Bonn region had not been given a special financial status. Even today there is no permanent subvention of their budgets by the federation, and no centrally planned investment policy for the region. Like all other local communities, the towns and rural communities of the Bonn region finance their budget by means of local taxes, the income of public enterprises, and money coming from a state fund, which pays subsidies based on the number of inhabitants. It was only in the year 1966 that the state of NRW acknowledged the special burdens of the communities of the Bonn region. The Act governing the state fund was revised so that these communities would receive an additional ten million marks per year, of which the city of Bonn got five million. Moreover, they receive for special needs caused by the presence of the federal government ad hoc subventions from the budgets of the respective ministries of NRW.

The federation, too, pays only ad hoc subventions in those cases in which Article 106 (7) of the constitution offers the possibility of compensation. This article determines that the federation shall compensate in the necessary amount the state or local unit in which the federation causes the installation of special institutions which immediately involve additional expenditures or a decrease of receipts. During the years 1959 to 1966, the federation paid to the town of Bonn 23 million marks, and to all the communities of the county 26 million, as subventions and compensation for expenditures related to the construction of new buildings for public purposes. These subventions have been paid by reference to the mentioned article of the constitution, but voluntarily and without acknowledging a right to them in the individual case. Moreover, they have been given only for buildings, which means that many other burdens caused to the communities by the presence of the government still remain without compensation. In 1967 the federation paid for the first time a compensation to the cities of Bonn and Bad Godesberg for representative purposes.

The conclusion is that we are only at the beginning of a general planning for public financing and investments in the capital area. Until 1969 public subventions were still paid by various state and federal authorities to the city of Bonn and to 22 other local communities in the area without any planning or co-ordination.

The problem of metropolitan government

The mere fact that 23 independent local units were directly affected by the presence of the federal government showed that a rational administration of the whole area was extremely difficult. As the federation itself did not elaborate a plan for the territorial distribution of its offices, it is not surprising that the city of Bonn and the county and its local communities, which were not directly interested in the functioning of the federal capital, could not come to an agreement on the future infrastructure of the area.

According to Sec. 2(1) of the Federal Construction Act (Bundesbaugesetz), the local units were, apart from the planning of supra-local roads, only entitled to planning in their own territories. Consequently a regional plan for the capital area would have needed the voluntary agreement of all affected communities. This could not be achieved because Bonn and the county, along with its local communities, differed in their views. Both sides agree that a reorganization of local administration in the area is necessary but they strongly disagree on the nature of this reorganization.

The city claimed that only a realization of a greater Bonn by means of an extension of its boundaries could provide for its optimal functioning as the capital. It has always rejected the idea of forming a voluntary union with the communities of the county for the administration of matters of common concern, contending that the voluntariness of co-operation would lead to very uncertain results. Instead it supported a report made at the request of the state government by District President Stakemeyer. This report proposed the inclusion of all urban communities bordering Bonn, plus Beuel (the town across the river) in a local super-unit with about 300,000 inhabitants. Some of the existing communities would retain a restricted form of local government within this greater unit. As under these circumstances the county would not remain capable of existing, the remaining communities, with about 80,000 people, would be included in the remote counties of Cologne and Euskirchen.

In the face of this proposal, the county developed another concept which was oriented towards not only a reform and simplification of the administration but also an improvement in the future living conditions of the whole capital area. Instead of continuing the concentration of people and buildings in a local super-Bonn, this plan proposed the development of eight local communities as centres.[14] They are about 4–7 kilometres apart and would possess excellent communications with Bonn, which would remain the main centre of the region. Regarding the organization of space, this plan offered two important advantages: the development of the new towns would stop the unplanned building which devastates the landscape; and the towns would secure in the whole region a satisfactory supply of the population of all the requirements of daily life, while special needs such as luxury shopping, attending the theatre, concerts, the university, etc., could be satisfied in Bonn. These towns would retain their local governments. But to rationalize the structure of local government the many small communities in the county would be integrated into them. Together with the city of Bonn and the town of Bad Godesberg the other seven towns would be integrated into a new greater county, which would administer matters of concern to the whole region. As the actual County Act of NRW does not provide for such a super-county, a new law would have been required for the Bonn region, giving it special status and transferring certain matters of planning and government from the competence of the communities to that of the new county.

In January 1969, however, the government of North Rhine Westphalia published a bill which followed the previously mentioned Stakemeyer plan and the wishes of Bonn by providing for a super-Bonn. On the Bonn side of the river Rhine the town of Bad Godesberg and the communities of Buschdorf, Duisdorf, Lessenich, Lengsdorf, Röttgen, and Ippendorf, and on the opposite side the town of Beuel and the communities of Holzlar and Oberkassel, were to be integrated into the new Greater Bonn. The latter would have about 300,000 inhabitants and cover an area of about 140 km² (54 sq. mi.). The integrated communities would not retain any rights of local government.

Most of the communities concerned, above all the towns of Bad Godesberg and Beuel and the county of Bonn, protested vigorously and organized their opposition. In Beuel the idea of a plebiscite against the law was discussed. Opinions of experts were published to demonstrate that other ways of reorganizing the area would be more rational and that the government's proposition was not in accordance with the Local Government Act and with the Constitution of North Rhine Westphalia.

Contrary to all criticism and resistance, the Parliament of North Rhine Westphalia passed the law in May 1969, against the votes of the Christian Democratic opposition. The opposition argued that Germany lacks experience in the administrative reorganization of large and densely populated areas and that the science of space organization offers but few and contradictory models. Apart from that they deplored the loss of democratic participation by the citizens in the administration of their local communities. They also feared that, according to the proclaimed intentions of the government, the Bonn model would become the model of a future reorganization of the industrial region of the Ruhr too. Local opposition to the plan, even in the ranks of the Social Democrats, who have a majority in nearly all local governments of the region, was very strong. The Christian Democrats hoped to improve their position by supporting this opposition.

The government coalition of Liberals and Social Democrats, however, had from the beginning proclaimed territorial reorganization of local government to be one of the main points of their program. Reorganizing the capital area was to be a milestone of this part of the program and therefore should be completed before the elections to Parliament in 1970. In view of these political circumstances, arguments based on more rational considerations had no chance.

The new law was to come into force on 1 July 1969. But the county of Bonn and nearly all the communities concerned, including the towns of Bad Godesberg and Beuel, raised an action before the Constitutional Court of North Rhine Westphalia, claiming that the law was unconstitutional. The court suspended the law for a few weeks to have time enough for deliberation, but then consented to its coming into force on 1 August 1969, pending the final judgment of the court within a few months.[15] Up to then the court had rejected all actions against laws to reorganize local government. Hence, as expected, the court finally approved the law.

1 See Konstantin Frantz, *Der Föderalismus* [*Federalism*] (Mainz, 1879), 265.
2 See R. Suthoff-E. Luther, *Verfassung und Verwaltung der Reichshauptstadt Grosz-Berlin* [Constitution and Administration of the capital of the Reich, Berlin] (Berlin, 1938).
3 For the history of this development, see: A. Wandersleb, "Wie und warum Bonn zur Hauptstadt wurde," *Das Parlament* (No. 35/36, 1967), 3.
4 Likewise it is said that the capital of the US would not have been constructed where it is if President Washington had not had his farm nearby.
5 In December 1965, 17,700 citizens of Bonn worked in the federal administration, while a total of 33,600 persons (22.4 per cent of Bonn's population of about 140,800) lived on their incomes.
6 See footnote 1.
7 See ["Bonn, a Federal District?"] *Christ und Welt* (4 November 1966).
8 On local government in NRW, see K. Zuhorn and W. Hoppe, *Gemeindeverfassung* (Siegburg, 2nd ed., 1962).
9 Stadt Bonn (ed.), *Bericht über die Probleme, die sich für eine Stadt durch ihre Bestimmung zur Haupstadt ergeben* [*Report on the difficulties Involved in Turning a City into a Capital*] (Bonn, 1966), 4. (Typewritten.)
10 Zurnieden, P., "Bonn – Portrait einer Residenz" [Bonn – Portrait of a Residency] (Bonn, 1965), 8.
11 Landkreis Bonn (ed.), *150 Jahre Landkreis Bonn* [*150 years of the County of Bonn*] (Bonn, 1966), 92.
12 Stadt Bonn, *op. cit.*, 13. A West German mark was worth about 27 US cents in 1970.
13 Stadt Bonn, *op. cit.*, 17.
14 The basis of this proposal is the intensive study by A. Machtemes, *Gutachten zur Raumordnung des Landkreises Bonn* [*Report on Space Planning in the County of Bonn*] (Bonn, 1964).
15 See *Frankfurter Allgemeine Zeitung* (2 July and 1 August 1969), and *Die Zeit* (4 July 1969).

Donald C. Rowat **OTTAWA***

THE PROBLEM OF DIVIDED CONTROL

Ottawa is a good example of a federal capital governed by the laws of a single province or state in a federation. When a federal capital is not located within a territory governed exclusively by the central authority, there arise serious problems of government for the capital area. This is especially true if the federation is decentralized, because the government of the province or state within which the capital city is situated, is the sovereign governing authority for all provincial and local functions, and the federal government has little control over its own capital city. Thus, in Canada, which has a decentralized federation, the federal capital is mainly controlled by the government of Ontario, the most populous of the ten provinces. In 1970 Ontario had more than seven million inhabitants, or over one-third of Canada's population of about 21 million, while Quebec, the adjacent French-speaking province, had about six million.

For local and provincial purposes, there are now three levels of government controlling Ottawa: the city municipality, which has an elected council of 27 members including, as the executive authority, a mayor and four controllers; a new regional government for the Ottawa area, which includes the mayor and sixteen members of Ottawa's council; and the government of Ontario, which regulates all municipalities in the province, and whose laws govern the citizens of Ottawa. The provincial government therefore controls the government, planning and development of Ottawa and its adjacent municipalities. Under Canada's constitution, the federal government has no jurisdiction over local governments, and it therefore has no direct control over the capital city or its surrounding territory.

This situation is complicated by the fact that Ottawa is located on the south side of the Ottawa river; on the north side is a different province, Quebec, and another city, Hull. The city of Hull has its own elected council,

* Based on the author's study for the Ontario Advisory Committee on Confederation, *The Proposal of a Federal Territory for Canada's Capital* (Toronto, 1966); the Chairman of the Committee is thanked for permission to reproduce portions of that study.

it is regulated by the municipal laws of Quebec, and its citizens are governed by the laws of that province. Recently, for instance, the government of Quebec created a separate regional government for the Hull area. Yet Ottawa and Hull are twin cities, which, along with their adjoining municipalities, form a single metropolitan area. In 1970 Ottawa's estimated population was about 300,000, Hull's was about 60,000, while that of the whole census metropolitan area was about 550,000. If a federally governed district were to be created for Canada's capital, it would therefore almost necessarily include both cities and additional territory on each side of the river in both provinces.

An unusual feature of local government in Canada is that elections are generally non-partisan. Since the political parties do not run candidates in the local elections in the Ottawa-Hull area, there is therefore no possibility of purely partisan disagreements between the central and city governments. Another odd feature of local government in the area is that there are two independent municipalities as islands within the boundaries of Ottawa. One of them is the city of Vanier (formerly Eastview), which had a population of about 25,000 in 1970. The other is the village of Rockcliffe Park, the wealthy embassy area, with a population of 2,500. Like Vanier, it has managed to maintain its independence from Ottawa, and therefore does not have to pay taxes to support services in the main city. Outside the boundaries of Ottawa and Hull are several other urban municipalities and also a number of rural townships which are becoming rapidly urbanized. All of these have their own elected governments. Hence, there is not only a lack of federal control and a division of control between two different provincial governments in the national capital region, but also a fragmentation of local government, which has been only partly overcome by the recent creation of regional governments for the Ottawa and Hull areas.

Historically, how did this situation arise, and what has been the role of the federal government in attempting to control and develop its own capital?

THE ORIGIN OF THE PROBLEM

It was mainly an accident of history that the federal government's present area of interest for the development of the national capital covers two cities in two different provinces as well as territory beyond the cities in both provinces. Before 1867 Ottawa had already been for a few years the capital of the province of Canada (now Ontario and Quebec). When Ottawa was chosen as the capital for the new Canadian federation in 1867, scant attention was paid to the fact that now part of the urban population would be living across the river in the new province of Quebec. It was not at that time realized, of course, that the building of bridges across the Ottawa river would to a large extent remove the river as a barrier between the two populations on each side, and that the whole area would develop into one vast interdependent urban complex. Nor was it thought that the relationships between the central government and the city of Ottawa would be at all complicated. Those were the days before the age of the welfare state, when the civil service was extremely small. It was therefore expected that the federal land on "Barracks Hill" would be sufficient to contain the Parliament buildings and all federal administrative offices for the foreseeable future. It is perhaps for this reason that no one at the time of Confederation seems to have seriously proposed a federal territory for the capital, despite the precedent established by the creation of the District of Columbia in the United States long before this.

The difference between the choice of Washington and Ottawa as capitals is that Washington had been created as a new capital after the formation of the United States, whereas Ottawa was a thriving lumber town and the capital of the province of Canada before Confederation. Since Toronto and Quebec were the obvious choices for the capitals of the newly created provinces of Ontario and Quebec, it seemed logical to leave Ottawa as the capital of the new Dominion, and simply to place the new federal Parliament and its administration in the buildings that had just recently been completed for the Parliament and administration of the former province of Canada.

There was an inherent flaw and source of future friction in this arrangement, however. Any extension of the federal government's interest beyond the immediate boundaries of Parliament Hill was bound to involve differences of interest and delicate relations with the city of Ottawa, and ultimately with the city of Hull, the municipalities surrounding these cities, and the provincial governments of Ontario and Quebec, under whose control they came for all provincial and municipal purposes. Moreover, the Ontario side of the river was mainly English-speaking, Protestant, and governed under the English common law, while the Quebec side was soon to become mainly French-speaking and Roman Catholic, and was governed under the radically different Quebec civil code, which had been inherited from French law.

EARLY ATTEMPTS TO MEET THE PROBLEM

It was almost the turn of the century before the government began to recognize its special responsibilities for developing the area in which its seat of government was situated. The 1890s had seen a great quickening of interest throughout North America in city architecture and planning. In June of 1893, while leader of the opposition, Wilfred Laurier had stated that Ottawa should become the "Washington of the North," and this idea had begun to fire people's imaginations toward the future development of a great capital city. But until after 1895 – the end of the "Great Depression" – the federal government was chronically hard up. Just before Laurier's accession to power in 1896, two city councillors, Fred Cook and Robert Stewart, succeeded in getting Ottawa's council to appoint a committee to make a study of the principal capitals in the British Empire, in order to demonstrate to the federal government both its opportunities and its obligations for the development of the federal capital. In 1897, the city made use of this information in a petition to the Laurier government. The petition pointed out that the United Kingdom government paid municipal rates to London on all its properties, including the houses of Parliament, and noted that the tax-exempt properties owned by the Crown within the city of Ottawa in 1897 were valued at (Can.) $14 million.[1] Also the city had received no compensation from the federal government for the city's large outlay on public works, in contrast with the practice in other parts of the world. This petition no doubt had considerable influence upon the federal government, for in 1899 it initiated an annual grant to Ottawa of $60,000 to meet these claims. It also created the Ottawa Improvement Commission, which consisted of four commissioners, three chosen by the federal government and one by the city of Ottawa, and which began its work with an annual grant of $60,000.

In the early years of this century the Ottawa Improvement Commission did much good work in beautifying Ottawa's parks and driveways. But, as Wilfrid Eggleston has noted, it was "handicapped by insufficient funds, restricted powers, and possibly, by lack of imagination. As it was not created as a town planning body, and in any event lacked authority in that field, its remedies were bound to be superficial rather than basic."[2] Although it had hired a landscape architect, F.G. Todd, who had submitted a plan for the future development of the Ottawa area as early as 1903, architects and others began to realize that the Ottawa Improvement Commission was incapable of meeting the problem. In 1911, for example, a deputation of members of the Royal Architectural Institute of Canada presented a brief to the new prime minister, Robert Borden, complaining about the lack of planned development of the capital, and pointed to the difficulties of finding a satisfactory site for new government buildings and to the still-existing need for relocating the railways and amending the street system of the city.

The Holt and Cauchon proposals

As a result, in 1913 the Borden Government appointed a Federal Plan Commission, chaired by Herbert S. (later Sir Herbert) Holt of Montreal, with five other members, including the mayors of Ottawa and Hull. The terms of reference instructed the commission to "draw up and perfect a comprehensive scheme or plan, looking to the future growth and development of the city of Ottawa and the city of Hull, and their environs..." This was the first time that the federal government had officially recognized any responsibility for the development of the Hull side of the river or even the environs of Ottawa. The Holt Commission, which reported in 1915, developed a comprehensive and impressive plan for the future development of Ottawa, Hull, and the surrounding area. It recognized that the power to implement the far-reaching proposals it had made (which involved the reconstruction of a good deal of Ottawa) came constitutionally under the jurisdiction of the governments of Ontario and Quebec and of the municipalities in the area. Foreseeing the difficulties of divided jurisdiction involved, the commission proposed the outright creation of a federal district and federal control over local government.

Unfortunately, the report of the Holt Commission was badly timed, coming as it did in the midst of the first world war, and just at the time that the Parliament building burned down. The building, which burned on 3 February 1916, required ten years and $12 million to rebuild, enlarge, and furnish. As a result, except for raising the annual grant to the Ottawa Improvement Commission in 1917 to $150,000 a year, nothing much was done for ten years about the recommendations in the report, even though Noulan Cauchon, planning consultant to the city of Ottawa, had in 1922 produced an updated revision of the plan.

Cauchon had proposed, as his administrative solution to the problem, a federal commission which would have authority over the physical features and public utilities of a "federal district," but which would preserve provincial and municipal autonomy in other respects. Being essentially an architect and planner, he did not seem to realize that, constitutionally, even the federal Parliament did not possess this authority and so could not delegate it to a commission. Hence the commission would not have had the power to implement the plans for redevelopment that he and the Holt Commission had proposed. Yet those who read his report may have been led to believe that all that was needed to implement the plans was for the federal government to establish a more powerful body with jurisdiction over an enlarged "federal district," and that therefore the creation of a federally governed territory would be unnecessary.

At any rate, in 1927 the Ottawa Improvement Commission was reconstituted as the Federal District Commission, with broadened powers and the extension of its interests into Quebec. The (by then) eight members of the older commission were increased to ten, of which one was to be a resident of Hull. Thus, for the first time, Hull was officially recognized as being part of the federal capital. In the twelve years from 1927 to 1939 the FDC parks area was enlarged to 900 acres, and the length of the federally owned and maintained driveway was increased to 22 miles, including an extension across the Champlain Bridge into Quebec. But the constitutional limits to the FDC's powers, the long depression of the 1930s, and the outbreak of the war discouraged any more ambitious attempts to implement the Holt Report of 1915.

Meanwhile, the growth of the welfare state in the 1920s and 1930s had caused a gradual encroachment by the federal government into the heart of Ottawa for buildings to house its administrative personnel. The great influx of military and civilian personnel connected with the second world war, of course, greatly accelerated this trend. The total space in the city coming to be occupied by the federal government through construction, purchase, or rental could not help but create tensions and difficulties between crown and town. Eggleston (p. 177) lists a total of 23 permanent buildings that had been erected between 1918 and 1945 and notes that no fewer than fourteen wartime so-called "temporary" buildings had been built in assorted locations throughout Ottawa. These properties of course were all tax-exempt, and often occupied the space of former businesses that had been paying property and business taxes to the city. At the same time they required the continuing provision of all normal municipal services. The growing number of foreign embassies and headquarters of crown corporations, which were similarly tax-exempt, exacerbated the problem.

This was a problem which could be largely solved by larger grants to the city. But the problem created by the constitutionally restricted powers of the Federal District Commission to redevelop the cities of Ottawa and Hull and their surrounding area could not be so easily solved.

THE EVOLUTION OF THE NATIONAL CAPITAL REGION, 1944–58

The federal government responded to Ottawa's claim for "better fiscal terms" by setting up a special Joint Committee of the Senate and House in 1944. Although the Committee did not accept the city's contention that an annual payment of nearly $1,600,000 was needed to offset the loss of taxes from government tax-exempt property, it did recommend that for a period of five years the annual grant to Ottawa should be raised to $300,000, and the government accepted this recommendation. Part of the government's difficulty was that it could not pay adequate compensation to Ottawa without recognizing a similar responsibility for its tax-exempt properties in other cities of Canada. In 1949, however, it recognized these responsibilities by passing the Municipal Grants Act, and by 1955 Ottawa was receiving under this Act an amount substantially larger than that requested in 1944. It also agreed to pay grants in lieu of taxes on embassy properties, and required crown corporations to pay similar grants. However, the city still complains that the total of these grants is far from equal to the loss in taxes.

By 1945 the prime minister had become convinced that the redevelopment of the entire national capital area should be undertaken as a national memorial of Canada's participation in the war. Apparently he had been persuaded that this project could be brought to fruition without the creation of a federal territory. He therefore brought to Ottawa M. Greber, a French planner, to prepare a new plan for the capital, and an Order-in-Council was passed in 1945 defining some 900 square miles as the National Capital District for purposes of this plan.

The National Capital Plan

The proposals for redevelopment contained in the resulting *Plan for the National Capital*, published in 1950, were much more far-reaching than those of the earlier Holt Report. Since meanwhile Ottawa and Hull had developed without a plan and the National Capital District now took in many municipalities surrounding Ottawa and Hull, the problem of correcting the errors and implementing the plan would be that much more difficult. However, the report of 1950 recommended no change in the status and powers of the Federal District Commission, and clearly indicated that it was depending upon the co-operation of the governments of Ontario and Quebec and of all the municipalities in the new National Capital District for the successful implementation of the plan. But the problem of what would happen if these governments did not co-operate was never squarely faced. The fact is that the Federal District Commission had no power to enforce any part of the plan that did not affect federally owned territory.

Because the city of Ottawa co-operated whole-heartedly in taking the initial action necessary to control the development of its urban fringes and to preserve the plan's proposed greenbelt around Ottawa, this difficulty was not clearly revealed for some time. In 1947 Ottawa took steps under the Ontario Planning Act of 1946 to establish the Ottawa Planning Area Board, whose planning area included not only the city of Ottawa, but also the town of Eastview, the village of Rockcliffe Park and the townships of Gloucester, Nepean, March, Torbolton and Fitzroy – all the municipalities that were within the boundaries of the Ottawa side of the National Capital District. Membership on the Board was weighted in favour of the city, with usually five from Ottawa, one from the Federal District Commission, one from the Central Mortgage and Housing Corporation, and only two from the surrounding municipalities (e.g. Gloucester and Nepean). The city also applied to the Ontario Municipal Board to annex those parts of the townships of Nepean and Gloucester which lay within the inner ring of the proposed greenbelt. But it met opposition from Nepean and also from the county of Carleton (which surrounded most of the city and which contained Nepean). Because of this, the size of the original area asked for was reduced by the Ontario Board. As a result, a considerable gap was left between the new southern boundary of the city and the inner ring of the greenbelt in Nepean. Gaps were also left at the western boundary of the city, and at the eastern boundary in Gloucester. Other effects of the annexation, which became effective at the beginning of 1950, were to enclose Rockcliffe Park and Eastview completely within the boundaries of the city, and to multiply the city's area by five times, to its present area of 45.4 square miles.

The effective implementation of a city plan, of course, requires a comprehensive zoning by-law, or at least zoning by-laws for those parts of a municipality which are undergoing rapid subdivision and urban development. The older city had had no master plan, no detailed plan of land use, and no comprehensive zoning by-law. Although Ottawa was now at least in a position to begin work on these matters within its own territory, none of the other municipalities in the area had zoning by-laws or any facilities for implementing the National Capital Plan. The Ottawa Planning Area Board was staffed by the city's planning department, and tended to ignore the planning needs of the surrounding municipalities. Although the Board had approved in principle the proposals of the National Capital Plan for the Ottawa side of the river, it did not have adequate facilities to control urban development, especially beyond the boundaries of the city and in particular in the area designated as the greenbelt. Nor, of course, did it at that time have any facilities to plan and carry out redevelopment. On the Hull side of the river, no adequate planning machinery existed for implementing that side's share of the plan, nor was any created.

Yet when the plan was presented in 1950, the Ottawa metropolitan area was on the verge of one of the most dramatic periods of urban expansion that it had ever seen. Since there existed no adequate machinery to control this development, the result was urban sprawl on both sides of the Ottawa river, and inevitably developments that went contrary to the plan. The most striking example of this was the township of Nepean. For financial reasons developers tended to jump beyond the new boundaries of the city and even into the proposed greenbelt. Nepean had a population approaching 25,000 in 1949. When the annexation was complete Nepean was left with an almost exclusively rural population of only 2,500. Yet in the next five years the outflow from the city again raised the population to 8,000, largely urban. The township of Gloucester showed a similar pattern. Its population was cut from 10,000 to 5,000 by the annexation, but by 1956 its population had again jumped back to 11,500. Indeed the pace of urban subdivision in the proposed greenbelt proceeded so fast that it forced the federal authorities to redefine the greenbelt and to extend its inner boundary, making it in places even farther from the boundaries of the city. The fact was that the greenbelt was nothing more than an attractive dream drawn on a map, and it would never be realized unless something were done quickly.

The difficulty, inherent from the beginning, was a genuine conflict of interests between the federal and local governments in the area. While the federal government was interested in developing a national capital worthy of Canada, the local governments were, individually, incapable of meeting this challenge, especially since the financial burdens fell upon them unequally. There was a similar but lesser conflict of interest between the federal and provincial governments in implementing the plan. So long as the provincial governments remained responsible to their electors in the national capital area, they could not be expected to turn a deaf ear to representations from local citizens desiring action contrary to the plan. Nor could they be expected to have any very positive incentive to create the governmental and planning machinery that would be necessary to enforce the plan.

As a result of these difficulties another parliamentary joint committee was appointed in 1956 and the evidence given before that committee well illustrates this conflict of interests, especially regarding the preservation of the greenbelt. The committee devoted a good deal of its report to the problems of divided jurisdiction and conflict of interests, but it did not feel, as did the committee of 1944, that the proposal for a federal territory should be studied. It probably felt that the federal government was already too heavily committed to a program of voluntary co-operation with the provincial and municipal governments concerned. At any rate, it concluded that there was still a reasonable hope of achieving the objectives of the plan through such co-operation, especially if the federal government were prepared to spend enough money in a program of assistance to the local municipalities and of control over the use of land through purchase or expropriation. However, its plea for co-operation from the provincial and municipal governments was unsuccessful, and if any further time had been lost in trying to secure co-operation the battle to preserve the greenbelt would have been lost. In 1958, therefore, the federal government decided to proceed with a program to purchase or appropriate all the land necessary to preserve the greenbelt.

The National Capital Act

In 1958 the federal government also implemented two other recommendations of the 1956 report. A new National Capital Act was passed changing the name of the Federal District Commission to National Capital Commission, and the National Capital District was officially renamed the National Capital Region and doubled in size (from 900 square miles to 1,800 square miles, most of the increase being on the Ottawa side of the river, to 1,050 square miles. The Region now took in all or part of 66 municipalities in Quebec and Ontario. This of course further complicated the problem of divided jurisdiction.

At the same time, the new Act removed the mayors of Ottawa and Hull from the commission. Instead it specified that, of the twenty commissioners, the governor-in-council must appoint one from each of the provinces and a minimum of two local residents from Ottawa, one from Hull, and two others – from the other municipalities on each side of the Ottawa river. Since 1958, local representation on the commission has customarily consisted of four residents of Ottawa, two others from the Ottawa side of the river, one from Hull and the other from the Hull side of the river. Also, the commission was given the direct power "to prepare plans for and assist in the development, conservation and improvement of the National Capital Region in order that the nature and character of the seat of the Government of Canada may be in accordance with its national significance."

The financial resources of the commission were also greatly enlarged. From now on the federal government would attempt to solve the problem of divided jurisdiction with money – through massive purchase and expropriation of property, by paying the full cost of many projects vital to the success of the plan, sharing a large proportion of the cost of many others, and by providing free technical help and advice on planning and other matters to the municipalities in the Region.

RECENT PROGRESS AND FUTURE DIFFICULTIES

Federal expenditure

Since the federal government's decision in 1958 to provide a massive increase in its financial support for the National Capital Plan, great progress has been made in implementing the main provisions of the plan. The annual report of the National Capital Commission for 1965–66 shows that between 1 April 1947 and 31 March 1966 it spent a total of $156 million for development and improvement within the National Capital Region. Of this total it spent $87.8 million on property acquisitions, including $34.4 million for the greenbelt. It also spent $20.2 million on the relocation of the railway facilities.

On projects requiring the sharing of expenditures with Ottawa or other local municipalities, and in some cases also with the provincial governments, the commission spent $13.4 million, or about nine per cent of its total expenditures, including $312,000 for research, studies and other types of assistance. Its contribution to local governments for research and other technical assistance was certainly money well spent, for it has stimulated the local municipalities and the two provinces to take some of the action necessary to implement their share of the plan. The staff of the commission, which now numbers about 750, including professional engineers, architects, and planners, have also been generous in their provision of technical assistance and advice. Thus, the commission has tried to follow the recommendation of the committee of 1956 that the municipalities and the provinces should be brought more closely into the arrangements for implementing the plan.

There is no doubt that the federal government has managed to overcome many of the difficulties inherent in divided jurisdiction through its program of massive land acquisition and its co-operation with and assistance to the provincial and local governments. By 1966, the major projects contained in the Greber Plan of 1950 had been successfully completed or were well on the way to completion. The greenbelt had been saved, the Queensway had been built, the railways were being relocated, opening the way for many improvements in the downtown area of Ottawa, the parkway system and the development of Gatineau Park were almost complete, and many of the key bridges had been built.

This has not been accomplished, however, without considerable dissatisfaction and complaint on all sides – from the local municipalities, from groups of local citizens, and from the federal government. The removal in 1958 of the representatives named by Ottawa and Hull to the Federal District Commission meant that the local municipalities in the area had no direct representation on the National Capital Commission. Not surprisingly, there were some rather bitter comments from the local municipalities regarding this change, especially since the National Capital Commission was still represented on the Ottawa Planning Area Board.

Similarly, the expropriation program led to a good deal of opposition, especially in the greenbelt. The Expropriation Act had not been revised, as recommended by the 1956 committee, to ensure that procedures were scrupulously fair, and complaints were made that the National Capital Commission was acting arbitrarily and without regard to the rights of local citizens. In fact, one of the land owners in the greenbelt even brought an important test case before the Exchequer Court questioning the constitutional right of the federal government to expropriate land for the purpose of preserving a greenbelt on the ground that this interfered with provincial powers over the property, civil rights and, in particular, zoning. This case was appealed to the Supreme Court of Canada, and in *Harold Munro v National Capital Commission* (28 June 1966), was decided in favour of the federal government because expropriation for the purpose of implementing the National Capital Plan comes under its general power to make laws for the "peace, order, and good government of Canada."

On the other hand, although the federal government is now pouring millions of dollars into the centre of the Region in the form of development projects, joint sharing of development, and grants in lieu of taxation to the cities of Ottawa and Hull, it has no direct control over or representation on any of the local councils which would give it a chance to help to determine how this money will be spent. As already noted, the National Capital Commission had spent $156 million in the Region by April of 1966. Also, by 1964 the municipalities in the Region were receiving about $6.6 million annually from federal grants in lieu of taxation. The largest recipients were Ottawa ($5.7 million), Hull and its school commission ($500,000), Gloucester ($90,000), and Nepean ($80,000).[3] Ottawa got the largest grant in Canada, the next largest being Halifax ($1.7 million). In 1966 Ottawa received for its current budget about $8.4 million in federal grants, about 23 per cent of its own city budget (but only about 9 per cent of the city's current gross expenditures, including schools, compared with 19 per cent from provincial grants, 42 per cent from taxes, and 30 per cent from other sources). In addition, between 1966 and 1970 the city expected to receive $15 million in federal grants toward its capital budget.[4] Impressed by these contributions to the city, Hon. George McIlraith, then President of the Privy council and MP for an Ottawa constituency, proposed in 1964 that the federal government should be represented on Ottawa's city council. Paul Tardif, MP for Russell and for many years a member of Ottawa's council, endorsed this suggestion. The reaction of the council was to reject the idea vigorously and to demand city representation on the National Capital Commission instead.[5]

Examples of difficulties

That the difficulties of divided jurisdiction have by no means been overcome may be illustrated by two examples. The parliamentary committee of 1944 had stressed that the pollution of the Ottawa river was already serious, and the committee of 1956 had placed this as the number one priority on its list of problems to be solved. Yet in 1966, over twenty years later, some ten million gallons of raw sanitary sewage were dumped into the Ottawa river every day by the municipalities in the capital area.[6] The municipalities on the Quebec side were the worst offenders, since most of them had no sewage treatment whatsoever. In addition, tons of industrial wastes were discharged into the river daily from the pulp and paper mills of the E.B. Eddy Company and the Canadian International Paper Company.

The second example was the problem of implementing the freeway and street plan proposed in the Ottawa-Hull Urban Transportation Study. This plan, which involved the technical co-operation of all three levels of government, was prepared in 1965 by private firms under a contract with the city of Ottawa. Though the National Capital Commission paid part of the cost, the plan was not produced by the NCC as part of the National Capital Plan. Yet it is revolutionary in its proposals for the construction of a new freeway system and the reconstruction of a good deal of downtown Ottawa, involving fundamental revisions of municipal Master Plans and of the National Capital Plan. However, the fragmentation of municipal responsibility in the area was such that, although the main municipalities concerned approved the plan in broad principle, there was no assurance that they would adhere to the plan. Moreover, the projected cost was tremendous, requiring $435 million over the next twenty years. Of this, $103 million would be needed in Quebec and $332 million in Ontario, with expenditures in Ottawa alone accounting for $226 million, or over half the total. Who was going to pay for this redevelopment? Since the federal government did not produce the plan, it could easily disclaim major financial responsibility. Partly for these reasons, and partly because of opposition to the plan itself, its main features have not been implemented to date.

Despite the impressiveness of the national capital projects completed to date, and despite considerable private rebuilding of Ottawa's business core in recent years, parts of the centres of Ottawa and Hull still remain a disgrace to the nation. "To apply cosmetics to the decayed body of a disorganized city," as Wilfrid Eggleston notes (p. 280), "will not achieve the purpose for which the [National Capital] Commission exists." Nor has the existing planning machinery prevented a great deal of uncontrolled and undesirable urban sprawl, which still continues beyond the boundaries of Ottawa and Hull. Unfortunately, the plain facts are that, constitutionally, the National Capital Commission cannot control development or redevelopment on land that it does not own; that the planning, land use, and zoning controls by the local municipalities in the area are in many ways still unsatisfactory; and that the provinces of Ontario and Quebec and the cities of Ottawa and Hull are not prepared to pour the amount of money into urban and road redevelopment that would be necessary to create a capital worthy of Canada's growing stature as a nation.

The problem of urban growth

Recent urban growth in the area has been so great that it has required a change of Greber's original concept of an urban centre surrounded by a greenbelt with only small satellite towns beyond it. The Greber Plan had projected that the urban population of the national capital area would reach 500,000 by 1980, but this population figure was reached in 1963. The growth has been so marked that between 1956 and 1961 Ottawa-Hull was the fastest growing metropolitan area in eastern Canada and third in Canada, exceeding even Toronto. A forecast made in 1964 indicated that the National Capital Region might have a population of over 800,000 by 1980, and possibly a million by the year 2000. Though these predictions were revised somewhat downward by a new NCC forecast in December 1969, the growth is such that the Region will soon contain as big a population as any of the Atlantic provinces.

A study of the future urban growth pattern made in 1964 by the technical co-ordinating committee for the Ottawa-Hull Area Transportation Study predicted that this growth will take place in five specific areas: to the west, south, and east of the greenbelt surrounding Ottawa, and north of the Ottawa river on the west and east sides of the Gatineau river. The study also predicted that by the year 2000 Ottawa's population may reach 540,000 and of that the present Aylmer-Hull urban area may be about 160,000. The 1969 forecast, however, indicates that these figures should be somewhat reduced. The populations of the four new satellite cities will also be large. Indeed, the one to the west of the greenbelt may be larger than Aylmer-Hull, while the ones east of Hull and south of the greenbelt may be almost as large. The study also indicated that the percentage distribution of the population in the year 2000 may be about as follows: 38 per cent within the greenbelt, 40 per cent beyond the greenbelt on the Ontario side of the river, and 22 per cent on the Quebec side. Since the residents of the whole metropolitan area will depend for their employment mainly upon the federal government, a large proportion of them will travel to work in the urban core on high-speed traffic arteries. This situation will be considerably different from Greber's vision of small self-contained satellite towns far beyond the greenbelt.

The projected speed and pattern of this urban development will require, for its effective control, a reorganization of government in the Region much more fundamental than that which took place in 1950 through Ottawa's expansion of its area by five times in an attempt to control urban development within the proposed greenbelt. The existence of the greenbelt, and the expectation that the new urban areas in the south will be established along widely separated traffic arteries and that urban Hull will grow rapidly and split into two big urban areas separated by the Gatineau river, mean that simple annexation and integration of governmental services will no longer be the answer. It is clear, as it was before 1950, that the full implementation of a comprehensive plan for a metropolitan area requires a governmental authority over the area which has control over all the services of local government that have relevance to planning and development. Except for Ottawa, the existing local governments cannot provide the finances, expertise and control necessary to make them viable units for implementing a national capital plan or even a metropolitan plan.

The new regional governments

For this reason, the idea of a basic reorganization of local government on the Ontario side of the Ottawa river had been gaining ground in recent years, and finally came to fruition in 1968. In that year the government of Ontario passed legislation creating a second tier or regional level of government, with a council made up of representatives from the city and sixteen surrounding municipalities. The area of the region is somewhat smaller than that of the National Capital Region on the Ontario side of the river (16 versus 21 municipalities). One wonders why the boundaries were not made coterminous.

The first council chairman was appointed by the provincial government in mid-1968 for a term of four and a half years, but thereafter the "super-mayor" will be chosen by the regional council itself. In addition to the chairman, the council has 30 members, of whom 16, a majority, are from Ottawa's council, and the remaining 14 are from the other 16 municipalities, some of which are so small that their councils must choose representatives jointly. The regional government exercises certain functions for the whole Region, and charges the cost to the local municipalities. Although its powers are rather limited, additional ones will probably be added as it gains experience. In creating this type of regional authority, the Ontario government was no doubt influenced by the successful operation for many years of a similar metropolitan government for the Toronto area. In 1969 it completed the reorganization by consolidating the numerous school boards in the region into four: one public and one separate school board covering Ottawa, Vanier and Rockcliffe, and one public and one separate school board for the rest of the region.

A basic flaw in the new regional scheme was that it did not include Hull or its metropolitan area. The problems of a unified governing authority for the Hull side and for the whole Ottawa-Hull area remained unsolved.

On the Hull side, the same need for reorganization existed. Hull's present urbanized area is split up among four municipalities west of the

Gatineau river (Hull, Lucerne, Deschenes and Aylmer), and four east of it (Gatineau Point, Templeton-West, Gatineau, and Templeton). These municipalities have experienced the usual problems arising from a lack of co-operation. The old municipality of Hull South, for example, feared that part of it would be swallowed by Hull, or that Hull would gobble up the whole potentially urban area west of the Gatineau river. To avoid too intimate association with Hull, Hull South had its name changed to Lucerne, and then made overtures to Aylmer and Deschenes for an amalgamation with them as a sort of counterbalance against Hull. Then, following the lead of Ontario, the government of Quebec decided to create second-tier regional governments for some of the province's metropolitan areas, including Hull. At the end of 1969 Quebec's assembly passed legislation creating a regional government for Hull and 31 of its surrounding municipalities, called the Outaouais Regional Community. The Community is a large one, encompassing much rural and uninhabited land to the north, and its boundaries even go beyond those of the National Capital Region on the Hull side of the river. The regional government's main organs are a council made up of the mayors of the 32 municipalities, and a seven-man executive committee, of whom six are elected at large and the chairman is appointed by the provincial government. Because of objections that the Community is too big, in November 1971 the Quebec government announced that it planned to abolish the two-tier regional government and instead to consolidate the 32 municipalities into five regional single-tier units, two urban and three rural.

Even though regional governments have been created on both sides of the river, the Ottawa-Hull metropolitan area is still split into two parts governed by the independent actions of two different provincial governments and two different sets of local and regional authorities. If the federal government had exclusive jurisdiction over the National Capital Region, it could create a single governing authority for the whole area. It could do this without abolishing the existing municipalities or even the regional governments, simply by creating a higher level of government for the whole Region and delegating to it the equivalent of provincial powers plus certain federal functions.

THE BILINGUAL-BICULTURAL ISSUE

Until recent years the national capital was thought of mainly in terms of physical development – as an efficient place for members of Parliament and civil servants to work and live, and as an impressive place worthy of a capital city for Canadians and representatives of foreign governments to visit, conduct their business, and reside. Not much attention was paid to the development of the capital as a symbol of the successful uniting of Canada's two main ethnic groups into a single nation. Ottawa remained predominantly an Anglo-Saxon city in an English speaking province.

The relevance of Hull

The relevance of Hull to the national capital was virtually ignored for sixty years after Confederation. Since Hull had been cut off more definitely from Ottawa by Confederation and was from then on governed by a different legislature in a new province, this is perhaps not surprising. Even after 1927, when Hull was specifically named as part of the capital district to be improved, little was done to recognize Hull as part of the national capital. It is true that the Champlain bridge was completed, the federal driveway was extended to the Quebec side, and a beginning was made at acquiring the land north of Hull necessary to form Gatineau Park, which is now an important recreation area for Ottawa. But it was not until after the second world war that the first important federal building, the Printing Bureau, was constructed in Hull.

Why was Hull's claim that it should be regarded as part of the national capital ignored for so long and then so grudgingly admitted? From an employment point of view it had always been closely tied to the national capital. At the hearings of the parliamentary committee in 1956, the mayor of Hull pointed out that by then between 5,000 and 6,000 residents of Hull were working in the federal civil service, and that half of the population depended upon the presence of the federal government for their employment. One can argue that if the federal government had been more forthright in its recognition of Hull as part of the national capital by placing federal buildings there, and more generous in its financial support and in the representation of Hull on successive federal capital commissions, co-operation from Hull and from the government of Quebec would have been much better.

At any rate, in May 1969 the federal government, under Prime Minister Trudeau, made a dramatic change in policy designed to cement Hull's marriage with Ottawa as part of the national capital. It unveiled a $200 million plan for the construction of federal buildings and aid to municipal services in downtown Hull over the next twenty-five years. The government proposes to direct about 25 per cent of its new office space to that area and expects that by 1995 it will accommodate 36,000 public servants. Early in 1970 the federal government also announced, apparently without consulting the governments of either Ottawa or Ontario, that a new bridge was to be built from Ottawa to downtown Hull. The implications of a massive shift of public servants to Hull have not yet been fully realized. It is likely to result in large-scale moving of English-speaking residents to the Hull side of the river and a drastic change in the linguistic, religious, and ethnic composition of the Hull area's population.

English-speaking Ottawa

From Quebec's point of view, the difficulty has always been that Ottawa alone was regarded as the national capital. To the people of Quebec, it is an alien capital in alien territory. The culture and language of Ottawa are predominantly Anglo-Saxon and English-speaking, and it is governed under a different system of judicial and provincial law. French-speaking Canadians who came to live in Ottawa as members of Parliament or as federal civil servants found that they were cut off from their cultural roots and were forced to speak, read, and write English most of the time. They disliked living in Hull because it was only a run-down lumber town and a poor cultural home for educated French-Canadians. On the other hand, if they lived in Ottawa, they became part of an alien minority who lacked equal linguistic and educational rights under Ontario law. And in the city government there was always a strong majority of English-speaking Canadians. French-speaking Canadians tended to congregate in an old central section of the city known as Lower Town, or to migrate to Eastview (now Vanier).

This no doubt explains Vanier's continuing existence as a separate municipality even though it is now an island within the boundaries of Ottawa. The annexations of 1950 tended to overwhelm the French-speaking minority in Ottawa, and Eastview became a kind of French-speaking bastion through its majority control of that municipality's council and other local institutions. Vanier, for example, is one of the few municipalities in Ontario which conducts its council business in both languages and which has bilingual by-laws, tax bills, and traffic signs, and a bilingual public high school where several subjects are taught in French. French is the mother tongue of about half the teachers and over two-thirds of the students.

Ontario's public school system provides little elementary schooling for French-speaking students. Since most French-Canadians are Roman Catholic, the separate schools are expected to meet nearly all of their language needs. These are Roman Catholic schools which are administered separately from the public schools. Most of them are elementary schools, but some teach grades 9 and 10. Separate school supporters pay a separate local education tax.

Historically, under Ontario's educational system French-speaking children, like the children of immigrants, were expected to learn English as soon as possible. The curriculum for the separate schools required certain subjects, such as science and mathematics, to be taught in English, with progressively more English expected in the upper grades. It is true that in recent years inroads have been made into this policy. In areas where the parents are predominantly French-speaking, the separate schools were at first allowed to teach the first three grades almost entirely in French and to continue several subjects in French into the higher grades. Then in 1968 the Ontario government decided to allow these bilingual schools to use French as the language of instruction. As a result, about half of the large number of separate schools in Ottawa and most of those in Vanier have now become French schools. But there are still no public elementary French schools in Ottawa or Vanier for the children of French-speaking parents who do not want them to attend the separate schools. In 1965 Ottawa's Public School Board even refused the request of a group of French-speaking parents for an elementary bilingual school.

It should also be noted that until recently separate school supporters had to pay higher taxes than public school supporters, and that the standard of the buildings, facilities, and instruction in the separate schools was much lower than in the public schools. Although provincial grants for separate schools have increased markedly in recent years, they have not entirely made up for these past deficiencies. Moreover, local tax and provincial support for the separate schools does not go beyond grade 10. Until 1968 there were seven private Roman Catholic French-speaking high schools, but they were costly to the parents and provided a much lower standard of instruction than the public high schools. Although Ottawa's Collegiate Institute Board took over the operation and financing of these schools in 1968, schooling in French at the elementary and secondary levels is still regarded as inadequate by the French-speaking community.

The language situation

As a result of these educational difficulties and of the overwhelming predominance of the English language in the federal and local public services, in business, and in everyday living, French Canadians in Ottawa are threatened with the gradual loss of their language and culture. The 1961 census statistics for the Ottawa metropolitan area reveal that this has already taken place to some extent. Of Ottawa's total population of 268,000 in 1961, nearly 70,000, or about one-quarter, gave their ethnic origin as French. On the other hand, only 57,000, about one-fifth, gave their mother tongue as French, indicating some loss of the French language from one generation to the next. The whole metropolitan area on the south side of the river, except for Eastview, shows a similar loss. Hull, on the other hand, actually shows a slight gain, indicating that some children of English-speaking parents have adopted French as their mother tongue. Out of Hull's population of 57,000 in 1961, only 5,500 or under 10 per cent did not give their mother tongue as French. Because of the existence of some English-speaking communities in the Hull metropolitan area, however, this area as a whole shows no gain for the French language. Exactly the same proportion, 85 per cent, gave French as their ethnic group and mother tongue.

The figures on official language show a similar predominance of English and French, respectively, on the south and north sides of the river, and also indicate the extent to which the metropolitan area is bilingual. In the Ottawa area south of the river, whereas nearly 70 per cent of the total population stated that of the two official languages they could speak English only, a mere 15,000, or under five per cent stated that they could speak French only. The Hull metropolitan area, and in particular the city of Hull, shows almost the reverse situation. In Hull a mere 3,200 spoke English only, while over 25,000, or nearly half, spoke French only. In Ottawa, only about one-quarter spoke both English and French, while in Hull and in its whole metropolitan area, there were more people who spoke both English and French than who spoke French only, indicating the much greater degree of bilingualism north of the river. In Hull almost exactly half of the population are bilingual. The reason, of course, is the predominant influence of English-speaking Ottawa. Much of the French-speaking population has been required to learn English in order to work in Ottawa, whereas in Ottawa the English have not had to learn French.

The comparative figures on religion show that, as might be expected, the number of people in the Hull metropolitan area who give their religion as Roman Catholic is about the same as those who give their ethnic group as French. The Ottawa metropolitan area, however, and Ottawa in particular, indicates a surprisingly larger number of people who are Roman Catholic than are of French origin; in Ottawa in 1961 about 128,000 were Catholic, nearly half the total population. This is because of the presence of a considerable number of Irish Catholics in the area.

In view of the disadvantageous situation of the French minority in Ottawa, it is not surprising that the federal Public Service Commission has found it difficult to attract French-speaking civil servants to Ottawa and to keep them there. Coming from a French-speaking culture in Quebec, they find living in Ottawa an unpleasant shock. As a result, many of them resign and return to their home province. After the reform government of Jean Lesage came into power in Quebec and began hiring well-qualified provincial civil servants, some of the best French-speaking federal civil servants left Ottawa for Quebec. In recent years, the federal government has been making valiant efforts to meet one of the chief sources of French-Canadian dissatisfaction: the neglect of the French language in the civil service. A massive program has been launched to teach French to English-speaking civil servants, and the federal service is gradually becoming more bilingual. A new spirit is now developing among English-speaking civil servants. Many of them want their children to become fluently bilingual by taking their schooling in French, and would also like to see the position of the French-speaking minority in Ottawa improved.

The city government in Ottawa, however, at first remained relatively untouched by these developments. True, in 1966, the council decided to introduce bilingual traffic signs in one French-speaking ward, and to print its tax bills in both languages. But it also decided that bilingual letterheads and by-laws would be too costly. And when the Royal Commission on Bilingualism and Biculturalism began looking into the use of the French language by the civic administration, and the relative proportions of English- and French-speaking civic servants, it received a singular lack of cooperation from the city government, which at first objected to any inquiry being conducted and later refused to allow a questionnaire on language practices to be distributed. The inquiry was part of a larger survey of language and culture in the capital area, the results of which, edited by my colleague, Kenneth McRae, were published as a Commission study in 1969. This study revealed the extent to which governmental institutions on the Ottawa side of the river were unilingual, including even the courts, in contrast with those on the Hull side. It also noted that historically, Ottawa has elected very few French-speaking controllers, and had not elected a single French-speaking mayor in over twenty years.[7] Pressed by the publicity given to its anti-bilingual stand, the city council finally adopted a policy of bilingualism for its civic departments in October 1970.

The attitude of French-Canadians to the capital city, then, is not hard to understand. They – and also many fairminded English-speaking Canadians – are beginning to ask questions such as these: Is it right that the national capital, which is necessarily the home of many French-speaking MPs and civil servants, should provide an atmosphere which to many of them is hostile? Is it right that they should be deprived of their own cultural environment, especially the use of their own language? Is it fair that they should not have equal educational services and linguistic rights? Isn't Ottawa as the national capital a special case – shouldn't it be a symbol of the two founding peoples and cultures, and become a model of bilingualism and biculturalism for the rest of Canada?

The basic problem, however, as with the physical planning and development of the national capital, is that the federal government has no control over Ottawa. A number of people have recently come to believe, therefore, that the problem can only be solved by cutting the Ottawa area adrift from the overwhelming English-speaking majority and Anglo-Saxon culture and laws of Ontario, and combining it with the Hull area as a separate federal territory. This explains the origin of the proposals to this effect made to the Royal Commission on Bilingualism and Biculturalism.

A FEDERAL DISTRICT?

In recent years it has been widely admitted that the federal capital area has developed serious problems of planning, transportation, metropolitan government, bilingualism, and biculturalism. The first in the series of final reports by the Royal Commission on Bilingualism and Biculturalism, which was issued in 1967, stressed the far-reaching changes required to solve these problems. On the language question, the commissioners recommended:

A that the English and French languages should have full equality of status throughout the area;
B that all services should be available at all levels of public administration in the two languages;
C that the use of both English and French should be permitted in the deliberations of all local government bodies, that all by-laws and regulations should be recorded and printed in the two languages;
D that all courts should permit pleadings in the two languages, and that the lower courts should be equipped to function in both;
E that publicly supported education should be as available in French as in English and should be of the same quality;
F that the two provincial governments concerned and the federal government should discuss and negotiate the necessary measures.[8]

In their supporting commentary the commissioners significantly added:

But in our view the fact that it is the federal capital means that more than the establishment of a linguistic regime is required. We shall devote a later Book to the other aspects of the problem and to the concerted action which we envisage on the part of the provincial and federal governments.[9]

Although the report did not specifically recommend a federal district, this statement could easily have been taken as implying that their later book might do so, especially since the Commission's staff was in the process of conducting a costly and comprehensive study of the capital area.

On 29 November 1967, former Prime Minister Pearson said during a television interview that he thought a federal district should be created for Ottawa. The next day, in reply to a question in the House of Commons, he stated that the government was discussing the implementation of this project with the two provinces concerned. A few weeks later, on 31 January 1968, he and the prime ministers of Ontario and Quebec jointly announced that they had appointed a committee of officials to make proposals for the Ottawa area. But their proposals were not to involve "changing basic constitutional jurisdictions or existing provincial boundaries." Since a federal district could not be created without such changes, one wonders why Mr Pearson agreed to this restriction on the committee's study and why he did not insist on keeping the question of a federal district open.

In the statement jointly issued by the three prime ministers announcing their appointment of the study committee, the objectives for the federal capital were stated to be as follows:

That the necessary steps should be taken for the further development of the capital region of Canada, within appropriate geographic boundaries, which would extend on both sides of the Ottawa river, and include the cities of Ottawa and Hull and suitable neighbouring areas; that the capital region of Canada should be so constituted and developed as to reflect fully the linguistic and cultural values of the two founding peoples and the contribution of Canadians of other origins, and thus encourage in all Canadians a feeling of pride and participation in, and attachment to, their capital.[10]

One wonders whether these far-reaching objectives can be fully achieved under existing constitutional arrangements and without creating a federal district. Yet in proposing substantially the same objectives to the federal-provincial Constitutional Conference in February 1969, the three governments secured the conference's agreement that:

A The cities of Ottawa and Hull and their surrounding areas shall be the Canadian Capital area.
B No changes be made to provincial boundaries or to the constitutional responsibilities of the governments concerned.
C The boundaries of the Canadian Capital area are to be established by agreement of the governments concerned.
D In line with the aforementioned objectives, steps must be taken so that the two official languages and the cultural values common to all Canadians are recognized by all governments concerned in these two cities and in the Capital Region in general, so that all Canadians may have a feeling of pride and participation in, and attachment to their Capital.
E That the study committee on the Canadian Capital continue its work, giving particular importance to the following:
(a) the definition of adjacent areas which would eventually constitute, along with the cities of Ottawa and Hull, and their surrounding areas, the Canadian Capital Region.

(b) the study of the administration and the financing of a tripartite organization.[11]

Nothing was said about the nature of this "tripartite organization," but the term seemed to imply some kind of governing body for the Capital Region which would have powers delegated to it by the federal and the two provincial governments, and which would include representatives from these governments and perhaps also from the local governments in the Region. One wonders how such a government could be created and could operate with no changes made "to the constitutional responsibilities of the governments concerned." It would be in the virtually unworkable legal position of being controlled by and responsible to three different governments whose powers are constitutionally divided. So far, the study committee has issued no public report or proposals.

The Royal Commission seems to have been influenced not only by this determination of the three governments to try to solve the capital's problems without creating a federal territory but also by their idea of a "tripartite organization." When at last it published its Book Five, *The Federal Capital*, in June 1970, although it promoted the idea of a federal territory eventually, and even included a long appendix on possible institutional arrangements for the territory, it weakly recommended instead as the only structural reform for the immediate future, a "tripartite agency." Thus it even adopted the same term, "tripartite," as was employed by the Constitutional Conference. Perhaps recognizing the constitutional difficulties inherent in a tripartite governing organization, however, it proposed that this "tripartite agency" should at first be only advisory and should be restricted to co-ordinating plans for the development of the capital area.

It seems highly unlikely that such an agency could achieve the Commission's far-reaching objective of bilingual and bicultural equality in the area. Even if it were later granted some executive powers, its decisions might be rejected by any one of the three senior governments or ignored by the local governments. It would certainly be no solution to the other serious problems of governing the area. After about a year of frustration in office, the new chairman of the National Capital Commission, Mr Douglas Fullerton, also came to this conclusion, and has publicly stated that a more drastic reorganization is necessary.

It is often assumed that a federal district is out of the question because it would be so difficult for the federal government to secure the agreement of Ontario and especially Quebec to the necessary constitutional change. Yet to achieve the desired objectives in the absence of a federal district would require not only their initial agreement but also their continuing co-operation and continual new agreements on every detail of implementation, an unlikely eventuality. A federal district, on the other hand, would require only one master constitutional agreement at a single point in time. If this agreement is to be secured, however, it must be such as to satisfy Quebec that the benefits to be gained in bilingualism and biculturalism will more than offset her loss of territory. In view of the importance of the objectives, as agreed by the three prime ministers, it seems strange that they did not initiate a thorough investigation of the problems of governing the capital area, and also of the solutions tried in other federal capitals, before deciding whether the idea of a federal district should be excluded.

Despite this stand of the senior governments and the opposition of many local politicians, available evidence indicates that a large proportion of the population, both outside and within the capital area, favours a federal district. Although no systematic survey of the general population has been conducted, a number of organizations in Ontario and Quebec polled their own membership on the question in preparing their briefs for the Royal Commission, and found that a substantial majority favoured a federal district. Also, scattered surveys of opinion within the capital area have shown that a large proportion of its residents supports the idea.[12]

Historically, local politicians have fostered a prejudice against a federal district through their constant references to the absence of local self-government in Washington and Canberra, and their unwarranted assumption that a federal district necessarily implies the abolition of all voting rights and self-government. Yet, as the other essays in this book demonstrate, the citizens of most federal districts elect representatives to the national legislature, and several federal districts have enjoyed a considerable degree of self-government. Even Washington had self-government for almost a century, and only went into federal "receivership" as a result of overspending in trying to build a fine capital. Significantly, Washington once again has a mayor and councillors who, though appointed, are more representative of the local population. There is also a growing movement for self-government in Canberra, and several interesting proposals for its government have been made in recent years.

In considering whether a federal district may be desirable for Canada, then, there is thus much to be learned from examining carefully and fully the experience of federal district capitals elsewhere, especially capitals such as Caracas and Delhi, where a more desirable balance between national and local interests has been worked out. At the same time the Ottawa-Hull area is in some ways unique. It has a special problem of balancing the interests of the populations on each side of the Ottawa river. These populations have not only different dominant languages and religions but also different traditions and systems of law. Canada would therefore have to design a scheme of district government suited to the special needs of the area.

1 One Canadian dollar worth was about 98 US cents in 1970.
2 *The Queen's Choice* (Ottawa, 1961), 166.
3 B.W.G. Marley-Clarke, *The Policy and Administration of the Municipal Grants Act, 1951, As Amended* (MA Thesis, Carleton University, 1966), Appendix.
4 For such purposes as urban redevelopment ($9.0 million), the Civic Hospital ($2.8 million), bridges and roads ($1.4 million), and elimination of railway crossings ($1.5 million). See City of Ottawa, *1966 Current Expenditure Budget,* Part I, 3; and *Minutes of the City Council,* 28 February 1966, 690-1.
5 *Ottawa Citizen,* 25 and 27 July 1964.
6 See story by Donna Dilschneider, *Ottawa Citizen,* 6 August 1966.
7 *The Federal Capital: Government Institutions* (Ottawa, 1969), 148-51 and 163-4. The full correspondence between the Commission and the City regarding the inquiry into Ottawa's language practices was reproduced in an appendix.
8 Royal Commission on Bilingualism and Biculturalism, *Report,* Book I: *The Official Languages* (Ottawa, 1967), 119.
9 *Ibid.,* 117.
10 *Ottawa Journal,* 1 February 1968.
11 Constitutional Conference, Second Meeting, Ottawa, February 1969, *Conclusions of the Meeting* (Document No. 96, mimeographed), 5-6.
12 See Royal Commission on Bilingualism and Biculturalism, *Report,* Vol. V: *The Federal Capital* (Ottawa, 1970), Appendix II, "A Note on Public Attitudes," 105-108. See also, D.C. Rowat, "Ottawans prefer federal district to metro," *Ottawa Citizen* (2 May 1967), 7.

Conclusion*

Our comprehensive study reveals that nearly all federations, and especially relatively decentralized ones, face difficult problems regarding the government of their federal capitals. Common to all federations is the problem of what degree of self-government should be granted to the capital city. And all of them must decide whether it is better for the capital to be within a federal district under the exclusive control of the central government. The cases of Kuala Lumpur and Islamabad, however, demonstrate that it is possible to have alternative constitutional arrangements which, though not creating an exclusively federal territory, give the central government almost complete legal control over the capital. Common to nearly all federal capitals is a problem characteristic of all large and rapidly growing cities in the world: the explosion of population beyond the legal boundaries of the central city and the difficulty of providing an adequate scheme of government for the whole metropolitan area or potentially urban region. This problem is made the more difficult in the case of federal capitals because of the division of powers between the central government and the states, so that even if the central government controls the capital city, it does not control the surrounding urban territory.

Our study also reveals that, of the three main types of constitutional arrangement for the government of federal capitals – a federal district, a city-state and government under state law – none has been entirely satisfactory, and each has its own peculiar problems. Let us review each of them in turn to see what these problems are.

CAPITALS IN FEDERAL DISTRICTS

Since many federations have chosen the federal district arrangement, the question naturally arises whether this is not the best way of governing a

---

* These concluding comments are based on my article, "The Problems of Governing Federal Capitals," *Canadian Journal of Political Science*, 1 (September 1968), 345–57. I should like to thank the editor of the *Journal* for permission to reproduce portions of that article.

federal capital. It is frequently argued that, as a matter of principle, the capital of a federation should not be governed by the laws of any one state in the federation. There is a danger that the government of the state or of the capital city may interfere with the proper functioning of the organs of the central government. Also, the state subjects the capital to its own legal and cultural dominance. This is the complaint that French-Canadians make about Ottawa. Furthermore, the central government does not have sufficient control over the planning and development of its own capital.

Although a federally governed district solves these problems, at the same time it presents the danger of too much central control over the local residents. They may not be granted local self-government or the normal political rights enjoyed by the citizens of the states. It is commonly known in the English-speaking world that the residents of Washington and Canberra have no locally elected government. This is also true of several other capitals in federal districts: Brasilia, Buenos Aires, and Mexico City. Of all these capitals, Brasilia is the most extreme case. Not only does it not have a locally elected government but it does not elect any representatives to the national Congress. In Brasilia, the residents have no vote of any kind. This was also true of Washington's residents until 1961. They now have the right to vote in presidential elections, and have a non-voting representative in Congress. In all other federal districts, however, the residents elect voting members to the national legislature.

In the US, Australia, and especially Canada, many of those who discuss this problem assume the absence of local self-government to be a necessary characteristic of a federal district. Yet even in the US and Australia there has been strong opposition, particularly in recent years, to the absence of self-government in the federal capital. There are special reasons why self-government has not been granted to Washington. Most of the white population have moved into the surrounding metropolitan area in Maryland and Virginia, where they have local governments and full voting rights, leaving a large Negro majority in the city. The southern Democrats in control of the Congressional committees which govern the federal district are reluctant to create an elected city council having a Negro majority. On the other hand, Canberra has had a locally elected Advisory Council for many years, and the Australian government is at present considering greater self-government for the capital territory.[1]

The newly built federal capitals – Canberra, Brasilia and Islamabad – had to be planned and constructed by the central government, and at first had no local population. It is therefore not surprising that the first residents were not given self-government. Islamabad, however, is being constructed beside an existing city, Rawalpindi, which contains much of the new capital's population, and which has had its own elected city government. Pakistan's former capital, Karachi, had self-government as a federal district, as did Brazil's former capital, Rio de Janeiro. Also Lagos had an elected local government before the civil war broke out in Nigeria. During the long periods when Argentina was governed under a constitutional regime, Buenos Aires always had an elected city council. Local elections have been suspended under the present dictatorship, but if Argentina returns to constitutional government Buenos Aires will no doubt again have an elected local government. These cases show that the absence of self-government is by no means a necessary characteristic of federal districts.

In addition, there are two examples of federal districts which at present have a considerable degree of self-government: Caracas and Delhi. Dr Brewer's essay reveals that Caracas has a fully elected governing council which chooses its own mayor. At the same time, the President of Venezuela appoints a governor for the district, and the division of powers between the governor and the elected council represents an interesting balance between national and local interests in the federal capital. In recent years the mayor and a majority of the district's council have usually belonged to a different party from that which dominates the federal government. Clearly then, it is quite possible to have a considerable degree of self-government within a federal district.

From this point of view, the Union Territory of Delhi is perhaps the most interesting of all the federal districts. As Dr Singhvi points out, the Union Territory, which was created in 1956, has a population of about four million. It includes three adjacent cities: Delhi (with a population of over three million); New Delhi, the official capital (with about 400,000); and the cantonment (about 60,000). The latter is a military-residential-commercial area governed by the local military commander on the advice of a council mainly appointed by him but also partly elected by the local residents. The Territory also includes a large rural area with about 360 villages, which elect local councils. While New Delhi is governed by an appointed committee, Delhi, like British cities, has a huge elected council of 106 members. On the executive side, Delhi has a commissioner, an executive officer resembling a city manager, except that he is appointed by the central government.

Before 1966 the Union Territory was governed for federal and state purposes by a Chief Commissioner and his Advisory Council, who were responsible to the Minister of Home Affairs. The Advisory Council consisted of the members of Parliament from the Territory, the mayor of Delhi, the chairman of the New Delhi municipal committee, and four members appointed by the federal government. In 1966 a Metropolitan Council was created for the Territory, with five members appointed by the federal government and 56 directly elected. The title of the Chief Commissioner was changed to Administrator, and he now chairs an Executive Council of four members who are appointed by the federal government from among the members of the Metropolitan Council. Thus a second tier of territorial government has been created above the existing local units. It is like the regional government recently created for Ottawa, except that it covers the whole capital territory and is supervised by the federal government in recognition of the facts that the Union Territory is the federal seat of government and that the territorial council must necessarily deal with federal and state-level matters. As in Caracas, a party different from the one in power at the federal level has had a majority at the local level, not only in Delhi's government but also in the Metropolitan Council. This party has even held all the seats on the Executive Council.

The experience of Delhi demonstrates that within a capital territory under the exclusive jurisdiction of the federal government it is possible to have elected local governments and also an elected or predominantly elected council for the whole territory. This was one of the suggestions I made in my report on a federal territory for Ottawa.[2]

Although the creation of federal districts has helped to solve the problem of metropolitan government for federal capitals, it has by no means solved this problem completely. Except for Brasilia, the federal districts in North and South America were created near the turn of the century or earlier. Although they were made large enough to contain expected urban growth, no one at that time could conceive of the tremendous pace of urbanization that the world has experienced since the second world war. The result has been that the urban population of these four federal districts (Buenos Aires, Caracas, Mexico City, and Washington) has by now spread well beyond their boundaries, and serious problems of metropolitan government have developed. The most extreme case is Washington, where two-thirds of the population of the metropolitan area live outside the boundaries of the district in about sixty separate municipalities governed by the states of Maryland and Virginia. Since the boundaries of a federal district must be provided for in a federation's constitution, they are difficult to change. If a federal district is to be created, then, the obvious lesson is that it should be made large enough to include any conceivable future growth of the capital city's urban area.

CAPITALS AS CITY-STATES

Let us now consider the idea of turning a federal capital into one of the states of the federation. This is an intriguing idea, and has been proposed recently for Ottawa's national capital region.[3] A unit which is a city and at the same time one of the states of a federation is outside the experience of people in most federations, and seems very strange. Yet there are several examples of city-states of this kind. In Western Germany there are the city-states of Hamburg and Bremen, and Berlin is a kind of city-state. These city-states seem to work very well within the West German federation. In 1962 I became interested in this idea and proposed that the metroplitan areas of Montreal and Toronto should become city-provinces, in order both to help solve their problem of metropolitan government and to reduce the huge populations of Quebec and Ontario, which tend to dominate the Canadian federation.[4]

Lagos and Vienna, then, are not unique as city-states. But they are unique as city-states which are also federal capitals (though Delhi was a state for a short period before 1956). The example of Lagos is not very helpful because it is so recent. Vienna, on the other hand, was one of the original states of the Austrian federation in 1920, and is by far its most populous state. Austria's experience with this type of arrangement, however, has not been an entirely happy one. In fact, Austria's political history may be summed up as a struggle between the central government and Vienna.

Because of the degree of autonomy acquired with full statehood, turning the federal capital into a state may give the centre even less control over its own seat of government than it has when the capital is governed by a state from outside. Also, if the city-state is not made big enough at the time of its creation, the urban population may eventually spread far beyond its boundaries into other states, and create a serious problem of metropolitan government. Vienna has not had to face this problem yet because, as the former capital of the Austro-Hungarian empire, it was too large to be economically supported by the Austrian federation. Its population actually declined between the world wars, and has been growing only slowly since then.

Where the capital of a federation is very large, like Vienna, and has many industrial and other interests not directly related to its functions as the capital, there may be a case for its being an autonomous city-state. But the arrangement is not likely to work very successfully, for the obvious reason that the centre needs some kind of control over the government and development of its own capital. Therefore, in a decentralized federation the federal capital should not be as autonomous as a state.

CAPITALS UNDER STATE LAW

What are the problems of governing a federal capital that comes under the laws of one of the states? In a genuine, relatively decentralized federation, the chief problem is that the federal government has no direct control over its own capital city. Although it has a definite interest in developing the capital as a symbol of the nation, it does not have the constitutional power to do this. Usually the powers in the constitution are divided in such a way that the central government has no jurisdiction over city planning or local government. The rapid growth of urban areas and the spread of the urban population into many municipalities surrounding the capital city has intensified this problem. Furthermore, the laws, influence and culture of the governing state dominate the capital city and make it unrepresentative of the nation as a whole. As my own essay shows, Ottawa provides a typical example of these difficulties.[5]

Five of the federal capitals that are not in federal districts have not experienced the same difficulties as Ottawa because they are in relatively centralized federations. These are Yaoundé (Cameroon), Moscow (USSR), Belgrade (Yugoslavia), Islamabad (Pakistan), and Kuala Lumpur (Malaysia). Cameroon, the USSR, and Yugoslavia are all one-party countries, while Pakistan has been under military rule. Though Islamabad and Kuala Lumpur are not in federal districts, they are governed almost exclusively by federal law. In most of these federations, too, the state in which the capital city is located is the largest one, and dominates the federation. In such federations there is little likelihood of serious disagreement between the state and the central government, and the centre manages to control its capital city to its satisfaction.

Cameroon is of special interest because it has a language situation almost the reverse of Canada's. It is a two-state federation with four million people in the French-speaking Eastern State and one million people in the English-speaking Western State. However, the position of its capital is not at all like that of Canada's. As Dr Enonchong points out, the country has only one political party, and Yaoundé is the capital of both the federation and the larger Eastern State. Therefore, the possibility of a dispute between the federal government and the capital city or its governing state is rather remote.

In the relatively decentralized federations of Switzerland and West Germany, on the other hand, the problems of divided jurisdiction over the federal capital and its metropolitan area are surprisingly similar to those in Canada.

Bern, like Ottawa, cannot be controlled directly by the federal government. For instance, the central government cannot control the planning and development of the Bern area. In fact, it cannot even control its own construction. If it wishes to put up a building, it has to secure approval of the design from the city planning department. Bern is growing like most cities of the world and is overflowing into the suburbs. A serious problem of planning and metropolitan government is therefore developing there, as it has in Ottawa.

Another interesting way in which Bern parallels Ottawa is in language usage. Bern and Belgrade are the two federal capitals most like Ottawa in this respect. Although Switzerland has four national languages (German, French, Italian, and Romansch), the two main languages are German and French, and French is in much the same minority position as it is in Canada. Bern is in the German-speaking part of the country. It is a German-speaking city governed by a German-speaking canton, just as Ottawa is an English-speaking city governed by an English-speaking province. Like the province of Ontario, the canton of Bern has a French-speaking minority in the north and in the federal capital. Therefore the problem arises of the rights of the French-speaking minority, particularly the federal civil servants. They naturally wish not only to work in their own language but also to have their families use it in daily life, and to have easy access to their own culture.

But the language problem in Bern is not as acute as in Ottawa for several reasons. In the first place, the German-speaking majority in Switzerland have been more generous in meeting the language requirements and wishes of the minorities. For instance, nearly all of the educated majority have learned to speak French, and usually make a point of doing so socially when French-speaking persons are present. They even go more than half way in this respect by not expecting a French-speaking social group to speak German when German-speaking persons are present. Also, the French-speaking population are well represented in the federal civil service. French is used more there than in the Canadian federal civil service, partly because French rather than German is the traditional diplomatic language. The French-speaking minority are therefore over-represented in the Ministry of Foreign Affairs.

On the other hand, the language policy in Switzerland is that, though minority language rights are guaranteed at the federal level and in the canton of Bern, the official language in each district is the majority language of that district. This means that Bern's city government, school system, and working language are German. Such a cultural environment does not fully satisfy the needs and wishes of the French-speaking civil servants. For instance, there is not a single French-speaking public school in Bern to which they can send their children. The federal government can do nothing about this because public education is a state matter. As my colleague, Kenneth McRae, has pointed out, in recent years the problem has been partly solved in an informal way by the federal and state governments making grants to a *private* French-speaking school.[6] Since Bern is a small city, one school has been enough to meet the immediate problem. This use of federal money to overcome a problem in the capital caused by divided constitutional jurisdiction is strikingly similar to Ottawa's case.

Another similarity is that Bern's street signs are in the majority language only, and there are other language usages of this nature which are likely to become a basis for complaint. In fact, I have the uneasy feeling that, as in Ottawa only a few years ago, the majority in Bern are much too complacent about how well they are meeting the language needs of the minorities. I was in Bern not long after General de Gaulle's visit to Canada in 1967, and the joke then travelling around was that de Gaulle's next visit would be to Switzerland where he would similarly urge the French-speaking minority to throw off their chains. Since jokes often express underlying emotions, in my opinion the language problem in both the canton and the city of Bern will become more serious. In fact, the French-speaking minority in Switzerland are likely to be influenced directly by recent developments in Canada, including the separatist movement in Quebec.

Of all the federal capitals, Bonn seems to be the closest parallel to Ottawa. In the first place, the city has had a long history of independent self-government. Second, it is one of the few state-governed federal capitals that is not also the capital of the state in which it is situated. Like Ottawa, it is governed from a state capital, Düsseldorf, which is a considerable distance away. Like Ontario, the state of North Rhine Westphalia, which governs Bonn, is the most populous one in the federation, and its government has several larger cities to worry about. Like the residents of Ottawa and Hull, the citizens of Bonn feel that they are being neglected by the state government. Third, the federal government has no direct control over or financial responsibility for Bonn or its surrounding area. The residents and local municipalities complain that the federal government does not pay a large enough share for new facilities, such as bridges, highways, and cultural centres, which are required because Bonn is the capital city; others complain that it is not a capital worthy of West Germany; and so on, in much the same phrasing that one hears about Ottawa. A fourth interesting parallel is that Bonn's metropolitan area is divided by a river and there is a smaller city across the Rhine, Beuel, which corresponds to Hull across from Ottawa. This has created similar transportation and bridge-building problems. Important differences, however, are that Hull is governed under the laws of a different province and the great majority of the residents speak a language different from that of the capital city.

A fifth similarity between Ottawa and Bonn is in their problems of metropolitan government. In the past two decades the urban population in both capital areas has spread far beyond the boundaries of the central city. As Dr Beck points out, because Bonn was much too small as a capital, the embassies had to locate outside its boundaries. There is therefore a special embassy area, Bad Godesberg, which corresponds to Ottawa's separate village of Rockcliffe Park except that the latter is much smaller. Several federal ministries were also located outside Bonn's boundaries, mainly in a community to the west, called Hardtberg. Until recently, no action had been taken to solve Bonn's metropolitan problems because Bonn was regarded as only a temporary capital. The government of North Rhine Westphalia had been considering a plan for a second tier of regional government in the Bonn area that was surprisingly like Ontario's new system for the Ottawa region. Instead, however, in 1969 it greatly extended Bonn's boundaries to include Bad Godesberg and several other communities. Though Dr Beck seems to regard this as an inadequate solution to Bonn's metropolitan problems, it is to be noted that the new Bonn also includes Beuel, the city across the river. The new regional government for Ottawa, however, does not, and constitutionally cannot, include Hull. Recently the government of Quebec has had to create a quite separate regional government for Hull and its surrounding communities, even though the whole Ottawa-Hull region forms a single metropolitan and national capital area.

From this comparative survey it is clear that, though state-governed national capitals in decentralized federations usually enjoy a high degree of self-government, they suffer from serious problems of divided jurisdiction, financial insufficiency, cultural domination by the governing state, inadequate metropolitan government, and the inability of the central government to control the capital city or its development in the interests of the nation.

THE QUESTIONS OF A FEDERAL DISTRICT AND SELF-GOVERNMENT

Let us now turn to the two central questions posed in the Introduction: the desirability of a federal district, and of self-government for federal capitals. What conclusions can be drawn from our comparative study regarding these questions?

On the question of where a federal district is appropriate, some negative, though useful, generalizations may be stated. For instance, one cannot say that a federal district is undesirable because it exists only in centralized federations. Some federations, like the US and Australia, are relatively decentralized and have federal districts; others like the USSR and Cameroon, are centralized and do not have federal districts. Nor can one say that a federal district is inappropriate for federations with relatively small capital cities. Several federal districts, like those in Argentina and Mexico, contain by far the largest city in the country, but others, as in Australia, contain a relatively small city. A federal district certainly seems desirable for the construction of new capitals, since the federal interest is direct and there is from the very beginning no local population with pre-existing state loyalties. But one cannot conclude from this that a federal district is desirable only for the construction of new capitals. Most of the federal districts were created around existing old cities.

Where a federal district seems to be particularly appropriate is in decentralized federations. It is here that the sharp division of powers between the central and state governments prevents the central government from having any effective control over its own capital. This lack of control violates the federal principle that the capital of a federation should not come under the predominant legal control and cultural influence of only one of the states in a federation. On the other hand, even in a decentralized federation it might be possible to solve this problem without going so far as to create an exclusively federal district. In the constitution, the central government could be given predominant but not exclusive control over the capital area, as in the case of Kuala Lumpur and Islamabad, or it might be given at least concurrent control.

Alternatively, the central government and the state concerned might try to agree on extra-constitutional measures of voluntary co-operation to overcome the problems of divided jurisdiction. As mentioned in my essay on Ottawa, this is the approach now being taken in Canada by the governments concerned. But in Canada such an approach is complicated by the fact that two provincial governments are involved, so that the success of the plan will depend upon the continuous voluntary co-operation of three governments. It is therefore difficult to believe that it could succeed. To be effective, joint control would require special constitutional arrangements which give the central government at least a limited, if not an overriding, control over the federal capital area.

Turning now to the question of self-government for federal capitals, we find that state-governed capitals and federal districts tend to be at opposite ends of a spectrum. In the case of state-governed capitals, the problem may be too much local control, while in federal districts there is likely to be either no self-government or very little. In fact, there is a real danger of local interests being disregarded in a federal district. Very few countries having a federal district have provided the local residents with a significant measure of self-government. On the other hand, the experiences of Caracas and Delhi indicate that it is possible to provide a balance between national and local interests and even to preserve local government within the district.

History shows that when a federal government built a new capital, it did not ordinarily provide the inhabitants with any locally elected government. The only exception was Washington in the early years. On the other hand, where a federal district was created around an old city which already had an elected council, at least some self-government was provided.

Certainly if a capital is large, and a large proportion of its inhabitants are not working for the government, a considerable degree of self-government seems desirable. Where no self-government is provided, a serious problem of co-ordinating the activities of the various federal departments and agencies concerned with governing the district seems to develop. A single, multi-purpose governing authority for the district would no doubt help to solve this problem. The authority could be made responsible for co-ordinating all federal and state-level services in the area.

Our survey of experience in federal districts suggests that the predominant legal, financial, and political power of the central government tends to tip the balance between local and central interests strongly in favour of the central government. Provisions for local political rights and self-government should therefore be laid down and protected by the constitutional provisions for the district. Since the central government would still possess over-riding authority, there seems to be no good reason why the federal constitution should not provide the district with an elected governing council, which would exercise at least state-level and metropolitan powers. At any rate, in the interests of enhancing democratic government, the constitution should provide a federal district with the highest degree of local self-government that is consistent with protecting the national interest in the federal capital.

Since a federal government has a great stake in the central, state-level, and even metropolitan services provided within its capital, only a limited independence could be granted to a federal district's council, and the federal government might insist on sharing in the membership of either the council or its executive body, or both. Hence the district government could not be fully self-governing. In order to increase the element of self-government within federal districts, therefore, I would suggest that a second tier of locally elected governments should be created beneath the district government, to deal with municipal matters. Their boundaries would be drawn so as to correspond as much as possible with identifiable communities within the urban and rural zones.

There are many precedents in other large metropolitan areas of the world for a two-tier system such as this – in London, Toronto, Berlin, Belgrade, and Moscow, to name only a few. In the case of a capital within a federal district, since the central government's interest must necessarily weigh heavily in the over-all planning, development, and financing of the capital, a lower level of local government would provide a valuable way to increase the element of self-government for the residents of the district.

1 See J.D. Miller, "Self-Government for Canberra?" 26 *Public Administration* (Australia, September 1967), 218–26; also, Australia Ministry of Interior,

Self-Government for the Australian Capital Territory: A Preliminary Assessment (Canberra, 1967).

2 "The Proposal for a Federal Territory for Canada's Capital," in Ontario Advisory Committee on Confederation, *Background Papers and Reports* (Toronto, 1967), 268–74.

3 Frank Flaherty, "Gift Suggestion for Canada's 100th Birthday: Make Ottawa Our 11th Province," *Weekend Magazine* (29 June 1963), 1–4, 23; see also A.R. Kear, "Provincial Status for the National Capital Region," a brief to the Royal Commission on Bilingualism and Biculturalism, 19 August 1964, 16 pp. mimeographed.

4 "Toronto and Montreal Should Be Provinces," *Maclean's* (16 June 1962), 46–7; reproduced in expanded form in my *The Canadian Municipal System* (Toronto, 1969), 94–8. The same proposal was made again, and quite independently, by Senator Keith Davey in *Maclean's* (August 1969), 14.

5 For a full account of the numerous difficulties that have been caused by divided jurisdiction over Canada's national capital, see Wilfrid Eggleston's excellent history, *The Queen's Choice* (Ottawa, 1961).

6 *Switzerland: Example of Cultural Coexistence* (Toronto, 1964), 68.

Selected bibliography

A MATERIALS IN ENGLISH

GENERAL

Bureau of Municipal Research, *Reference Handbook on Metropolitan Areas* (Toronto: the Bureau, 1967). Includes Belgrade and Buenos Aires.

Busey, James L., *Latin America: Political Institutions and Processes* (New York: Random House, 1964)

Davies, Howell (ed.), *The South American Handbook 1967* (London: Trade and Travel Publications, 1967)

Dreyfus, Simone, "Capital Cities: A Jurists View," 5 *Local Government Throughout the World* (December 1962), 59–61

–, "Capital Cities: Their Legal-Constitutional Status." Translated by Ruth Atkins for National Capital Development Commission (Canberra, 1964), 163 pp. mimeographed

Fodor, Eugene (ed.), *Fodor's Guide to South America* (New York: David McKay Co., 1966)

Gottmann, J., "Great Capitals in Evolution," 54 *Geographical Review* (January 1964), 124–7

Humes, S., and Martin E.M., *The Structure of Local Governments Throughout the World* (The Hague: Martinus Nijhoff, 1961)

International Union of Local Authorities, *Metropolis: A Selected Bibliography on Metropolitan Areas* (The Hague: Int. Union of Local Authorities, 1968)

Mackenzie, W.J.M. (ed.), *The Government of Great Cities* (Manchester: Univ. of Manchester, 1952)

Overall, J.W., "The Form and Development of National Capitals (with special reference to Washington and Ottawa)" (Canberra, 1963), 23 pp. mimeographed, plus charts

Peaslee, A.J., *Constitutions of Nations*. (The Hague: Martinus Nijhoff, 1965)

Perry, J. Harvey, *Report on the Financial and Administrative Arrangements in Capitals of Federal Countries* (Nigeria: Government Printer, 1953)

Robson, W.A. (ed.), *Great Cities of the World: Their Government, Politics and Planning* (London: Allen and Unwin, 2nd ed., 1957)
– , "Metropolitan Government: Problems and Solutions," 9 *Canadian Public Administration* (March 1966), 45–54
Rowat, D.C., "How Federal Capitals are Governed," 3, 2 *Indian Administrative and Management Review* (July–Sept. 1970), 38–47
"Special Problems of New Capital Cities," in *Report of the United Nations Symposium on the Planning and Development of New Towns* (New York: UN ST/TAO/Ser. C/79, 1964), Ch. v, p. 48
Statesman's Year-Book (Toronto: Macmillan, annual), for brief but current information
Watts, Ronald L., *New Federations: Experiments in the Commonwealth* (Oxford: Clarendon Press, 1966)

Belgrade

BOOKS AND DOCUMENTS

Benes, V., Gyorgy, A. and Stambuk, G., *Eastern European Government and Politics* (New York: Harper & Row, 1966), Ch. 6, "Yugoslavia," by George Stambuk
Fisher, Jack C., *Yugoslavia, a Multinational State: Regional Difference and Administrative Response* (San Francisco: Chandler, 1966)
Hondius, F.W., *The Yugoslav Community of Nations* (The Hague and Paris, 1968), 375
Kovačević, Živorad, *The Yugoslav Commune* (Belgrade, 1965)
Petrović, R., *Local Self-Government in Yugoslavia* (Belgrade: Publicity and Publishing Enterprise Jugoslavia, 1955)
Serbia, Constitution, *Constitution of the Socialist Republic of Serbia* (Belgrade: Institute of Comparative Law, Collection of Yougoslav Laws, Vol. 8, 1964)
Standing Conference of Towns of Yugoslavia, *Amalgamation or Cooperation*, Yugoslav Report for the IULA Stockholm Conference (Belgrade, 1967)
– , *The Commune in the New Yugoslav Constitution* (Belgrade, 1963), 37
– , *Local Government Structure and Organization in Yugoslavia* (Belgrade, 1961)
Yugoslav Embassy Information Office, *Local Government in Yugoslavia* (London, 1954), mimeographed
Yugoslavia, Constitution, *The Constitution of the Socialist Federal Republic of Yugoslavia*. Translated by Peter Mijuskovic (Belgrade: Secretariat for Information of the Federal Executive Council, 1963), 91

ARTICLES

Dermastija, M., "The New Local Government System in Yugoslavia," *International Union of Local Authorities Bulletin* (2, 1956)

Djordjević, Jovan, and Pašić, Najdan, "The Communal Self-Government System in Yugoslavia," 13 *International Social Science Journal* (3, 1961)

– , "Local Self-Government in Yugoslavia," 12 *American Slavic & East European Review* (April 1953)

Fisher, Jack C., "The Yugoslav Commune," *World Politics* (April 1964)

Kovačević, Živorad, "Local Government in Yugoslavia," 4 *Local Government Throughout the World* (May–June 1965), 44–8

Mirić, Branislav, "Yugoslavia's Search for the Optimum Size of Commune," I *Comparative Local Government* (The Hague, IULA, 1967)

Neoričić, Milijan, "From Blueprint to Reality: 'Novi Beograd,' Belgrade's Modern Sector," 4 *Local Government Throughout the World* (May–June 1965), 50–2

Scott, D.J.R., "The Development of Local Government: Yugoslavia's Experience," 6 *Journal of African Administration* (July 1954)

Bern

Codding, Geo. Arthur, *Federal Government of Switzerland* (Boston: Houghton Mifflin, 1961)

Friedrich, Carl J., and Cole, Taylor, *Responsible Bureaucracy: A Study of the Swiss Civil Service* (Cambridge: Harvard Univ. Press, 1932)

Huber, Hans, *How Switzerland is Governed*. Translated by Mary Hottinger (Zurich: Schweizer Spiegelverlag, 1963)

Hughes, C.J., *The Parliament of Switzerland*, published for the Harvard Society (London: Cassel, 1962)

McRae, Kenneth D., *Switzerland: Example of Cultural Coexistence* (Toronto: Candian Institute of International Affairs, 1964), pp. 74

Bonn (and Berlin)

Adam, C., "Capital Life at Bonn," 67 *New Statesman* (5 June 1964), 876

"Administrative Reorganization of Greater Berlin," 19 *National Municipal Review* (June 1930), 440–2

Norden, W., "Berlin's New Government," 20 *National Municipal Review* (December 1931), 697–703

Plischke, Elmer, *Berlin: Development of its Government and Administration* (Berlin: Office of the US High Commissioner for Germany, 1952)
– , *Government and Politics of Contemporary Berlin* (The Hague: Martinus Nijhoff, 1963)
"Problems Confronting the Berlin Administrative Area," 19 *National Municipal Review* (Janury 1930), 14–17
Wells, Roger H., *German Cities* (Princeton: Univ. Press, 1932)

Brasilia (and Rio)

Alexander, Robert J., "Brazil: New Capital, New Hope," 43 *New Leader* (22 February 1960), 8–10
"Brasilia: A New Type of National City," 113 *Architectural Forum* (November 1960), 126–33
"Brasilia Neurosis," 65 *Newsweek*. (3 May 1965) 66
Brazil at a Glance 1967, sponsored by Banco Central do Brasil (Rio de Janeiro: Editôra Banas SA, 1967), 254. Chapter on "The Structure of Government"
"Brazil's New Capital," 194 *Economist* (27 February 1960) 820
Bruno, Zevi, "Brasilia: A Kafka Nightmare," 2 *Atlas* (January 1961), pp. 26–8. Translated from *L'Espresso* (Rome, October 1959)
"Capital becoming a capital," 86 *Time* (9 July, 1965), 36
"Crisis in Brasilia: Problems Facing the New Capital," 3 *Atlas* (February 1962) pp. 120–50. Translated from *Jornal do Brasil* (14–15 November 1961)
Crist, Raymond E., "Why Move a Capital? Brasilia's Origins," 15 *Américas* (August 1963), 13–17
Freyre, Gilberto, "A Brazilian's Critique of Brasilia," 22 *Reporter* (31 March 1960), 31–2
Knox, John and France, *Brasilia* (Munich: Wilhelm Andermann Verlag, 1966), 66
Mello, Diogo Lordello de, *Local Government in Brazil* (Rio de Janeiro: Brazilian School of Public Administration, 1958)
Rios, José Arthur, "Rio de Janeiro," in W.A. Robson (ed.), *Great Cities of the World* (London: Allen and Unwin, 1957), 489–516
Sherwood, Frank, *Brazil's Municipalities: A Comparative View* (Los Angeles: Chandler, 1967)
Skidmore, Thomas E., *Politics in Brazil: an Experiment in Democracy* (New York: Oxford Univ. Press, 1967)
"Two Faces of Brasilia," 20 *New Statesman* (27 August 1960), 268–9.

Buenos Aires

Abell, Mac., *Buenos Aires Through Bifocals* (Buenos Aires: Guillermokraft, 1961)

Biesla, Rafael, "Buenos Aires," in W.A. Robson (ed.), *Great Cities of the World* (London: Allen and Unwin, 1957), 167-90

Hauser, Philip M. (ed.), *Urbanization in Latin America* (Paris: UNESCO, 1961), Chapter 8

Lewald, H., *Buenos Aires: A Cultural Reader* (Boston: Houghton Mifflin, 1967)

Macdonald, Austin F., *Government of the Argentine Republic* (New York: Crowell, 1942), Chapter on Buenos Aires

Mouchet, Carlos, "The Federal Concept in Community Development," in L.V. Padgett (ed.), *Community Development in the Western Hemisphere*, Selected Papers, Public Affairs Research Institute (San Diego: San Diego State College, 1961), 70-80

Pendle, George, *Argentina* (London: Oxford Univ. Press, 3rd ed; 1965)

Scobie, James R., *Argentina: A City and A Nation* (London: Oxford Univ. Press, 1964)

Canberra

Archer, R.W., "The Costs of Canberra," XXIV *Public Administration* (Australia, June 1965), 146-58

Australia, Australian Capital Territory, *Advisory Council Ordinance, 1936-1962*

Australia, Department of the Interior, *Reports on the Administration and Development of Canberra and the Australian Capital Territory* (Canberra: Commonwealth Government Printer)

– , *Self-Government for the Australian Capital Territory* (Canberra: Commonwealth Government Printer, 1967)

– , Planning Section, "Canberra its Origin; A Brief History of its Government; A Survey of some Proposals for Reform" (Canberra, 1956), 17 pp. mimeographed

Australia, National Capital Development Commission, *Report on the Development of Canberra for the five year period, July 1962-June 1967* (Canberra, 1967)

– , *Tomorrow's Canberra* (Canberra, 1970), 244 pp.

Australia, Parliament, *Seat of Government Acts, 1908–1959,* as amended to 1963, *Australian Capital Territory Representation Act, 1948–1959,* as amended to 1966, and *National Capital Development Commission Act, 1959–1960*
– , Senate, *Development of Canberra,* Report from the Select Committee (Canberra: Commonwealth Government Printer, 1955)
Borrie, W.D., and others, *Canberra: the Next Decade* (Canberra, 1963)
Buxton D., "Self-Government for the Australian Capital Territory?" 37 *Australian Quarterly* (Sydney, March 1965), 40–8
Canberra Chamber of Commerce, "Canberra: Your National Capital" (Canberra, 1960), 16 pp.
Higgins, Benjamin, "Canberra: A Garden Without a City," I *Community Planning Review* (August 1951), 88–102
Linge, G.J.R., "Canberra After Fifty Years," 51 *Geographical Review* (August 1961 and April 1962), 239–44, 476–86
Miller, J.D.B., "Self-Government for Canberra?" XXVI *Public Administration* (Sydney, September 1967), 218–26
Overall, J.W., "Canberra will be symbol of federalism," *The Financial Times* (London, 7 May 1962), 57
White, H.L. (ed.), *Canberra – A Nation's Capital* (Sydney: Halstead Press, 1954)
Wigmore, Lionel, *The Long View: A History of Canberra, Australia's National Capital* (Melbourne: I.W. Cheshire, 1963)

Caracas

Henion, Doris Volz, *Venezuela: Land of Bolivar, the Liberator* (New York: Charles Frank, 1964), 56–7
International Bank for Reconstruction and Development, *The Economic Development of Venezuela* (Baltimore: Johns Hopkins Press, 1961)
Laquian, Aprodicio A. (ed.), *Rural-Urban Migrants and Metropolitan Development* (Toronto: Intermet, 1971), Chapter 3
Moron, Guillermo, *History of Venezuela* (New York: Roy, 1963)
Shoup, Carl S., Harriss, C.L. and Vickrey, W.S., *The Fiscal System of the Federal District of Venezuela: A Report* (Baltimore: Garamond, 1960)

Delhi

Chandra, Jag Parvesh, *Delhi: A Political Study* (Delhi: Metropolitan Book, 1969), 135 pp.

Delhi, Municipal Corporation, Finance Branch, *Delhi Corporation Finances (General Wing), 1958–59* to *1964–65* (Delhi, 1965)

India, Administrative Reforms Commission, *Report on Administration of Union Territories and NEFA*. (New Delhi: Government of India, 1969), 56 pp.

India, Delhi Administration, *Annual Report, 1964–1965* (Delhi, 1965), 44 pp.

India, Ministry of Home Affairs, *The Delhi Municipal Corporation Act, 1957.* (New Delhi: Government of India, 1961)

– , *The Delhi Municipal Corporation (Amendment) Bill, 1966* (New Delhi: Government of India, 1966)

– , *Report 1965–66* (New Delhi, 1966), 62 pp.

India, Parliament, *The Delhi Administration Bill, 1966*

– , *The Punjab Municipal (Delhi Amendment) Bill 1966*

Khanna, Y., "The Traffic Problem and the City Government," 5 *India Journal of Public Administration* (July–September 1959), 333–41

Mitra, Asok, *Delhi – The Capital City* (New Delhi: Thomson, 1970), 129 pp.

Nath, Dharmindra, "The Governmental Set-up of Delhi," v *Indian Political Science Review* (April–Sept. 1971)

Raheja, B.D., "How Delhi should be governed," *Civic Affairs* (Kanpur, June 1965), 5–13

Rao, V.K.R., and Desai, P.B., *Greater Delhi: A Study in Urbanization 1940–57* (New York: Asia Publishing House, 1965)

Spate, O.H.K., "Aspects of the City in South Asia; Delhi: An Example of Current Problems," 7 *Confluence* (Spring 1958), 23–7

Vira, Dharma, *Expert Report on Planning Metropolitan Delhi* (Tokyo : Seminar on Metropolitan Planning in Asia, 1964)

– , "The Planning of Delhi: Its Progress and Problems," 3 *Local Government Throughout World* (November–December 1964), 103–7

Islamabad

Feldman, Herbert, *Revolution in Pakistan: A Study of the Martial Law Administration* (London: Oxford Univ. Press, 1967), esp. 91–3

Hussain, Farhat, "Some Thoughts on Administration in Islamabad Metropolitan Area" (Rawalpindi: Capital Development Authority, 1963), 15 pp. typed

"Islamabad, New Capital for a New Nation," 3 *Local Government Throughout the World* (May–June 1964), 51–2

Pakistan, *Capital Development Authority Ordinance* (Lahore, W. Pakistan: Superintendent of Government Printing)

Pakistan, Provincial Administration Committee, *Report* (Lahore: Superintendent of Government Printing)
Pakistan, Provincial Re-organization Committee, *Report, Part* I – *West Pakistan* (Lahore, Superintendent of Government Printing)
Pott, Janet, "Impression of Islamabad – West Pakistan," 13 *Housing Review* (London, March–April 1964), 49–52

Kuala Lumpur

American University (Maday, Bela C., and others), *Area Handbook for Malaysia and Singapore* (Washington, DC: Government Printing Office, 1965)
Development Administration Unit, Prime Minister's Department, *Organization of the Government of Malaysia, 1967* (Kuala Lumpur: Government Printer, 1967)
Laquian, Aprodicio A. (ed.), *Rural-Urban Migrants and Metropolitan Development* (Toronto: Intermet, 1971), Chapter 6.
Malaysia, Parliament, *Federal Capital Act No. 35/60* (Kuala Lumpur: Government Printer, 1960)
Milne, R.S., *Government and Politics In Malaysia* (Boston: Houghton Mifflin Co., 1967)
Papineau, Aristide J.G. (ed.), *Kuala Lumpur: Capital of Malaysia* (Singapore: Andre Publications, 1964)
The Straits Times (13 and 14 September 1960)

Lagos

BOOKS

Action Group, *Lagos Belongs to the West* (Ibadan: Action Group Secretariat, 1964)
Awa, Eme O., *Federal Government in Nigeria* (Berkeley: Univ. of California Press, 1964)
Blitz, L. Franklin, *The Politics and Administration of Nigerian Government* (New York: Praeger, 1965)
Cowan, L.G., *Local Government in West Africa* (New York: Columbia Univ. Press, 1958)
Harris, P.J., *Local Government in Southern Nigeria* (Cambridge: University Press, 1957)
Hicks, U.K., *Development from Below* (Oxford: Clarendon, 1961)

Jakande, L.K., *The Case for a Lagos State* (Lagos: John West Publications, 1966)

Jones, G.C., and Lucas, Keith B., *Report on the Administration of Lagos Town Council* (Lagos: April 1963)

Williams, Babatunde A., and Walsh, Annmarie H., *Urban Government for Metropolitan Lagos* (New York: Praeger, 1968)

Wraith, Ronald, *Local Government in West Africa* (London: Allen and Unwin, 1964)

REPORTS AND DOCUMENTS

Koenigsberger, Otto, and others (for the Government of Nigeria), *Metropolitan Lagos* (New York: UN TAA, 1964)

Lagos Executive Development Board, *Annual Report and Accounts* (1956–), and *Board News* (Quarterly Journal)

Lagos Town Council, *Annual Reports, 1961–62 to 1964–65* (Lagos: Town Council, 1965)

– , *Memorandum Submitted to the Commissioner of Inquiry (Saville) Into the Administration of the Lagos City Council* (Lagos: Town Clerk, 1966)

Nigeria, Commission on Lagos Local Government, *Report by Sir John Imrie into the Relationship between the Federal Government and the Lagos Town Council* (Lagos: Federal Government Printer, 1959)

Nigeria, Government, *The Lagos Local Government Law, 1953*, 2 Supplement to the Western Regional Gazette, No. 25, July 1953 (Lagos: Government Printer, 1953)

– , *The Laws of the Federation of Nigeria and Lagos* (Chapters 56, 97, 98, 99) (Lagos: Government Printer, 1959)

– , *National Development Plan, 1962–1968* (Lagos: Federal Ministry of Economic Development, 1962)

– , *National Development Plan Progress Report* (Lagos: Government Printer, 1964)

– , *Proceedings of the Commission of Inquiry into the Administration of the Lagos City Council (Saville Commission)* (Lagos: Federal Government, 1966)

– , *Report on Education Development in Lagos* (Lagos: Government Printer, 1957)

– , *Report on the Nigeria Federal Elections* (Lagos: Government Printer, 1959)

– , *A Report of the Registration of Title to Land in Lagos* (Lagos: Government Printer, 1957)

Rapson, R.N., *Report of an Inquiry Into Alleged Irregularities by the Lagos Town Council in Connection with the Collection of Money and the Allocation of Market Stalls in Respect of Proposed Ereko and Oko-Awo* (Lagos: Government Printer, 1959)

Simpson, S.R., *Report of a Work Party on Registration of Ownership of Land, in Lagos* (Lagos: Federal Government, 1960)

Storey, Bernard, *Report of the Commission of Inquiry Into the Administration of the Lagos Town Council* (Lagos: Government Printer, 1953)

Mexico City

Almond, Gabriel A., and Verba, S., *The Civic Culture* (Princeton: Princeton University Press, 1963)

Cardenas, L., Jr., "Contemporary Problems of Local Government in Mexico," 18 *Western Political Quarterly* (19 December 1965), 858–65

Cline, H.F., *Mexico: Revolution to Evolution, 1940–1960* (London: Royal Institute of International Affairs, 1962)

Martínez Corbalá, Gonzalo, "Growth Problems of Mexico City" (Philadelphia Institute for Environmental Studies, University of Pennsylvania, 1969)

"Mexico Federal District" and "Mexico City" in 15 *Encyclopaedia Britannica* (1970 edition)

Oldman, Oliver, and others, *Financing Urban Development in Mexico City: A Case Study of Property Tax, Land Use, Housing, and Urban Planning* (Cambridge: Harvard University Press, 1964)

Parkes, H.B., *A History of Mexico* (Boston: Houghton Mifflin, 3d 1960)

Tucker, William P., *The Mexican Government Today* (Minneapolis: University of Minnesota Press, 1958)

Moscow

BOOKS

Allakhverdyan, D.A., *Soviet Financial System* (Moscow: Progress Publishers, 1966) (The best full account in English of central and local finance)

Barfivala, L.D., *Local Government in the USSR* (Bombay: All-Indian Institute of Local Self-Government, 1958). (Last section deals with Moscow)

Churchward, L.G., *Contemporary Soviet Government* (London: Routledge & Kegan Paul, 1967) (The best account of the Soviet political system, with a full coverage of local government)

Mote, M.E., *Soviet Local and Republic Elections* (Stanford: Hoover Institution, 1965) (A critical account of the elections in Leningrad in 1963)

Parkins, Maurice F., *City Planning in Soviet Russia* (Chicago: Univ. of Chicago Press, 1953)

Saushkin, Yuri, *Moscow* (Moscow, 1966) (The best guide book available in English)
Simon, Sir Ernest Darwin, *Moscow in the Making* (London: Longman, 1937)
Statistical Administration of Moscow City, Moscow in Figures During the Years of Soviet Power (1917–1967), A Short Statistical Handbook (Moscow: Statistical Publishing House, 1967)

ARTICLES

Davydov, M., "Moscow's Oktyabrsky District," *Culture and Life* (November 1967)
Mote, M.E., "The Budget of Greater Leningrad, 1956–1960," *Soviet Studies* (October 1967), 245–54 (The most detailed account in English of a city budget)
Oliver, James H., "Citizen Demands and the Soviet Political System," 63 *American Political Science Review* (1969), 465–75
Posokhin, M., "The Moscow of Tomorrow," *Culture and Life* (Moscow, July 1967), 2–5 (Mr Posokhin is the chief architect of Moscow)
Rothstein, A., "In a 'Rayon' (Borough) of Moscow," 35 *Municipal Review* (London, December 1964), 752–3
Simon, Rogers, and Hookham, Maurice, "Moscow," in W.A. Robson (ed.), *Great Cities of the World* (London: Allen and Unwin, 2nd ed. 1957), 383–412
Swearer, H.R., "The Functions of Soviet Local Elections," 5 *Midwest Journal of Political Science* (May 1961), 29–49
– , "Popular Participation: Myths and Realities," IX *Problems of Communism* (September–October 1960), 42–51
Tucker, R.C., "Field Observations on Soviet Local Government," 18 *American Slavic and East European Review* (December 1958), 526–38
Vyshinsky, Andrei Y., *The Law of the Soviet State*. Translated by Hugh W. Babb (New York: Macmillan, 1948)
Wesson, Robert G., *Soviet Communes* (New Brunswick, NJ: Rutgers Univ. Press, 1963)
– , "The Soviet Communes," 13 *Soviet Studies* (April 1962)

Ottawa

BOOKS

Bond, Courtney C.J., *City on the Ottawa* (Ottawa: Queen's Printer, 1961)
Brault, Lucien, *Hull 1800–1950* (Ottawa: Les Editions de l'Université d'Ottawa, 1950) (in French)

Brault, Lucien, *Ottawa Old and New* (Ottawa: Ottawa Historical Information Institute, 1946)

Davies, Blodwen, *The Charm of Ottawa* (Toronto: McClelland, 1932)

Eggleston, Wilfrid, *The Queen's Choice; a story of Canada's capital* (Ottawa, Queen's Printer, 1961)

Ketchum, Carleton J., *Federal District Capital* (Ottawa: Runge, 1939)

Ross, A.H.D., *Ottawa past and present* (Toronto: Musson, 1927)

REPORTS AND DOCUMENTS

Canada, National Capital Commission, *A Propos of the Capital of Canada* (Ottawa, Queen's Printer, 1964), 72 pp.

–, *Annual report* (Ottawa: the Commission)

–, *Statistical Review with Explanatory Notes; National Capital Region* (Ottawa: the Commission, 1964), 156 pp.

Canada, National Capital Planning Service, *Plan for the National Capital: General Report* (Ottawa: King's Printer, 1950), 307 pp.

–, *Plan for the National Capital: Preliminary Report* (Ottawa: King's Printer, 1948), 137 pp.

Canada, Parliament, "An Act respecting the Development and Improvement of the National Capital Region" (1958, 7 Elizabeth II, Chap. 37)

–, Joint Committee of the Senate and the House of Commons on the Federal District Commission, *Minutes of Proceedings and Evidence* (Ottawa: Queen's Printer, 1956), 1056 pp.

Canada, Royal Commission on Bilingualism and Biculturalism, *Report*, Vol. 5, Book V: *The Federal Capital* (Ottawa: Queen's Printer, 1970)

Coleman, Alice, *The Planning Challenge to the Ottawa Area* (Ottawa: Queen's Printer, 1969), 98 pp. plus maps

Culliford, Paul, *Metro Government: Ottawa-Carleton* (Ottawa: Carleton University MA essay, 1970), 149 pp. typed

De Leuw, Cather & Co., and Beauchemin-Beaton-Lapointe, *Ottawa-Hull Area Transportation Study* (Ottawa: prepared for the City of Ottawa, 1965), 154 pp.

Hull City Planning Commission and General Planning Committee of the City of Hull and Its Environs, *Master Plan for Hull, Aylmer, Hull South, Deschenes, Hull West (part)* (Hull: City Planning Commission, 1964?), 94 pp.

–, *Urban Renewal Report: Hull 1962* (Hull: City Planning Commission, 1963), 205 pp.

McRae, Kenneth D. (ed.), *The Federal Capital*, Studies of the Royal Commission on Bilingualism and Biculturalism, No. 1 (Ottawa: Queen's Printer, 1969), 270 pp.

Ontario, Department of Municipal Affairs, *Ottawa, Eastview and Carleton County Local Government Review* (Toronto: the Department, 1966)

Ontario Legislative Assembly, *An Act to Establish the Regional Municipality of Ottawa-Carleton* (Toronto: Queen's Printer, 1968), 80 pp.

Ottawa, Department of Planning and Works, *Urban Renewal* Study (Ottawa, 1959-63)

Perry, J.H., *Report on the Financial and Administrative Arrangements in Capitals of Federal Countries* (Lagos: Government Printer, 1953) (Study of Canberra, Ottawa and Washington)

Quebec National Assembly, *Outaouais Regional Community Act* (Quebec Official Publisher, 1969), 82 pp.

Quebec, Commission d'étude sur l'intégrité du territoire du Québec, *Rapport, No. 1: les problèmes de la région de la capitale canadienne* (Quebec, Government Printer, 1968?), 7 vols.

Rowat, Donald C., *Ottawa's Future Development and Needs*, a brief prepared for submission by the City of Ottawa to the Royal Commission on Canada's Economic Prospects (Ottawa: City of Ottawa, 1956), 57 pp. plus tables and charts

– , *The Proposal of a Federal Territory for Canada's Capital* (Toronto: Ontario Advisory Committee on Confederation, 1966), 136 pp.; later printed in the Committee's *Background Papers and Reports* (Toronto: Queen's Printer, 1967), 215–82; and final chapters reprinted in Rowat, *The Canadian Municipal System* (Toronto: McClelland, 1969)

Smith, Larry & Co., *Economic Prospects of the National Capital Region, Ottawa, Canada* (Toronto: prepared for the National Capital Commission, 1963), 107 pp.

Western Quebec Regional Economic Council, *The Quebec Territory of the Region of the National Capital* (Hull: the Council, 1967), 55 pp.

ARTICLES

Bruce, Harry, "The Crusade to Make Canada's National Capital a Tale of Two Cities," *Maclean's* (October 1970), 33–40

Eggleston, W., "Not too late to make Ottawa federal district," *Ottawa Journal* (19 March 1962)

Flaherty, Frank, "Gift suggestion for Canada's 100th birthday: make Ottawa our 11th province," *Weekend Magazine* (29 June 1963), 1–4, 23

Gibson, James A., "How Ottawa became the capital of Canada," 46 *Ontario History* (August 1954), 213–22

Perry, J.H., "We don't want a Federal District for Ottawa," 31 *Canadian Business* (February 1958), 84–6, 88-91

"Why Capital District sought – and fought – by Ottawans," 59 *Financial Post* (29 May, 1965), 73. (Special issue on Ottawa)

Vienna

Barea, Ilse, *Vienna, Legend and Reality* (London: Secker & Warburg, 1966)
Concise Information about Vienna (Vienna: Municipal Administration, Dept. of Public Works, 1960), mimeographed
Crane, W., "The Errand-Running Functions of Austrian Legislators," *Parliamentary Affairs* (1962), 160
– , *The Legislature of Lower Austria* (London, 1961)
Feiler, Margaret, *The Viennese Municipal Service 1933 to 1950*, PHD thesis, New York University (Ann Arbor, Michigan: University Microfilms, 1965), 330 pp.
Gerlich, Peter, *Local Government and Local Politics in Austria, A preliminary survey* (Vienna: Institute of Advanced Studies, 1967), mimeographed
Humes, Samuel, *The Structure of Local Governments throughout the World* (The Hague: Martinus Nijhoff, 1961), 268–72
International Union of Local Authorities, *Local Government in the XXth Century* (The Hague: Martinus Nijhoff, 1963), 13–25
McGuigan, Dorothy, *Vienna Today: A Complete Guide* (New York: Vanoos, Arthor, 1966)
Pinner, F.A., "On the Structure of Organizations and Beliefs: Lagerdenken in Austria" (Annual Meeting of the American Political Science Association, Chicago, 1967), mimeographed
Rickett, Richard, *A Brief Survey of Austrian History* (Vienna: Prachner, 1966)
Shell, K., *The Transformation of Austrian Socialism* (New York, 1962)
Vienna at a Glance (Vienna: Municipal Administration, Dept. of Public Works, 1964), mimeographed

Washington

Bain, H.M., *The Governing of Metropolitan Washington* (Washington, DC: US Government Printing Office, 1958), 98 pp.
– , *The Development District* (Silver Spring, Maryland: The Maryland-National Capital Park and Planning Commission, 1968)
Caemmerer, H. Paul, *Historic Washingon* (Washington, 1954)
Connery, R.H., and Leach, Richard H., *The Federal Government and Metro-Areas* (Cambridge: Harvard University Press, 1960)

Derthick, Martha, *City Politics in Washington* DC (Cambridge: Harvard University Press, 1962)

District of Columbia Government, *Annual Report Fiscal Year 1969* (Washington, 1969)

Ecker-Racz, L.L., *Financing the District of Columbia* (Washington: DC Government, 1968), 57 pp.

Fletcher, Thomas W., *Managing the Nation's Capital* (Washington: Washington Center for Metropolitan Studies, 1970)

Grant, D.R., "The Government of Interstate Metropolitan Areas," 8 *Western Political Quarterly* (March 1955), pp. 90–107

Green, Constance (McLaughlin), *The Secret City, A History of Race Relations in the Nation's Capital* (Princeton, NJ: Princeton University Press, 1967)

– , *Washington*, 2 vols. (Princeton, NJ: Princeton University Press, 1962–63,) pp. 445 and 558

Grier, George W., DC *Reorganization: Making it Work* (Washington: Washington Center for Metropolitan Studies, 1967), 47 pp.

Hanson, Royce, *The Anatomy of the Federal Interest* (Washington: Washington Center for Metropolitan Studies, 1967), 86 pp.

– , *The Politics of Metropolitan Cooperation: Metro. Washington Council of Governments* (Washington: Washington Center for Metropolitan Studies, 1964)

– , and Ross, B. H., *Governing the District of Columbia: An Introduction* (Washington Center for Metropolitan Studies, 1971), 26 pp. An extended version of their essay for this book

Harman, B. Douglas, *The National Capital Planning Commission and the Politics of Planning in the Nation's Capital* (Washington: Washington Center for Metropolitan Studies, 1968), 97 pp.

Hopking, Andrew, and Ridgeway, J., "Washington the Lost Colony," *New Republic* (23 April 1966), 13–17

Metropolitan Washington Council of Governments, *Annual Report, 1968* (Washington, 1971)

Ross, Bernard H., Boesel, A., and Webster, W., *The Delegate and the District Building: The Potential for Conflict or Cooperation* (Washington: Washington Center for Metropolitan Studies, 1971)

Rutherford, Geddes W., *Administrative Problems in a Metropolitan Area: The National Capital Region* (Chicago: Public Administration Service, 1952), 63 pp.

– , "Reorganization of the Government of the District of Columbia," 33 *American Political Science Review* (August 1939), 653–55

Schmeckebier, Laurence F., *The District of Columbia: Its Government and Administration* (Washington: The Brookings Institution, 1929)

–, and Willoughby, W.F., *The Government and Administration of the District of Columbia: Suggestions for Change* (Washington, 1929)

United States Congress, Congressional Record, "Home Rule for the District of Columbia – Appointment of Conferees" (5 April 1966), 7269–71

United States Congress, House of Representatives, Committee on Government Operations, Executive and Legislative Reorganization Subcommittee, *Hearings* (13, 14, 15, 21, and 22 June 1967), on *Reorganization Plan No. 3 of 1967 (Government of the District of Columbia)* (Washington: US Government Printing Office, 1967)

United States Congress, Joint Committee on Washington Metropolitan Problems, *Progress Report: Growth and Expansion of the District* (Washington: US Government Printing Office, 1958), 56 pp. with maps

–, *Hearings, Senate reports and staff studies and reports* (Washington: US Government Printing Office, 1958)

–, *Final Report: Meeting the Problems of Metropolitan Growth in the National Capital Region* (86th Congress, 1st session, Senate, Report No. 38) (Washington: US Government Printing Office, 1959)

United States, National Capital Planning Commission, *The Proposed Comprehensive Plan for the National Capital* (Washington: the Commission, 1967)

–, *Proposed Physical Development Policies for Washington*, DC 1965–85 (Washington: US Government Printing Office, 1965)

Waldrop, F.C., "D.C. Home Rule," letter, 152 *New Republic* (17 April 1965), 45

"Washington, D.C.," in 23 *Encyclopaedia Britanica* (1970 edition)

Winters, J.M., *Interstate Metropolitan Areas* (Ann Arbor: University of Michigan Law School, 1962)

Yaoundé

Ardener, Edwin, "The political history of Cameroon," 18 *World Today* (August 1962), 341–50

"Cameroon" in *The Europa Year Book,* 210–20, esp. "The Constitution," 215

"Cameroun" in *West Africa Annual* (1967), 11

Cowan, L.G., *Local Government in West Africa* (New York: Columbia Univ. Press, 1958)

Enonchong, H.N.A., *Cameroon Constitutional Law: Federalism in a Mixed Common-Law and Civil Law System* (Yaoundé: Centre d'Edition et de Production de Manuels et d'Auxiliaires de l'Enseignement, 1967)

–, "The Position of Cameroon State in Litigation," *Abbia* (No. 11, 1965)

Foulon, Bernard, "The Language Problem in Cameroon," 5 *Comparative Education* (February 1969), 25–49

France, Government, Direction de la documentation, *Les constitutions des républiques africaines et malgaches d'expression française, 1 avril 1963* (Paris, 1963)

Jackson, Vernon, *Language Schools and Government in Cameroun* (New York: Teachers College Press, Columbia Univ., 1965), 26 pp.

Le Vine, Victor T., *The Cameroons: From Mandate to Independence* (Berkeley: University of California Press, 1964)

– , "The New Cameroon Federation," *Africa Report* (December 1961)

"One party state for Cameroon?", *Africa Report* (November 1962)

B MATERIALS IN OTHER LANGUAGES*

GENERAL

Les capitales du monde (Lausanne: Edition Margerat, 1959).
Préface de Georges Duhamel

Gosset, R.P., *Capitales Latines-Américaines* (Paris: Fasquelles, 1950)

"Le Problème des capitales en Amérique Latine," 3 *Caravelle* (Toulouse, 1964). Whole issue devoted to this theme

Union des Capitales de la Communauté Européenne, Etude présentée par la ville de Bonn, "Comparaison de la Structure Administrative des Six Capitales de la Communauté Economique Européenne" (9e Session Plénière, Paris, 15–17 juin 1966), 10 pp. mimeographed

Belgrade

ITEMS IN FRENCH

Bjeličić S., "Le système communal en Yougoslavie", *Jugoslavija* (Belgrad, 1962), 122

Carcasses, L., "L'Organisation communale en Yougoslavie," 65 *Revue politique et parlementaire* (Paris, January 1963)

Jovičić M., "Le gouvernement local", in *La Constitution yougoslave de 1963* (Paris: Editions Cujas, 1966)

– , "Le rôle et la position de la commune (et de l'arrondissement) dans la

---

* Since most English-speaking readers will be able to divine the contents of items in French, Portuguese and Spanish even if they do not know these languages, only the titles in German and Russian have been translated.

Fédération yougoslave", in XVIII *Annales de la Faculté de Droit et des Sciences Politiques et Economiques de Strasbourg*

Vratuša A., "La commune en Yougoslavie," *Questions actuelles du socialisme* (1965), 104–23

Bern

ITEMS IN GERMAN

Baertschi, Ernst, *Wie Bern Bundesstadt wurde* [Former mayor of Bern; How Bern Became the Federal City] (Bern, 1948)

Burckhardt, Walter, *Kommentar der Schweiz Bundesverfassung* [Commentary on the Swiss Constitution] (Bern, 1931)

Eidg. Gesetzessammlung 1851, 1934, 1947 (Federal laws concerning the political and safety guarantees of the federal authorites)

Giacometti, Zaccaria, *Schweiz Bundesstaatsrecht* [Swiss Constitutional Law] (Zurich, 1949)

Markwalder, Hans, *Bern wird Bundessitz* [Former town clerk of Bern; Bern Becomes the Seat of the Federal State] (Bern, 1948)

Rappard, William E., *Die Bundesverfassung der Schweiz. Eidgenossenschaft 1848–1948* [History of the Swiss Federal Constitution] (Zurich, 1948)

Schweiz Bundesblatt (Swiss Federal monitor; 1848 and the following years)

Verwaltungsberichte und Akten betreffend die Gemeinde Bern und ihre Beziehungen zum Bund (Official reports and documents concerning the relations between the city of Bern and the federal government, mainly in the municipal archives of Bern)

Bonn

ITEMS IN GERMAN

Das Parlament [The Parliament] (Nr. 35/36, 30 August 1967; special no. of the weekly newspaper on the capital of Bonn)

Landkreis Bonn (ed.), *150 Jahre Landkreis Bonn* [150 Years of the County of Bonn] (Bonn, 1966)

– , *Verwaltungsbericht 1959–1964, Landkreis Bonn sorgt fur heute – plant für morgen* [Administration Report 1959–1964; County of Bonn Provides for Today – Plans for Tomorrow] (Bonn, 1964)

Machtemes, A., *Gutachten zur Raumordnung des Landkreises Bonn* [Report on Space Planning in the County of Bonn] (Bonn: County of Bonn, 1964)

Stadt Bonn (ed.), *Bonner Zahlen, Statistische Berichte der Stadt Bonn* (Statistical Reports of the City of Bonn; Bonn, 1966)

–, *Bericht über die Probleme, die sich für eine Stadt durch ihre Bestimmung zur Hauptstadt ergeben* [Report on the Difficulties Involved in Turning a City into a Capital] (Bonn, 1966)

Stakemeyer, *Gutachten zur Neuordnung Bonner Raum, herausgegeben vom Regierungspräsidenten* [Report of the District President on the Reorganization of the Area of Bonn] (Cologne, 1966, typewritten)

Zurnieden, P., "Bonn, Portrait einer Residenz" ["Bonn, Portrait of a Residence"] Sonderdruck aus Bonn 1955-1964. Verwaltungsbericht (herausgegeben vom Oberstadtdirektor der Stadt Bonn; Bonn, 1965)

Brasilia

ITEMS IN PORTUGUESE

Branco, Elivia Lordello Castello, "Administração descentralizada do Distrito Federal," *R. Adm. Municipal,* Rio de Janeiro (57): 134-152, mar/abr, 1963

"Brasilia," in Richardson, Ivan L., *Bibliografia brasileira de administração pública e assuntos correlatos* (Rio de Janeiro: FGV, 1964), 775-782

"Concurso para o planejamento e urbaniza ção da futura capital," *Notícias Municipais,* Rio de Janeiro (16): 12-13, maio/jun, 1956

Cortesão, Jaime, "Brasília-síntese histórica," *R. bras. Municípios,* Rio de Janeiro (39/40); 205-210, jul/dez, 1957

Costa, Lúcio, "Relatório sôbre o plano pilôto de Brasília," *Notícias Municipais* (21): 21-40, mar/abr, 1957

Distrito federal. Leis, decretos, etc., *Distrito Federal e sua nova estrutura administrativa* (Brasília, Sec. do Govêrno, s.d. 4 v.)

Freitas, M.A. Teixeira de, "A localização da nova Capital da República. I-Carta ao General Djalma Poli Coelho. II-Brasília, capital do Brasil," *R. bras. Municípios* (6): 273-295, abr/jun, 1949

Jardanoviski, Isaac, "O zoneamento de Brasília, uma experiência fascinante," *Notícias Municipais* (25): 12-14, nov/dez, 1957

Martins, José Eurico, "Argumentos em favor da mundança da capital da República," *R. bras. Municípios* (16): 495-505, out/dez, 1951

Werneck Jr., Américo, "Financiamento da construção da futura capital federal," *R. bras. Municípios* (31): 210-216, jul/set. 1955

Buenos Aires

ITEMS IN SPANISH

Mouchet, Carlos, "Criterios y bases legales para el ordenamiento de la ciudad de Buenos Aires y de su area metropolitana," in 103 *La Ley* (Buenos Aires, 1961)

– , "El financiamiento municipal en Latino America," paper presented to the Conference on Municipal Financing in Latin America organized by the Inter-Amerinca Development Bank, Washington, 1966

– , *La legalidad en el municipio* (Buenos Aires: Editorial Perrot, 1966)

– , "Ordenamiento y gobierno de las areas metropolitanas: El caso de Buenos Aires," in 24 *Revista de Administracion Public* (Buenos Aires, January–March 1967)

Caracas

ITEMS IN SPANISH

Aurelio-Vila, Marco, *Area Metropolitana de Caracas* (Caracas: Ediciones del Cuatricentenario de Caracas, 1965)

Brewer-Carías, Allan-Randolph, "El Area Metropolitana de Caracas y la Cooperatión Intermunicipal en Materia de Urbanismo," en *Revista de la Facultad de Derocho de la Universidad Central de Venezuela* (Caracas, No. 35, 1967)

– , "La Intergración del Area Metropolitana de Caracas y la Coordinación de los Serviciós de Transporte Urbano," en *Revista Taller Facultad de Arquitectura* (Caracas, No. 20, 1966)

– , *El Régimen de Gobierno Municipal en el Distrito Federal Venezolano* (Caracas: Publicaciones de la Gobernación del Distrito Federal, 1968)

Carmona-Romay, Adriano G., "Estructura Política y Funcional del Distrito Federal de la capital de la República," en *Revista de la Facultad de Derecho de la Universidad del Zulia* (Maracaibo, No. 11, 1964)

Dana-Montano, Salvador M., "El Régimen Municipal en la Nueva Constitución Venezolana," en *Revista de la Facultad de Derecho de la Universidad del Zulia* (No. 3, 1961)

Estudio de base para la formulación de una tesis sobre el Area Metropolitana de Caracas (Caracas: Oficina Municipal de Planeamiento Urbano, 1963)

González-C. Jesús, *Caracas y su Régimen Municipal* (Caracas, 1941)

Hill-Peña, Aníbal, *Historia de la Creación del Distrito Federal* (Caracas: Publicaciones de la Secretaría General de la Comisión del Cuatricentonario de Caracas, No. 5, 1955)

Maza-Zabala, D.F., *Condiciones Generales del Area Metropolitana de Caracas para su Industrialización* (Caracas: Ediciones del Cuatricentenario de Caracas, 1966)

Moles-Caubet, Antonio, "Los Límites de la Autonomía Municipal," en *Revista de la Facultad de Derecho de la Universidad Central de Venezuela.* (No. 26, 1963)

Tamayo-Gascue, Eduardo, *Sociología del Municipio* (Caracas, 1960)

Mexico City

ITEMS IN SPANISH

González Casanova, Pablo, *La Democracia en México* (Ciudad de México: Ed. Era., 1969)

Informes Anuales del Departamento del Distrito Federal (1969)

Ley Orgánica del Departamento del Distrito Federal (1940)

Ley Orgánica del Distrito y Territorios Federales (1940)

Unikel, Luis, *Demografía y Economía* (Ciudad de México: El Colegio de México, 1968)

Moscow

ITEMS IN RUSSIAN

Executive Committee of Moscow City Soviet, *Bulletin* (Moscow, issued every two months)

Golovin, B., et al., "Moscow Tomorrow and the Day After," in *Report from the Chief Architectural Planning Administration* (Moscow, January 1967), 147-61

Konovalov, M.F., and Yesuitov, V.M., "Moscow Soviet, its Tasks and Activities," *Gosudarstvo i Pravo (Soviet State and Law*, April 1967) (This is the most detailed account of the work of the Moscow city soviet. Konovalov is head of the organization department of the city soviet)

Lepeshkin, A.I., *Soviets, the People's Power, 1936-1967* (Moscow: Judicial Literature Publishers, 1967) (The most detailed account in Russian of the work of local soviets)

Mikheev, V.E., "Moscow Budget," *Gorodskoe Khozyaistvo Moskvy* (*Moscow Municipal Economy*: February 1968) (From which details of the 1968 budget have been derived, in the essay on Moscow)

Promyslov, V., "An Important Stage in the Development of the Capital," *Kommunist* (January 1970), 73–82 (The author is chairman of the executive committee of Moscow city soviet)

Rubinov, A., *City Fathers* (Moscow: Moscow Worker, 1966) (A comparison of the composition and working of the Moscow city duma and city soviet)

Selivanov, T., "Plan for the Development of the Municipal Economy of the Capital," *Stroitel'stvo i Arkhitektura* (*Building and Architecture*; January 1970), 1–3 (The author is deputy chairman of the executive committee of Moscow city soviet)

Shupta V. (deputy chief of Moscow town financial department), "The Work of the Financial Organs of Moscow in the New Situation," *Finances of USSR* (July 1967), 14–18

Vienna

ITEMS IN GERMAN

General

Handbuch der Stadt Wien [Handbook of the City of Vienna], vols. for 1967–70 (Wien: Verlag für Jugend und Volk)

Jahrbuch der Stadt Wien [Yearbook of the City of Vienna], ed. by the Statistische Amt der Stadt Wien, vols. for 1965–70 (Wien: Magistrat)

Österreichisches Jahrbuch [Austrian yearbook], ed. by the Bundespressedienst, vol. for 1968 and 1969 (Wien: Österreichische Staatsdruckerei)

Österreichischer Amtskalender [Austrian official almanac], vols. for 1967–71 (Wien: Österreichische Staatsdruckerei)

Statistisches Handbuch für die Republik Österreich [Statistical handbook for the Republic of Austria], ed. by the Österreichische Statistische Zentralamt, vols. for 1967–70 (Wien: Österreichische Staatsdruckerei)

History

Goldinger, Walter, *Geschichte der Republik Österreich* [The history of the Republic of Austria] (Wien: Verlag für Geschichte und Politik, 1962)

Till, Rudolf, *Geschichte der Wiener Stadtverwaltung in den letzten zwreihundert Jahren* [The history of the Vienna city government during the last two-hundred years] (Wien: Verlag für Jugend und Volk, 1957)

Zöllner, Erich, *Geschichte Österreichs von den Anfängen bis zur Gegenwart* [Austrian history from the beginnings to the present day], 3rd edn. (Wien: Verlag für Geschichte und Politik, 1966)

The legal situation

Adamovich, Ludwig, *Handbuch des österreichischen Verfassungsrechts* [Handbook of Austrian constitutional law], 6th edn. (Wien: Springer, 1971)

Antoniolli, Walter, *Allgemeines Verwaltungsrecht* [General administrative law] (Wien: Manz, 1954)

Koja, Friedrich, *Das Verfassungsrecht der österreichischen Bundelsänder* [The constitutional law of the Austrian provinces] (Wien, New York: Springer, 1967)

Schütz, Eduard, *Die Verfassung der Bundeshaupstadt Wien* [The Constitution of the Municipality of Vienna] (Wien und München: Verlag für Jungend und Volk, 1969)

Verfassung der Bundeshauptstadt Wien samt Nebengesetzen sowie Organisationsstatut für die Unternehmungen und Betriebe der Stadt Wien [Constitution of the federal capital of Vienna plus by-laws and administrative regulations of the municipal undertakings] (Wien: Verlag des Wiener Magistrats, 1960). Supplements

Werner, Leopold, and Klecatsky, Hans, *Das österreichische Bundesverfassungsrecht* [Austrian constitutional law] (Wien: Manz, 1961). Supplements

Vienna's finances

Berichte und Informationen. Weekly of the Österreichische Forschungsinstitut für Wirtschaft and Politik, Salzburg

Melichar, Erwin, "Die österreichische, Finanzverfassung" [Austrian financial system], in Andreae, Clemens-August, Handbuch der österreichischen Finanzwirtschaft [Handbook of the Austrian financial economy] (Innsbruck, Wien, München: Tyrolia Verlag, 1970)

The political situation

Berchtold, Klaus, ed., *Österreichische Prateiprogramme 1868–1966* [Austrian party programs] (Wien: Verlag für Geschichte und Politik, 1967)

Czeike, Felix, *Wirtschafts- und Sozialpolitik der Gemeinde Wien in der ersten Republik (1919–1934)* [The economic and social policy of the city of Vienna during the First Austrian Republic (1919–1934)], 2 parts (Wien: Verlag für Jugend und Volk, 1958, 1959) (*Wiener Schriften*, 6, 11)

Danneberg, Robert, *Die sozialdemokratische Gemeindeverwaltung 1918–1928*
[The Social Democratic administration of the city, 1918–1928] (Wien: Wiener Volksbuchhandlung, 1928)

Gerlich, P., and Kramer, H., *Abgeordenete in der Partiendemokratie* [Representatives in Party Democracy] (Wien: Verlag für Geschichte and Politik, 1969)

Jehly, Eduard, *Zehn Jahre rotes Wien. Eine Kritik der Jahre 1919 bis 1929* [Ten years of Socialist Vienna: a critical account of the years 1919 to 1929] (Wien: Verlag des Generalsekretariates der Christlichsozialen Partei, 1930)

Patzer, Franz, *Der Wiener Gemeinderat von 1918–1934. Ein Beitrag zur Geschichte der Stadt Wien und ihrer Volksvertretung* [The Vienna city council from 1918 to 1934: a contribution on the history of the city of Vienna and its parliament] (Wien: Verlag für Jugend und Volk, 1961) (*Wiener Schriften*, 15)

Stiefbold, Rodney, and others, *Wahlen und Parteien in Österreich* [Elections and parties in Austria], vol. 3 (Wien: Österreichischer Bundesverlag, Verlag für Jugend und Volk, 1966, supplement)

Winkler, Gunther, "Das österreichische Konzept der Gewaltentrennung in Recht und Wirklichkeit " [The Austrian system of balance of powers—concept and reality], in *Der Staat* [The State] (Berlin: Dancket and Humbolt, 1967)

The functions and problems of Vienna

Kaufmann, Albert, *Demographische Struktur und Haushalts- und Familienformen der Wiener Bevölkerung* [Demographic structure and household and family patterns of the Viennes population], unpublished PHD thesis (Wien, 1966)

Nieuwolt, Simon, *Die funktionelle Gliederung von Wien* [The functional structure of Vienna], unpublished PHD thesis (Wien, 1957)

Raumordnung in Österreich [Regional planning in Austria] (Wien: Österreichisches Institut für Raumplanung, 1966)

Wien, special issue of the periodical *Die Vereinten Nationen und Österreich* (1966)

Ziak, Karl, ed., *Wiedergeburt einer Weltstadt* [The rebirth of a metropolis] (Wien, München: Verlag für Jugend und Volk, 1965)

Yaoundé

ITEMS IN FRENCH

Le Cameroun, aspedgeo graphique, historique, touristique, économique et administratif du territoire (Paris: Alépéa, 1953)

"Cameroun" and "Togo," in *Encyclopédie de l'Afrique française* (1951)
Commune de plein-exercice de Yaoundé (Yaoundé: L'Imprimerie St-Paul, 1957)
Mreng, Englebert, *Histoire du Cameroun* (Paris: Presence Africaine, 1963)
La Population de Yaoundé (Yaoundé: Service de la Statistique, Ministry of Economic Planning, 1962)

FEDERAL CAPITALS THROUGHOUT THE WORLD

(Prepared September 1968 by Projects and Legislation Branch, Australian Department of the Interior, in collaboration with Professor D.C. Rowat, Carleton University, Ottawa)

Country (Population) m	Capital (Population) m	No. of States	Federal District	The Federal Capital is also a State Capital	Federal Capital overflows into adjoining units	Governing authority in the capital			Elected representation in the Capital			Homogeneity of population in the Capital	Remarks
						Federal	State	Local	Federal	State	Local		
Switzerland (6.0)	Bern (0.2)	22	No	*				*	*	*	*	No	Has growth problem due to suburban growth outside borders of city. Federal Government has no direct control over city.
West Germany (60.0)	Bonn (0.2)	10+ Berlin	No		*			*	*	*	*	Yes	Temporary capital only. State Capital Düsseldorf. Federal Government has no direct or financial control over city.
Yugoslavia (20.0)	Belgrade (0.7)	6	No	*			*	*		*	*	No	Two-tier municipal government with a central and local councils. Federal control is achieved by democratic centralism.
USSR (236.0)	Moscow (6.5)	15 Union Republics	No	*			*	*		*	*	Yes	Two-tier government with a central and local Soviets. Federal control is achieved by democratic centralism and by State/Party ownership of land and buildings.
Cameroon (5.0)	Yaoundé (0.1)	2	No	*			*	*		*	*	No	Not a true federation as it is a one-party state. President appoints Prime Ministers of both States.
Canada (20.0)	Ottawa (0.5)	10	No		*		*	*		*	*	No	Federal Government has no direct control over city, but has National Capital Commission for federal projects and lands. Two-tier regional-local government in capital area. Provincial capital Toronto.
Austria (8.0)	Vienna (1.7)	9	City State	*		*	ø		*	ø		Yes	ø One body acts as State and local government.
Nigeria (60.0)	Lagos (0.5)	12	Yes, then City State	*		*		ø			*	Yes	Complete federal control since 1967 when civil war abolished elected local government. ø Until 1967.
USA (200.0)	Washington (0.8)	50	Yes		*	*			ø			No	Had local government till 1871. President appoints local council of 9 (since 1967). Control by Committee of Congress. ø Participate in electing President only, from 1964.
Australia (12.0)	Canberra (0.1)	6	Yes			*			*			Yes	Administered by Federal Government. Has partly elected Advisory Council. Planning, development and construction by National Capital Development Commission.

Brazil (86.0)	Brasilia (0.4)	22	Yes		•	Yes	An appointed governing council. Constitutional provisions for elected reps. at federal and local levels not yet in operation.
Mexico (46.0)	Mexico City (3.5)	29	Yes		•	Yes	Governed by an appointed Governor who is a member of the President's cabinet.
Malaysia (10.0)	Kuala Lumpur (0.5)	13	ø	*New one being built	•	No	Appointed Commissioner and advisory board. City council abolished in 1961. ø Federal Government does not have exclusive control (e.g. transfer of land still controlled by surrounding State).
Argentina (23.0)	Buenos Aires (3.5)	22	Yes		•	Yes	Constitution of 1853 provides for elected Council. This Constitution not in effect while a dictator is in power.
Venezuela (9.3)	Caracas (1.0)	20	Yes		• •	Yes	Governor appointed by President administers nearly all services for elected Council and Mayor. Federal opposition as majority on Council.
Pakistan (107.0)	Islamabad (0.1)	2	ø		ø •	Yes	ø Developed and governed by a federal agency but State still has some jurisdiction. Rawalpindi (adjacent) has own local government.
India (151.0)	Delhi (3.0)	17 States 10 Territories	Yes		• •	No	Two-tier system of 56 elected and 5 federally appointed Metropolitan Council and elected local councils. Federally appointed Administrator and Executive Commission; latter chosen from majority party on Council. Executive Commissioner of city of Delhi and New Delhi municipal body are federally appointed.

www.ingramcontent.com/pod-product-compliance
Lightning Source LLC
Chambersburg PA
CBHW020239030426
42336CB00010B/543